PHILOSOPHIZING THE AMERICAS

Philosophizing the Americas

Jacoby Adeshei Carter
Hernando A. Estévez
EDITORS

Funding for this book was provided in part by the Helen Tartar Memorial Fund.

Copyright © 2024 Fordham University Press

All rights reserved. No part of this publication may be reproduced, stored in a retrieval system, or transmitted in any form or by any means—electronic, mechanical, photocopy, recording, or any other—except for brief quotations in printed reviews, without the prior permission of the publisher.

Fordham University Press has no responsibility for the persistence or accuracy of URLs for external or third-party Internet websites referred to in this publication and does not guarantee that any content on such websites is, or will remain, accurate or appropriate.

Fordham University Press also publishes its books in a variety of electronic formats. Some content that appears in print may not be available in electronic books.

Visit us online at www.fordhampress.com.

Library of Congress Cataloging-in-Publication Data available online at https://catalog.loc.gov.

Printed in the United States of America

26 25 24   5 4 3 2 1

First edition

*Jacoby Carter's Dedication:
To my sons, Elijah Yussef and Ilyas Ezra,
may you both inhabit a better world*

Contents

Introduction: Prolegomena to Inter-American Philosophy
Jacoby Adeshei Carter 1

PART I – INTER-AMERICAN PHILOSOPHY: THEORIZING THE AMERICAS

1. Inter-American Philosophy: Born of Struggle?
Daniel Fryer 11

2. Bringing Africa to the Americas: The Creolizing of Afro-Caribbean Philosophy
Chike Jeffers 28

PART II – INTER-AMERICAN PHILOSOPHY OF INDEPENDENCE AND STATE FORMATION

3. The 1812 Constitution of Cádiz: From Colonialism to Independence
Hernando A. Estévez 49

4. Martin Delany and José Martí: Two Thinkers, Two Cubas
Dwayne A. Tunstall 68

PART III – INTER-AMERICAN HISTORICISM

5. Illuminated in Black: Arturo Alfonso Schomburg's Revolt against Colonial Historicization—An Anti-Colonial Reflection on the Philosophy of (Black) History
Tommy J. Curry 93

6   Chaos in the House of Reason: Positivism in the Americas, 1780–1900
    Adriana Novoa   117

PART IV – CURRENT TRENDS AND FUTURE POSSIBILITIES

7   Latin American Philosophy Has No Quine, So What?
    Susana Nuccetelli   147

8   Latin American Thought as a Path toward Philosophizing from Radical Exteriority
    Alejandro A. Vallega   162

9   Afro-American Writing: Motifs of Place
    James B. Haile, III   193

PART V – INTER-AMERICAN PHILOSOPHY OF RACE

10 Alain Locke, José Vasconcelos, and José Martí, on Race, Nationality, and Cosmopolitanism
    Jacoby Adeshei Carter   235

11 Reason, Race, and the Human Project: Sylvia Winter, Sociogenesis, and Philosophy in the Americas
    Michael Monahan   261

12 Race, Multiplicity, and Impure Coalitions of Resistance
    Lee A. McBride, III   284

PART VI – INTER-AMERICAN FEMINISM

13 La Negra's Provocation: Corporeal Consciousness in *Nuestra Señora de la Noche* by Mayra Santos-Febres
    Nadia V. Celis Salgado   307

14 Decolonial Feminisms and Indigenous Women's Resistance to Neoliberalism: Lessons from Abya Yala
    Andrea J. Pitts   326

15 The Menstruating Body Politic: José Martí, Gender, and Sexuality
    Stephanie Rivera Berruz   350

LIST OF CONTRIBUTORS   367

INDEX   371

PHILOSOPHIZING THE AMERICAS

Introduction: Prolegomenon to Inter-American Philosophy

Jacoby Adeshei Carter

Philosophizing the Americas exists as a prolegomenon to Inter-American philosophy. Scholars accepted the challenge to step beyond their disciplinarity and embrace the task of doing philosophy in an unfamiliar way. The results break new ground. This text invites scholars to expand their idea of what it means to do (Inter-) American philosophy. The chapters of this book are a foundation for a distinctly Inter-American philosophical discourse and field of study. Many chapters shed new light on well-studied figures, as well as on race and patriarchy. Others offer insights into unfamiliar thought traditions that are influential in the Caribbean or Latin America. Several essays contain thoughtful considerations of better- and lesser-known figures. Still others pose deep questions about what distinguishes Inter-American philosophy and whether to defend or criticize those features.

The most distinctive feature of *Philosophizing the Americas* is that it treats not American philosophy, but *Inter*-American philosophy. Fine volumes exist on the various schools of mainstream American philosophy. Fewer in number, but equally fine, are books on African American, Africana, Latin American, and Afro-Caribbean philosophy. But there does not exist a single text that consciously seeks to bring these traditions together as this volume does.

Latin American, Caribbean, and African American philosophy are three distinct philosophical traditions found across the Americas. Each has struggled with questions of legitimacy. There are differences between these traditions that are important for understanding each as a subfield of philosophy. Overlooking these differences obscures comprehension of the unique philosophical contribution provided by these intellectual traditions. However, difference is not the only relative characteristics of these philosophical traditions. There are similarities in subject matter, historical figures, methodologies, and critical orientation among these otherwise diverse traditions. Moreover, there is the fact that Latin American, Caribbean, and African American philosophy are all American philosophical traditions. This does not make them the same or provide grounds for a seamless integration between them. The historical, social, geopolitical, religious, economic, and cultural phenomena that constitute modernity have had far-reaching effects throughout the Americas—though not, of course, with equal effect in every sector. Exceptional is the American nation with no historical relation to the destruction of Indigenous cultures, the trans-Atlantic slave trade, European settler or exploitation colonialism, or national identity formation among diverse cultural populations. This list is merely illustrative. Latin American, Caribbean, and African American philosophy have all weighed in on such topics in novel and insightful ways, though not always—in fact rarely—in conversation with one another. This volume aims to change that in at least two ways. First, by intentionally bringing these diverse American philosophical traditions into conversation with one another, and second, by exploring further the possibilities created by that exchange between traditions.

Importantly, this assemblage of essays brings all three traditions up to date. The authors do not simply rehash older problems or questions in their respective fields. Instead, they engage the most current debates, such as those surrounding gender, race, and sexuality. Each in some way connects Africana and African American thought to Caribbean and Latin American thought. Essays explore the idea of creolizing the canon, racial realism, and Indigenous resistance. Scholars are increasingly interested in these areas, and efforts to "decolonize" philosophy are motivating explorations of philosophy beyond Europe and the U.S. The present text represents two novel interventions into these fields. First, it undoubtedly contributes to each of the three specific areas of philosophy. Second, it brings all three fields into dialogue with one another. It does this by exploring points of intersection and departure as themselves interesting subject matter for philosophical exploration.

Philosophizing the Americas draws an impressive range of philosophical traditions and figures into dialogue with one another. Some are familiar, such as José Martí, Sylvia Wynter, Martin R. Delany, José Vasconcelos, Alain Locke, and others. But some, such as Arturo Alfonso Schomburg, Hilda Hilst, and George Lamming, have not been written about extensively by philosophers. The volume is interdisciplinary in scope and focus. Most authors are philosophers, others are scholars from literary studies, history, Latin American studies, and anthropology. A few essays in the philosophy of literature consider philosophical ideas expressed in fictional or poetic form.

Philosophizing the Americas constitutes something quite new, needed, and original in both substance and approach. By coherently integrating an Inter-American perspective derived from various traditions it helps to develop a new philosophical discourse. This anthology is a new beginning. It voices a new perspective that meets important, hitherto unmet and unrecognized needs. The book is an organized vehicle for voices that share numerous philosophically and politically important themes. In some respects, these voices are already "out there," though not yet brought into dialogue with each other. The philosophy done in this book is instrumental for creating an Inter-American philosophy. It takes a particular view about which methods, concepts, or perspectives constitute Inter-American philosophy, yet it remains open to what Inter-American philosophy could be.

There is in fact a persistent editorial refusal to take a definitive position on what is most distinctive and important about this anthology. Is the aim to motivate a new type of philosophical dialogue among the Americas? And if so, what is the intellectual need for it, and what will it achieve that is unachieved without it? Should the aim be to show that there are resources for an emerging cultural and intellectual self-knowledge in the Americas and that it involves elements not yet clearly understood? And if so, does significant openness remain, or is it possible to identify and explicate its main contours now? Arguably, the cultural, intellectual, and philosophical concerns of this project capture something deeply particular and distinctive about the Americas beyond what one would expect of any large, diverse geographical region with a complex history.

Philosophizing the Americas contains numerous features concerning subject matter, topical content, methodology, and explanatory idiom. All are equally important, and the chapters of this book reflect that fact. There is an openness to a multiplicity of ways of framing and understanding Inter-American philosophy. There is no litmus test controlling entry. There are scholars in Africana, Caribbean, and Latin American philosophy for whom an achievement of the sort that this book can be is vitally important. This work responds to an intellectual need, even if others have not yet perceived it.

Offered here is a novel approach to philosophical inquiry, grounded in engagement with and between African American, Latin American, and Caribbean philosophers. The volume places particular emphasis on marginalized traditions of thought and resistance, especially Africana philosophy, Indigenous American philosophy, and feminist philosophy. There is an irreducibly critical element to the very notion of Inter-American philosophy. Doubts about the veracity of claims by "American" and European philosophers to describe and analyze humanity, reason, and human societies in the abstract motivate this project. Such philosophies justify formal and informal imperialism, racial inequities, patriarchy, and heteronormativity. Building from a broad base of cultural experiences, Inter-American philosophy demonstrates the inadequacy of US and European philosophers' universalist pretensions. This opens the way to insights relevant to struggles against the political, legal, and social formations those pretensions have helped sustain.

One may question the focus in some essays on thinkers of European descent who were perhaps more sympathetic to European than to American philosophy and politics. Most of the thinkers engaged in this text wrote in European languages and engaged deeply and not in a uniformly critical manner with European philosophy. If their thought is revolutionary, then arguably, that is not because the theorists are non-European. Plausibly, it is because they are theorizing from non-European—Inter-American—contexts. Arguably, greater emphasis should be placed on the contexts from which Inter-American philosophy emerges than on the identity of its proponents. This contention is at issue in several of the essays in this volume, which investigate theorists from the perspective of those whose humanity European thinking questions or denies, those who face intellectual and existential challenges to their humanity. Absolute rejection of European intellectualism is a non-starter in much of the Americas. Not every American thinker is subject to the dehumanizing intellectual constructs on which they reflect. While others philosophize from their perspective as members of dehumanized populations. Whether as targets or expounders of criticism, these thinkers focus in numerous ways on those often left out of European understandings of humanity and personhood. This is a fundamental, ubiquitous, and characteristic philosophical problem in the Americas.

The critical reader will ask how to differentiate American philosophical traditions so that instances of engagement between them amount to Inter-American philosophy. The question then becomes how to define American philosophical traditions such that we can make sense of which engagements between them count as Inter-American philosophy. Scholarly attention to an explicitly Inter-American philosophy lies at the center of this text but this anthology does not state definitively what counts as Inter-American philosophy. Some of the essays are prescriptive of such a philosophy. Others offer pensive proposals or suggest contestable avenues for development. At a minimum, a distinctive and characteristic feature of Inter-American philosophy is engagement across and between American philosophical traditions. This is more than mere juxtaposition. Engagement between American philosophies requires practitioners to substantively and critically take up the problems, arguments, and concepts of other traditions. Cursory interlocution is insufficient. The depth and breadth of exchange is a function of which problems, arguments, concepts, or figures are engaged. Predetermined accounts of how projects should look threatens to impede philosophical engagement and stifle creation of a sphere of discourse at the intersections of diverse American intellectual traditions.

Antecedent definitions or conceptions of American traditions are unavoidable in preliminary explorations of Inter-American philosophy. However, static, or dogmatic presuppositions are not necessary at an incipient stage. They could function as working hypotheses, tentative starting points to inaugurate inquiry. By remaining flexible to change, revision, or modification, insightful interaction across traditions may restructure present and historical understanding of concomitantly engaged traditions. Such intellectual possibilities are the purview of scholars interested in the philosophical terrain this volume helps to unearth. Such work begins here in earnest. The task is not complete in this single text. This is, however, a promising step towards defining, developing, and doing Inter-American philosophy.

Associated questions arise concerning who has done or presently does Inter-American philosophy. The anthology describes few instances where American intellectuals engaged with theorists from other parts of the Americas. The question arises whether Inter-American philosophy is solely a contemporary concern? Are there past iterations of Inter-American philosophy? Are past iterations worthy of our present attention? This anthology gives an affirmative answer to all three questions. The essays demonstrate superbly the potential for philosophical insight available when scholars draw together thinkers who did not themselves directly interact. The answer to the second question is weaker. Scholarship on the historical foundation and precedent of Inter-American philosophy is sorely needed. This anthology may serve as a clarion call to some to take up that task.

There are in fact few historical instances of the philosophical approach advocated in *Philosophizing the Americas*. It is not that there are none, but this book is more than an attempt to recover and comment on that history. This anthology provides intellectual resources for an Inter-American approach to philosophy in the present and the future. That project is usefully informed by understanding past intellectual exchanges, but a historical focus is not the only way forward. This anthology contends that Inter-American philosophy is something that contemporary philosophers should pursue, and a historical study of such engagements in the past is useful, but not required, for present efforts.

Many chapters in this anthology engage substantively with all three philosophical traditions brought together in this text. This is the first proposed feature of Inter-American philosophy. A few go further to include Indigenous philosophical perspectives, feminist philosophy, and African philosophy. They forge a dialogue on philosophical questions germane to the Caribbean, North, and Latin America. These essays situate arguments and concepts in a broadly American, and in some instances diasporic, context. Sometimes authors have an extremely specific, other times a general, focus. The volume explores ways that marginalized American traditions transform American philosophy.

This collection exemplifies the thought of marginalized American intellectuals as primary sources, rather than as foils to the thought of European intellectuals. This is the second suggested feature of Inter-American philosophy. It centers marginalized thinkers whose work focuses on philosophical problems unique to the Americas. Moreover, an Inter-American philosophy should frame such thinkers and works as appropriate objects of study, and not as tangential, parasitic, or subordinate to the work of European or mainstream American philosophers. Philosophical reflection on the populations, places, persons, politics, and histories of the Americas by those whose experiences were shaped by those phenomena is the crux of Inter-American philosophy. Such a perspective is a radical break from the way many marginalized figures are understood as critical interpreters of their own experiences, histories, identities, or socioeconomic realities.

Whether race is a modern invention or an antiquated phenomenon, it is a phenomenon of paramount human concern throughout the Americas. The philosophical examination of race touches on such fundamental humanistic concerns as what it means to be human, the nature of freedom and liberation, the proper formation of a state, the meaning and aim of revolution, the meaning and prospect of civilization, and the proper formation and exercise of democracy. Throughout the Americas the concept of race is a crucial and indispensable feature of philosophical inquiry. Here, by example, is a feature of Inter-American philosophy. Namely, an explicit focus on phenomena or concepts that are ubiquitous American concerns. Often such phenomena have specific and unique dimensions in the Americas relative to other parts of the world. A concept such as race can serve as a prism for investigating the Americas more broadly. Race functions as an entry point to various sectors of the Americas, be they regional, linguistic, religious, political, national, etc. The phenomenon or concept of race is merely indicative of this methodological approach. Other concepts such as nationality, democracy, coloniality, or revolution could equally serve as the paradigm through which to develop an Inter-American philosophy. The idea again is to identify concepts and phenomena that open multiple and intersecting avenues of investigation to all or most of the Americas simultaneously while also narrowing the scope of such inquiries.

Inter-American philosophy furthers human knowledge. Take for example the time-honored philosophical concern with humanity. What does it mean to be a full human person? What are the characteristics, and possibilities of such a being? How is personhood understood by those denied that status? Humanity and personhood are quintessential philosophical concerns, not only of Western European philosophy. Members of populations whose humanity European thinkers denied produced profound reflections on the subject. But more than a counter-assertion against European denials, Inter-American philosophy creates an interlocution between marginalized perspectives.

A single society in isolation is unlikely to furnish a proper understanding of humanity. Full understanding of humanity in all its intricacies requires contributions from a broad set of human perspectives. In some instances, fecund and profound philosophical insight into the nature of the human results from the perspective of those whose humanity is in question. Philosophizing from the existential position of a humanity denied is a creative precursor to philosophical insights that define traditions. Such revolutionizing reflections on humanity from the perspective of non-European thinkers exist throughout the Americas. In the Latin American intellectual tradition, it exists in the work of such thinkers as De las Casas, Rodo, Anibal Quijano, and José Martí. In Afro-Caribbean thought such reflections are present in such thinkers as Frantz Fanon, Sylvia Wynter, and Edward Blyden. And in the context of the United States the philosophical perspectives of a denied humanity come from thinkers like Frederick Douglass, David Walker, Anna Julia Cooper, or Martin Delany.

There is another possible task of Inter-American philosophy. It can interrogate within past and present contexts the problems and possibilities of using philosophy, even Anglo-European instantiations in service of liberation. Struggles against coloniality are ubiquitous throughout the Americas. This makes a characterization of Inter-American philosophy as anti-colonial struggle possible. Such characterization applies to Afro-Caribbean, Indigenous, Latin American, and African American philosophy. If anti-colonial struggle is an appropriate way to characterize some marginalized American philosophies, then such a notion can frame coherent conceptions of a philosophical tradition that reaches throughout the Americas.

Epistemically centering populations such as Indigenous or African descendant peoples provides a conceptual framework that challenges hegemonic tendencies. This is a fourth possible framework for Inter-American philosophy. Philosophizing the Americas in part offers a critical feminist perspective through similar epistemic centering. There is an opportunity here to connect various parts of the Americas. Black feminist and womanist thought are North American feminist positions that take seriously the intersection of race, class, and gender oppression. Coupled with Indigenous and Latina feminist perspectives, these feminisms can provide an excellent bridge for connecting decolonial feminist theorists in North America with the global South. Feminist resistance movements can discursively reshape various (Inter-)American feminisms. This indeed is an essential aspect of the anthology. The chapters reveal new conceptual and theoretical spaces as sometimes intended, and other times unforeseen, consequences of venturing into initially epistemically foreign conceptual territory.

Philosophical inquiry is importantly contextual. Investigations across contexts are less likely to privilege one context over another. There is an irreducibly critical element to the very notion of Inter-American philosophy, particularly in those cases where the object of investigation has broadly human significance. Inter-American philosophy challenges European traditions that claim universality. Inter-American philosophy is critical in its assertion that philosophical exploration of reason, ethics, knowledge, freedom, and the political cannot be thoroughly investigated from the privileged vantage point of a culture that has enjoyed political and imperial dominance. Some American philosophies question aspects of European philosophies. These philosophies address fundamental human concerns that relate to non-European populations in the Americas.

Inter-American philosophy affords the opportunity to better understand a multiplicity of systems of colonial and imperial domination, even while these are set in a wider and more diffuse geopolitical context. The critical orientation toward colonial impositions were not all analogous and do not all originate in the same condition of colonial imposition. This produced a variety of critical perspectives aimed at different colonial powers. The critical standpoint of various thinkers in the Americas varied with differences in place, race, gender, and social condition. Various populations in the Americas resisted European colonial domination. The kind and degree of domination varied, as did the resistance in thought or deed they were able to muster.

Philosophizing the Americas explores the possibilities of Inter-American philosophy in several ways. The essays in this volume provide examples of various methodologies and features of an Inter-American philosophy. This book makes no pretension regarding the success of any of these approaches. Future philosophical inquiry will collectively determine our understanding of Inter-American philosophy. The central problems it addresses, its method, the figures it considers will be the result of this inquiry.

Here is an initial foray into the possible field of Inter-American philosophy. If successful, this volume will stimulate philosophical exchanges beyond present disciplinary boundaries and fields throughout the Americas. *Philosophizing the Americas* is offered therefore as a prolegomenon to Inter-American philosophy.

PART I
*Inter-American Philosophy:
Theorizing the Americas*

1
Inter-American Philosophy: Born of Struggle?
Daniel Fryer

Introduction

In the opening sentence of his groundbreaking anthology *Philosophy Born of Struggle*, Leonard Harris writes that "philosophic texts, if products of social groups doggedly fighting to survive, are texts born of struggle."[1] So begins a collection that has become pivotal in African American philosophy. In fact, the phrase "born of struggle" is now used by many African American philosophers to describe their work, self-construction, and the overlap of the two.

They invoke it to explain the lived realities of their philosophy: how, that is, the questions they pursue academically are informed by the adversity they face as persons racialized as Black in the United States.[2] For the past three decades, an annual conference, "Philosophy Born of Struggle," has addressed philosophical questions pertinent to the African American community. For many, the recognition that they are members of an oppressed group in an American society and their philosophies are interconnected. This binds them to other philosophers whose projects are similarly associated with their condition. As a result, the "struggle" these philosophers confront creates a sense of community—a "we-ness"—that connects philosophical work done from many different angles to formulate a tradition.

Yet there is little written about when it is appropriate to designate a philosophy born of struggle. African American philosophers in the past few centuries have created bodies of literature while overcoming adversity and facing oppression that justifiably warrant the label "born of struggle". But should the phrase be reserved only for texts produced in the African American philosophical tradition? Given conversations at the recent "Philosophy Born of Struggle" conference—and the organization's apparent efforts to expand the conversation to include voices from other marginalized communities[3]—one might think that the label "born of struggle" has a larger scope than is suggested by its virtually exclusive use among those in the African American philosophical tradition.

But these efforts have not been followed by a philosophical attempt to determine the limits of the expression. Which means it's dangerously vulnerable to being misunderstood—or at least becoming too capricious a label for many forms of philosophy that differ in principle from the philosophy that Harris, and others, are referencing when they describe their philosophy as born of struggle.

This chapter explores some of the limits of this expression while attempting to characterize what it means to designate a philosophy "born of struggle". I argue that some of the diverse philosophical traditions throughout the Americas could be labeled as philosophies born of struggle and identify common praxes among them. My aim is to make a case for why it makes sense to understand various philosophical traditions throughout the Americas as philosophies born of struggle. Theses philosophies confront "American Philosophy" by raising challenges to standard conceptions about what issues are important, forcing a reevaluation of what "American" and "philosophy" actually mean.

The purpose of this chapter, however, is not to create an artificial unity between distinct philosophical traditions and ignore the nuances of the particular problems persons writing in these traditions encounter. On the contrary, the expression "born of struggle" emerges out of an attempt to make sense of different— sometimes conflicting—judgments of the world. In this respect, "[i]t heralds not one movement, but several."[4] This chapter provides an initial proposal for a unified conception of the various philosophical movements throughout the Americas that have challenged traditional ways of conceiving the world. By articulating what a philosophy "born of struggle" is, we could illuminate similarities between the African American philosophical tradition and other complex philosophical systems composed by persons who have faced oppression—that is, it could allow us to see connections between different, but "overlapping struggles." Clarity around the phrase forces us to consider the cultural and political linkages through which we could ground a philosophical discourse.

This chapter begins by reviewing Harris's use of "born of struggle" and demonstrating why extrapolating his use may not provide a sufficient account of what other African American philosophers are expressing when they use the phrase. I then provide three different interpretations of the expression: a broad interpretation that includes all philosophy written from positions of struggle; a narrow interpretation which includes philosophy written from African American experiences; and a third, intermediate, interpretation which situates various philosophies throughout the Americas as philosophies born of struggle. I make a case for the third interpretation by highlighting how philosophies born of struggle emerge through members of oppressed groups that challenge dominant conceptions of what it means to be "American" and what it means to do "philosophy." My hope is to initiate discussion between traditions that have often ignored each other. I conclude by discussing some apparent reasons why this step, although important, is only a small one toward the ultimate goal.

What Is Philosophy "Born of Struggle"?

The classification of a philosophy as born of struggle emerges directly out of an effort by Harris to introduce a genre of American philosophy to a world in which it was largely hidden.[5] In an attempt to provide a clear articulation of what it means to be a philosophy born of struggle, then, it makes sense to first turn toward what Harris attempted to convey when he introduced the expression. While we need not think that Harris's understanding of the term provides the definitive word on the matter,[6] examining his original use of the expression could shine light on the role the phrase has in the African American philosophical tradition, where Harris's work is often cited when invoking the expression.[7]

However, attempting to understand the meaning of the expression "born of struggle" through Harris's eyes creates a few problems. First, Harris does not go through much trouble to analyze the phrase and its limitations. In fact, it is in the opening sentence of *Philosophy Born of Struggle* that we find the only use of the expression in his entire anthology. While initially this may seem unusual, Harris's goal for the anthology is to demonstrate what a philosophy "born of struggle" is rather than to define it. Since Harris is contributing to the creation of the very tradition that he is commentating on, he is less worried about constructing a set of necessary conditions for the label born of struggle than he is with setting the stage for a compilation of articles that illustrates why African American philosophy is a philosophy born of struggle. Regardless, Harris's scarce use of the phrase creates a problem for anyone who wants to provide an interpretation solely through a strict conceptual focus. If examination were restricted to his use of the phrase "born of struggle," then we would have an inadequate understanding of its intended meaning. Thus, the search for Harris's position requires extrapolation from several comments throughout his work without a strict focus on when the label "born of struggle" is used.

Second, while Harris is interested in providing a text with various interpretations of the world by African Americans using mediums that are germane to African American culture for intellectual reasons, he also has a political agenda in mind. Formally, his aim is to present a "family of texts" with "various perspectives" that serves "as a guide to the ideas of modern Afro-American philosophers."[8] For this reason, a presentation of distinct arguments by philosophers facing similar struggles serves as a demonstration of what work in the tradition of African American philosophy looks like. However, an important consequence of Harris's anthology is the recognition of the philosophy of the Black experience as a legitimate area of inquiry. Harris provides reasons why philosophy, as an academic discipline, ought to be more receptive of philosophers writing in the tradition of African American philosophy. Thus, Harris also has a practical goal of attempting to get more Black scholars working as academic philosophers in American institutions.[9] This practical goal of Harris may distort how Harris characterizes a philosophy born of struggle. His almost exclusive attention to African American philosophy in his anthology need not be taken as evidence of him suggesting that African American philosophy is the only philosophy born of struggle. The restricted focus on African American philosophy could be viewed as political—not theoretical. One should not take Harris' lack of attention to other philosophies as evidence against him understanding them to be born of struggle. His presentation of African American philosophy suggests that it is *a* philosophy born of struggle, not *the* philosophy born of struggle.

I mention these two interpretative obstacles at the outset to suggest some leeway in our hermeneutical exercise. They are relevant to our purpose because they suggest a broad range of arguments could be viewed as consistent with Harris's intended meaning of the expression "born of struggle." To determine whether it is appropriate to use the label to ground an inter-American discourse, one should assess some of the alternative interpretations to decide the limitations and practical issues when articulating a philosophy born of struggle.

Three Interpretations of Philosophy Born of Struggle

There are, at least, three interpretations to deal with here. The first interprets the phrase "philosophy born of struggle" broadly and suggests that the expression denotes any philosophy written from a position of struggle. On this interpretation, the label could be used as a descriptive tool for a variety of texts produced under conditions of struggle without making any specifications to the particular conditions or the persons producing these texts. In Harris's sole use of the phrase in the first edition of his anthology, he speaks as if there is a plurality of social groups whose philosophies warrant the label born of struggle and does not engage in a discussion of whether there are particular, relevant struggles that limit the expression's applicability. While Harris is concerned with the way it applies to one particular philosophy—namely, African American philosophy—his understanding of the expression may be much broader. In fact, given that African American philosophy is often commended for its "politics of inclusion" and "seemingly infinite capacity to be compatible with any number of philosophical traditions,"[10] it may be unsurprising if Harris understands "born of struggle" as an umbrella term that captures this inclusivity.

A second, narrower, interpretation of the expression limits the applicability of the label to African American philosophy. If *Philosophy Born of Struggle* does anything, it provides the reader with an understanding of what philosophizing from the Black experience looks like. African American philosophers endure a unique struggle, as Black people's experience of the American society has never coincided with the philosophical principles that are said to form the foundation of a democratic United States. The history of African Americans being deemed sub-persons and incapable of rationalization leads to Black people engaging in a socio-existential struggle when reflecting on conditions in a society that views Black people as inferior. African Americans were not part of intellectual discussions because African Americans were viewed as incapable of possessing the faculties that were required to participate in a professional field of inquiry. In this sense, a philosophy born of struggle situates reflective thought in the lived experiences of African Americans—a group of people deemed as inferior, different, and unimportant.

A third interpretation of the phrase situates the expression born of struggle somewhere between the broad and narrow interpretations described above. This view takes the label born of struggle to be more exclusive than the philosophy produced by persons under the conditions of struggle, yet more inclusive than the philosophy written from the African American experience. From this perspective, philosophizing from the African American experience is a paradigmatic, but not exhaustive, case of a philosophy born of struggle. In addition, this interpretation of the label places significance on particular kinds of struggles, precluding the universal application of expression to all struggles. This interpretation of philosophy born of struggle aims to show how African American philosophy, and other philosophies of a similar character, diverge from traditional philosophical practices and endorse a strategy of inquiring about the world from the position of an oppressed subject attempting to overcome adversity.

Evaluating the Three Interpretations of Philosophy Born of Struggle

With these three interpretations in the background, we can now assess the merits of each. The first interpretation gets its appeal from being consistent with the inclusionary practice that has become common in African American philosophy.

On this interpretation, the label born of struggle is quite flexible: it could be used to describe any philosophical text written from the position of struggle. Taking the phrase straightforwardly, this understanding of philosophy born of struggle includes the production of any philosophical text that is produced under challenging conditions.

The risk here, however, is that if one interprets the expression too broadly then the expression may capture philosophical texts that Harris's anthology was unmistakably meant to separate African American philosophy from. While Harris does not tell us what philosophies are not born of struggle, he is aware of the importance of exclusion when formulating traditions[11] and does not appear to intend for the label "born of struggle" to apply to all philosophical texts written from a position of struggle. He wanted the expression to capture texts by a particular group of persons facing distinct challenges inside and outside of the academy. The philosophical tradition has many cases of members of social groups attempting to achieve survival through their writing; however, it is not clear that all of these would be what Harris had in mind when he states that texts are born of struggle.

Take, for instance, the seventeenth century English philosopher John Locke, who was part of a group of equality radicals whose work emphasized revolutionary responses to political systems that wrongfully denied equality. John Locke wrote from a position of struggle as he confronted real political systems that claimed to be legitimate despite this denial of equality to their citizens. His struggles were both academic and social. His period in exile in the Dutch Republic is intimately connected to some of the themes of his work, and much of Locke's philosophical contributions are inseparable from his core beliefs. Locke struggled as a person who believed that an injustice occurred when people were denied their basic rights. The views in John Locke's *Letter* and *Second Treatise* are the views of a radical who is fighting for survival in a time that was dismissive to his thoughts.[12] Similar views also led to his removal as a student from Oxford.[13] Although the illiberal position advocating for the divine right of kings based on patriarchalism dominated at the time, Locke stood by his liberal commitments even through exile for accusations of treasonable activity.[14] For this reason, it seems the work produced by John Locke would warrant the label "born of struggle" if we take a broad understanding of the expression as suggested by the first interpretation.

Yet, it seems clear that John Locke's work is not what Harris has in mind when he discusses philosophical texts that are born of struggle. Describing his work as such betrays the expression. While Locke separated himself from his peers when he expressed his sentiments through his writings, prior to the expression of these views he was accepted by his society and had unrestricted access to the larger philosophical community. His case seems vastly different than, to use one of Harris's examples, Broadus N. Butler, who, after graduating with a doctoral degree from the University of Michigan in 1952, discovered that his advisers' letter of recommendation stated ". . . a good philosopher, but of course, a Negro." The one-line response he received from one of the institutions he applied to was of similar spirit: "Why don't you go where you will be among your own kind."[15] Harris's intention is to identify a struggle by a group of people who, like Butler, are deemed outsiders because of their identity—they are external to the philosophical community because of who they are, not just what they write. While John Locke's philosophy could be viewed as born of struggle if we take a broad understanding of the phrase, it does not seem that his writings would be born of struggle in the sense that Harris, and others writing in the tradition of African American philosophy, understand the phrase. The expression denotes a struggle against "a world unduly reluctant to embrace, and unwilling to avow, messages of truth, insight, sound arguments, or cogent messages *because of their source.*"[16] The broad interpretation, then, seems inconsistent with the spirit of the expression.[17]

Perhaps, then, there ought to be a limited understanding of the expression that does not include everyone writing from a position of struggle. The second, narrower, interpretation of a philosophy born of struggle provides just that. On this interpretation, philosophy born of struggle represents a set of texts that foreground the social and historical struggle of persons racialized as Black in the United States. If the source of the philosophical work is what makes it born of struggle, then it may seem reasonable to conclude that Harris intended the expression to solely capture philosophical work done from the African American experience. To separate cases like Broadus Butler from those like John Locke's we could interpret "born of struggle" to mean philosophical reflections of the human condition by those who are often denied a philosophical voice because their identity deems them unphilosophical.

Since Black people have often been on the margins of European and American societies, there has not been much concern for reflective thoughts of African Americans. As George Yancy writes, "[t]o think of the history of western philosophy as constituting a family with cross-generational (monochromatic) ties, it is important to note that Black people were never even part of the family; they were already outsiders, deemed permanently unfit to participate in the normative philosophical community."[18] Using the work of Harris and other African American philosophers as a guide, Yancy's discussion of African American philosophy is meant to transcend "the familial 'Oedipal conflict' subtext that is often associated with so many thinkers who eagerly unseat the patriarch of modern philosophy."[19] Given the persistent oppression of persons of

African descent, Yancy follows Charles Mills in arguing for a different, non-Cartesian, approach to philosophy that challenges the philosophical assumptions that much of Western philosophy stands on. For Yancy, the "reinforced sub-personhood status" of African Americans creates a discipline that "looks suspiciously upon and rejects the a-historical nature of the epistemic subject."[20] Contrary to Cartesian epistemology, Yancy writes, "Black self-understanding grows out of a social matrix of pain and suffering; a site where the Black body is a site of marked inferiority, difference, and deviance."[21] Echoing Mills' comments about why Cartesian skepticism would be an inadequate approach for most African American philosophers who are interested in theorizing about their lived experience, Yancy declares that "[l]ynch mobs make a mockery of Cartesian hyperbolic doubt." This is because "the vitriol of white racism forces one to be ever cognizant of the existence of other minds, not in vats, but as embodied and raced." It seems rational to believe that "solipsism has no place in a world where Black bodies are mutilated and burned for the pleasure of others." Hence, Yancy concludes, "for Black people, the philosophical problem is not whether one exists or not, but how to collectively resist a white supremacist world of absurdity where one is degraded, marginalized, humiliated, oppressed and brutalized."[22] As long as Black people face discrimination and oppression from the philosophical community and the general society, African American philosophical thought will be linked by a shared struggle and support a particular epistemological and social ontological approach.

If we recognize philosophies born of struggle as limited to philosophical work done from the African American experience, then Yancy's discussion of African American philosophy provides us with an understanding of the socio-existential struggle African American philosophers endure and how it informs African Americans' approach to philosophizing about a lived experience. While Yancy does not aim to reduce African American philosophy to struggle, he suggests that the discipline's starting point presupposes an oppressed subject.[23] So interpreting philosophy born of struggle in this narrow way—that is, as a philosophy from the African American experience—allows us to understand the philosophical site where African American philosophy takes place. On this view, labeling African American philosophy as a philosophy born of struggle does a particular kind of epistemological work as it informs us that the critical reflection and philosophical engagement is aimed at changing the world by a group of oppressed persons. This starting point is arguably different than the one held by traditional figures often discussed in philosophical discourse.

There is little doubt that Harris agrees that there are particular features of African American philosophy that distinguish it from other forms of philosophy.

In addition to the rejection of the universal self and insistence on starting from the place of oppression, African American philosophers are also often expected to understand the history of Western philosophy and validate their ideas by showing its connection to canonized thought. As Harris writes, "[since] the white world accords little status to philosophic activities, couched in the Black heritage, the Black philosopher must banter contributions between two worlds."[24] These, and many other features, are common to philosophizing from the Black experience in the United States and this cultural matrix is believed to create a distinct genre of philosophy.

But rather than exploring the distinguishing features of African American philosophy, the question then becomes whether other philosophies share the features with African American philosophy that make it a philosophy born of struggle. This is not to deny that there is something distinct about African American philosophy. My focus here is not on what makes African American philosophy distinct, but what renders African American philosophy a philosophy born of struggle. If we specify *that* struggle as deriving from the African American experience alone, then we preclude the possibility of other philosophies being appropriately described as such. However, if we treat African American philosophy as a paradigmatic, though not exhaustive, case of what a philosophy born of struggle looks like, then we can use it to detect philosophies of a similar character. I am not suggesting that we take a phrase that has importance in the African American philosophical tradition and appropriate it to a wide variety of philosophical projects that would collapse the phrase into a descriptor for any type of philosophy that share similarities with African American philosophy. Instead, I offer an interpretation of philosophy born of struggle that provides us with insight into various philosophical conditions that derive from persons enduring similar struggles from similar sources. But then we must ask: What grounds this view?

The third interpretation of "philosophy born of struggle" extends the applicability of the label beyond the African American philosophical experience but falls short of suggesting that all philosophy written from a position of struggle qualifies as "born of struggle." Philosophies born of struggle, at bottom, are philosophical productions by members of oppressed groups who are striving for social and political freedom. A site of power that dictates what (and who?) is important often denies this freedom to them. African American philosophy, as a philosophy born of struggle, challenges the nature of American philosophy by showing how certain principles that are viewed as important to laying the philosophical foundation of an American society—principles such as equality, liberty, etc.—are not universally distributed. Like those in the African American philosophical tradition, all philosophies born of struggle approach the world from a different epistemological context than philosophies from those in dominant positions. Philosophies born of struggle conceptualize the world from a consciousness where the person stands as victim to or outcast from a larger society.

Broadus Butler's essay on Frederick Douglass in *Philosophy Born of Struggle* illustrates this point. As Butler notes, "[t]he philosophical context from which the metaphysical and social world outlook of Frederick Douglass emerged in the nineteenth century United States is very different from that of Thomas Jefferson even when interpreting the same words of the same fundamental documents and ideas. Yet each purported to define the deepest meaning of America."[25] However, the Americas that these figures knew were radically different. Douglass wanted to construct an understanding of a nation that was contingent on the rights that were granted to African Americans. In this spirit, Butler notices a difference between Douglass's constructions of the world and those who approach similar questions from a dominant position:

> Those constructions were not part of the mindset of the Jeffersons or even the more recent liberals among traditional American philosophers. Frederick Douglass as distinguished from Thomas Jefferson in the realm of political thought or William James, John Dewey, Alfred North Whitehead, George Mead, or George Santayana in the philosophical arena addressed conceptual and analytical questions from a humanicentric perspective. That is, a perspective that presupposes that all human being are equal qua humans and does not base human equality upon political and economic premises. The others, by contrast, address such matters from a systems-centric and an institutional analysis based upon European political, philosophical, and economic theories and systems rather than broader human universalities.[26]

Although appealing to the same principles as his contemporaries, Douglass aims to demonstrate that these principles extend further than normally considered. The problem is not that abstract philosophical ideas do not provide recognition of the importance of freedom. The problem is that the documents that form the basis of the society "did not contemplate the peer status of Black Americans or of women or of Native Americans within the purview of the polity."[27] Douglass's voice stands in to show that the understanding of the reality of the philosophical principles that ground American philosophy would be incorrectly understood unless it includes the existence of persons who are not white men and, consequently, their reflection on reality.

The point is that philosophies born of struggle provide alternative voices to a hegemonic system that often works toward silencing the voices of those in non-dominant positions. These voices form the basis of the African American philosophical tradition, but may also ground feminist philosophy, Afro-Caribbean philosophy, Latin American philosophy, Native American philosophy, Asian American philosophy, and lesbian and queer philosophy.[28] A historical, racial, cultural, and gendered force has traditionally created a framework where these voices are considered "other" voices outside of the philosophical milieu. Once they are let in, they then become confrontational voices sitting on the bottom end of the philosophical hierarchy that presumes a universal grasp of the totality. The voices that are grounding philosophies born of struggle then become "contestatory voices," that are "deemed anthropologically interesting only and lacking in sophistication and rigor."[29]

This perception by the dominant members in the discipline could also have a negative effect on marginalized groups, compelling them to question the legitimacy of their philosophical tradition and the importance of the philosophers in their community. In this vein we get the Brazilian academic Afranio Coutinho, denying the philosophical capacities of Brazilians at the First Inter-American Conference of philosophy in 1943:

> One cannot speak of a Brazilian philosophy or of Brazilian philosophers as distinguished from thinkers. We have neither. We have not even a philosophical mind. Our creative capacity expresses itself in poetry and music, both of them having been elevated in our country to the highest level of greatness.[30]

At a conference devoted to facilitating a wider understanding of the various philosophical contributions of groups throughout the Americas, Coutinho unreluctantly states that Brazil, because of its "colonial mentality," has not been able to produce philosophers who have made original contributions.[31] This statement is strikingly close to the statement by E. Franklin Frazier in 1962 that Harris mentions in the introduction to *Philosophy Born of Struggle*. Frazier, a prominent African American sociologist, writes:

> We have no philosophers or thinkers who command the respect of the intellectual community at large. I am not talking about the few teachers of philosophy who have read Hegel or Kant or James and memorized their thoughts. I am talking about men who have reflected upon the fundamental problems which have always concerned philosophers such as the nature of human knowledge and the meaning or lack of meaning of human existence.[32]

To these scholars the meaning of philosophy connotes something beyond the contributions of what was being produced by the members of their community.

The dominant position that members of their group are unable to make philosophical contributions is internalized by some of the members of the group. As a result, the important work being done by Brazilian and African American thinkers at the time are not deemed worthy of the label "philosophy." The issue of philosophical heterogeneity, then, penetrates different oppressed communities, where diverse philosophical voices are undervalued and go unrecognized as philosophy. Philosophies born of struggle work to demolish the hegemonic influence that sits both internal and external to their communities.

In rethinking "born of struggle" as a label for examinations of the world by various oppressed groups that are dismissed because of features of their identity, there is still indeterminacy to the scope of the phrase. I have followed Harris in speaking about particular genres of American philosophy that are philosophies born of struggle. These philosophies challenge the dominant conception about what it means to be "American" and what it means to do "philosophy" by presenting alternative voices that challenge the prevailing norm. I have suggested that the term could be applied to various texts produced in multiple traditions—including feminist philosophy, Afro-Caribbean philosophy, Latin American philosophy, Native American philosophy, Asian American philosophy, and lesbian and queer philosophy—that work toward destabilizing some of the oppressive barriers that ground some of the outdated, established views of the philosophical canon. Like much of the work in the African American philosophical tradition, these traditions challenge what it means to do philosophy in America. Philosophical traditions, such as the philosophy of liberation out of Latin America and Negritude philosophy out of Caribbean America, are also examples of philosophies born of struggle that have provided sophisticated analyses of a "postcolonial" reality[33]—a subject that Harris notably views as lacking in African American philosophy.[34] Harris notes that, on his account, "philosophy is most valuable when its authors and texts are decidedly dedicated to liberation."[35] In a society tormented with misery, "the pursuit of liberation is at least laudable."[36] The philosophical traditions mentioned above share a common feature of being harmed by American philosophy and American philosophy's exclusionary practices. Thus, the scope of philosophies born of struggle may extend to the diverse philosophical discourses that work to combat the traditional American racist and heterosexual philosophical framings. "Liberation from such social consequences and critiques by theories tending to legitimize reprehensible conditions," we might say, "are the distinguishing marks of"[37] philosophies born of struggle.

Which philosophical traditions that exist outside of the American context would warrant the label is a question that I will not attempt to answer at this moment. Given the epistemological work that labeling something "born of struggle" does, it is likely that those who face comparable struggles in other parts of the world could appropriately use the label to describe their condition. I have in mind not philosophers like John Locke, but perhaps philosophers such as Margaret Cavendish or Anton Wilhelm Amo, who provided philosophical voices despite the oppressive social conditions that were operative in the societies that they lived in. Much more needs to be said about the epistemological working of philosophies born of struggle and how we interpret work in the history of philosophy that are written under these oppressive conditions before we could begin to consider an exhaustive list of philosophies born of struggle.[38] But rather than deal with the possibility of this expansion here, I end by noting a different question that is at the heart of this inquiry. Up until now, I have been speaking about when it is suitable to label a philosophy "born of struggle." I have suggested that various forms of philosophical works by marginalized groups contributing to the deconstruction of the wrongful perception of what it means to be an "American" and to do "philosophy" may be considered philosophies born of struggle. This departs from a myopic view of the phrase, but also avoids permitting expansive applications that would go against the spirit of the term. At this point, we may ask: what is at stake in all of this? What, that is, happens once these various philosophies become recognized as philosophies born of struggle?

Conclusion

Once philosophies born of struggle acknowledge each other as such it opens the possibility for a discourse that functions simultaneously as a site of unity and as disunity. Philosophies born of struggle have become accustomed to engaging in abstractions about identity claims and unjustified means of oppression that offer a principle of unity against the hegemonic power. Thus, they exploit the perceived differences that often ground the unequal treatment between those in marginalized groups and those in the dominant group by using principles or arguments that are accepted by those in the dominant group to say "look, we are the same as you" or "ain't I an American?" As a result, these various philosophical traditions have become accustomed to constantly looking at the work of the oppressive power while only occasionally glancing at the works of each other. Even when we fight similar problems—from a similar location—we are not sufficiently united with those who face similar struggles because of different identities. As an example, Gregory Fernando Pappas writes, "Blacks and Hispanics in many of our cities have not engaged sufficiently together in a more general inquiry about racism. Many somehow find it difficult to 'distance' themselves enough from the particular problem they suffer to learn from the similar problem of another."[39] What I am arguing for here is not to ignore the historical factors contributing to these groups' oppression—nor to release oneself from the problems that contribute to these groups' struggle—but to emphasize the importance of a joint effort to confront the dominant force. It is only through this joint effort that we may confidently secure freedom for people with similar identities as ours without obstructing the attainment of freedom for other groups with marginalized identities. An inter-American philosophical discourse among the various marginalized groups of society, groups whose philosophies are born of struggle, allows for the redefining of American philosophy using concepts that have traditionally grounded American philosophy but showing reasons why they have different extensions.

Up to a point, then, philosophies born of struggle already engage in a similar project. The problem is not creating commonalities for philosophies born of struggle, but being conscious of them. Once we become aware of the overlapping struggles that we face, we are able to form our own "family" of philosophy that works toward understanding the problems that corrupt our liberation. It is only then that we could begin to collectively break down the barriers that we have, until now, only chiseled at independently.

Notes

1. Leonard Harris, *Philosophy Born of Struggle: Anthology of Afro-American Philosophy from 1917* (Dubuque, Iowa: Kendall/Hunt Pub. Co., 1983), ix (italics added).

2. For an example of this, see George Yancy, *African-American Philosophers: 17 Conversations* (New York: Routledge, 1998).

3. See Tommy J. Curry and Leonard Harris, "Philosophy Born of Struggle: Thinking through Black Philosophical Organizations as Viable Schools of Thought." *Radical Philosophy Review*, 18, no. 1 (2015): 1–10, at 2. Despite these efforts to expand conversations, including with "Latino/a philosophers and LGBTQ scholarship," Curry and Harris state that philosophy born of struggle "maintain[s] a singular focus: philosophies within the African American resistance tradition." Curry and Harris, "Philosophy Born of Struggle." In many ways, this chapter asks: What happens if we move beyond that singular focus?

4. See "Introduction" in Harris, *Philosophy Born of Struggle*, xi

5. See George Yancy, "Leonard Harris," in Yancy, *African-American Philosophers*, 214.

6. Indeed, after this chapter was submitted, an edited volume of Harris's work was published with a newly printed essay articulating Harris's conception of philosophy. See Leonard Harris "What, then, is 'Philosophy Born of Struggle?': *Philosophia Nata Ex Conatu*: (Philosophy as, and Sourced by, Strife, Tenaciousness, Organisms Striving)" in *A Philosophy of Struggle: The Leonard Harris Reader*, ed. Lee McBride

(Bloomsbury, 2020), 13–39. In his essay, Harris notes that "[t]here is no one 'philosophy born of struggle;'" "[p]hilosophy born of struggle should always make possible epistemological, metaphysics, aesthetics that include the excluded;" and "[e]xceptionalism is always dangerous." Yet his essay is primarily an exercise of rejecting other conceptions of philosophy—not articulating the boundaries of a philosophy born of struggle or examining whether the phrase should be reserved only for texts produced in African American philosophical traditions. Regardless, this chapter is concerned about whether various philosophies throughout the Americas *could* be designated a philosophy born of struggle as the phrase is commonly used in African American philosophical thought. It is less concerned about whether Harris *would* accept this as so. Although his inclusive approach suggests that there may be room to extend the phrase to other philosophies throughout the Americas, the analysis here does not require that Harris adopts this approach.

7. This is not to suggest that Harris was the first African American philosopher to use the phrase. The expression goes back as least as far as Frederick Douglass, who declared that "the whole history of the progress of human liberty shows that all concessions yet made to her august claims have been *born of earnest struggle.*" John Blassingame, *The Frederick Douglass Papers, series Three, Speeches, Debates, and Interviews, Vol. 3, 1855–63* (New Haven: Yale University Press, 1985), 204 (italics added). Indeed, even some of Harris's contemporaries sought to adopt the notion of struggle to explain the condition of Black philosophers prior to the publication of *Philosophy Born of Struggle*. In fact, Curry and Harris lists Lucius Outlaw's "Black Folk and the Struggle in Philosophy" as one of two essays that "carved out a theoretical geography marking the foundation of Black perspectives in philosophy." See Curry and Harris, "Philosophy Born of Struggle: Thinking through Black Philosophical Organizations as Viable Schools of Thought," 4 (citing Lucius Outlaw, "Black Folk and the Struggle in Philosophy," *Radical Philosopher's News Journal* 6 (1976): 21–30).

8. Harris, *Philosophy Born of Struggle*, xxi.

9. This aim is more visible in the introduction to the second edition of *Philosophy Born of Struggle* and other articles by Harris in that volume such as "Believe It or Not."

10. See Tommy J. Curry, "On Derelict and Method," *Radical Philosophy Review* 14, no. 2, (2011): 139–164 at 139–140.

11. See Leonard Harris "Horror of Traditions" in John Pittman, ed. *African-American Perspectives and Philosophical Traditions* (New York: Routledge, 1997), 96.

12. It is worth noting that the *Two Treatises* and *The Letter Concerning Toleration* were both published anonymously. These texts express controversial intuitions that would have jeopardized anyone's reputation and wellbeing in seventeenth century England. But Locke believed in the arguments expressed in these writings and continued to defend them against objections years after they were first published. Part of his life was a *struggle* to provide coherent defenses of the liberal views that were rejected by the society in which he lived.

13. See Laslett's "Introduction" in John Locke, *Two Treatises Of Government*, ed. Peter Laslett (Cambridge England: Cambridge University Press, 1988), 23.

14. Laslett, "Introduction," p. 20

15. Leonard Harris, *Philosophy Born of Struggle: Anthology of Afro-American philosophy from 1917.* (Dubuque, Iowa: Kendall/Hunt Pub. Co.BOS 1st Ed., 1988), ix.

16. Harris, *Born of Struggle* (1988), ix (italics added).

17. For other features of Harris's philosophy that concur with my refutation of this broad interpretation of philosophy born of struggle, see Leonard Harris, "Philosophy of Philosophy: Race, Nation, and Religion." *Graduate Faculty Philosophy Journal* 35, nos. 1–2 (2014): 369–380.

It is worth noting, too, that Locke's ownership of stock in slave trading companies, and his other involvement with slavery in the Americas, would make him an awkward target for the designation "born of struggle" in the sense that African American philosophers have used the phrase. The broad reading would curiously entail that we apply the label to a person some believe to be a racist who tried to justify slavery and the seizure of Native American lands. For a discussion of the racism in Locke's work, see Robert Bernasconi and Anika Mann, "The Contradictions of Racism, Locke Slavery and the Two Treatises," in *Race and Racism in Modern Philosophy*, ed. Andrew Valls (Ithaca, NY: Cornell University Press 2005), 89–107. But see Wulliam Uzgalis, "John Locke, Racism, Slavery, and Indian Lands," in *The Oxford Handbook of Philosophy and Race*, ed. Naomi Zack (Oxford University Press, 2017), 20–30, for an explanation for why Locke's *philosophy* is not racist (even if Locke was).

18. See George Yancy, "African-American Philosophy: Through the Lens Of Socio-Existential Struggle," *Philosophy & Social Criticism* 37, no. 5 (2011): 551–574, at 552.

19. Yancy, "African-American Philosophy."

20. Yancy.

21. Yancy, 554.

22. Yancy, 556.

23. Yancy, 554.

24. See Leonard Harris, "Philosophy in Black and White." *Proceedings and Addresses of the American Philosophical Association* (American Philosophical Association, 1978), 418.

25. See Broadus Butler's "Frederick Douglass: The Black Philosopher in the United States," in Harris, *Philosophy Born of Struggle*.

26. Harris, *Philosophy Born of Struggle*, 5.

27. Harris, *Philosophy Born of Struggle*, 4.

28. For a demonstration of multiple philosophical voices discussing problems they confront as part of these traditions, see George Yancy, *Philosophy in Multiple Voices* (Rowman & Littlefield, 2007).

29. George Yancy's "Introduction" in Yancy, *Philosophy in Multiple Voices*, 8.

30. Afranio Coutinho, "Some considerations on the problem of philosophy in Brazil," *Philosophy and Phenomenological Research* 4, no. 2 (1943): 186–193 at 186.

31. In a recent essay, Harris discusses what could be viewed as a slightly mitigated version of this mentality that continues today when discussing the impact of

colonialism on formerly colonized societies: "One of the saddest commentaries on the colonial heritage is that the formerly colonized tend to grant high honors, in the form of financial rewards, titles, and awards for books to scholars of the former colonizer. Of the fifteen honored lecturers at the Centre for Logic, Epistemology and the History of Science at the Universidade Estadual de Campinas, Brazil, by 2007 thirteen were from Europe and two were from Latin America." See Leonard Harris, "Philosophy of Philosophy, 373.

32. See Harris, *Philosophy Born of Struggle*, xii.

33. See e.g. Walter D. Mignolo, "The Geopolitics of Knowledge and the Colonial Difference," *The South Atlantic Quarterly*, 101, no. 1 (2002): 57–96; Luis Fernando Restrepo "Colonial Thought," in *A Companion to Latin American Philosophy*, edited by Susana Nuccetelli, Ofelia Schutte, and Otávio Bueno (Malden, MA: Wiley-Blackwell, 2010), 36–52; Aimé Césaire, *Discourse on colonialism* (New York: Monthly Review Press, 2001).

34. Leonard Harris, "Telos and Tradition: Making the Future—Bridges to Future Traditions," *Philosophia Africana* 16, no. 2 (2014): 59–71 at 62–63.

35. Harris, "Telos and Tradition," 62.

36. Harris, "Telos and Tradition."

37. Compare Harris, *Philosophy Born of Struggle*, xv (stating that this is the distinguishing mark of African American heritage).

38. This is not meant to imply that we can have an exhaustive list. It is possible that given that new conceptions of liberation are likely to occur (ones that we have not even considered), it is possible that the expression "born of struggle" will be continuously evolving. I thank Leonard Harris for pointing out the possibility of this indeterminacy to me.

39. See Gregory Pappas "Distance, Abstraction, and the Role of the Philosopher in the Pragmatic Approach to Racism," in *Pragmatism and the Problem of Race*, eds. Bill E. Lawson and Donald F. Koch. (Indiana University Press, 2004), 22–32, at 29.

2
Bringing Africa to the Americas: The Creolizing of Afro-Caribbean Philosophy

Chike Jeffers

In my first publication as a budding philosopher, I offered a constructive critique of the Antiguan sociologist and philosopher Paget Henry's landmark book, *Caliban's Reason: Introducing Afro-Caribbean Philosophy*.[1] I argued there that, in *Caliban's Reason*, Henry misleadingly represents the study of philosophical content in traditional African thought as less controversial in nature, more standardized in method, and more uniform in results than it is because of his mission to position traditional African philosophy as a resource to be drawn on in developing Afro-Caribbean philosophy. In this chapter, as part of the effort to philosophize the Americas and encourage inter-American dialogue, I wish to develop the constructive aspect of my earlier treatment of Henry's book. Despite my argument that he misrepresents the ease with which this is possible, I want to defend Henry's view that drawing upon philosophy from the African continent and particularly from its precolonial traditions should be viewed as essential to the advancement of the practice of philosophy in the African diaspora across the Americas.

In the chapter's first section, I will describe the engagement with and investment in traditional African philosophy in *Caliban's Reason*. In the second section, I will bring up a possible criticism of this treatment of the importance of African thought. One might worry that it involves a kind of racial essentialism. In response to this objection, I will explain and defend how Henry's position grows out of the need to resist the cultural dimension of the system of white supremacy. In the third and final section, I will consider whether Henry's imperative to engage with African thought applies equally to African American, Afro-Latin, and African Canadian philosophy. I will argue that his argument carries over.

Henry's Use of Traditional African Philosophy

Henry aims to provide us in the first chapter of *Caliban's Reason* with "a systematic outline of traditional African philosophy."[2] He tries to capture and express what he takes to be the religious vision informing traditional African philosophy, describing its cosmogonic ontology and its existentialist, ethical, and epistemological dimensions. He draws on studies by philosophers and anthropologists of various African peoples and societies, including the Akan, the Yoruba, the Igbo, the Luba, the Tallensi, the Dogon, and the Kingdom of Dahomey. On the basis of his readings of these studies, he produces a picture of traditional African philosophy clearly intended to be comparable to the discernment of larger patterns and trends in Western philosophy or Eastern philosophy.

One of the most important themes in traditional African philosophy, according to Henry, is the relationship between the individual self and the spiritual world. Influenced by the Ghanaian philosopher Kwame Gyekye, Henry is particularly fond of the example of the Akan concepts, *okra* and *sunsum*. The *okra*, or "soul," is a "divine spark" that every human being has, encoded with a divine message that determines for each individual what his or her destiny will be.[3] It is not, however, the conscious part of the self. The *sunsum*, which Henry refers to as the "ego," is the conscious part.[4] This distinction between parts of the self introduces the possibility of conflict between the conscious, active *sunsum* and its destiny as encoded within the *okra*. As Henry puts it, there can be "gaps between the message that was spiritually encoded in the *Okra* and the projects of being that our egos create for themselves."[5] Thus, while the achievement of fulfillment in life requires that the *sunsum* develop within the guidelines of the *okra*, it is common for us to end up striving in directions that put us at odds with the destiny bestowed upon us by the Creator. Henry speaks of the process of seeking to live in accord with one's destiny as involving the resolution of a conflict between "self-determination" and "spiritual determination" in favor of the latter (and this, of course, can require attaining spiritual knowledge through such means as divination or spirit possession).[6]

Having introduced traditional African philosophy in his first chapter, Henry returns to it repeatedly throughout the rest of the book. The second and third chapters concern two major Afro-Caribbean philosophical minds: C.L.R. James of Trinidad and Frantz Fanon of Martinique. In both chapters, Henry expresses what he finds powerful in their thought but then mounts a critique of their work concerning their lack of engagement with traditional African philosophy. James is criticized for having accepted an understanding of the distinction between the modern and the premodern that makes paying any attention to the content of traditional African thought unnecessary: "its truth claims were part of a larger group of premodern claims that James did not feel any necessity to affirm or reject."[7] Fanon is criticized for having appropriated the language of European existentialism in order to explore the Afro-Caribbean psyche while having neglected the potential insights of African existentialist discourse: "At the same time that it was helping to destroy racist discourses, the linguistic coding of Fanon's existentialism reinforced Caribbean philosophy's overidentification with Europe and underidentification with Africa."[8]

In the fourth chapter, where Henry discusses the philosophical vision of the Guyanese novelist and literary critic Wilson Harris, things go differently. Harris' notion of a universal consciousness that can intrude upon the self-enclosure of the individual consciousness and whose intrusions ought to be welcomed if we are to be authentic and find fulfillment seems to Henry to point the way toward fruitful engagement with traditional African philosophy. Henry argues that, for both traditional African existentialism and Harris, "the philosophical subject is open to its spiritual ground and to its experiences of being constituted and voided by the latter."[9] This beckoning toward productive engagement with traditional African philosophy continues in later chapters.

I wish to affirm the general principle behind this call for engagement: Afro-Caribbean philosophy should be viewed as significantly weaker when carried out with no attention to traditional African thought, and thus the future healthy development of Afro-Caribbean philosophy necessitates paying attention to this source of ideas. In affirming this general principle, I do not undertake the responsibility of supporting Henry's particular description of traditional African philosophy. His understanding of it as among the world's "ego-critical philosophies" is fascinating but requires a thorough and comprehensive defense, and providing such a defense is not necessary or even helpful for my purposes.[10] It is not his specification of content but rather his general principle that I wish to endorse.

Is Henry Promoting Racial Essentialism?

There are, of course, a number of worries one might have about the view I am endorsing. One would be that the very idea of "traditional African philosophy" as an identifiable, unified category seems problematic. Firstly, how do we decide what counts as traditional? Do Islamic and Christian intellectual traditions count, for example? There are concerns here about how we distinguish between that which belongs to Africa and that which does not. Secondly, even if we resolve the question of what counts as traditional, thinking about the diversity on so large a continent may lead us to worry that not much concrete can be said about "traditional African philosophy" as a whole, as compared with "Akan philosophy," "Zulu philosophy," etc.[11] There is also the question of what counts as philosophy when we are talking not about philosophical writing but rather various aspects of oral traditions.

For the purposes of this chapter, though, I would like to take for granted that the worries above are not irresolvable. Grant that we can speak meaningfully of that which is *traditional,* usually intending to refer to that which has clear roots in societies existing in Africa before European colonialism. Grant also that we can speak meaningfully of that which is *African,* despite the continent's size. We ought to avoid homogenizing Africa and African thought, no doubt, but note, first, that Henry recognizes this and makes an effort to acknowledge diversity among traditions (as when he differentiates between the "predestinarian" existentialism of the Akan and the "vitalist" existentialism of the Luba).[12] More importantly, we need not believe that discerning trends and patterns across the traditions of various peoples is an illegitimate and impossible enterprise. It is not the same as saying that all Africans believe the same thing and it is not the case that looking at the diversity of sub-Saharan African traditions turns up no commonalities.[13] Finally, grant that we can speak meaningfully about *philosophy* even in the absence of literary traditions and that, through studying such things as proverbs and talking to those knowledgeable about the beliefs of the ancestors, we can encounter and critically reflect upon *traditional African philosophy.*[14]

Even granting all this, one can raise a significant objection against Henry's general principle. Being able to talk coherently about traditional African philosophy is one thing. Being required to do so is quite another thing. Why should those who are invested in developing Afro-Caribbean philosophy feel an obligation to make connections in their work to traditional African philosophy? It is true that the "Afro-" in "Afro-Caribbean" is a reference to the African ancestry of the people in question, but it should not be seen as obvious that being of African ancestry means needing to pay attention to traditional African philosophy. Some who have considered the matter have thought the opposite. In *Prophesy Deliverance! An Afro-American Revolutionary Christianity,* Cornel West writes:

> Afro-American philosophy expresses the particular American variation of European modernity that Afro-Americans helped shape in this country and must contend with in the future. While it might be possible to articulate a competing Afro-American philosophy based principally on African norms and notions, it is likely that the result would be

theoretically thin. Philosophy is cultural expression generated from and existentially grounded in the moods and sensibilities of a writer entrenched in the life-worlds of a people. The life-worlds of Africans in the United States are conceptually and existentially neither solely African, European, nor American, but more the latter than any of the former.[15]

West suggests that Africans in the diaspora may acknowledge themselves as such without thereby being led to the conclusion that "norms and notions" derived from African traditions are of great relevance to their culturally grounded philosophizing. James may have meant to suggest something similar to this in a statement Henry quotes: "I, a man of the Caribbean, have found that it is in the study of Western Literature, Western Philosophy and Western History that I have found out the things I have found out, even about the underdeveloped countries."[16]

Without assuming that the positions articulated by West and James are above reproach, we can explain the objection here further by identifying its major concern as the threat of *racial essentialism*. The idea that people of African descent interested in philosophy ought to be particularly motivated to study traditional African philosophy seems like it might be based on the idea that it is simply natural for black people to seek out and identify with that which is authentically black, here understood as that which is authentically African. Thinking in terms of what is natural and what is authentic when it comes to being black, though, often involves consciously or unconsciously believing in racial essences, that is, sets of mental and behavioral traits and tendencies that individuals inherit by virtue of being members of particular races. From a scientific point of view, though, such a belief seems clearly erroneous. It is also a dangerous belief, not only because it has been the foundation of racist ideas about the limited capacities of non-white peoples but also because, even when the characteristics ascribed to a race are positive, racial essentialism pressures people to fit into molds that they need not fit into and thus unnecessarily and unfairly circumscribes their sense of freedom. This, then, is the worry about Henry's position: could it be that it treats the study of traditional African philosophy as incumbent upon Afro-Caribbean people because African traditions are somehow in their blood, waiting to be acknowledged? Could the suggestion be that people like James and Fanon are to be criticized because their investment in European thought meant the suppression of inborn African tendencies? If this were the case, I would agree that Henry's position ought to be rejected for its racial essentialism.

I do not, however, think this is the case. Rebutting this objection will require, firstly, looking more carefully at Henry's understanding of what he is proposing and how that understanding points us away from rather than toward racial essentialism. The key concept at work in Henry's understanding of his proposal is the concept of *creolization*. This refers to the process whereby elements of cultures from elsewhere combine in a new setting and create something culturally novel. While creolization in this anthropological sense can happen anywhere, usage of the term has been inspired predominantly by discussions of the creole languages and identities of the Americas and especially of the Caribbean. The Martinican thinker Édouard Glissant is particularly well-known for his use of the idea of creolization, and Henry cites him shortly before offering the following definition: "creolization is a process of semio-semantic hybridization that can occur between the arguments, vocabularies, phonologies, or grammars of discourse within a culture or across cultures."[17]

What does creolization have to do with traditional African philosophy? Henry's thought is that we can compare different aspects of Caribbean culture with regard to whether they are *more or less creolized*. He takes music, dance, and creative literature to be examples of aspects of Afro-Caribbean culture that are significantly more creolized than philosophy. He writes:

> compared to the other Afro-Caribbean cultural forms, such as dance or literature, Afro-Caribbean philosophy is the least creolized of these important media. That is, the African, European, and Indian elements in it are the *least integrated*. If we take Afro-Caribbean fiction, Calypso, and Reggae as examples of well-integrated creole forms, then Afro-Caribbean philosophy has a long way to go.[18]

The cultural elements of Afro-Caribbean philosophy are so much less integrated, in Henry's view, because of the sociopolitical dynamics of colonialism. He characterizes Caribbean thought at one point as emerging historically out of "a series of extended debates over projects of colonial domination between four major social groups: Euro-Caribbeans, Amerindians, Indo-Caribbeans, and Afro-Caribbeans," and, at another point, as consisting in "a series of extended dialogues that arose out of European projects of building colonial societies around plantation economies that were based on African slave labor."[19] Given this origin and the resulting need for the European power structure to establish its authority and legitimacy within the context of the colonized, slavery-based Caribbean, it is not hard to see that non-European intellectual production in general and African thought in particular faced from the beginning an uphill battle in any struggle for recognition. The hegemonic discourse within the colonial social structure "inflated European identities while deflating African identities" and a crucial component of this project of inflation and deflation was the ascription of the capacity for philosophical thought to Europeans alone and the corresponding denial that others had previously generated and remained capable of generating philosophical traditions.[20]

Key, then, to Henry's claim that Afro-Caribbean philosophy is the least creolized dimension of Afro-Caribbean culture is the observation that an important step in the subjugation of Africans was the denial that they had ever shown any talent for rational thought, an aspect of their identity deflation harsher and more complete than any other: "Euro-Caribbean texts of the tradition repeatedly recognized the dancing, dramatic, oratorical, religious, and musical capabilities of Africans but never their philosophical capabilities."[21] Thus African traditions of thought were rendered invisible and African philosophy a contradiction in terms. Henry's view is that this discursive starting point was so influential that even as intellectual heroes like James and Fanon engaged in philosophical discourse in ways that were combative of colonialism, they were unable to attack this basic component of the colonial structure. They ended up instead reinforcing the pattern of overemphasizing the richness of European thought and leaving African thought hidden from view. Afro-Caribbean philosophy is thus overly reflective of the Caribbean's European heritage and not reflective enough of its African heritage—that is to say, Afro-Caribbean philosophy is insufficiently creolized.

We may now see why we have good reason to think it cannot be the case that Henry is promoting racial essentialism. To speak of Caribbean creolization as an anthropological fact and to encourage creolization as a sociocultural project is to speak in what are generally understood to be not just non-essentialist but *anti-essentialist* terms. Racial essentialism generally evokes and orients us toward ideals of purity, upholding the possibility and desirability of racial groups having stable characters that differentiate them from each other and remain constant across time (e.g., centuries) and space (e.g., oceans). Creolization is the opposite of purity: it is mixture, the interpenetration of cultures as a result of their juxtaposition and the interaction of peoples once distinct but now linked, intertwined, and often no longer clearly distinguishable.[22] Henry's call for the study of traditional African philosophy should not be mistaken for a demand that black people in the Caribbean maintain something like a purely African identity because Henry's talk of creolization conspicuously indicates that he does not believe Afro-Caribbean people have or should seek the option of doing such a thing.

It is to Henry's credit, however, that, while he recognizes Caribbean hybridity not only as an inescapable reality but also as something in many ways positive, he acknowledges and calls our attention to the ways in which hybridity is also a site of inequality and struggle. Stuart Hall, the Jamaican-born Afro-British pioneer of cultural studies, writes in an essay that

> in black popular culture, strictly speaking, ethnographically speaking, there are no pure forms at all. Always these forms are the product of partial synchronization, of engagement across cultural boundaries, of the confluence of more than one cultural tradition, of the negotiations of dominant and subordinate positions, of the subterranean strategies of recoding and transcoding, of critical signification, of signifying. Always these forms are impure, to some degree hybridized from a vernacular base.[23]

It is tempting, when speaking of hybridity, to latch onto the exhilarating novelty made possible by "engagement across cultural boundaries" and the "recoding and transcoding" of cultural elements. It is extremely important, however, to grapple with the ways that hybridity involves *"negotiations of dominant and subordinate positions."* Henry tells us as early as the preface to *Caliban's Reason* that, for him, talk of creolization in relation to Caribbean philosophy "raises explicitly the issue of *power relations* in determining the ways in which African, Indian, and European philosophies come together to constitute a regional philosophy."[24] He often speaks of Caribbean creolization in ways that suggest that it has been both powerfully productive but also ethically compromised in its means and patterns of creating newness and disrupting forms of life:

> The history of discursive violence in the region has produced high levels of mutual decentering and interculturation between the African and European worlds, the European and Indian worlds, and the Indian and African worlds. This violence has left parts of these systems fairly intact, other parts highly mixed, and others damaged beyond repair.[25]

Henry's project in *Caliban's Reason* is to suggest a path forward for Afro-Caribbean philosophy in light of this history of discursive violence and interculturation. This path will not lead away from but rather toward further creolization and hybridity, but in a self-consciously anti-colonial manner necessarily different from the processes of cultural mixing that created the Caribbean as we know it.

This is what motivates Henry's call for the study of traditional African philosophy. He claims that "Caribbean philosophy must creolize itself by breaking its misidentifications with European and African philosophies and allowing them to remix within the framework of more organic relations with local realities."[26] The misidentifications here, once again, are over-identification with Europe and under-identification with Africa. Henry's vision of creolization aims to "indigenize" Caribbean philosophy by facilitating the "full functioning of its African, Indian, and European dimensions."[27] In his chapter on James, as previously mentioned, Henry points to the investment that thinkers like James have had in the importance of the modern vs. premodern distinction as part of the problem. Henry claims that "since European categories of modern and premodern have been invested with so many anti-African connotations, these categories need to be reassessed" and the judgments of traditional African thought that flow from them need to be reconsidered and revised.[28] Looking with new eyes at African traditions means creating new connections between Africa and the Caribbean that involve no obligatory subordination of Africa to Europe as before: "there is the need for Afro-Caribbean philosophy to undertake an independent dialogue with traditional African philosophy and develop its own arguments for accepting or rejecting its truth claims."[29]

I support this goal of making the pursuit of anti-Eurocentric perspectives on traditional African philosophy one of the central tasks of the project of constructing a newly self-conscious tradition of Afro-Caribbean philosophy. Such perspectives would be critical and not given to automatic glorification or acceptance of claims but nevertheless characterized by charitable, sympathetic reconstructions preceding evaluations. Also, supporting this goal does not mean believing that everyone who contributes to Afro-Caribbean philosophy must take up the task equally because, as I understand the claim, it is not individual instances of Afro-Caribbean philosophy but the field that is being positioned as needing to develop in this particular way. How culpable an individual philosopher would be for not paying attention to African philosophy would, on my view, depend on the relevance of existing work on African philosophy by others to the individual's work—but the work of individuals is not the main issue. What matters are broader trends.

The reason these broader trends matter—and why I support Henry's call—is that white supremacy as a sociopolitical system functioning on global and local levels must be fought and I believe Henry has pointed out one of the ways in which it ought to be attacked. Charles Mills, the late Jamaican philosopher, did perhaps the most among professional philosophers to conceptually organize the analysis of white supremacy as a sociopolitical system. He argued that it should be understood as "a multidimensional system of domination, encompassing not merely . . . the juridico-political realm of official governing bodies and laws" but also as "economic, cultural, cognitive-moral, somatic, and in a sense even 'metaphysical.'"[30] When discussing the cultural dimension of white supremacy and its roots in the history of colonialism, Mills notes that all colonized peoples suffered denial of the worth of their cultures but also that "the centrality of African slavery to the project of the West required the most extreme stigmatization of blacks in particular."[31] Africa was portrayed as "lost in a historyless and cultureless vacuum, to be redeemed only by a European presence."[32] Black people in the Americas were seen as "tainted by their association with such a barbarous origin" and "African cultural survivals were actively suppressed."[33]

Undertaking an independent dialogue with African traditions of thought, as Henry advocates, provides a way for Afro-Caribbean philosophy to repudiate and work to undo the legacy of stigmatization, distortion, disrespect, disregard, and active suppression of African culture that has shaped the lives of people of African descent in the Caribbean. It is true that all people interested in philosophy should fight the legacy of colonialism by approaching traditional African thought with an open mind. People of African descent in the Caribbean, however, have additional reasons to do so. Taking pride in having African ancestry is part of overcoming the identity deflation perpetuated by the colonial system and having such pride makes it possible to view the cultural legacy of precolonial Africa as part of one's inheritance, that is, as part of one's own culture. This makes it possible to understand Afro-Caribbean philosophical inquiry into traditional African thought as a means of philosophical self-exploration. Henry also points out that properly understanding the creolized culture of the Caribbean—especially Afro-Caribbean religions—may require a deeper understanding of the traditional African elements that served as antecedents.[34] This means that further creolizing Afro-Caribbean philosophy by seeking to overcome its lack of engagement with African thought can provide insight into the already well- or at least better-creolized aspects of Caribbean culture, thus once again and in an even more exact sense enabling philosophy to serve as self-exploration.

This is not racial essentialism. Some may be uncomfortable with the notion of taking pride in ancestry, worrying that it reveals belief in the biological inheritance of cultural characteristics and responsibilities to carry forward past traditions. Biological reproduction is indeed an important part of the story I have told. This story is compatible, however, with acknowledging that to be born to certain parents and to look a certain way as a result does not, as a matter of pure genetics, necessitate a particular cultural path. The inheritance of culture is a *social* process. As such, it is also a process fraught with *politics* and the denigration of African culture ingrained in Afro-Caribbean minds under colonialism is one such culturally inherited and transmitted political dynamic. Henry's call for the study of African philosophy as part of the self-conscious development of Afro-Caribbean philosophy is equally political. It involves Afro-Caribbean people *choosing* to inherit a certain valuable cultural legacy in order to break with another problematic one. We need not fear that the idea is that black people everywhere just naturally gravitate to traditional African philosophical positions because these are carried in the blood. The problem to be addressed is the way that the cultural dimension of white supremacy has long made it natural to ignore Africa when searching for philosophical thought. Henry's proposal helps us denaturalize such tendencies for the benefit of philosophy and for the benefit of Afro-Caribbean people.

Creolizing Beyond the Caribbean

I mentioned Cornel West earlier as an example of a philosopher who thinks it unlikely that a vibrant tradition of philosophy among people of African descent requires paying attention to traditional African philosophy. It is reasonable to wonder: have I now explained why he is wrong? I think so. It is understandable, however, that some would doubt this. First, there is the question of what exactly West is rejecting. What would it mean for a diasporic tradition of philosophy to be "based principally on African norms and notions"? Is that not more ambitious than Henry's exhortation to undertake an independent dialogue with philosophy from the continent? This difference matters little, I think. If West does not reject exactly what Henry calls for, he certainly suggests that it is unnecessary, and Henry, for his part, certainly suggests that we should be open to the possibility of African norms and notions becoming in some sense foundational. A more fundamental concern would be that it is illegitimate for me to position West's claim as relevant to Henry's claim because West is talking about "Afro-American philosophy" and not Afro-Caribbean philosophy. Why should we see West as rejecting what Henry calls for if Afro-Caribbean thought is not his concern? Why should we see Henry as showing why West is wrong if Afro-Caribbean thought *is* his concern? Answering these questions will allow me to make clear why it is important to see Henry as contributing not merely to the development of Afro-Caribbean philosophy but *Africana philosophy* more widely and also, of even greater importance given the goal of this volume, not merely to Caribbean philosophy but to *philosophy of the Americas* more widely.

In bringing up the relevance of Henry's call to what West said and to African American philosophy more generally, I am following Henry himself, who discusses this in the sixth chapter of *Caliban's Reason*. The chapter's opening line quickly confirms that, as Henry sees it, the philosophizing of black people in the United States is a topic closely related to that of his book: "From within the Afro-Caribbean intellectual tradition, it is difficult not to see Afro-American philosophy as a brother or sister discourse with Africa and Europe as our parents."[35] He distinguishes between two positions on the most appropriate context within which to set this discourse: the "American reading of Afro-American philosophy," which emphasizes "the connections between Afro-American philosophy and the American pragmatist tradition," and the "Africana reading," which emphasizes connections to "traditional African philosophy and to the discourses of the global struggles of African peoples for liberation from colonialism and racial domination."[36] Henry identifies West as a proponent of the American reading and explains that he will provide an Africana reading.

When evaluating an Africana reading, it is worth taking note of the version provided by one of the pioneers of African American philosophy as a professional enterprise: Lucius Outlaw. In the article that first popularized the term "Africana philosophy," Outlaw laments:

> there is a striking aspect to the recent work of African American philosophers: namely, for the most part this work is conducted with little or no knowledge of, or attention to, the history of philosophical activity on the African continent or elsewhere in the African diaspora. At the very least, this lack of awareness and attention may well contribute to deficiencies in our historically informed self-understandings . . . African and African-descended philosophers are perhaps long overdue for coming together for a sustained, systematic, critical reconstruction of our intellectual histories.[37]

Outlaw is careful to add that

> the historical connections and more or less similar experiences of persons of African descent in the United States, in the African diaspora generally, and on continental Africa, do not warrant uncritical appropriations and celebrations of our racial connectedness, nor of the glories of philosophical insight from the African "Motherland" to which we should all turn to be shown the way to the primordial "ancient wisdom" that simply waits to be reclaimed.[38]

Uncharitable readers of Henry might take this warning to apply to him but I would argue that it is simply a demand for an anti-essentialist approach to African thought and, as such, it is compatible with Henry's own anti-essentialism.[39] Outlaw shares Henry's worry that a lack of attention to philosophical thought from the African continent is detrimental to diasporic African philosophical traditions, thus adding a voice from within African American philosophy in opposition to West's position.

One might worry, though, that this does not yet address the main issue: African American life and culture differ from the life and culture of black people in the Caribbean and so it is questionable to assume, simply because both groups have African ancestry, that what applies to one will apply to the other. One might think that it should not be assumed that the relevance of traditional African culture to Afro-Caribbean culture is mirrored in the case of African Americans, given the differences between a context in which diasporic Africans numerically predominate (the Caribbean) and one in which they are a minority in a population predominantly European in origin (the United States). It is often thought that Afro-Caribbean people have retained more of the culture of their ancestors than African Americans, and, if this is the case, it may seem plausible that traditional African philosophy could be relevant to Afro-Caribbean philosophy in a way that it is not to African American philosophy.

As a matter of fact, it is not at all clear whether it is more of a priority to study traditional African philosophy where the experience of slavery has done less to erase the culture of the ancestors. It seems just as plausible, in my view, to argue that the more distant a group of African-descended people is from African culture, the more important it is for the group's philosophers to work toward generating awareness of and interest in Africa's intellectual riches. West leads us to worry that for African American philosophers to be strongly invested in African thought is for them to stray from the cultural reality that ought to be inspiring their philosophical activity. This is, however, problematically conservative. If a people's distance from their cultural roots has come about through a history of stigmatization and suppression, aiming to reconnect with those roots in a critical manner is a goal much more progressive than simply accepting that the damage is done and that the ancestral connection has therefore become irrelevant. Seeking to revive cultural links affirms agency in the face of historical oppression.

As for whether it is the case that African Americans, in comparison to Afro-Caribbean people, lack cultural ties to Africa, this is a misconception. While there is much that could be said about why, it is useful for my purposes to draw an example from Henry, one which involves acknowledging differences between black culture in the United States and in the Caribbean:

> Although rooted in the great Protestant revivals of the 1700s the processes of Christianization in the Caribbean and Afro-America were quite different. In the main, Caribbean Christianity was the product of classic colonial churches that did not become independent until the 1960s. By contrast Afro-American Christianity emerged from black churches that were autonomous by the start of the American Civil War. In the Caribbean we have the two extremes produced by these processes of Afro-Christian syncretism: the survival of predominantly

African religions such as Shango and Vodou, on the one hand, and highly Europeanized churches, on the other . . . In Afro-America, there has been a uniform and intermediate pattern of syncretism that has produced a distinct Afro-American Christianity. This Christianity is more African in tone than the classic colonial churches of the Caribbean, but less so than religions like Shango or Vodou.[40]

Henry's claim that African American Christianity is syncretistic and reflective of African origins is a common and well-supported one.[41] His positioning of this syncretism as midway between two Caribbean extremes also shows us, first of all, the kind of complexity to be recognized when comparing black religion across regions. Secondly, though, it is nicely indicative of the suitability of Henry's talk of creolization to the African American context. We can understand him as saying that African American Christianity is highly creolized and thus impressive in its integration of African and European elements. It is easy to guess the next steps of the argument: African American philosophy, like Afro-Caribbean philosophy, can be seen as less creolized and the sensible way to deal with its comparative failure to incorporate African antecedents is to encourage more attention to traditional African philosophy.

This argument connecting the Caribbean and the United States can be extended further as we recognize the struggle of black people to flourish culturally and otherwise in the wake of slavery as a struggle that spans the Americas. I will speak first about Latin America and then say something about my own part of the Americas, i.e., Canada. Latin America is, of course, not mutually exclusive with the Caribbean as the Spanish-speaking islands of the Caribbean are major sites of Afro-Latin culture. It is useful to include them in considering the prospects for Afro-Latin philosophy, especially given the fact that they receive less in-depth treatment from Henry than the English and French-speaking islands.[42] The possibility of building Afro-Latin philosophy as an institutionalized area of study has received even less attention than Afro-Caribbean philosophy, at least in research written or available in English.[43] As it develops and grows, however, as it undoubtedly will, it will be highly beneficial if, like Henry and Outlaw, some of those who give Afro-Latin philosophy its shape call for and demonstrate engagement with African thought.

Part of what would make such engagement fruitful is the distinctive set of problems associated with being black in Latin America. On the one hand, the powerful influence of African traditions in the creolized cultures of some parts of Latin America (for example, in the form of religions like Santería in Cuba or Candomblé in Brazil) is well-recognized. On the other hand, across all of Latin America, Cuba and Brazil included, scholars have described a history of the "invisibilization" of Afro-Latin people.[44] The distinctness of black populations has often been denied, their numbers often underestimated, their historical contributions often forgotten, and the discrimination and disproportionate poverty they suffer often ignored. The fiery Afro-Brazilian thinker and activist Abdias do Nascimento wrote of the pursuit in his country of the "physical and spiritual genocide of Black people" through "the manipulative mystique of whitening the Brazilian population."[45]

This paradox of prominent Africanness and disregarded blackness forms an important part of the background against which future contributions to Afro-Latin philosophy will be made. So too, though, do recent struggles by Afro-Latin social movements that have succeeded over the course of the past few decades in gaining increasing recognition for the disadvantages suffered by Afro-Latin people.[46] It seems to me that these two background conditions make possible a special utility for engagement with traditional African philosophy. To undertake a new philosophical dialogue with Africa in situations where African cultural influences in forms such as music and religion have often been noted and celebrated but where people of predominantly African ancestry have not been equally valued would seem to offer philosophers the opportunity to help people re-envision what it means to explore and celebrate African cultural heritage. The creolizing tactic of looking toward Africa rather than Europe as a source of philosophical ideas could serve as symbolic of the need to go beyond prominent but circumscribed valuations of African identity in order to destroy all forms of racial hierarchy in Latin America.

I offer the foregoing in humble speculation, and I want to close by saying something about a place with which I am more familiar—Canada, my home. As Lewis Gordon has noted, talk of Africana philosophy in North America has most often meant philosophy from the United States because, while there are a number of notable professional philosophers contributing to Africana philosophy "whose academic credentials were acquired at Canadian universities, no Africana philosophical movement has developed there."[47] As Henry has sought to encourage the development of Afro-Caribbean philosophy as a disciplinary formation, I have recently made a similar effort with regard to African Canadian philosophy.[48]

Unsurprisingly, it is my view that Henry's call for the study of traditional African philosophy applies to African Canadian philosophy too. There are interesting things to be said, though, about why. Canada is unique within the Americas in having a sizable black population the vast majority of which is of recent immigrant background (it is, in this way, more similar to Western European countries with significant black populations).[49] The most common among places of origin for black people differs based on where one is in the country. In

Toronto, the largest city, it would be Jamaica; in Montreal, the largest predominantly French-speaking city, it would be Haiti; and in Ottawa, the nation's capital, it would be Somalia. In Nova Scotia, the province where I live, the majority of black people are not of recent immigrant background but are descended from freed African Americans transported from the United States after the Revolutionary War or the War of 1812. Clearly, African Canadians are a diverse lot.

African Canadian philosophy, to be worthy of the name, will have to reflect this diversity. Nevertheless, to be worth treating as a distinct category, it will also need to reflect some kind of unity. This sets up African Canadian philosophy as a remarkable forum for discourse about what black people share. Here is where I imagine the study of traditional African philosophy has a distinctive, experimental role to play. To what extent can ideas and motifs drawn from African traditions serve as unifying forces for black people today? Can the pride in African heritage reflected in taking traditional African philosophy seriously itself be a basis for unification? The fact of diversity in Canada's black population and the fact that so many have come just recently from elsewhere arguably provide us with a black cultural world that is not yet creolized or which at least has only just begun to be. To the extent that a path of creolization, hybridization, and integration lies ahead for African Canadians, Henry helpfully teaches us to view creolization as a project we can actively direct with anti-Eurocentric cultural and political aims rather than merely a process we passively undergo.

Notes

1. Chike Jeffers, "Strategies of Organization: Paget Henry and Traditional African Philosophy," *The C.L.R. James Journal: A Review of Caribbean Ideas* 10 (Winter 2004): 13–23. This article was first presented as a paper at the inaugural meeting of the Caribbean Philosophical Association in Barbados in May 2004. I had just finished my undergraduate education, knew where I was going but had not yet started graduate school, and this was my first academic conference. Henry, when replying to me and others on the panel discussing his book, was incredibly gracious and humble, conceding much of my critique. In doing so, he not only gave me confidence as someone embarking on a career in philosophy but also provided me with a model of how to engage honestly and openly with critics. I am happy to honor him with a defense rather than a critique in the present piece.

2. Paget Henry, *Caliban's Reason: Introducing Afro-Caribbean Philosophy* (New York: Routledge, 2000), 21.

3. Paget Henry, *Caliban's Reason*, 27, 28.

4. Paget Henry, *Caliban's Reason*, 27. The choice of "ego" shows Henry's independence from Gyekye, because Gyekye argues that "ego" is not ideal as a translation

of *sunsum* and prefers "spirit." See Kwame Gyekye, *An Essay on African Philosophical Thought: The Akan Conceptual Scheme*, revised ed. (Philadelphia, PA: Temple University Press, 1995), 102, 88.

5. Paget Henry, *Caliban's Reason*, 34.
6. Henry, 35.
7. Henry, 56.
8. Henry, 83.
9. Henry, 103.
10. Henry, 63.
11. Brian Meeks has raised this concern, claiming that Henry has not succeeded in making "a watertight case for common features, sufficiently widespread and accepted as such, to conclude decisively that there is an African or even a West African philosophy." See his "Reasoning with Caliban's Reason," *Small Axe* 6 (March 2002): 165.
12. Henry, 34–36.
13. The existence of common features in African intellectual traditions has notably been defended by John Mbiti and by Gyekye. See John S. Mbiti, *African Religions & Philosophy* (London: Heinemann, 1969) and Gyeke, *An Essay on African Philosophical Thought: The Akan Conceptual Scheme* (Philadelphia: Temple University Press, 1995), 189–212.
14. See Gyekye for a good example of the methodology I have just described.
15. Cornel West, *Prophesy Deliverance! An Afro-American Revolutionary Christianity*, anniversary ed. (Louisville, KY: Westminster John Knox Press, 2002), 24.
16. Quoted in Henry, 50.
17. Henry, 88.
18. Henry, 8. Emphasis mine.
19. Henry, 68.
20. Henry, 69.
21. Henry, 75–76.
22. It should be noted that it is certainly possible to value mixture while endorsing forms of racial essentialism. José Vasconcelos, for example, believes that distinctive character traits are carried in the blood of different races (black people, for example, are "eager for sensual joy, intoxicated with dances and unbridled lust") but holds that it is the special mission of Latin America to herald through its mixed-race population the future fusion of all the world's races. See José Vasconcelos, *The Cosmic Race/La raza cósmica*, trans. Didier T. Jaén (Baltimore, MD: The Johns Hopkins University Press, 1997), 22. That being said, creolization as conceptualized by Henry, Glissant, and most others who use the term to refer to cultural mixture is not based on any belief in biological essences.
23. Stuart Hall, "What is This 'Black' in Black Popular Culture?" *Social Justice* 20 (Spring-Summer 1993): 110.
24. Henry, xi. Emphasis mine.
25. Henry, 15. It is interesting that Henry does not mention indigenous Caribbean worlds in this passage, despite having previously characterized Afro-Caribbean

philosophy as arising out of debates among four social groups including "Amerindians," as quoted above. One wonders if the implicit claim here is that the Amerindian world counts as "damaged beyond repair."

26. Henry, 89.

27. Henry, 87, 88. Note, once again, the lack of reference here to an indigenous Caribbean dimension, made even more striking by Henry's talk of the need to "indigenize." Does Henry not think there is any need to pay attention to the traditional thought of the first peoples of the region? I suspect this is merely a slip rather than a principled distinction. Many will think it eminently forgivable given that most of the island nations of the Caribbean have no remaining self-identified indigenous population. It is not the case, however, that none at all remain. Dominica (the country my father is from) has the Kalinago Territory, or the Carib Reserve as it was called until recently, where descendants of the island's original inhabitants live and elect a local council. When we look beyond the islands to countries like Guyana (where my mother is from) and Belize, which are culturally and politically part of the Caribbean, we find indigenous peoples comprising significant portions of the population. Belize not only has the Maya who are indigenous to Central America but also the Garifuna people, descended from Africans and the Kalinago of St. Vincent, who ended up in Belize through relocation by the British. The indigenous heritage of the Caribbean should definitely figure in efforts to construct Caribbean philosophy, even as problems of indigenous languages being extinct or under threat of extinction make it harder in some cases to preserve the insights of indigenous intellectual production. For more information on the indigenous peoples of the region, see Samuel M. Wilson (ed.), *The Indigenous People of the Caribbean* (Gainesville, FL: University Press of Florida, 1997).

28. Henry, 58.

29. Henry, 67.

30. Charles W. Mills, *From Class to Race: Essays in White Marxism and Black Radicalism* (Lanham, MD: Rowman & Littlefield, 2003), 186.

31. Charles Mills, *From Class to Race*, 189.

32. Mills.

33. Mills.

34. For example, having contrasted James' conception of the self with the spiritualized traditional African conception, Henry writes: "Can we understand Afro-Caribbean religions such as Rastafarianism [sic] and Vodou without this African conception of the self? Can we understand how we got from one to the other without a more sustained exchange between these two views?" Henry, 60.

35. Henry, 144.

36. Henry, 145.

37. Lucius Outlaw, "African, African American, Africana Philosophy," *Philosophical Forum* 24 (Fall–Spring 1992–1993): 71–72.

38. Lucius Outlaw, "African, African American, Africana Philosophy," 72. For another consideration of how traditional African philosophy might be relevant to African American philosophy that similarly demands a critical approach, see

K. Anthony Appiah, "African-American Philosophy?" *Philosophical Forum* 24 (Fall–Spring 1992–1993): 11–34.

39. Note that Henry writes in the sixth chapter that we can affirm "the formative influences of African symbols and discourses" while acknowledging that they are "not timeless essences" but rather "have been changed by different processes of hybridization and creolization." Henry, 155.

40. Henry, 158.

41. For a classic study, see Albert J. Raboteau, *Slave Religion: The Invisible Institution in the Antebellum South* (New York: Oxford University Press, 1978).

42. Henry admits this and also acknowledges his failure to address the Dutch-speaking Caribbean in the conclusion of *Caliban's Reason*. Henry, 273–274.

43. Among English language researchers, one of the few people working on Afro-Latin philosophy is Gertrude James-Gonzalez de Allen. See, for example, her "Recipe of a Life: The Sediments, Fragments, and Flow in an Afro-Latin Caribbean Identity," *International Studies in Philosophy* 39.4 (2007): 15–34.

44. I take the quoted term here from Jean Muteba Rahier, "Introduction: Black Social Movements in Latin America: From Monocultural Mestizaje and "Invisibility" to Multiculturalism and State Corporatism/Co-optation," in Rahier (ed.), *Black Social Movements in Latin America: From Monocultural Mestizaje to Multiculturalism* (New York: Palgrave Macmillan, 2012), 3.

45. Abdias do Nascimento, *Brazil: Mixture or Massacre? Essays in the Genocide of a Black People*, 2nd ed., trans. Elisa Larkin Nascimento (Dover, MA: The Majority Press, 1989), 59.

46. A book from the 1990s discussing the activism and conditions in various Latin American countries is tellingly titled *No Longer Invisible: Afro-Latin Americans Today*, ed. Minority Rights Group (London: Minority Rights Publications, 1995).

47. Lewis R. Gordon, *An Introduction to Africana Philosophy* (Cambridge, UK: Cambridge University Press, 2008) 91. Some of the philosophers he must have had in mind are Mills, Bernard Boxill, Clarence Sholé Johnson, Nkiru Nzegwu, and Olufemi Taiwo.

48. See Chike Jeffers, "Do We Need African Canadian Philosophy?" *Dialogue: Canadian Philosophical Review/Revue canadienne de philosophie* 51 (December 2012): 643–666.

49. According to census information, a little more than half of Black Canada is foreign-born and less than a tenth of Black Canadians were born to parents born in Canada. See Statistics Canada, "Immigration and Ethnocultural Diversity in Canada" (2013), http://www12.statcan.gc.ca/nhs-enm/2011/as-sa/99-010-x/99-010-x2011001-eng.cfm.

PART II
Inter-American Philosophy of Independence and State Formation

3
The 1812 Constitution of Cádiz: From Colonialism to Independence

Hernando A. Estévez

Ortega y Gasset's conceptual distinctions, especially those between belief and idea, have provided the bases for illustrating different perspectives of a given historical moment, in particular the transition from subject to citizen. Furthermore, Ortega y Gasset's philosophy has also problematized this historical moment insofar as it has provided an analysis of a historical reality. Specifically, Ortega y Gasset's notion of historiology, rather than history, "grants an immediate analysis of the res gesta, of the historical reality" by asking, "What is its [historical reality] ontological texture? Of what ingredients is it [historical reality] composed? and Which are its [historical reality] primary dimensions?"[1]

Ortega y Gasset's notion of historical reality questions history in terms of the use of the concept of historical reason and the understanding of history as a system providing the tools to evaluate both the beliefs as well as the ideas of a historical moment. An analysis from historiology of the 1812 Constitution of Cádiz, demands attention to both the individual life and the collective life in a given moment of history. An approach to the life of citizens as well as to the notion of citizenry in terms of historiology will reveal the status of the individual as well as the collectivity in its social reality since historiology provides an evaluation of the relation between individual life with collective life by forming what Ortega y Gasset calls social life:

> [social life] involves those individual lives and it [historiology] exerts total pressure over them. Therefore, it is necessary to transcend once more and from the inter-individual perspective move forward to a live ampler whole that comprehends both what is individual and what is

collective: in sum, social life. This new reality, as announced, transforms the vision that each has of itself.[2]

The notion of the social, and in light of Ortega y Gasset's notion of historiology, makes possible the elaboration of a new perspective about the influence of the 1812 Constitution of Cádiz in the independence movements insofar as it distinctively emphasizes the intimate relation between the individual and the collective in his political circumstance. This relation between the individual and her circumstance is now the individual's social life that recognizes the historical aspect of life in the circumstance's manifestation: "which comes from a past, in other words, of another prior social life, and it goes toward a future social life."[3] In other words, the historical character of the social life endorsed by the relation between the individual and his/her circumstance emanates from the understanding of reality as a historical reality.

The historical and political reality of Latin American nations during the transition from subject to citizen is mediated by the implementation of the 1812 Constitution of Cádiz. In the following pages, I will analyze the 1812 Constitution of Cádiz with the intention of unmasking the concealed influence of its articles and decrees over the Spanish territories in Latin America. Let's remember that this constitution was the political blueprint for Latin American countries, and that its legal content regulated the relationships between individuals, institutions, and the state. Furthermore, an analysis of the influence of the constitution cannot be done without first evaluating the historical context and the concrete circumstances of its elaboration.[4] Regardless of our findings, it is safe to argue at this point that the 1812 Constitution of Cádiz had impacted political life in Latin America by promoting ambivalent political, and in many cases contradictory, assertions about what constitutes governance, citizenry, citizenship, and the basis for national stability.

An unmediated acceptance of the 1812 Constitution of Cádiz by the newly formed states in Latin America and the need to establish a form of government that could legitimize the transition from colony to state defined social and political life during the initial moments of the transition by first accepting a system of classes as a necessary condition to create and maintain social and economic order; and second, by allowing the use of natural law as a legitimizing instrument for an absolute authority and power. These assertions as stated on the first articles of the constitution contributed to the rise of a political crisis reflected on a lack of political identity insofar as it promoted and justified the absence of a concrete understanding of what it means to be a citizen or the notion of citizenship from a specific historical reality within its circumstances.

As a result, the concrete circumstance of Latin America was initially perceived by the collective and the individual as a dual relation with its own historical and political moment: on the one hand, the will for political freedom and liberty from Spain depended upon what the constitution could legitimize as a political right; and on the other hand, the need for a political ideology that could provide the principles and laws of what it meant to be an independent nation was perceived as the result of the influence of Spain's own historical moment. This dual relation of Latin American history in the midst of independence has resulted in what I would like to call the dilemma of political identity: sovereignty or submission. In the following pages I would like to explore in detail the sources of this political dilemma and identify its causes. From a philosophical perspective this dilemma demands the positioning of the notion of political identity as the central axis for the understanding of Latin American concrete reality and political dilemma. Given that during the political and social transition from subject to citizen many political interests were lost and many others were created, this analysis requires a clear distinction between the independent movements and the formation of nation-states.

The historical events that participated in an effective manner during the independence movements in Latin America played different roles but all of them contributed to the formation of nation-states. Economic, social, political, and ideological situations gave rise to the necessary conditions for the culmination of a colonial period as well as the beginning of an independence and state formation. These situations allowed the transition from subject to citizen but not all of them had the same impact in the construction of nation-states. Some situations ignited an independent sentiment, others simply augmented the force of independence, and others were simply witnesses to the events. Economic situations and the exhaustion of a colonial system were solely fueled by the interest of an elite and the concentration of their power, which gave rise to a social crisis within the political institutions charged with maintaining a social and political stability.

An understanding of the transition from subject to citizen requires us to carefully look at the 1812 Constitution of Cádiz and its influences upon both Spanish territories in America and Spain during and after the independence movements. Overall, the following study of the constitution's text aims to recognize its influence upon the political ideas of the newly formed states and simultaneously understand the political circumstance surrounding Spain during the formation of the nation-states in Latin America. According to Jorge Mario García Laguardia:

> Still during the colonial regime, a preceding fact of great importance for our constitutional law is the Constitution of Cádiz, which was promulgated in 1812 in that Spanish city, and was effective for several years in several Latin American countries before and after the independence, and from where our first electoral experiences were produced.[5]

García Laguardia's analysis of the 1812 Constitution of Cádiz and its influence in Latin America during the formation of states helps to identify the most prominent European political traditions affecting the transition from subject to citizen insofar as it reveals both the causes for the development of the constitution and the political and social effect of the document in the Spanish territories of America. For García Laguardia the inclusion and participation of Americans[6] in the discussions and elaboration of the constitution gave rise to the first "popular" elections and to a mixed system of political participation. This step towards the representation of "all" constituted one of the first political aberrations affecting the colonies due in part to the unequal participation in the election process of members who supported the constitution. García Laguardia also reminds us that the elaboration of the constitution was an interruption of continuity with the old Spanish regime and therefore a break from traditional colonialism. Once the new government replaced the Central Junta[7] the government dedicated its first legislative moments to introducing pivotal ideas of a liberalism in Spain and the Spanish territories in America. For García Laguardia, the introduction of the free press, the abolition of the inquisition, the elimination of the Santiago vote, incorporation of the nation of all jurisdictional *senõrios*,[8] abolition of subjects, suppression of nobility proof, abolition of *mitas*, and *repartimientos* of Indians, free enterprise, and free commerce[9] constituted the fundamental step for a political rupture with monarchy's absolute power but not a disruption of colonial power and its structures in Latin America.

García Laguardia's analysis is important because it contributes to the understanding of Latin American political circumstance during the transition from subject to citizen insofar as it recognizes the most influential ideological repertoire, which has defined and informed citizens' belief system, namely, constitutionalism, nationalism, and the division of power. It also reasserts how and why an ambivalent form of power was always part of the transition from colony to independent state. The most influential political decisions and changes found in the 1812 Constitution of Cádiz according to García Laguardia were:

1) Constitutionalism: which not only limited the governors' power but also mediated political power through the creation of institutions for such aim; 2) National Political Representation: which introduced the concept of modern national representation based upon the idea of individualism which did not exist before; the creation of intermediate social groups between the nation and the individual where the citizen had the same rights as the rest, making the citizen the only justification for political organization; 3) National Sovereignty and the Division of Power: which established three distinct forms of power, namely the legislative, judicial, and executive.[10]

Without oversimplifying the political and social force of the independence movements and the different causes that promoted and incited the transition from colony to independent state in Latin America, I argue that it was precisely the elaboration of the 1812 Constitution of Cádiz and the participation of Americans in the discussions and debates which served as a preamble for an independent political ideology which in turn began to corrode colonial institutions. The most important and influential political decision made by the 1812 Constitution of Cádiz for the Latin America political situation was the establishment of political representation and the division of power. These decisions not only redefined the concept of power, in Spain as well as in the Spanish territories, but they also reestablished the nation's sovereignty and the individual's legitimacy before the institutions while creating the conditions for a possible change in the individual's political position. The individual's political representation within the state became the foundation for a new political organization and her political position shifted from an economic participatory level in colonial institutions to a more political and social interaction in political decisions, formulating new parameters for the political relations between Spain and its colonies. Of all the political decisions derived from this new form of individual political power, as a result of the implementation of the constitution in Latin America during the transition from subject to citizen, it was political representation which contributed the most to the elaboration of the notion of citizenship by providing the framework for the notion of political identity. However, political identity and political representation were filled with ideological ambivalences that inevitably produced contradictory roles during the period of independence especially for the citizens in the Spanish territories.

At this time, I would like to give particular emphasis to the contents of some articles of the Constitution and especially to those defining the notion of citizenship to identify the root of the ambivalences and contradictions mentioned earlier. The aim of this examination within the historical circumstance of the constitution outlines not only the ideological content of the notion of citizenship, but it also examines the relationship between the individual and her circumstance while understanding the political repertoire acting over the individual's political tasks (*los quehaceres politicos*) during state formation in Latin America. In other words, once we establish the individual's political repertoire in her political context, we can then diagnose the beliefs of the individual or the people. This in light of Ortega y Gasset's need for understanding the circumstance of a given individual and collective to diagnose and identify the beliefs vivifying their life.

The first chapter of the constitution "Of the Spanish Nation" defines the nation as "the reunion of all Spanish individuals from both hemispheres."[11] In its fourth article, this chapter states that, "the nation is obligated to preserve and protect, through wise and just laws, civil liberty, property and the rest of legitimate rights of all individuals belonging to the nation."[12] These new definitions, or more precisely redefinitions of nation and who is authorized to participate in national affairs as well as international affairs, opened the debate about the role political institutions had in relation to an individual's rights. On the other hand, the second chapter, "Of the Spanish" reduces the possibilities for a true political participation when it defines in its fifth article "Spanish citizen" in terms of the relation of the individual to the land: "A citizen is: First, a man that has been born free and within the vicinity of Spanish dominions as well as his sons. Second, foreigners that have obtained naturalization. Third, men who have lived in the vicinity of any town of the Monarchy for ten years. Fourth, free men who have obtained freedom in Spanish territories."[13] In the Fourth Chapter, "Of Spanish Citizens", citizens are those whose lineage originated in territories belonging to Spanish dominions from both hemispheres as well as those who have lived in the vicinity of any Spanish territory. Furthermore, this fourth chapter defines Spanish citizens as those legitimate sons of foreigners living in both Spain and Spanish territories in America, those born in Spanish territories that have never left without governmental license, and those individuals who have become residents of a town in Spain and Spanish owned territories by practicing some profession, work or engaging in some useful industry.[14]

The articles of the 1812 Constitution of Cádiz mentioned earlier made a clear and important mediation between the nation and the individual. The relation between the individual and the nation as described in these articles provides to the notion of citizen a sense of belonging to a given geographical region which in turn legitimized the "right to be" a citizen. In other words, an individual is a Spanish citizen by living within the boundaries and limits of the Spanish nation, but the individual does not have the same citizenship rights unless the law legitimizes her political status. From these articles, we can infer that the concept of nation gained a new dimension of sovereignty while reaffirming its autonomy but only through the exclusion of some individuals as citizens and simultaneously the inclusion of all belonging to the nation in terms of their geographical limits. It is interesting to notice how the first articles of the constitution do not address the notion of citizenship until the physical boundaries of what it means to be a nation, a Spanish nation and a Spanish citizen, have been established. These geographical precisions are important for our understanding of citizenry insofar as they reflect Spain's political interest of maintaining political control over the territories and show the need to promote a different way to exercise political power in their territories. According to Carlos Meléndez Chaverri's essay, "Las Cortes de Cádiz en sus Circunstancias Históricas Orígenes de la Constitución de Cádiz de 1812," the true antecedent events for the elaboration of the 1812 Constitution of Cádiz were Spain's need to legitimize[15] its representatives and to change the political status of its territories in America. The constitution wanted to redefine and reorganize the territories in America not as colonies, but as an essential part and member of the Spanish Monarchy by declaring that the kingdoms, provinces, and islands that formed the territories must have national representation and constitute a part of the Government of the Kingdoms of Spain through their deputies.[16] This inclusive representation meant for Spain the need to unite, for the first time since the colonization of America, all national representatives from Spain and from America, as well as to consider, at least in theory, equality between the Spanish and the Americans. Spain's need to maintain authority and power over the territories in America shows how the independent movements in the newly formed states of Latin America were first motivated by the intention of settling a territorial dispute. Briefly put, while Spain defended its territories from the French and English, the people of Spanish America were beginning to contemplate the possibility of liberating and defending what they now considered their territories. This interest of the Spanish territories, purely territorial, displaced and postponed the possibility of establishing what it could mean to be a citizen, not solely in terms of belonging to a region, but also to have representation within the territory, given that to have a sense of belonging to a territory would mean to still belong to Spain. Within this theoretical framework, the concept of a nation, initially understood as a delimited territory, overshadowed the possibility of defining the state in relation to the citizen. This primary interest, I contend, hindered the need to define what it is to be a citizen in Spanish territories, since all that was necessary to have some form of political status was to be recognized as having a sense of belonging by way of living in a territory independent of Spain. This could be interpreted as an initial need to establish a difference between Spain and the newly independent territories, which in turn became an oversimplified response to the question of political identity while establishing some form of difference between the Kingdom of Spain and its colonies, namely, cultural differences between Spain and what is now called Latin America. This cultural difference is what Carlos Meléndez Chaverri calls Americanism:

> I understand by Americanism, a common identity; for having situations and needs equally common, which were transformed into demands, which the Americans had to live. In spite of the evident isolation in which some men lived from others in the New World, the mere fact of having come to America constituted an important tie, which shaped common struggles and eagerness.[17]

Although Meléndez Chaverri considers the notion of Americanism from the social aspect of political representation and prior to equality among both Spanish and Americans as stated in the Cortes of Cádiz, I argue that political Americanism was subsequent to the sense of belonging to region: For the inhabitants of Spanish territories in America, one is American because one was born in America, and then one is American because one understands what is to be American. But to understand what it is to be an American one must first recognize the cultural traits that provide difference and define them negatively; it also implies not to have been defined politically. Given that cultural identity during colonialism often arose in adversarial circumstances, there was no easy way to reconcile culture with politics. It should be apparent that cultural values and political values are not the same. Often, the subject of colonialism had to choose between belonging to a region or participating politically in the institutions. This means that cultural values were not simply overshadowed by political differences, but they were part of the historical tradition of the colonial period that creates ideological matrices to prevent the consolidation of political identity capable of producing people's emancipation. There was no shortage of getting a political identity that called for transformation of the very cultural identity that served to provide a given person with an identity in the face of what it meant to be Spanish. To make sense of such political independence we must see it as advancing the interests of Spain while stripping the individual of political recognition or an authentic political identity. This need for a political identity was superseded by what it meant to be Latin American culturally. Culture became the set of values and actions that identify the individual with a sense of belonging to a given region, but with no regard for having a clear and concrete understanding of the political circumstance in which they could be legitimized as political actors of their own circumstances. In other words, belonging to a region meant to have cultural roots and values capable of providing to the individual a sense of both ownership and belonging, but it limited the individual of the independence from a true transition from subject to citizen: Culture alone provided identity. We can describe the relation established by the 1812 Constitution of Cádiz between Spain and America with a little more precision. In particular, the notion of citizen seems to have the following sort of structure: First, it requires that some people were recognized as members of a given region to guarantee some sort of participation in the social arena. A second element of the notion of citizen is the internalization of cultural values by way of certain criteria of ascription, such that part of the individual identity of at least some of those who bear the sense of belonging—blacks, Indians, mestizos, Spanish, etc.—adopted a sense of citizenship. The availability of these terms in the colonial as well as the independence discourse demanded that newly formed Latin American states became first geographically independent from Spain, culturally independent but not politically independent.

Joaquín Santana Castillo's essay "Identidad Cultural de un Continente: Iberoamerica y La America Sajona. Desde la Doctrina Monroe hasta la Guerra de Cuba"[18] provides a concise study of the theoretical distinctions and genesis of what constitutes the cultural identity of the American continent. His study argues that the geographical differences between Iberia-America and Anglo-Saxon America make cultural differences more evident because of the existence of two easily defined regions: Iberia-America and Anglo-Saxon America, located respectively in the south and north of the continent. His essay alludes to cultural, religious, judicial, and political differences among others and concludes that both Americas, South and North, have their origin in the colonial models enacted by Spain and Portugal on the one side and England on the other.[19] Santana Castillo is part of a tradition of authors who emphasize cultural identity and colonial processes such as *mestizaje* and the coexistence of social and ethnic-cultural groups in the American Continent as evidence for explaining the difference between sources for Latin American political ideology and North American ideology, a difference that endures despite their belonging to the same continent. According to Santana Castillo:

> In a general sense, it could be asserted that the American (American Continent) is no less ballasted by prejudices and ancestral customs. Less dependent upon traditional values, this attitude is a psychological component that should have been taken into account to explain the causes it took for the creoles to rebel against colonial power, without negating the determinant role of economic and political motivations. Also there can be seen characteristics less reverent to traditional viewpoints with respect to identity, understanding it solely as a new identity. But

in this case, other cultural factors and elements have greater importance in what differentiates between one America and the other. Thus, identity is not a problem for the American of the North. S/he does not think nor reflect upon it, either because his/her utilitarian temperament is less given to speculation; or because s/he has not mixed with others and does not share this problem or even because the revolution they made did not seek the construction of a new society but rather because they sought the restitution of economic and civil rights which were affected by the regulations of the English Crown.[20]

The cultural and historical specificity of the Latin American people (*pueblo*) is without a doubt what guided Latin Americans to conceive a cultural identity as the central axis of their own politics. However, cultural identity could only create a transition for social change while leaving the colonial political structure intact. Independence movements reach an ample economic redistribution of lands and markets through the revaluation of social relations, but current political ideologies of exclusion, of social castes, and marginalization created an ambivalent and contradictory process of state-formation and consequently of the notion of citizen.

The concept of citizen elaborated in the first chapter of the 1812 Constitution of Cádiz is primarily related to Europe's traditional political theory insofar as it addresses the relation between the individual and the sovereign in terms of loyalty. The French and American Revolutions rescued the individual from the vestiges/traces of an absolute power by making him/her into the main character of public life and providing the possibility of differentiating between the citizen of a national state and the subject of a monarchy. The work of Francisco Colom, *Razones de Identidad*, puts forward cultural pluralism and political integration as the basis for identity especially in those states that have used ethnicity and geographical conditions for the justification and legitimization of individuals' rights and self-governance of the people. Colom's book looks primarily at European and North American democracies to study the notions of citizenry and nationality. His study becomes relevant for the understanding of Latin American politics because his approach to the notion of citizenship emphasizes the historical principles that have defined citizenship in relation to the "sense of political belonging" (*pertenencia politica*) as an essential element in the establishment of individual rights within a national state. Accordingly, the author argues that the notion of citizenship in the European tradition was characterized by the abolition of structures that mediate political divisions between the individual and the state as well as by the citizens' active participation in public affairs. Colom asserts that:

The Republic, was not based upon the ontological primacy of the individual nor upon the defense of particular rights, but rather upon a shared life style, an ethics that presupposed personal disposition to the abnegation of sacrifice in view of the survival of the political community.[21]

Colom's understanding of citizenship in light of the political tradition that had informed Europe and North America reveals important assumptions regarding the political recognition of the individual as citizen: On the one side, liberal rights were affirmed in contrast to those of the community to which the individual belongs, condensing the individual judicial conditions in the right to public participation. On the other hand, an individual's capacity to manage his affairs privately becomes limited due in part because for republicanism, a citizen can only be free when his duties and personal interest coincide.[22]

I argue that it was this approach to citizenship that preceded the definition of citizenship in the 1812 Constitution of Cádiz. Also, that from this definition of citizenship arose a model of sovereignty in the Latin American states that placed the individual in opposition to the collective. In other words, although independence required some form of social and political integration of all individuals belonging to the state in terms of its geographical limits, independence in view of the constitution's principles did not allow for an inclusion of different cultural identities; sovereignty depended upon the inclusion of all. Sovereignty was constantly negated, yet it was affirmed by that very negation. It was thwarted by inequality and exclusion; it was affirmed by the individual desire for political participation and recognition. Righteously, Andrés Bello would question the United States and especially Thomas Jefferson's writings, which excluded equality for Indians and the abolition of slavery from the republican and liberal model.[23]

Our discussion of citizenship and the theoretical bases for its elaboration force us to attend to the problem of governability. The political relationship between the citizen and the state is not only mediated in terms of duties and rights that are conceded or granted by either party, but they presuppose the necessary conditions for such a relation to exist or at least to be established. In other words, it is necessary to study the political "circumstances" that make possible governance while providing us with the diagnosis of the ideas and beliefs informing them.

Antonio Annino's essay "Ciudadanía versus Gobernabilidad Republicana en México" defines governability, as:

> the conditions which make possible governing a country, or as to highlight the capacity that established forms of authority have to be obeyed without having recourse, unless in extreme cases, to force.

This second meaning that I use here, is closer and it even becomes identical with legitimacy.[24]

Although, for the author the notion of citizenship "was disseminated prior to the independence," given the use of the concept by the indigenous communities to defend themselves from the liberal state, and by "its intention to destroy collective identity," Annino's reference to the origins of citizenship provide us with a theoretical framework with which to differentiate the process of elaboration of the notion of citizenship in relation to the context in which can find a practical use. For Annino, the modern notion of citizenship has always wanted to impose collective mono-identities that could replace poli-identities from ancient regimes. This imposition, especially from the elites, is what has always led them to consider the people (*el pueblo*) as incapable of adopting the necessary conditions for self-governance or for the establishment and embracing of the values for citizenship. The reason for such a mistaken approach to citizenship, according to Annino, is based on the mere fact that republicanism made of all communities means for all judicial institutions and transformed the *comuneros*[25] into citizens; in other words, they become new subjects without any connection to their past. Annino also makes reference to the articles of the 1812 Constitution of Cádiz to insist that the concept of citizenship was elaborated from a "slip of citizenship" (*desliz de la ciudadania*). This slip was the conceptual mistake that did not redefine citizenship but that rather procured the extension of the notion of citizenship not from the political representation but rather from geographical extension:

> The citizen of Cádiz, and then of the Republic, was in effect the neighbor (vecino), the old political subject of both Spanish and American cities. Without a doubt this character had much in common with the French bourgeois and with the English householder of the Whig era, but these characters knew liberalism with a new judicial definition which enhanced the requirements that in turn guaranteed the State and its control agents over them. On the contrary, the old/prior notion of neighbor (vecino) was not modified in the 1812 Constitution; it was only extended to new subjects (the Indians), while it preserved all its traditional indetermination to the extent that for the historian it is difficult to comprehend the which profile the subject preserved in 1812 for the mentality of the collective.[26]

Here the concept of neighbor, "local,"[27] is of great interest for this author as well as for this work insofar as it provides a first glance at the way in which the notion of citizenship begins to be elaborated during the transition from subject to citizen.

Once the local is a citizen, his political representation becomes mediated by his participation in political decisions through voting. The right to vote is without a doubt the most practical way to integrate individuals into the political affairs of the state. Voting presupposes a relationship between the individual and the institutions, which in turn serves as a mechanism for some form of political and socio-cultural cohesion. In other words, voting, at least in theory, accomplished a certain level of equality among individuals of different ethnic groups and cultures once the state established as the starting point of its governability political participation of all citizens. It is worth asking then, if the individual, the local, now a citizen—a status given solely by the territorial inclusion as proposed by the 1812 Constitution of Cádiz—could have exercised her citizenship rights, or if her beliefs as a local simply allowed her to accept the role of citizen as a mere idea?

During colonialism the local belonged to a place by the mere fact of having been born near such a place; her sense of belonging rested upon the relation with the environment and with the loyalty shown to the established form of authority. To believe him/herself as subject provided an identity as a participant of a circumstance defined by the authority of a system of power. The identity of the local was defined in terms of his/her ethnicity and culture; the local's sense of belonging, the criteria defining what is to be a citizen, was articulated by contrasting Spanish values and culture to that of the values of political identity, namely political participation. The local had a sense of belonging to the state in terms of her difference rather than in the commonalities with other culturally or ethnically similar individuals. The local's identity was based solely on cultural and ethnic differences, and it was always elaborated in reference to the already established Spanish culture in Spanish territories, making her political identity an instrument for participation in national values and a tool for exclusion and marginalization. This double use of the notion of identity had a great impact upon the idea of nationalism during the years of independence. The nation-state after independence attempted to formulate its political principles under the parameter of both social and political inclusion from the political representation given by the sense of belonging but without guaranteeing cultural inclusion. In other words, the citizen of the independent nation was an extension of the concept of local but it was not enough to make the individuals of the newly formed states in Latin America believe in their political status; a status that would have provided the bases for diagnosing the circumstances surrounding their reality and therefore help them attain a concrete understanding of their reality. Such concrete understanding, according to Ortega y

Gasset's theoretical framework, would have propelled a true historical transition, one that would have also promoted the possibilities of developing the theoretical framework of a collective ideology concerned with political identity in light of a political system belonging to Latin America.

Although this new form of political inclusion promoted by the 1812 Constitution of Cádiz contributed to the formation of the nation-state in Latin America, the basis for its legitimacy and sovereignty was solely based upon the inclusion of all individuals while ignoring the role of political representation with the state. According to Francisco Colom:

> the nation-state, on the contrary, exercises its sovereignty in a totally new way: it does so directly over the individuals, in a coherent territorial ambiance and through the use of judicial and fiscally homogeneous instruments.[28]

The citizen of the newly formed state in Latin America received the idea of citizenship not from the need to build a new national state capable of understanding and responding to her unique social and cultural needs, but rather from an idea of citizenship which had arisen from the imposition of neo-feudal structures—a kind of false autonomy in the face of Spanish and European ideological influence. The state proposed by the 1812 Constitution of Cádiz forewarned of the formation of a nation that extended the social and cultural bases of political power through the establishment of territorial autonomy and dependant upon the administrative institutions, while leaving aside the citizen at the mercy of a fragile nationalism: As a result, the citizen's identity has its origin not in Latin American circumstances but rather in nationalist foreign ideologies. Thus, the first ideas of nationalism in Latin America were defined under a model of exclusion and inequality. The development of a national consciousness was marked by a cultural and political ambivalence. We cannot invalidate the role of cultural identity in the construction of nationalism nor the contributions of intellectuals[29] (*letrados*) in the formation of the state and their effective participation in the unfolding and preservation of values. Though there was no conflict of cultural loyalty among citizens during the nation-state, there was an intensification of a lack of congruence between cultural identity and political identity, creating a sense of nationalism which allowed for the participation of citizens in politics, while simultaneously approving and justifying the accentuation of social and economic differences, still latent and active in Latin America. According to Francisco Colom:

> The politization of ethnic identities, that is, their political awakness in terms of their national consciousness, unleashed since the XIX

century a series of internal and external conflicts between existent state organizations, since the conflicts belonging to them rarely coincide with those of ethno linguistic communities. In this manner a double aim movement was generated: nationalism in search for a State belonging to the communities and a State committed to the cultural assimilation of their citizens.[30]

As argued earlier, European tradition transferred to Latin American countries a political ambivalence coming from a tradition of debate between republicanism and liberalism as well as a great political-judicial insecurity in regard to the best way to establish and maintain both sovereignty and legitimacy during the transition prompted by ideologies inviting independence and beliefs still rooted in a cultural and political dependency. In the same manner, it was shown how this ambivalence promoted and forged in Latin American political life a concept of the citizen lacking a rooted understanding of her circumstance, an understanding which would allow a clear position in front of the institutions legitimizing her place within the state. These political deficiencies, what I would like to call political mistakes, have created diverse political experiences all with the same results: In Latin America, individuals' political status was granted under the imposition of alien notions to their concrete realities, creating false representations of their political conditions.

Carmen McEvoy's essay "La Experiencia Republicana: Política Peruana 1871–1878" discusses Peruvian republicanism to disclose the theoretical contradictions and ambiguities of the creation of the state while identifying the conceptual axis of the formation of the citizen. Her work is motivated in part by the debate over the institutionalization of Peru's constitution in 1822. According to McEvoy, the Peruvian republic was born:

> from a double ambiguous and contradictory inheritance. On the one hand, a constant appeal to the spirit of a body attending the constitution for a stronger benefit for all its members, even by promoting an indissoluble union between the state and society; and on the other, a strong defense of private rights and private property for each individual of the 'Peruvian family.' This ambivalence, republican inheritance was the historical matrix of the cultural-political contradiction that emerged during the national period.[31]

This political inheritance not only incited a contradiction about what should constitute the national state, but it also developed models of citizenry that were contaminated by the same type of ambivalence. The consolidation of a national project was not centered around an inclusive citizenship, even though the elites perceived in republicanism a powerful unifying ideology capable of promoting the institutionalization and social control necessary for the formation of the state.[32] The notion of citizenship, although defined from a totalizing discourse upon an active and comprehensive participation of the citizen, had to accept class difference and discrimination to prevent an economic crisis that could contribute to acute social conflicts. For McEvoy, this situation gave rise to the acceptance of an "elastic" notion of citizen always attached to labor, which at the end was no more than the development of a hegemonic project of belonging for the elites to maintain their own superior economic status without politics becoming a threat to their privileges. Decency, order, morality, and discipline became indispensable elements to better social control and were also required for attaining the status of citizenship. The author concludes that during the formation of the Peruvian state, political ambivalence became a legitimizing category that simultaneously made possible the emergence of elite cultural circles whose political values as citizens were defined in terms of power, social control, justice, and identity.[33]

Culture as an axis for social integration meant once more the displacement of a political understanding of reality that made inevitable the convergence of political identity with culture, augmenting in this way the ambiguity of what it means to be a Latin American citizen.

Notes

1. José Ortega y Gasset, "Hegel: La Filosofía de la Historia y la Historiología," *Revista de Occidente*, VI, No. LVI, (February 1928): 173. (Un analisis inmediato de la res gesta, de la realidad historica- Cuál es la textura ontológica de esta? De qué ingredientes radicales se compone? Cuáles son sus dimensiones primarias?)

2. Ortega y Gasset, "Hegel," 175. (Que envuelve a aquellas [vidas individuales] y ejerce presiones de todo orden sobre ellas. Es preciso, por lo tanto, transcender nuevamente y de la perspectiva interindividual avanzar hacia un todo viviente mas amplio que comprende lo individual y lo colectivo: en suma, la vida social. Esta nueva realidad, una vez advertida, transforma la vision que cada cual tiene de si mismo.)?

3. Ortega y Gasset, "Hegel," 175. (Es ésta (la circumstancia) algo que viene de un pasado, es decir, de otra vida social preterita, y va a hacia una vida social futura.)

4. This, to be consistent with what we have learned from Ortega y Gasset's philosophical system.

5. Jorge Mario García Laguardia. *La Constitución de Cádiz y su Influencia en América (175 Años 1812–1987)*, (Costa Rica: Centro Interamericano de Asesoría y Promoción Electoral/IIDH, 1987), 8. (Todavía durante el régimen colonial, un antecedente de gran importancia para nuestro derecho constitucional es la Constitución de Cádiz, que se promulgo en el año 1812 en esa ciudad española,

y que estuvo vigente varios años en varios países latinoamericanos antes y después de la independencia, y con base en la cual, se produjeron nuestras primeras experiencias electorales.)

6. Americans in this context means those born in in the Spanish territories in America.

7. *Junta* is the name of a type of administrative institution belonging to the Hispanic monarchy and continues to administratively operate in Spain; also a military or political group that rules a country after taking power by force, e.g., the country's ruling military junta.

8. *Señorio* is an institution of medieval and modern Spain; in many ways similar to feudal system where land and subjects are inherited or are part of a payment for services.

9. Jorge Mario García Laguardia, *La Constitución de Cádiz*, 11–17. (Libertad de imprenta, abolicion de la Inquisición, supresión del tributo del voto de Santiago, incorporación a la nación de todos los señoríos jurisdiccionales, abolición de los dictados de vasallos y vasallaje, supresión de pruebas de nobleza, abolición de las mitas y repartimientos de indios, libertad de industrias, libre comercio.)

10. García Laguardia, 12.

11. A. Fernandez García, *La Constitución de Cádiz (1812) y Discurso Preliminar a La Constitución*. (Madrid: Clasicos Castalia, 2002), 89. (La Nación española es la reunión de todos los españoles de ambos hemisferios.)

12. García, *La Constitucion de Cádiz*, 89. (La Nación está obligada a conservar y proteger por leyes sabias y justas la libertad civil, la propiedad, y los demás derechos legítimos de todos los individuos que la componen.)

13. García, *La Constitucion de Cádiz*, 90–91. (Primero: Todos los hombres libres nacidos y avecinados en los dominios de las Espanas, y los hijos de estos. Segundo: Los extranjeros que hayan obtenido de las Cortes carta de naturaleza. Tercero: Los que sin ella lleven diez años de vecindad, ganada según la ley en cualquier pueblo de la Monarquia. Cuarto: Los libertos desde que adquieran la libertad en las Españas.)

14. García, *La Constitucion de Cádiz*, 96–97. (Son asimismo ciudadanos lo hijos legitimos de los extranjeros domiciliados en las Españas, que habiendo nacido en los dominios espanoles, no hayan salido nunca fuera sin licencia del Gobierno . . . se hayan avecinado en un pueblo de los mismos dominios, ejerciendo en el alguna profesion, oficio o industria util.)

15. Carlos Meléndez Chaverri, "Las Cortes de Cádiz en sus Circunstancias Históricas Orígenes de la Constitución de Cádiz de 1812," in *La Constitución de Cádiz y su Influencia en América (175 Años 1812–1987)*.

16. Carlos Meléndez, citando el Archivo Nacional de Costa Rica. Complementario Colonial 2050. fol. 15. (Como parte esencial e integrante de la Monarquia Española declarando que los reinos, provincias e islas que forman los referidos dominios, deben tener representación nacional inmediata a la real persona y constituir parte de la Junta Central Gubernativa del Reino por medio de sus correspondientes diputados.)

17. Meléndez Chaverri, "Las Cortes de Cádiz." (Entiendo por americanismo la común identidad, por ser igualmente comunes las situaciones y necesidades,

transformadas en demandas, que tuvieron que vivir. Pese al aislamiento evidente que vivían unos hombres de los otros en este Nuevo Mundo, el solo hecho de venir de América, constituyo un lazo importante que se plasmo en comunes luchas y afanes.)

18. Joaquin Santana Castillo, "Identidad Cultural de un Continente: Iberoamerica y la América Sajona. Desde la Doctrina Monroe hasta la Guerra de Cuba," in A. A. Roig, *El pensamiento social y politico iberoamericano del siglo XIX*. (Madrid: Editorial Trotta, 2000), 19–39.

19. Santana Castillo, 20. (Las dos Américas, Sur y Norte, tienen su origen en los modelos coloniales implementados por España y Portugal de un lado e Inglaterra del otro.)

20. Santana Castillo, 24. (En sentido general, pudiera afirmarse que el americano (continente americano) no está menos lastrado por los prejuicios y costumbres ancestrales. Esta actitud menos dependiente ante los valores tradicionales es un componente psicológico que debía ser tenido en cuenta para explicar las causas que llevan al criollo a sublevarse contra el poder colonial, sin negar por el ello el papel determinante de las motivaciones económicas y políticas. También pueden verse rasgos de este comportamiento menos reverente ante la tradición en las propias posiciones con respecto a la identidad, al entender esta como una identidad solamente nueva. Pero en este caso tienen una mayor importancia otros factores culturales y los elementos que diferencian a una y otra América. Así, la identidad no se presenta como un problema para el americano del norte. No piensa o reflexiona sobre ella, ya porque su temperamento utilitario sea menos dado a la especulación, ya por que no se ha mezclado y no comporta este problema o bien por que la revolución de independencia que realizo no buscaba la construcción de una sociedad nueva y si la restitución de sus derechos económicos y civiles, afectados por las nuevas regulaciones de la corona inglesa.)

21. Francisco Colom, *Razones de Identidad Pluralismo Culturale Integración Política* (Barcelona: Anthropos Editorial, 1998), 207. ([L]a república, pues, no se asentaba sobre la primacía ontológica del individuo ni sobre la defensa de sus derechos particulares, sino sobre un modo de vida compartido, sobre un ética a la abnegación que presuponía la disposición personal al sacrificio en aras de la supervivencia de la comunidad política.)

22. Colom, 207–208.

23. Andrés Bello, Investigaciones sobre la influencia de la conquista y el sistema colonial de los Españoles en Chile, Obras Completas, vol xix, Caracas.

24. Antonio Annino, "Ciudadanía versus Gobernabilidad Republicana en México," in *Ciudadanía Política y Formación de las Naciones: Perspectivas Históricas de América Látina*, ed. Hilda Sabato, (México: El Colegio de México/Fondo de Cultura Económica, 1999), 62. (El conjunto de las condiciones que hacen posible gobernar un país, o para subrayar la capacidad de as autoridades constituidas para hacerse obedecer sin recurrir, a os en casos excepcionales, al uso de la fuerza. Esta segunda acepción, que utilizare aquí, se acerca y casi se identifica con la de la legitimidad.)

25. *Comuneros* refers to individuals in Spain or Latin America who organize and participate in an armed uprising against the established form of government.

26. Annino, "Ciudadanía" 68. (El ciudadano de Cádiz, y luego el de la Republica, fue en efecto el vecino, el antiguo sujeto político de las ciudades ibericas y americanas. Sin duda esta figura tenia mucho en común con el bourgeois francés y el con el householder ingles de la época whig, pero estas figuras conocieron con el liberalismo una definición técnico-jurídica nueva, que amplio los requisitos y garantizo al Estado y a sus agentes de control sobre ellos. En cambio, en la Constitución de 1812 no fue modificada la definición anterior de vecino; solo fue extendida a nuevos sujetos (los indios), pero conservó toda la indeterminación formal de la tradición, tanto que para el historiador resulta difícil comprender qué perfil conservaba en 1812 en la mentalidad colectiva.)

27. The original text in Spanish is *vecino*; its literally translation is "neighbor," however throughout this work, I use the English notion of "local" to signify a sense of belonging to a geographical region, an essential distinction when defining the notion of citizen during the period of state formation in Nineteenth century Latin America.

28. Colom, *Razones*, 209. (El estado-nación, por el contrario, ejerce su soberanía de una forma totalmente novedosa: lo hace directamente sobre los individuos, en un ámbito territorial cohesionado y a través de instrumentos jurídicos y fiscales homogéneos.)

29. Andrés Bello, Simón Rodríguez, and Domingo Faustino Sarmiento, among others, with their interest in governability and culture, contributed to the formation of the state and the discussions surrounding the need to civilize America or preserve its cultural authenticity.

30. Colom, *Razones*, 219. (La politización de la identidades étnicas, esto es, su despertar político en términos de conciencia nacional, desencadeno desde mediados del siglo XIX toda una seria de conflictos de orden interno y externo entre las entidades estatales existentes, ya que los confines de las mismas raramente coincidían con los decomunidades etnolinguisticamente afines. Se genero así un movimiento de doble sentido: nacionalismos en búsqueda de Estado propio y Estados comprometidos con la asimilación cultural de sus ciudadanos.)

31. Carmen McEvoy, "La Experiencia Republicana: Política Peruana, 1871–1878," in *Ciudadanía Política y Formación de las Naciones. Perspectivas Históricas de América Látina*, ed. Hilda Sabato, (México: El Colegio de México/Fondo de Cultura Económica, 1999), 256. (Con un doble herencia ambigua y contradictoria. Por un lado, una apelación constante a un espíritu de cuerpo tendiente a la consecución del mejor beneficio para todos sus miembros, incluso promoviendo una unión indisoluble entre el Estado y sociedad; por el otro, una tenaz defensa de los derechos y la propiedad privada de cada individuo de la familia peruana'. Esta ambivalente herencia republicana fue la matriz histórica de la contradictoria cultura política que emergió durante el periodo nacional.)

32. McEvoy, 259.

33. McEvoy, 263–267.

4
Martin Delany and José Martí: Two Thinkers, Two Cubas

Dwayne A. Tunstall

In this chapter I will compare Martin R. Delany's advocacy of Cuban independence from Spain during the mid-nineteenth century with José Martí's advocacy of Cuban independence from Spain during the latter decades of the nineteenth century. I will begin by explaining why Delany advocated for Cuban independence in the late 1840s and later in the early 1860s. Then, I will contend that Martí's advocacy of Cuban independence is an extension of his desire for "a new society, a new Cuban nation shaped by the vision of Cuba Libre."[1] Martí's imagined Cuba would be forged from the smithy of revolution and result in the formation of a collective national identity in which all Cubans, regardless of their racial, ethnic, and socioeconomic status, would simply be *Cubans*. Next, I will compare Delany's vision of a Black-led and U.S.-governed Cuba with Martí's vision of a race-neutral Cuba. I will end this chapter by identifying some problems with both Delany's and Martí's visions for Cuba.

Martin R. Delany's Imagined "Cuba"

In 1849, Delany published two essays on Cuba in *The North Star*. These two essays are his April 27, 1849, *North Star* essay, "Annexation of Cuba," and his July 20, 1849, essay, "The Redemption of Cuba." In them, he advances a concept of hemispheric U.S. solidarity in which free Blacks in the U.S. ought to identify with other people of African descent both in the U.S. and throughout the rest of the Americas. We can better understand the importance of hemispheric thinking to Delany's political thought from the 1840s by reconstructing Delany's arguments in those two essays.

Delany begins "Annexation of Cuba" with a warning to U.S. abolitionists and anti-imperialists that they should actively work to stop the annexation of Cuba, even though the chance that the U.S. federal government would annex Cuba seemed to be a distant one.[2] He reminds them that the annexation of Texas in 1845 also seemed unlikely when it was first proposed; yet, that annexation became a reality.[3] Given that the U.S. annexed Texas, which was a less desirable territory for the U.S. to acquire than Cuba, Delany thought that it would only be a matter of time before the U.S. would annex Cuba. After all, Cuba was located in a strategic military and economic location. Annexing Cuba would have led to the U.S. controlling one of the main trade centers in the Americas. The crown jewel of the acquisition would have been Havana.[4] In addition, annexing Cuba would legalize the importation of slaves from Cuba to the southern and western U.S.[5] It also would be an economic boom for the U.S. given that Cuba had, in Delany's estimation, over 600,000 slaves, with a conservative estimated worth of US$150,000,000, not to mention the value of property and land on that island.[6] Once one considers the prospects of foreign trade with Cuban sugar plantations and other businesses, Cuba would provide an excellent revenue source for the U.S. domestic economy, particularly for ports and markets dependent on the slave trade like Baltimore; Natchez, Mississippi; Washington, DC; Richmond, Virginia; and New Orleans.[7]

Delany reminds his abolitionist and anti-imperialist readers that annexing Cuba wasn't merely a lofty thought experiment by documenting how President James K. Polk had approved of a plan to pay Spain's debt to Great Britain and in exchange the U.S. would acquire the island of Cuba. That plan would have likely succeeded if the U.S. Congress hadn't seriously considered the Wilmot Proviso. That proviso would have banned slavery "in any of territory acquired from the Mexican War,"[8] and it scared many of the sugar cane plantation owners in Cuba. They didn't want to risk having Cuba become a U.S. territory, only to be required later to officially prohibit the importation and sale of slaves as well as ending slavery there. Yet, Delany still thought that abolitionists and anti-imperialists should not be fooled by the apparent resistance to U.S. annexation of Cuba by Cuban residents. Just as most Texans were gradually convinced to accept U.S. annexation after the Mexican War, he thought that most Cubans could be convinced to let the U.S. annex the island.[9]

Delany even provides some astute observations on the geopolitical realities of the western Hemisphere and the U.S.'s ambitions for Cuba in "The Annexation of Cuba." In fact, these observations can be interpreted as the seeds of his later political thought and moral psychology, as they are articulated in his 1852 book, *The Condition, Elevation, Emigration and Destiny of the Colored People of the United States, Politically Considered (Condition)*, and his 1854 essay,

"Political Destiny of the Colored Race on the American Continent" ("Political Destiny"). For example, Delany's moral psychology and emerging nationalist thought is on display in his explanation for why Great Britain wouldn't interfere with the U.S.'s annexation of Cuba.[10] He reasons that Britain would likely be amenable to negotiating with the U.S. to facilitate the annexation of Cuba rather than entering into a war with them over the matter.[11] Britain wouldn't desire to enter into a humanitarian conflict with the U.S. over an island where slavery is still practiced, even though Britain itself was actively anti-slavery in its international policies by the late 1840s.[12] In addition, Britain wouldn't have the resources to conduct a war with the U.S. over its annexation of Cuba if the U.S. chose to annex it.[13] Moreover, Britain wouldn't want to fight against the U.S. since doing so would put them against the most recent exemplar of republicanism, as demonstrated by the U.S.'s expansion of suffrage to all men of European descent, regardless of whether they owed property or were propertyless, and a welcoming place for western European immigrants.[14] Besides, there would be enough resistance from lower-class citizens of European nations to prevent any attempt to wage war against the U.S. to stop its annexation of an island colony mostly populated by enslaved Africans and biracial people.

Delany thinks that the most promising way to stop the possibility of the U.S. annexation of Cuba would be to empower the people of color living in Cuba to form their own government.[15] This would include the roughly 600,000 enslaved Africans residing on the island at the time. This advice is a precursor to his contention in "Political Destiny" that people ought to be governed by officials that represent their interests. After all, Spanish officials weren't representing enslaved Africans' interests.

Delany thinks that free people of color in the U.S., particularly Americans of African descent, should assist enslaved Africans in Cuba to be no longer governed under the yoke of a colonial power that profits from slave labor.[16] Delany held this view at a time where the majority of people of African descent, and the majority of colored people residing in the U.S., lived in the southern states as enslaved people. He ends the essay by calling for people of color residing both in the U.S. and in Cuba to revolt against the annexation of Cuba.

One could take Delany's call for revolution as a call for enslaved Africans to take control of their own destinies, both in the southern U.S. and in Cuba. He realizes that the destinies of people of African descent who were racialized as Black in the U.S. and Cuba weren't separate, but tied together owing to geopolitical and economic forces. Those forces could be seen as creating a collective transnational Black identity. This collective transnational Black identity would justify conceiving of Black people, whether they are enslaved or free, as viewing one another as members of the same group. This identity is a "positive shared identity"[17] that is essential for the liberation of Black people from an anti-Black political and social order. It is also an identity in which Black people can view themselves as members of a national (or in this case, a transnational Black community). As a member of a national (or transnational) Black community, one is obligated to act in accordance with the needs of that community. For Delany, Black people throughout the U.S. and Cuba, especially enslaved Africans residing in those two places, have a national obligation to protest any U.S. annexation of Cuba with revolution.

Delany's second *North Star* essay on Cuba, "The Redemption of Cuba," radicalizes his call for revolution in Cuba. He no longer recommends that enslaved Africans wait until Cuba is annexed by the U.S. to revolt. Rather, he takes it as their duty to *"take their cause in their own hands,* and use the means adequate to the ends—the means within *their reach"*[18] because no one else is in the position to assist them in this task. After all, they don't even have an active abolitionist movement working to end their enslavement like enslaved Africans of the southern and western U.S. have. If they don't fight for their own freedom, then no one else will likely do it for them. Nor should they care what their slaveholders and the enablers of slavery think about their revolt.[19] They should fight for their freedom because it is their right to be free and to be governed as citizens of a free state. If a bloody revolution against Spain is necessary to free enslaved Africans in Cuba, then he thinks that such a revolution should be fought. He even justifies this revolution by tying it to the European and U.S. tradition of striking "down tyranny and assert[ing] their right to civil liberty—if it were an act in France, worthy the commendation, praise, and honor of the American people, to strike down the oppressor, throw off the burden of an unjust government, and declare in favor of 'Liberty, Equality, Fraternity,' then will it be just and right. . . ."[20]

After Delany published his second essay on Cuba, the country of Cuba appeared infrequently in his political writings during the early 1850s. Nevertheless, the moral and political values undergirding Delany's justification for enslaved Africans to revolt against their white oppressors and pro-slavery creole collaborators are further developed in his political writings of the early 1850s. Of special importance are the following political principles and moral values: (1) *democratic citizenship,* (2) *self-governance,* and (3) *vigor.*[21] One could interpret Delany's calls for a Black-led revolution in Cuba in the late 1840s and Black emigration from the U.S. in the 1850s as the result of Black people being denied their citizenship rights in those places, not being able to represent themselves in the nations in which they reside, and being subservient to the dominant racial group.

Being a Black person in Cuba or the U.S. during the 1840s and 1850s meant that one wasn't recognized as a citizen of the country in which one resided. Without the rights of citizenship, they couldn't have "a fair opportunity to occupy positions of authority within the country in which [they] permanently [reside]."[22] Under those circumstances, Delany thinks that Black emigration from the U.S. and a Black revolution in Cuba are justifiable responses to the denial of citizenship rights to Black people in nations governed by non-Black people. This is especially the case when those who are governing Black people have interests that run counter to the best interests of Black people.

Black emigration or Black revolution is also a justified response to Black people living in a country where they cannot govern themselves. Without the right to self-governance, Black people cannot be part of the U.S. or the Spanish Empire. They remain a "nation within a nation," that is, a marginalized racial group (i.e., a group of people who have a common ancestry and cultural heritage) or a marginalized group of people sharing a nationality (e.g., Irish people in the mid-nineteenth century Britain) that resides within a nation-state. Being a marginalized group, that group lacks the right to represent itself and its own political interests.[23] The only means available for Black people in the U.S. and Cuba to govern themselves was to form their own nation, or a group of people who share similar cultural heritage, social practices, and ancestry that can govern themselves according to their own interests. This could be done in one of two ways. First, Black people could emigrate to a geographic location where they could work with other people of color to establish social institutions and governments that are strong enough to command respect from other nation-states. Second, they could overthrow their oppressors and replace the oppressive government with a Black-controlled government. Delany didn't think that Black people living in the U.S. could overthrow the U.S. federal government so he strategically recommended that Black people emigrate to more hospitable locations in the Americas.

Black emigration in the U.S. or Black revolution in Cuba is further justified because Black people living in these two countries were often subservient to paternalistic white institutions and white inflections of religions (particularly Christianity). Removing these paternalistic influences on Black people, either through violence or emigration, would create an environment where Black people could cease imitating their oppressors' mannerisms.[24] They could begin to cultivate their own talents. Rather than take up the false universalism of European culture, which degrades Black accomplishments and lives, Black people should embrace and celebrate their ingenuity and achievements.

This response makes sense in Delany's context. He had personally experienced degradation as he attempted to advance professionally in white-dominated institutions. He was accepted into Harvard Medical School in 1850 to complete his physician's training as one of the first three Black students enrolled there. Most of their classmates rejected the idea of learning medicine with Black students. Dean Oliver Wendell Holmes, Sr. of the Harvard Medical School expelled Delany and his fellow Black students due to white student outrage shortly after he began studying there. This act of disrespect was coupled with the passage of the Fugitive Slave Law that same year. This law effectively deputized all northern U.S. citizens to assist slave owners in returning escaped slaves to them. This law also allowed slave hunters to more easily enter free states to reclaim escaped slaves. Slave hunters also were in a position to capture free Black Americans and sell them into slavery if they couldn't produce adequate evidence that they were free (or if such evidence was forcibly taken from them by the slave hunters). With that law in place, no Black person living in the U.S. could feel that their rights could be protected.[25] Four years later, "the Kansas–Nebraska Act repealed the limits on the spread of slavery established by the Missouri Compromise of 1820–21 and essentially granted white settlers of any new territory the right to constitute themselves as a slave state should that be the desire of the majority of voters."[26] Of course, people of color weren't among the voters who could determine whether a new territory could become a Free State or a Slave State.

Under these circumstances, Delany realized that cultivating a Black professional class in the U.S. would be nearly impossible. Emigration to Central America, South America, or the Caribbean islands became his preferred means for free Black people living in the U.S., particularly free Black professionals, to amass wealth and help build a Black state, one that could eventually compete with and be respected by other states, including white ones.[27] This follows from his belief, which he acquired as a young man living in Pittsburgh in the 1830s under the tutelage of such leaders as Reverend Lewis Woodson, that economic self-determination is the cornerstone for elevating the entire Black race.[28]

The subject of Cuba reappears in Delany's writings in the late 1850s and early 1860s with the serial publication of *Blake*. However, Cuba's reappearance in Delany's writings is a curious one. By the publication of twenty-six chapters of *Blake* (chapters 1–23 and 29–31 of Part One) in *The Anglo-African Magazine* from January 1859 to July 1859,[29] the prospects for Black Americans being full participants in the U.S. republic were in tatters. The Supreme Court's majority decision in *Dred Scott v. Sandford* (issued March 6, 1857) codified into law what was tacitly accepted by most U.S. citizens, the federal government, and most state governments—namely, that Black Americans had no citizenship rights in the U.S..[30]

As U.S. civil society deteriorated and the threat of a Civil War loomed over the nation, Delany once again became a vocal proponent of Black emigration. But Delany had shifted "from an emigrationist program emphasizing Central and South America to an emigrationist program emphasizing Africa."[31] One can compare his advocacy for emigration to Central America, South America, or the Caribbean in 1852 and 1854 to his advocacy for emigration to West Africa, especially Liberia, from 1858 to 1862. He even traveled to the Niger Delta region as part of an expeditionary group to investigate whether Black Americans could relocate and establish settlements there. It took the Alake of Abeokuta's renouncing of the treaty he signed with Delany, which "gave [Delany] the land necessary to establish an African American settlement in West Africa,"[32] and President Lincoln's Emancipation Proclamation issued on January 1, 1863, before Delany put his emigrationist projects on hold.[33]

Blake's publication was one of the ways that Delany financed his failed emigrationist projects in West Africa.[34] To address the apparent oddity of Delany publishing a novel set in the U.S. and Cuba to finance his emigrationist projects in West Africa, Robert Levine interprets *Blake* as Delany's "effort to revise his 1852 and 1854 emigrationist texts by linking Black nationhood not to some mystical notion of Blacks' manifest destiny in the Americas but instead to the fact of Blacks' historical ties to the region, thereby imaginatively implicating himself, through his heroic surrogate, in the history of Cuba, the Caribbean, and Africa."[35] I think that reading Delany's *Blake* in this manner is a plausible interpretation of it. In addition, this reading preserves the continuity of Delany's thought, with him still hoping that Cuba would become a multiracial state (and, more specifically, a Black-led state) after enslaved Africans and their Creole allies have successfully ended colonial rule and slavery there.

For our purposes, the most important part of *Blake* is Part Two. The protagonist, Henry Blake, travels to Cuba to find his wife Maggie who had been sold from the plantation in the Red River region of Louisiana where they both lived. After he finds her, he buys her freedom. Henry then sheds the remaining vestiges of his slave identity and becomes a general in a Black insurgent group fighting for their freedom in Cuba. That part of *Blake* can be interpreted as a fictionalized presentation of Delany's earlier writings on Cuban independence in *The North Star*, particularly his advocacy of enslaved Africans revolting against their oppressive conditions in Cuba and his hope that a Black-led Cuban revolution would ignite a Black revolution that would overthrow slavery in the U.S.[36] The protagonist Henry Blake is the personification of Delany's hope for a Black-led Cuban and U.S. revolution that would topple slavery in both of those places. Of course, readers should be mindful that Delany took liberties with then-recent Cuban history to promote his political and social agenda.³⁷ First, Delany's sympathetic portrayal of Cuban creoles "subordinating their own biases for the greater good of a [B]lack-led rebellion is at variance with the large numbers of [Cuban creoles] who in actuality feared 'Africanization' [of the island owing to the larger number of Africans residing there]."³⁸ Second, Delany fictionalizes the lives of some important historical Cuban figures. For example, he takes the free mulatto poet-rebel, Plácido (Gabriel de la Concepción Valdés), who was executed on June 28, 1844, by Cuban authorities for being one of the people who led a vast conspiracy to overthrow Cuban colonial government,³⁹ and makes him an inspiration for "a rebellion set sometime in the 1850s as well as Henry Blake's cousin."⁴⁰

It is interesting to note how Delany challenges the then-prevalent view that pure Black people were inferior to mulattoes by having his protagonist be a "pure" Black man who is cosmopolitan yet proud to be racially Black. He also contrasts those mulattoes who were willing to cooperate with Blake to end slavery in the U.S. and Cuba (e.g., Plácido) with "those mulattoes who, by following the racist practices of whites, degraded and abused pure-blooded Blacks. Consequently, Delany depicts a mulatto slave-owner, discusses the anti-Black practices of the mixed-blood Brown Fellowship Society of Charleston and shows on two occasions mulattoes attempting to capture Henry."⁴¹ In *Blake*, then, Delany identifies the complexities of Black communities in the U.S. and Cuba, with some members of those communities adopting a pro-Black stance and other members adopting the dominant anti-Black racist stance of their societies. In such environments, Black people who desire to govern themselves need to take it upon themselves to end their oppression and create a prosperous Black state. That would be the most effective means for Black people to flourish in the world.

I think a good way to understand Delany's proposal for Black uplift in *Blake* is to view it as a fictional expression of his classical racialism. As a classical racialist, Delany holds "the view that races are biologically distinct populations of human beings, and that along with phenotypic makers of this difference, these populations manifest different capacities for various phenomena such as cultural aptitude, intelligence, moral character and aesthetic beauty."⁴² Delany's racialism is most evident in his 1879 work *Principia of Ethnology: The Origins of Race and Color*. In that work, he contends that members of the three main racial groups—Black (people of African descent), white (people of European descent), and yellow (people of Asian descent)—would desire to remain separate from one another owing to race affinity.⁴³ He claims that each of these racial groups has its own unique set of characteristics, aesthetic standards, cultural mores, etc. These three main groups originated as a result of the divine's "command to go forth through the earth," and the sons of Noah became the patriarchs of "three distinct peoples, of entirely different interests, aims, and ends . . . forever severing their connexion with each other, henceforth becoming different peoples and divided as though they never had been united."[44] He acknowledges that members of these racial groups can intermarry and produce biracial or multiracial children. Nevertheless, he would prefer that those children marry and produce children with people closer to being a member of one of the "pure" racial groups. If these biracial and multiracial people would continue to marry and reproduce with people of pure racial groups, then their descendants can once again embody the characteristics of one of the original racial groups.[45]

I should note that Delany's racialism doesn't seem to degrade to a form of racism.[46] For example, Delany's racialism doesn't require people of African descent to treat members of other racial groups badly or discriminate against them. His racialism just would obligate people of African descent to criticize ethnic groups and nationalities who have justified enslaving people of African descent and other oppressed peoples of the world. This is the spirit in which he criticizes U.S. Anglo-Saxons in the 1850s, for example. His racialism also would require Black people to assist other people of color by helping them form a colored state. And if the majority of the population of that colored state is Black, then Delany thinks that the state should be a Black-controlled one.

Delany's earlier proposal for Black professionals to emigrate to a colored state in Central America or South America is an expression of his desire for free Africans in the U.S. to work with people of color living in the Central America and South America to form a functioning Black state. That state would be a place not only where people of African descent can be protected from the predatory actions of European-controlled states and territories, but also create an environment for biracial and multiracial people to work with people of "pure" African descent to move the population closer to its African origins. One can understand why Delany would think that a society like Cuba's, in which most people are either pure Africans or biracial Afro-Cubans, ought to be governed by Black people and formally become a Black state.

Unfortunately, Delany's prosperous and Black-controlled state would not be built with all Black people working together as equals. Rather, it would be built primarily by the policies crafted by a transnational Black bourgeoisie. Many members of this bourgeoisie would come from the U.S. Most of them would likely view most Black people, especially residing on the African continent, as uneducated masses needing to learn how to be civilized by educated New World Black professionals.[47] Delany thought that some of these professionals should emigrate to West Africa, especially Liberia, and establish a prosperous, civilized Black nation-state by using the technological skills learned in western societies to improve the lives of indigenous peoples in sub-Saharan West Africa.

Yet, unlike many Black North American and Caribbean proponents of Pan-Africanism in the late nineteenth and early twentieth centuries, Delany apparently did not consider the African continent as the spiritual motherland of all African peoples. He became interested in West Africa as a place for Black professionals to relocate through his exploration of the Niger Delta region during the period 1859–1860. During that expedition, he learned firsthand that Liberia could be a hospitable location for professional Black Americans to emigrate and develop self-sufficient Black communities. Since the rest of this story takes us too far from our discussion of Cuba in Delany's political thought, we should end it here and move on to Martí's imagined "Cuba."

José Martí's Imagined "Cuba"

I think we can evaluate Martí's sociopolitical thought concerning how to achieve Cuban independence and form a more just Cuban state if we view Martí as a non-ideal political philosopher. Following Linda Martín Alcoff, I contend that Martí is part of a 200-year tradition of non-ideal philosophy in Latin America, in which philosophers "[consider] the questions of goodness, beauty and truth as questions for a very specific amalgam of people in a particular time and place, with a troubled tie to its cultural lineage, both European and indigenous."[48] As such, we can understand Martí's sociopolitical thought as "ask[ing] what justice demands in a society with a history of injustice."[49] Martí's non-ideal political philosophy, like other forms of non-ideal political philosophy, "is concerned with corrective measures, with remedial or rectificatory justice. . . ."[50] These corrective measures involve specifying and justifying "principles that should guide our responses to . . . deviations from ideal justice."[51] These deviations involve the failures "on the part of individuals or social arrangements to satisfy what the ideal principles of justice demands."[52] For the purposes of this section, the relevant deviations from ideal justice Martí's political philosophy is meant to address are the injustices of nineteenth-century Spanish colonial governance of Cuba.

If we wanted to formulate one of the most relevant questions that Martí's non-ideal political philosophy is meant to solve, here is a likely candidate: How can one form a sustainable Cuban nationalism when the Cuban population has been separated into factions whose interests are at cross purposes? Martí's proposed answer to this question is for Cubans to first end Spanish colonial rule and then establish a free Cuban republic—in a violent revolution, if necessary. That revolution will be carried out by loyal Cuban nationalists and allies who will provide financial and material support to the Cuban Liberation Army. Being a Cuban nationalist would require one to conceive of Cuba as a race-neutral state where Cuban identity is constructed from a shared language, a shared experience of colonial oppression, and a shared culture. What Martí's imagined race-neutral Cuba might look like will be discussed later in this section.

After reading the previous section, especially reading about Delany's reasons for imagining an independent Cuba as a Black-controlled state, I can imagine some readers wondering why Martí would recommend that Cuban nationalists view Cuba as a race-neutral state. I think Martí had two reasons for recommending that Cuban nationalists view an independent Cuba as a race-neutral state. The first and primary reason was strategic. The second reason was philosophical.

I would like to begin by explaining the first general reason for recommending that Cuban nationalists ought to view an independent Cuba as a race-neutral state. Martí realized that any war for Cuban independence fought after the first two Wars of Independence—namely, the Ten Years' War (1868–1878) and La Guerra Chiquita (The Little War) (1879–1880)—could not succeed until its military leaders, its soldiers, and its non-military Cuban supporters overcame the racial and class divisions that undermined the previous wars. Martí knew that he had to wrestle with the legacy of racial and class fragmentation from those previous wars. He knew that he had to reconcile Carols Manuel de Céspedes' initial strategy for winning Cuban independence (which included emancipating enslaved Afro-Cubans, starting with those enslaved Afro-Cubans he legally owned, and then forming an army of formerly enslaved Afro-Cubans) with later reformist strategies that downplayed emancipating enslaved Afro-Cubans to attract "slaveholders, so as to have the resources required to finance the war."[53]

At the heart of the Ten Years' War was an irresolvable dilemma. On the one hand, the first Cuban war of independence began with "El Grito de Yara" ("The Cry of Yara"), a cry in which Cuba's independence was announced alongside the emancipation of enslaved Africans. On the other hand, there were many Cubans who might have disliked Spanish colonial rule, but they feared an independent Cuba with a majority Afro-Cuban population more than they disliked Spanish colonial rule. After all, many sugar plantation owners and other Cubans economically dependent on that industry were afraid that armed and newly freed Afro-Cubans would enact retribution against their former masters and start a race war, similar to the one fought in Haiti.[54] Even many insurrectionists who fought against Spain, e.g., provisional government officials "and army commanders in effect defended slavery, at least in the short term, argu[ed] for gradual emancipation and indemnity for slave owners, both to take place after Cuban independence."[55] This strategy was meant to convince western plantation owners "in the provinces of Matanzas, Havana, and Pinar del Río"[56] to ally with the insurrectionist army forces against Spain. For those enslaved Afro-Cubans who enlisted in the "the insurrectionist army. . . . they were granted emancipation but pressed into service roles; many African-born enlistees, in fact, were sent back to the fields to work."[57]

This strategy wasn't successful, though. The insurrectionist forces were unable to effectively challenge the Spanish forces in western Cuba. By 1878, enough insurrectionist leaders were exhausted enough to end hostilities with Spain. They signed the Pact of Zanjón on February 10, 1878. The provisional government established as a result of that pact "agreed to local rule similar to that granted Puerto Rico, namely, amnesty for insurgents and legal freedom for former slaves and Chinese laborers who had joined the rebellion."[58] This pact was not an adequate agreement for some of the insurrectionist commanders, e.g., Antonio Maceo, Máximo Gómez, and Guillermo Moncada. Many of those who opted out of the pact and fought in the ensuing Little War were soldiers or commanders of African descent. This war lasted fewer than two years and ended with the forces disbanding in 1880.[59]

Martí, for his part, honestly wanted to establish a Cuban independence movement that wouldn't fragment owing to racial tensions. He thought that he could establish such a movement by unifying the fractious groups that once made up the insurrection with "Cuban expatriates in the U.S. and across the Caribbean, wealthy whites, poor Blacks, and working-class Blacks and whites [who] were all resentful of prolonged Spanish rule."[60] He did that by founding La Liga Antillana (Antillean League), a "black mutual aid and instructional society"[61] for Afro-Cubans and U.S. Puerto Ricans in New York, and opening another branch in Florida in 1890. He did that by founding *Patria*, which functioned as the official organ of the Cuban resistance movement in the U.S. from 1892 until the third War of Independence ended in 1898. He did that by participating in the formation of the Partido Revolucionario Cubano (Cuban Revolutionary Party) in January 1892 and serving as its elected leader for three years, or roughly the last three years of his life.[62] This party would be the organization that was instrumental in coordinating the preparations for the 1895 War of Independence. Later in 1892, Martí traveled to numerous places in his role as a leader of the Cuban resistance—to Florida, Haiti, the Dominican Republic, and Jamaica.[63] In 1893–1894, he traveled to many of the Cuban émigré communities in New York and Florida to organize and promote Cuban independence. As he traveled and organized the Cuban resistance movement, he gradually built a network of activists, organizations, and media. This network functioned as the means by which Martí could unite disparate groups whose members desired an independent Cuba. But the network wasn't enough. Martí had to provide the vision of Cuba Libre that would unite disparate groups into a coalition. This vision couldn't be one where races remained separated. This vision had to promote racial equality. Martí thought that the most effective way of promoting racial equality among the coalition of groups desiring an independent Cuba would be to downplay race and emphasize the commonalities among Cubans.

At this point, I can imagine some readers questioning how Martí's strategy of downplaying race and emphasizing the commonalities among Cubans would lead to a race-neutral Cuba. Wouldn't a race-neutral Cuba mean that racial identities would be either immediately or gradually eliminated from that state, leaving just Cubans? Not necessarily. The very concept of *race-neutrality* is an ambiguous one, yet its ambiguity fits Martí's apparent ambiguity with respect to how he conceived of an independent Cuba. In fact, Martí could be read as advocating at least three senses of *race-neutrality* in his efforts to liberate Cuba and establish an independent Cuban state.[64] First, *race-neutrality* could mean that people of different races can live together peacefully and respectfully as fellow citizens without requiring them to denounce their racial identities. In this sense of *race-neutrality*, racial identity would neither be a salient factor in formulating and implementing government policies nor a salient factor when citizens engage in ethical deliberations between themselves. Martí seems to advocate this sense of race-neutrality in some of his political writings, most notably his 1893 essay, "My Race."[65] Second, *race-neutrality* can mean that people initially possess distinct racial identities, but over the course of forming a nation-state their racial identities gradually meld into a unified national identity. Martí occasionally seems to advance this conception of race-neutrality when he discusses Cuban identity as an identity formed by the blending of different races and ethnicities into one people. I would contend that Martí's imagined race-neutral Cuba most likely would resemble a nation-state whose government implements its policies in the first sense of race-neutrality and Cubans view their own national identities in the second sense of race-neutrality.[66]

There is a third sense of *race-neutrality* that Martí sometimes entertains as the desired goal for Cubans to adopt, but it isn't the one on which he builds his political philosophy. This third sense of race-neutrality is one in which racial identities *do not exist*, even though people have mistakenly self-identified as being raced. Martí sometimes writes as though he is a skeptical racial eliminativist for political reasons, and other times he writes as though he is a normative racial eliminativist for ethical reasons. By "skeptical racial eliminativist," I mean someone who holds "the view that race terms are meaningless and that race-talk ought to be eliminated from public and private racial discourse because there are no natural racial essences, nor are races natural biological kinds."[67] By "normative racial eliminativist," I mean someone who thinks "that racial ascription, identification, and racism all harm human beings morally."[68]

One can read Martí as a normative racial eliminativist, at least in some of his writings, because he advances the views "that racial ascription violates individual autonomy"[69] and that "[r]acial identification unnecessarily truncates people's life projects as race often becomes a primary mode of identification to the exclusion of other valuable identities."[70] Martí articulates this view concisely when he writes in "My Race": "When you say 'men,' you have already imbued them with all their rights. Negroes, because they are black, are not inferior or superior to any other men. Whites who say 'my race' commit the sin of redundancy; so do Negroes who say the same. Everything that divides men, everything that specifies, separates or pens them, is a sin against humanity."[71] Of course, the quoted passage from "My Race" can be interpreted as evidence for the first or second sense of *race-neutrality*, but doing so makes it more difficult to connect this essay with other writings in which he states explicitly that *races* don't exist. For example, he writes toward the end of "Our America": "There can be no racial animosity, because there are no races."[72] Given the context in which it was written, I cannot help but interpret that sentence as advocating for the unreality of races. This interpretation would fit Martí's avoidance of discussing nation-states as the political manifestation of the will of a particular racial group. Rather, Martí discusses the creation of nation-states in more nationalist terms, where nation-states ought to be formed by people who have fought together against tyranny and forged a common national identity as a result of the struggle against tyranny.

The Cuban identity that would emerge because of a successful liberatory struggle would be a political identity with some quasi-ethnic import. By "quasi-ethnic import," I just mean that Cuban identity functions in a manner similar to an ethnic identity. Cuban identity would be in part a cultural one in the sense that Cubans share a similar language, live in a similar environment, have a shared history of colonial oppression, and value a similar set of virtues (e.g., loyalty, steadfastness).[73]

There is a lot more I could say about Martí's reasons for imagining Cuba as a race-neutral state. However, I think we have sketched out Martí's views on this issue enough for the purposes of this chapter.

Delany's Challenge to Martí's Imagined Race-Neutral Cuba

Anyone somewhat familiar with the history of post-independence Cuba realizes that Martí's vision of a race-neutral Cuba became the dominant vision of an independent Cuba. Martí's vision of Cuban independence became the ideological foundation for the third Cuban War of Independence and of the post-independence period. It still seems to resonate with the current Cuban government. It is probably the only ideology that has been shared by the pro-U.S. Cuban government in the early twentieth century and the Communist government from the latter half of the twentieth century until now. Even though Delany's vision for Cuba arrived in the world stillborn, I think Delany should have a chance to question Martí's imagined Cuba.

I would formulate Delany's challenge to Martí's imagined Cuba along these lines. Martí thinks that conceiving of Cuban identity in race-neutral terms would be able to integrate all Cubans into citizens and residents of an independent state. He thinks that Afro-Cubans and mulatto Cubans would become full-fledged citizens of a race-neutral Cuban republic and would likely become integrated into Cuban civic society as equals. Delany would challenge that presumption. Unlike Martí, Delany would contend that having Afro-Cubans and mulatto Cubans fighting for Cuban independence alongside white Cubans and mestizo Cubans isn't enough to foster the political and civic solidarity required to have Afro-Cubans and mulatto Cubans become integrated into Cuban political and civil society as equals. There would still be a lack of sympathy between the dominant groups of Cuban society—namely, racially white Cubans and mestizo Cubans who are phenotypically similar to white Cubans—and Afro-Cubans and mulatto Cubans, particularly those mulatto Cubans who are phenotypically similar to Afro-Cubans. That lack of sympathy would be an insurmountable obstacle for Cubans of African descent in being integrated into Cuban political and civil society as equals. The history of race relations in Cuba, particularly between Afro-Cubans, mestizo Cubans, and white Cubans, provides plenty of evidence for this contention.[74]

Delany would contend that Afro-Cubans are still unjustly discriminated against in Cuba because the groups in political power do not identify with Afro-Cubans *as Afro-Cubans.* They generally would not consider Afro-Cubans to be their equals unless those Afro-Cubans are willing to forsake their African heritage. Even then, there is no guarantee that Afro-Cubans will have an equal access to employment, educational attainment, income, and wealth.

This state of affairs wouldn't surprise Delany, for he would consider racialism to be an all-too-common feature of modern societies. For the most part, members of racial groups cannot help but to favor their own racial group owing to group self-interest. There would need to be some mechanism that promotes racial equality among the different racial groups residing in a polity. That is a realistic option only if each racial group has the right to nominate and elect representatives who would have their own interests in mind.

One can reject Delany's ethnology of race and still agree with him that non-Black people will be less likely to be sympathetic to the plight of African descended people than they are to their own people. This is a bad thing for people of African descent who live in societies governed by non-Black people whose self-interests don't align with their own self-interests. Cuba would be considered one of those societies even though most Cubans have some African ancestry. Racial disparities between people of African descent (Afro-Cubans in particular) and white Cubans in educational attainment, income, wealth, employment rates, and incarceration rates will be more difficult to address because the ones who disproportionately benefit from those disparities will not have enough reason to be sympathetic toward the ones who are disproportionately affected by these disparities. This would be the case even in a "socialist revolutionary society"[75] whose government officially works to alleviate social and economic inequality in its society, like Cuba's government apparently does.

I can imagine Martí objecting to Delany's racialism by claiming that Delany "takes too cynical, and indeed, too pessimistic a view of human nature."[76] Like Frederick Douglass, Martí would claim "that human nature has a higher side, rationality, which can be used to expand our imaginations, and enable us to identify with the whole human race."[77] Of course, he would likely contend that race neutrality in itself might not engender sympathy between Afro Cubans, mulatto Cubans, mestizo Cubans, and white Cubans. Nevertheless, he thinks that people could work to deemphasize racial identities as politically relevant categories, and hence undermine a major impediment to the development of such sympathy. Once that impediment is undermined, then the shared history of Cubans of all races fighting for Cuba and the subsequent efforts to build a Cuban state would foster the development of such sympathy.[78] Yet, Delany's observations that Euro-Americans and even Cubans of European ancestry often have less sympathy for people of African descent, whether they are African Americans or Afro-Cuban, than they do for fellow Euro-Americans in the U.S. or Cubans with Spanish ancestry in Cuba is still relevant. This is so even after a century of working to build the Cuban state.

I could imagine Martí being somewhat sympathetic to Delany's concerns about the obstacles that impede the development of sympathy needed to build political solidarity between Afro-Cubans, mulatto Cubans, mestizo Cubans, and white Cubans. He would probably classify Delany's racialism as a good form of racism, given that it is a means of affirming the humanity of people of African descent in a society that systematically undermines their humanity. Yet, even in "My Race," when he writes that there could be good racists and a good racism, privileging one's racial identity is counterproductive and even problematic in regard to forming a unified Cuban identity, one in which color is at best secondary to one's nationality. This Cuban identity will be forged from the smithy of revolutionary struggle, as people become comrades and fellow citizens, forming their own shared heritage, or it won't happen at all.

Even though Martí has a plausible reply to Delany's concerns about white Cubans not having enough sympathy for Afro-Cubans and mulatto Cubans to integrate them fully into Cuban politics and civil society, I still would not consider Martí's vision of a race-neutral Cuba as providing adequate resources for people to dismantle discriminatory practices and address racial disparities in numerous areas of Cuban society. In fact, Martí's vision has been and could continue to be unwittingly used to promote a colorblind society that would not only fail to eliminate racism, but also be used to reinforce white (color) dominance in a society.[79] What we are left with after comparing Delany's vision of a Black-led Cuban state and Martí's vision of a race-neutral state is an unrealized and likely unrealizable vision on the one hand and a vision that will, on the other hand, be unable to adequately address racial disparities between white Cubans and Afro-Cubans.

Notes

1. Mark A. Sanders, "Ricardo Batrell and the Cuban Racial Narrative." In *A Black Soldier's Story: The Narrative of Ricardo Batrell and the Cuban War of Independence*, edited and translated by Mark A. Sanders (Minneapolis, MN: University of Minnesota Press, 2010), xxii.

2. Martin R. Delany, *Martin R. Delany: A Documentary Reader*, edited by Robert S. Levine (Chapel Hill, NC: University of North Carolina Press, 2003), 116.

3. Delany, *A Documentary Reader*, 160–61.

4. Delany, 161.

5. Delany.

6. Delany, 162.

7. Delany, 161–62.

8. Delany, 162n5.

9. Delany, 163.

10. Delany, 163–64.

11. Delany.

12. Delany, 163.

13. Delany, 163–64.

14. Delany, 164.

15. Delany.

16. Delany, 165.

17. Tommie Shelby, *We Who Are Dark: The Philosophical Foundations of Black Solidarity* (Cambridge, MA: The Belknap Press of Harvard University Press, 2005), 11.

18. Delany, *Martin R. Delany: A Documentary Reader*, 167.
19. Delany, 168.
20. Delany, 168–69.
21. Shelby, *We Who Are Dark*, 33–35.
22. Shelby, 33.
23. Delany, *A Documentary Reader*, 190.
24. Shelby, *We Who Are Dark*, 35.
25. See Delany, "Political Destiny," in Delany, 278.
26. Robert S. Levine, "Editorial introduction to 'Part Three: Debating Black Emigration,'" in Delany, 181.
27. Delany, 254, 258.
28. Delany, 210.
29. Floyd J. Miller, "Introduction," in Martin R. Delany, *Blake; or the Huts of America*, edited by Floyd Miller (Boston: Beacon Press, 1970), xi–xii.
30. See, for example, Roger B. Taney, *Scott v. Sandford*, 60 U.S. 393, 407, Cornell University Law School, http://www.law.cornell.edu/supremecourt/text/60/393 (accessed July 22, 2014).
31. Levine, "Editorial Introduction to 'Part Three: Debating Black Emigration,'" in Delany, 185.
32. Levine, "Introduction," in Delany, 2.
33. Levine, "Editorial Introduction to 'Part Three: Debating Black Emigration,' " in Delany, 185.
34. Delany.
35. Robert S. Levine, *Martin Delany, Frederick Douglass, and the Politics of Representative Identity* (Chapel Hill, NC: University of North Carolina Press, 1997), 203.
36. Miller, "Introduction", xxii.
37. Miller, xiii.
38. Miller.
39. Jackie Vernon Willey, "Writing and Rebellion in Plácido's Poetry," Master's Thesis, Spanish, Vanderbilt University, 2010, 1.
40. Miller, "Introduction," xxiii.
41. Miller.
42. Jacoby Adeshei Carter, "Does 'Race' Have a Future or Should the Future Have 'Races'?: Reconstruction or Eliminativism in a Pragmatist Philosophy of Race." *Transactions of the Charles S. Peirce Society: A Quarterly Journal in American Philosophy* 50, no. 1 (Winter 2014): 34.
43. Tommy J. Curry, "Doing the Right Thing: An Essay Expressing Concerns toward Tommie Shelby's Reading of Martin R. Delany as a Pragmatic Nationalist in We Who Are Dark," *APA Newsletter on Philosophy and the Black Experience* 9, no. 1 (Fall 2009): 18.
44. Martin R. Delany, *Principia of Ethnology: The Origin of Races and Color with an Archeological Compendium of Ethiopian and Egyptian Civilization from*

Years of Careful Examination and Enquiry (Baltimore: Black Classic Press, 1991 [1879]), 37; quoted in Curry, 18.

45. Tommy J. Curry, "Doing the Right Thing,"19.

46. For a discussion of racialism and the forms of racism that often accompany racialism, see Kwame Anthony Appiah, "Racisms," reprinted in *Introduction to Philosophy: Classical and Contemporary Readings*, 4th ed., edited by John Perry et al (New York, NY: Oxford University Press, 2007), 663–673.

47. See Robert Carr, *Black Nationalism in the New World: Reading the African American and West Indian Experience* (Durham, NC: Duke University Press, 2002), 66–67.

48. Linda Martín Alcoff, "Philosophy's Civil Wars: Presidential Address Delivered at the One Hundred Ninth Annual Eastern Division Meeting of the American Philosophical Association." *Proceedings and Addresses of the APA* 87 (2013): 36.

49. Charles W. Mills, "Racial Liberalism," "*PMLA* 123, no. 5 (2008): 1384–85.

50. Mills, "Racial Liberalism, 1385.

51. Tommie Shelby, "Racial Realities and Corrective Justice: A Reply to Charles Mills," *Critical Philosophy of Race* 1, no. 2 (2013): 154.

52. Shelby, "Racial Realities and Corrective Justice, 153.

53. Mark A. Sanders, "Ricardo Batrell," xix.

54. Sanders.

55. Sanders.

56. Sanders.

57. Sanders.

58. Sanders, xx.

59. Sanders.

60. Sanders, xxii.

61. Lillian Guerra, *The Myth of José Martí: Conflicting Nationalisms in Early Twentieth-Century Cuba* (Chapel Hill, N.C.: University of North Carolina Press, 2005), 16.

62. José Martí, *José Martí: Selected Writings*, ed. and trans. Esther Allen (New York, NY: Penguin Books, 2002), xxxi.

63. Martí, *Selected Writings*, xxxi.

64. I thank the editors of this volume for prodding me on this point and forcing me to clarify what I mean by *race-neutrality.*

65. This is compatible with how Ofelia Schutte interprets Martí's essay, "My Race," in her chapter, "Undoing 'Race': Martí's Historical Predicament," in *Forging People: Race, Ethnicity, and Nationality in Hispanic American and Latino/a Thought*, edited by Jorge J. E. Gracia (Notre Dame, IN: University of Notre Dame Press, 2011), 99–123, especially on pages 114–117.

66. This is how Ada Ferrer characterizes Martí's discussion of Cuban identity in her chapter, "The Silence of Patriots: Race and Nationalism in Martí's Cuba," in *José Martí's "Our America: From National to Hemispheric Cultural Studies,"* edited by Jeffrey Belnap and Raùl Fernández (Durham, NC: Duke University Press, 1998), 228–249.

67. Carter 35–36.
68. Carter, 39.
69. Carter.
70. Carter.
71. José Martí, *José Martí Reader: Writings on the Americas*, 2nd ed., edited by Deborah Shnookal and Mirta Muñiz; translated by Elinor Randall, Mary Todd, Manuel Tellechea, and Carmen González Díaz de Villegas (New York, NY: Ocean Press, 2007), 172.
72. Martí, *José Martí Reader*, 129.
73. Martí, 173–74.
74. For a realistic assessment of the anti-Black racist conditions Afro-Cubans endured in post-independence Cuba during the first decade of the twentieth century, see Ricardo Batrell, *A Black Soldier's Story: The Narrative of Ricardo Batrell and the Cuban War of Independence*, edited and translated by Mark A. Sanders (Minneapolis, MN: University of Minnesota Press, 2010 [1912]). For a critical assessment of recent racial relations between Afro-Cubans and white Cubans, see Roberto Zurbano, "For Blacks in Cuba, the Revolution Hasn't Begun," *New York Times*, translated by Kristina Cordero, March 24, 2013, SR5, http://www.nytimes.com/2013/03/24/opinion/sunday/for-blacks-in-cuba-the-revolution-hasnt-begun.html?_r=0 (accessed August 1, 2014). For a more sympathetic account of recent race relations between Afro-Cubans and white Cubans in Cuba, see Esteban Morales Domínguez, *Race in Cuba: Essays on the Revolution and Racial Inequality*, translated by Gary Prevost and August Nimtz (New York, NY: Monthly Review Press, 2013).
75. Morales Domínguez uses this term to describe Cuban society since the Cuban Revolution of 1959 (*Race in Cuba*, 44).
76. Bernard Boxill, "Two Traditions in Africa American Political Thought," in *African-American Perspectives and Philosophical Traditions*, edited by John Pittman (New York, NY: Routledge, 1997), 133.
77. Boxill, "Two Traditions."
78. I thank the editors for pressing this argument in our correspondence about an earlier draft of this chapter.
79. See Chapter 8 of Ian Haney López, *White by Law: The Legal Construction of Race*, 10th anniversary edition (New York, NY: New York University Press, 2006).

Bibliography

Alcoff, Linda Martín. "Philosophy's Civil Wars: Presidential Address Delivered at the One Hundred Ninth Annual Eastern Division Meeting of the American Philosophical Association." *Proceedings and Addresses of the APA* 87 (2013): 16–43.

Appiah, Kwame Anthony. "Racisms." Reprinted in *Introduction to Philosophy: Classical and Contemporary Readings*. 4th ed. Edited by John Perry *et al*, 663–673. New York, NY: Oxford University Press, 2007.

Batrell, Ricardo. *A Black Soldier's Story: The Narrative of Ricardo Batrell and the Cuban War of Independence*. Edited and translated by Mark A. Sanders. Minneapolis, MN: University of Minnesota Press, 2010 [1912].

Boxill, Bernard. "Two Traditions in Africa American Political Thought." In *African-American Perspectives and Philosophical Traditions*. Edited by John Pittman, 119–135. New York, NY: Routledge, 1997.

Carr, Robert. *Black Nationalism in the New World: Reading the African American and West Indian Experience*. Durham, NC: Duke University Press, 2002.

Carter, Jacoby Adeshei. "Does 'Race' Have a Future or Should the Future Have 'Races'?: Reconstruction or Eliminativism in a Pragmatist Philosophy of Race." *Transactions of the Charles S. Peirce Society: A Quarterly Journal in American Philosophy* 50, no. 1 (Winter 2014): 29–47.

Curry, Tommy J. "Doing the Right Thing: An Essay Expressing Concerns toward Tommie Shelby's Reading of Martin R. Delany as a Pragmatic Nationalist in We Who Are Dark." *APA Newsletter on Philosophy and the Black Experience* 9, no. 1 (Fall 2009): 13–22.

Delany, Martin R. *Blake; or, the Huts of America*. Edited by Floyd J. Miller. Boston, MA: Beacon Press, 1970.

———. "Annexation of Cuba." In *Martin R. Delany: A Documentary Reader*. Edited by Robert S. Levine. Chapel Hill, NC: University of North Carolina Press, 2003.

———. *Principia of Ethnology: The Origin of Races and Color with an Archeological Compendium of Ethiopian and Egyptian Civilization from Years of Careful Examination and Enquiry*. Baltimore: Black Classic Press, 1991 [1879].

Ferrer, Ada. "The Silence of Patriots: Race and Nationalism in Martí's Cuba." In *José Martí's "Our America: From National to Hemispheric Cultural Studies."* Edited by Jeffrey Belnap and Raùl Fernández, 228–249. Durham, NC: Duke University Press, 1998.

Guerra, Lillian. *The Myth of José Martí: Conflicting Nationalisms in Early Twentieth-Century Cuba*. Chapel Hill, N.C.: University of North Carolina Press, 2005.

Haney López, Ian. *White by Law: The Legal Construction of Race*. 10th anniversary edition. New York, NY: New York University Press, 2006.

Levander, Caroline F. and Robert S. Levine. "Introduction: Essays Beyond the Nation." In *Hemispheric American Studies*. Edited by Caroline F. Levander and Robert S. Levine, 1–17. New Brunswick, N.J.: Rutgers University Press, 2008.

Levine, Robert S. "Editorial introduction to 'Part Three: Debating Black Emigration.'" In *Martin R. Delany: A Documentary Reader*. Edited by Robert S. Levine, 181–186. Chapel Hill, NC: University of North Carolina Press, 2003.

———. "Introduction." In *Martin R. Delany: A Documentary Reader*. Edited by Robert S. Levine, 1–22. Chapel Hill, NC: University of North Carolina Press, 2003.

———. *Martin Delany, Frederick Douglass, and the Politics of Representative Identity*. Chapel Hill, NC: University of North Carolina Press, 1997.

Martí, José. *José Martí: Selected Writings*. Edited and translated by Esther Allen. New York, NY: Penguin Books, 2002.

———. *José Martí Reader: Writings on the Americas.* 2nd ed. Edited by Deborah Shnookal and Mirta Muñiz. Translated by Elinor Randall, Mary Todd, Manuel Tellechea, and Carmen González Díaz de Villegas. New York, NY: Ocean Press, 2007.

Miller, Floyd J. "Introduction." In Martin R. Delany. *Blake; or the Huts of America.* Edited by Floyd Miller, xi–xxv. Boston: Beacon Press, 1970.

Mills, Charles W. "Racial Liberalism." *PMLA* 123, no. 5 (2008): 1380–1397.

Morales Domínguez, Esteban. *Race in Cuba: Essays on the Revolution and Racial Inequality.* Edited and translated under the direction of Gary Prevost and August Nimtz. New York, NY: Monthly Review Press, 2013.

Sanders, Mark A. "Ricardo Batrell and the Cuban Racial Narrative." In *A Black Soldier's Story: The Narrative of Ricardo Batrell and the Cuban War of Independence.* Edited and translated by Mark A. Sanders, ix–lxvi. Minneapolis, MN: University of Minnesota Press, 2010.

Shelby, Tommie. "Racial Realities and Corrective Justice: A Reply to Charles Mills." *Critical Philosophy of Race* 1, no. 2 (2013): 145–162.

———. *We Who Are Dark: The Philosophical Foundations of Black Solidarity.* Cambridge, MA: The Belknap Press of Harvard University Press, 2005.

Schutte, Ofelia. "Undoing 'Race': Martí's Historical Predicament." In *Forging People: Race, Ethnicity, and Nationality in Hispanic American and Latino/a Thought.* Edited by Jorge J. E. Gracia, 99–123. Notre Dame, IN: University of Notre Dame Press, 2011.

Taney, Roger B. "Opinion." *Scott v. Sandford.* 60 U.S. 393, 399–454. Cornell University Law School, http://www.law.cornell.edu/supremecourt/text/60/393 (accessed July 22, 2014).

Willey, Jackie Vernon. "Writing and Rebellion in Plácido's Poetry." Master's Thesis. Spanish. Vanderbilt University, 2010.

Zurbano, Roberto. "For Blacks in Cuba, the Revolution Hasn't Begun." *New York Times.* Translated by Kristina Cordero. March 24, 2013. SR5. http://www.nytimes.com/2013/03/24/opinion/sunday/for-blacks-in-cuba-the-revolution-hasnt-begun.html?_r=0 (accessed August 1, 2014).

PART III
Inter-American Historicism

5
Illuminated in Black: Arturo Alfonso Schomburg's Revolt against Colonial Historicization—An Anti-Colonial Reflection on the Philosophy of (Black) History

Tommy J. Curry

Introduction

In recent years, the project to conceptually supersede the historical geography of America's borders has established itself as a known polemic within the American philosophical tradition. While this geographic expansion from America towards the "Americas" has certainly increased the number of fair-skinned voices now able to guide *the marginalized* towards the sempiternal echoes of (white) pragmatists, the conceptual ramification of this emergent encroachment is the encapsulation of Latin American thought within the confines of America's racist structure. Because philosophy functions as an enterprise of white endeavor, whereby the act of philosophizing, and its product—what is taken to be philosophical—is indelibly marred by a deference to the fortified apparati of the discipline, Latin American philosophy finds itself a Pyrrhic victory in disciplinary pleas for recognition—subtly embraced for its loyalty toward all "Americana" but accepted as distinct and in many ways as oppositional to that which is "Africana."

Despite both the historical realities of slavery that placed most of the abducted Africans in direct contact with South America extending throughout the Caribbean, and the documented participation of Africans in the social, cultural, economic and political milieu of anti-colonial revolts throughout Brazil, Haiti, Venezuela, and Cuba since the 1930's, today Africa remains just as invisible in the newly discovered geographies of the "Americas" as it did within the confines of America.[1] While the anthologized literature of Latin American philosophy has only emerged within the last decade or so in the American philosophy community, Africana studies has been debating the complexities the *expanded* diaspora has on African identity since the 1970's.[2] This historical encounter with Latin America resulted in the coining of the term "Afro-Latin America" in 1979, and its further development in the work of Pierre-Michel Fontaine throughout the 1980s. Even today, there exists a rich body of scholarship highlighting the African constitution of Latin America, and the implication this cultural resistance to colonialism has in the conceptualization of an anti-colonial "perspective of coloniality." Walter Mignolo's book, *The Idea of Latin America*, illustrates this idea perfectly. Looking at history outside of the lens of modernity, those spectacles formulated on the repetitive blindness of white European descended peoples, not only yields a different view of *this* history, but also produces different materials that constitutes *that* history itself. In Mignolo's words, such a perspective would "introduce a non-European perspective, the perspective grounded on the memory of slave-trade, slave-labor exploitation, and its psychological, historical, ethical, and theoretical consequences . . . it would be a *perspective from coloniality and from Afro-Caribbean rather than Europe*."[3] Such an intervention is necessary as it highlights the very stark realities that in many ways define the boundaries between a pragmatist theory rooted in the "theory of experience," and the theories that emerge from the experience of African and Afro-Caribbean peoples. While the philosophical efforts to create conversations between white pragmatists and Latin peoples have been the strategy of some, African-descended peoples, as evidenced by the work done in Africana studies, have always sought to learn and exchange with their Latin and Caribbean kin. The emerging perspectives developed in the work of multiple scholars like George R. Andrews, Marco Polo Hernandez Cuevas, and of course the great Africana scholar Anani Dzidienyo continue to expand upon the historical, political, and philosophical implications of the Afro-Latin America paradigm.[4]

Unfortunately, what has not emerged in these extended discussions and scholarly works is a historically relevant figure that embodies the paradigmatic thrust of this Afro-Latin formulation. In an effort to remedy both the absence of such a figure and the disciplinary dependence of many Latin American thinkers on connections to white pragmatists, I aim to show how Arturo Alfonso Schomburg, a Black Puerto Rican philosopher of history, not only exemplified the complexity of Black internationalism, but enacts a philosophical disposition towards the history of African-descended people that directly challenges the pillars of American philosophy, namely white supremacy. Arturo Schomburg's refutation of white supremacism in history is rooted in a bold assertion—that the Negro, both past and present, has a history beyond the specter of white colonial domination. This anti-colonial historical method is readily apparent in "Racial Integrity: A Plea for the Establishment of a Chair of

Negro History in Our Schools and Colleges (1913)" and "The Negro Digs Up His Past (1925)." While previous works[5] have articulated Schomburg's exploration of Black diasporic history as a search for peoplehood, simultaneously personal and conceptual, I see Schomburg's method to be an unexplored illustration of the incongruence between Black personhood—their stake in a racial existence testifying to their incompatibility with *history*—and the concepts that have come to define humanity under white civilization. Rather than simply collecting materials that catalog Black history, Schomburg gives us a glimpse into the possibilities created by rejecting the fixture of Anglo-Saxon dominance in the world. In short, history is not the record of events, or the process of their unfolding, but rather the meanings given to the world by a people; meanings which function in Black history to insist that the idea of the white race ever having had possession of *civilization* is nothing more than myth.

Arturo Schomburg: A Case Study of Afro-Latin Philosophy

Arturo Schomburg was born in San Juan, Puerto Rico in 1874. It is a matter of scholarly consensus that Schomburg's early life was spent with relatives in the West Indies and Virgin Islands until his well-noted move to New York at the age of 21. In 1891, Arturo Schomburg left for New York with an apparently combative temperament and revolutionary spirit. In 1892, Schomburg founded the radical Los Dos Antilles (the two Antilles) Political Club with Rosendo Rodriguez and Raphael Serra.[6] Rosendo Rodriguez assumed the office of president while Arturo Schomburg took on the duties of secretary.[7] The Los Dos Antilles Club committed itself to advocating the revolutionary program of Jose Martí. As Elinor Des Verney Sinnette argues, "The twenty-three members of Las Dos Antillas gave their full endorsement to Martí's plans and pledged to work actively to assist in the independence of Cuba and Puerto Rico."[8] The minutes of the Dos Antilles club shows Schomburg cataloging rifles and machetes, a sign that his revolutionary sentiment was also an explicitly political commitment.[9] Such evidence only adds to the seriousness of the club's proclamation that "the club would not be disbanded while Cuba and Puerto Rico are not independent nations."[10] Schomburg's activism as a mark of his ethnic/racial Blackness has been under contention among scholars for some time. While it seems intuitive to many scholars that Schomburg's nationalist commitments were an expression of his racial-ethnic consciousness, some works have argued the opposite—suggesting that it is in fact his lack of a racial-ethnic loyalty that makes his activism possible.

Flor Piñeiro De Rivera's *Arthur A. Schomburg: A Puerto Rican's Quest for His Black Heritage* reads Schomburg as demonstrating an unshakeable racial-ethnic identity throughout his corpus. Commenting on Schomburg's participation in the Cuban Revolutionary Board Puerto Rico section held in New York on December 22, 1895, De Rivera argues that Schomburg's participation and presence at this meeting "so bound to the future of his country, proves that the young man—in proud display of his Puerto Ricanness— began his civic life in New York City."[11] Winston James on the other hand does not believe that Schomburg's Puerto Rican identity has any resonance to the larger race struggles of Black Americans. In *Holding Aloft the Banner of Ethiopia*, James argues that "Black Hispanics, and black Puerto Ricans in particular, gave little indication of the heightened race consciousness so sharply manifested in the United States by migrants from other parts of the Caribbean. The characteristic behavior of Afro-Hispanic migrants has historically been to close ranks with fellow Spanish compatriots—'black' and 'white' together—distinguishing themselves, deliberately or otherwise, from those classified as 'Negroes' in the United States."[12] In James's view, Schomburg, "the ardent Pan-Africanist, with definite black nationalist sympathies, wedded to the struggles and aspirations of Afro-America," was the "Puerto Rican political aberration."[13]

Jossianna Arroyo suggests that Schomburg's connections with Caribbean clubs, and later with the Masons, is necessary for "shedding light on the complexity of his racial politics."[14] Arroyo insists that "Schomburg confronted and negotiated the contradictions of being black and Puerto Rican in Puerto Rico and in the United States while creating, in Foucault's phrase, a 'technology of the self' through his writings."[15] Focusing on his transcultural identities, Arroyo identifies Schomburg's use of the pen name Guarionex while secretary of Los Dos Antilles as significant to his envisioning of his identity. As Guarionex is the name of an Indian chief from San Domingo in the sixteenth century as well as the name of the fictional intellectual companion of Bayonán during his political journey throughout the Caribbean in Eugenio Maria de Hostos's *The Pilgrimage of Bayonán* (1863), Arroyo maintains "the Indian rebel and the black are ethnic constructions that are not separated from each other, rather, they overlap in Schomburg's imagination, creating a complex view of his definition of Antillian, Caribbean mestizaje, and Puertoricaness."[16] In her later book entitled *Writing Secrecy in Caribbean Freemasonry*,[17] Arroyo theorizes that the secrecy rituals and practices of freemasonry allowed Schomburg to craft an affective politics revolving around the process of self-creation with "the discursive realm that the Arturo-Arthur binary brings forward [as] a subjective dilemma: how to be black and Puerto Rican in the United States."[18] Whereas Arroyo sees Schomburg's identity as a dialect-dialogic vacillation of a transcultural-transgeographic identity, Jesse Hoffnung-Garskof sees Schomburg's irresolution of the self as indicative of a change in political options and his elevation within the Black middle class society. Hoffnung-Garskof claims that "As prospects for Puerto Rican independence worsened—and national, racial, and social conflicts within the Antillean separatist movement intensified—he migrated more fully into black public life, particularly through Masonic activities."[19] There was a decidedly class dynamic behind his immersion into Black American life. Hoffnung-Garskof notes:

> Among Prince Hall Masons he found a community of middle-class black men that was multi-ethnic, pan-Africanist, and, like Schomburg, increasingly pessimistic about the prospect of racial advancement through liberal, integrationist, national projects like the Cuban independence movement. In the decade following 1898, he maintained some ties to black and mulatto activists in Cuba and Puerto Rico, hoping to build them into an international alliance of black intellectuals. But as these links to the islands of his youth faded he continued his intellectual commitment to racial internationalism. He dedicated his life to gathering evidence of "Negro" contributions to world civilization.[20]

From De Rivera to Lisa Sánchez González's "Arturo Alfonso Schomburg: A Transamerican Intellectual," there is an account of Schomburg's passion for Black history married to his indignation for white supremacist historiography. According to González, "The story goes that sometime during the 1880's in San Juan, the young Arturo Schomburg asked his school teacher about the contributions of Africans and their descendants to the Americas' history. When the teacher rudely answered that they had contributed nothing, Schomburg decided that his life's work would be to prove the teacher, and his textbooks, wrong."[21] The historian has become immersed with this mythology and debated Schomburg's program through the lens of which identity, Black or Puerto Rican, triumphed. This debate over his identity and his race consciousness has defined what little work is available on him for over three decades. The "trans-American/national/cultural" paradigm emphasized by scholars from the dawn of the twenty-first century is largely a reaction to the previous works on Schomburg emphasizing one heritage over the other. The current stance on Schomburg is that "he himself insisted that being Black and Puerto Rican were for him overlapping elements of the same proud identity."[22] But is identity in fact the most pronounced and accurate reconstruction of Arturo Schomburg as an intellectual figure and thinker in the 1800s? Is not the very question of his self-definition and our assumptions as to what politics follow from such designation part of the obscuring rationalizations of disciplinarity more generally?

Arturo Schomburg's intellectual genealogy consists of Cuban revolutionaries like Jose Martí, Black radicals like Prince Hall, and John B. Russworm as well as Afro-Puerto Rican revolutionaries like Rosendo Rodriguez. Despite our disciplinary theorizations, which tend toward the problematization of identities as the means by which we decide one's political commitments, our utilization of post-structural-colonial apparati do not offer scholars retro-cognition. Schomburg is a complex historical figure that no amount of theorization in the twenty-first century will resolve. Our attempts to recover him must be aware of the tendencies of our day, which simply make all historical figures relevant by the extent to which they represent or articulate the moralities of our time. Schomburg's perspective was molded on cultural/ethnological assumptions that largely determined the range of possible interpretations offered by his racial identity. His philosophical commitments and life's work to compile the material history of the Black race's civilization was simply not predicated on the divisions we have today between an exceptional Black or African American identity and Black or African diasporic identities. Race simply did not function in this way during the late nineteenth century.[23]

Like many profound and complex problems concerning race, the contributions of Schomburg have been lost as simply a historical footnote in ethnic and Latin American studies because he cannot be confined to a single geographic description or specific racial interest. The task of historiography cannot simply be the philosophical assertion of "the possible interpretation" of history, rather a historiography must be a philosophical claiming of an interpretation of history to explain a set of relations or events that remain invisible and unfathomable within our current conceptual paradigms of analysis. In an effort to extend the geography of thought, our discoveries often attempt to expand our paradigms as if their advancement is in fact a new territory. As DuBois famously remarked in "The Propaganda of History," "We have spoiled and misconceived the position of the historian . . . to be able to use human experience for the guidance of mankind, we have got clearly to distinguish between fact and desire."[24] Our disciplinary attempts to expand thought must be careful of its propagandist leanings; it must attempt to expand knowledge, especially historical knowledge, as it existed, since to do otherwise is to relegate history only to a mythology to be utilized toward our present ends. A correct history is indispensable for the philosopher to guard against propaganda. DuBois saw this danger and warned that "somebody in each era must make clear the facts with utter disregard to his own wish and desire and belief. What we have got to know, so far as possible, are the things that actually happened in the world. Then with that much clear and open to every reader, the philosopher and prophet has a chance to interpret these facts."[25]

The task for the philosopher is not to invent *their* Schomburg. Their task is to situate the purview Schomburg utilized in his gazing upon the territories of civilization so that we may learn from his insights and improve upon the blindness of his time. Schomburg is an important figure in Afro-Latin thought because he developed a philosophy of history that attempts to illuminate the activity of Blackness within modernity. He adamantly rejects the view of the Negro as uncivilized, and asserts that the Negro was in fact birthed within generations of civilizations nurtured beneath the shadows of towering African, Caribbean, and Haitian nations. Schomburg adamantly defends the birth and triumph of Black civilization. In "Is Hayti Decadent" for example, Schomburg notes both the economic vulnerability of Haiti to foreign powers and the symbolism it holds for the Black race the world over as an independent Black republic. He says, "I understand that a subject of this nature is of great importance to the young people, for it has the tendency to create love, to see and observe what others have done preceding them for the welfare of the race, and to inculcate the virility of ambition and manhood."[26] Rather than appeal to some external racial apparatus for Haiti's economic salvation, Schomburg draws from his own; remarking, "I only wish I was able to infuse in Hayti, graduates of Booker T. Washington's technical school that would lift the people to an ambitious love that would increase the material wealth of the people and country."[27] Schomburg did not appeal to the ideas of other racial groups; he believed the Black race was self-sufficient and told history as a demonstration of this assertion. He made no distinction in the history of the Black world; he only sought to give testament to its various pasts—its heroes and heroines—whose names have survived the centuries.

Why would such an enormous view of the world occupy Schomburg if indeed he was an intellectual defined and committed to knowledge through his identity? Schomburg was a prolific essayist and exhibited his commitments to Black internationalism throughout the choices of his subject matter. Schomburg constructed history upon the legacies of Black Haitians, Russians, Americans, and Cubans. He wrote of the Afro-Russian Alexander Pushkin, the Haitian hero Henri Christophe, the Cuban poet Placido, and Antonio Maceo easily; all within the organizing concept of race. The question before us is not how he identified himself, but how his work identified the organizing and enduring history of the Negro.

The Negro Society for Historical Research: The Chair of Negro History as the Foundation of a Black Philosophy of History

On April 9, 1911, Schomburg, along with John E. Bruce, the famous student of Martin R. Delany, founded the Negro Society for Historical Research

(NSHR).²⁸ While Alexander Crummell's organization, the American Negro Academy, was created from "seeing that the American mind in the general, revolts from Negro genius, the Negro himself is duty bound to see to the cultivation and the fostering of his own race capacity,"²⁹ and where its mission was "the encouragement of the genius and talent in our own race,"³⁰ the NSHR was predicated on a much more radical historical vision—"an organizational expression of Pan-Africanism."³¹ William H. Ferris quotes John Edward Bruce's radical intervention into what we would now think of as Black historiography in volume 2 of his *The African Abroad*. According to Bruce:

> It was to instruct the race and inspire love and veneration for its men and women of mark that the Negro Society for Historical Research was brought into being. Our principal aim is to teach, enlighten, and instruct our people in Negro history and achievement; to institute a circulating library, a bureau of race information, with a collection of all books, pamphlets, etc., by Negro authors and their friends, together with all data bearing upon race achievements in every form of endeavor. We believe that the race can be made stronger and more united if it can be made to know that it has done great things.³²

Bruce was the first president of the NSHR, so it is no surprise that his description of the society's aims coincided with his views on the distortion and manipulation of Black history and the Negro's intellect. In a 1917 essay delivered to the newly ordained ministers from the Virginia Theological Seminary at the Messiah Church in Yonkers, New York, Bruce argued that "Only the white man can speak of a heredity of intellect. We cannot. Moreover, modern learning is dispensed and obtained in the language of the white man. The Negro, in the universities and colleges of Europe and America, has to do his thinking and his reading in another, that is to say, the white man's language."³³ In an effort to popularize the movement begun by Arturo Schomburg's *Racial Integrity: A Plea for the Establishment of a Chair in Negro History* in 1913, which demanded a chair of Negro history in all Black institutions of higher learning, Bruce argues such a chair is necessary "so that the generations to come after us will know more about our race from reading and study than most of us now know, because the textbooks written by white men have been and are woefully silent on the Negro's contributions to the general knowledge of the world, legal, ecclesiastical and political. Our environment makes us think white, and some of us think white so persistently that we haven't time to think black."³⁴ Bruce articulates a problem in the training of Black intellectuals (clergy-men, teachers, and race-men) most popularly credited to Carter G. Woodson's 1933 monograph entitled *The Miseducation of the Negro*.³⁵

In *The Miseducation of the Negro*, Woodson argued, "When a Negro has finished his education in our schools, then, he has been equipped to begin the life of an Americanized or Europeanized white man, but before he steps from the threshold of his alma matter he is told by his teachers that he must go back to his own people from whom he has been estranged by a vison of ideals which in his disillusionment he will realize that he cannot attain."[36] Because the educated Negro sought to imitate that which he or she saw as "civilized," they in fact "decry any such thing as race consciousness."[37] Married to the universality of history, law, philosophy, and economics, these Black intellectuals sought to emphasize the commonality of all humans and advocate the assimilation of the Black race into the cultural-historical spirit of the Anglo-Saxon race. This is why Woodson reacts so strongly to this assimilationist tone held by Black intellectuals trained by white universities which elided the historical contributions and evidence of civilization created by the Black race. In his *Appeal*, written in 1921, Woodson warns that:

> civilization is best which confers the greatest good on the greatest number. The so-called white man's civilization primarily concerned with promoting the interest of Europeans and white Americans becomes, therefore, decidedly inferior to that of some of the natives of the jungles. Passing through Europe or America one finds abundant resources productive of riches, cities of splendor inhabited by people of luxury and ease, and governments controlling dominions almost encircling the globe, all made possible, however, by forcing to a lower level the man far down or by enslaving, plundering, or exploiting the weaker peoples of other lands. This is not in itself progress for mankind. It is merely the centralization of power in the hands of autocrats.[38]

Europe is not civilized. It is in fact barbarous and destructive, so the effort of the Negro to imitate such a racial temperament is a failure to understand history, and only offers proof of one's internalization of Black inferiority. For Black historians like Bruce and Woodson, the struggle for liberation and freedom was not only political but anthropological; it was freedom against the Western concept of man and the white template of civilization. For these thinkers, Blacks/Blackness stood firm on its incongruity with the white world, and was evidence of a different envisioning of civilization.

The NSHR was not simply guided by a "political" intervention into the telling of history. Politics, as is usually discussed in relation to identity, or rather, what all Black thought is reduced to under our post-structuralist/post-colonial era, is not a concern of Black thinkers and activists in the late nineteenth and early twentieth century. These societies were attempting to address the scientific underpinnings of one's understanding of the artifacts of history. The first occasional paper delivered at the NSHR by Dr. York Russell was entitled *Historical Research*.[39] Russell begins his investigation of the topic by making a distinction between historical research as "the philosophy of history," and "the part that geography plays in history."[40] Russell understood history as a linking of the actual to the conceptual, or as he states "history, par excellence, comes from the Greek word which means 'to know' and may be defined as the 'Science of the Relation of FACTS to IDEAS.'"[41] Rather than simply being a rote recalling and cataloging of "facts," the Negro Society for Historical Research was an organization dedicated to exploring the philosophy of Black history. Russell explicitly endorses a view of history which requires the articulation of the order and relations facts demonstrate not only in their time, but to the (raced) observer. Russell maintains that "The prime duty of the philosophic historian is therefore to demand of the facts what they signify. The idea which facts express; the relations which these facts sustain with the spirit of the epochs of the world, in the bosom of which, they make their appearance."[42] Russell concerned himself with the role philosophic history has in discovering the *rule of history*. Russell claimed that the recalling of every fact throughout history illuminates the general law of history, or "the law alone which causes it to be."[43] Particularity, then, is the treasure of the philosopher of history, since it is through the relation facts have to the conditions that enable them that one grasps the rules governing their time. Black history then was not only the demonstration of great African and Negro civilization throughout time, but an attempt to account for the ideas and motivations which gave such nations ascendency. Russell believes such ideas and motivations can be captured within three categories: the space or place of the civilization, its defining of humanity and/or nation, and its great men.[44] The scholars of the NSHR were attempting to create a philosophical anthropology which refuted not only the archival claim that Africa had no civilization, but offered an account of the race's historical temperament and personality—what was generally referred to as the race's gifts, or the race's vision of humanity and the values the race offered the world through their existence.

Similar to the view of his president, Mr. John E. Bruce, Russell articulates the aim of the "historical research" conducted by the society as an attempt to create an account of history—its general laws—that improve upon the current order and avoid the imitation of Europe. Russell notes:

> the illustrious past is the common property of the illustrious present. Take care of the present, the God of nations will take care of the future; and the past will take care of itself. If you make a success to-day, you

can create a past for yourselves. Because Europe is great today—all past Europe is great, and the greatness of other non-European nations is expressed in the same terms as Europe. That is Europe takes care of all aspirants for greatness. When Africa of the present is great, Africa of the past will loom into prominence, for then we shall become arbiters of our own destinies, write our own histories, make our own researchers, organize our own libraries, establish our colleges, create our own monuments. Now as there is a possibility to produce a better environment than any existing today, we have a golden opportunity, not merely to imitate, but to improve the existing order.[45]

As Russell's essay points out, the opportunity for oppressed Africans to gain liberation—their particular racial humanity—is a function of their ability to know, and thereby create contrary visions of humanity and knowledge. Russell insists that the Negro must not imitate the ontology of Europe. The race must articulate separate values which arise from their historical consciousness and societies. In short, Russell is arguing that liberation comes through self-possession, the ability of the non-European to actively construct for themselves a reality, a heritage, a past that propels them into the future—remember, for Russell, an illustrious present and future demands an illustrious past. Russell demands the race to muster the courage to be loyal to their history and the society dedicated to exploring the intricacies of colonial legacies we have been sublimated to ignore. Russell ends his occasional paper with a plea for loyalty: "A loyalty to a cause and an effort, a loyalty which if well directed will form an effective breakwater against the ever increasing and cumulative tide of prejudice and discrimination."[46] Russell is true to the thought of his time. Black history was thought to inspire the resistance of the Black race against white superiority. As Woodson famously argued:

> the teaching of history in the Negro area has had its political significance . . . It was well understood that if by the teaching of history the white man could be further assured of his superiority and the Negro could be made to feel that he had always been a failure and that the subjection of his will to some other race is necessary the freedman then, would still be a slave. If you can control a man's thinking you do not have to worry about his action. When you determine what a man shall think you do not have to concern yourself about what he will do. If you make a man feel that he is inferior, you do not have to compel him to accept an inferior status, for he will seek it himself. If you make a man think he is justly an outcast, you do not have to order him to the back door. He will go without being told; and if there is no back door his very nature will demand one.[47]

This is why a chair of Negro history was a revolutionary and necessary paradigmatic revolt against the academic tide of white supremacist historiography. In *Racial Integrity: A Plea for the Establishment of a Chair in Negro History*, the third paper delivered before the NSHR, Schomburg articulates an argument for institutionalizing a Black philosopher of history as the foundation of Black college curricula. A chair of Negro history claimed the intellectual legitimacy of studying Negro history against the dominant Eurocentric interpretation of history set forth by American and European universities and colleges. Schomburg insists the reader understand this point: "The white institutions have their chair of history; it is the history of their people and whenever the Negro is mentioned in the text books it dwindles down to a footnote."[48] The white historian tells history with the white race as the victor and protagonist of civilization. "The white scholar's mind and heart is fired, because in the temple of learning he is told how on the 5th of March, 1770, the Americans were able to beat the English, but to find Crispus Attacks it is necessary to go deep into special books. In the orations delivered at Bunker Hill, Daniel Webster never mentioned the Negroes having done anything, and is silent about Peter Salem."[49] The university, much as Bruce and Woodson have described, canonizes the invisibility of Black contributions to history. This erasure is a deliberate effort to allow whites to control the ideas and define the characters of the heroes and heroines of civilization. The white history of the academy provides the only possible substance that historical interpretation can draw from. It provides the actors, the background, and the motivations of races and nations, thus in making Blacks invisible, white history determines for generations the ideas and concepts used to justify the struggles of the present and the ideals aspired towards in the future.

"Where is our historian to give us, our side view and our chair to Negro History to teach our people our own history," Schomburg asks. With no Black scholar creating an account of Negro history, "We are at the mercy of the 'flotsam and jetsam' of the white writers."[50] Schomburg however made no assurances that such a chair would come from the Black intelligentsia. He wanted a scholar "who would give us the background for our future, it matters not whether he comes from the cloisters of the university or from the rank and file of the fields."[51] Knowledge of the history, the material subject to the laws of civilization, comprised the substance of racial development. To bring the race into the future, the Black people of his time had to possess the ideas of the past which birthed the great leaders and nations of the race. Without this knowledge, the Black race was condemned to mimicry—the unreflective imitation of the white races. Schomburg argues that our attempts to recover our historical relationships, where we see in ourselves the impending legacies of our peoples, and are inspired by the fury of our progeny against a world that confines them to invisibility, can only come about as we begin to erase our dependency on the European systems of thought. In this regard I leave you with the last words of Schomburg's *Racial Integrity*:

> The Anglo-Saxon is effusive in his praises to the Saxon Shepherds who lived on the banks of the river Elbe, to whom he pays blind allegiance. We need the historian and philosopher to give us with trenchant pen, the story of our forefathers and let our soul and body, with phosphorescent light, brighten the chasm that separates us. And we should cling to them just as "blood is thicker than water." When the fact has been put down in the scroll of time, that the Negroes of Africa smelted iron and tempered bronzes, at the time Europe was wielding stone implements; . . . we will feel prouder of the achievements of our sires. We must research diligently the annals of time and bring back from obscurity the dormant examples of agriculture, industry and commerce, upon these the arts and science and make common the battle of our heritage.[52]

Schomburg's Ante-Theory: A Premise of a Black Philosophy of History.

Schomburg's essay "The Negro Digs Up His Past" (1925) begins with a call similar to that of *Racial Integrity*: "The Negro must remake his past in order to make his future."[53] Schomburg alerts the reader to the importance the past has in legitimizing the Black race's claim to a place at the seat of humanity. "Though it is orthodox to think of America as the one country where it is unnecessary to have a past, what is a luxury for a nation as whole becomes a prime social necessity for the Negro," says Schomburg.[54] The past is the foundation of the Black race's rejection of the Eurocentric schema that defines Black people, Black nations, and Blackness itself as uncivilized/non-human/animal. Schomburg's emphasis on the past disproves Europe's exclusive claim to civilization and technological evolution, what Schomburg understands more generally as racial development. Whereas Schomburg's *Racial Integrity* (1913) offers accounts of notable Black activity throughout the centuries in an effort to substantiate the Black historian's and philosopher's argument that the Black race has participated in history, "The Negro Digs Up His Past" is an attempt to articulate the effect Black historical research has for our conceptualization of civilization, history, and humanity. Schomburg is optimistic, given the Black historian's ability to shift the thinking about Black history from mythology to science. We see Schomburg utilizing Dr. York Russell's ideas, as well as the approach to historical research explored in the NSHR throughout his 1925 work. Schomburg sees the effect of historical research to be paradigmatic. "Gradually as the study of the Negro's past has come out the vagaries of rhetoric and propaganda and become systematic and scientific, three outstanding conclusions have been established," says Schomburg.[55]

> First, that the Negro has been through the centuries of controversy an active collaborator, and often a pioneer, in the struggle for his own freedom and advancement. This is true to a degree which makes it the more surprising it has not been recognized earlier. Second, that by the virtue of their being regarded as something exceptional, even by friends and well-wishers, Negroes of attainment and genius have been unfairly disassociated from the group, and group credit lost accordingly. Third, that the remote racial origins of the Negro, far from being what the race and the world have been given to understand, offer a record of predictable group achievement when scientifically viewed, and more important still, that they are of vital general interest because of their bearing upon the beginnings and early development of culture.
> With such crucial truths to document and establish an ounce of fact is worth a pound of controversy. So the Negro historian today digs under the spot where his predecessor stood and argued.[56]

Schomburg begins his account of Black history with the success historical research has had in dismissing the propaganda of white supremacy and refuting the negation of Black existence committed by white civilization's erasure of Black activity throughout history. Historical research has shown that the Black race has in fact been an active collaborator in the development of civilization, that the race's great men and women are in fact of Negro stock and evidence of the group's achievement, and that the race's history offers proof of cultural development and evolution. The white account of history, however, asserts that Blackness is without consequence in the plane of civilization, that the race offered no ideas or activity motivating humanity's development. Blackness is non-being, without existence and cultural program. Racially, Blackness is such that it is possible to ignore it or assimilate it within the stories of "other" white nations and peoples. Blackness then is defined by (white) grand narratives because the Negro requires none of *his* own. How we come to know of the world, and the races, nations, and peoples that comprise it, remains idle and barren for Blacks under this order of knowledge, of which history is a part. Schomburg's project offers the material basis from which theory is established since it makes what is not visible, visible and able to be engaged by theory—an ante-theory (preceding of theory) so to speak.

Adalaine Holton's *Decolonizing History: Arthur Schomburg's Afrodiasporic Archive* (2004) observes a similar theme in Schomburg's work. For Holton, "The Negro Digs Up His Past" articulates a theory of recovery—it addresses the politics and processes of historical recovery."[57] Holton maintains that "Schomburg's accumulation of documents is an archive that extends and complicates our understanding of what an archive is and the role that it plays in the production of knowledge and in the creation and maintenance of political power."[58] Inspired by Foucault's understanding of the archive from the *Archaeology of Knowledge* as "the law of what can be said, the system that governs the appearance of statements and events,"[59] Holton's thinks "the archive is what organizes and hierarchizes statements and events in our historical memory."[60] Holton attempts to get at the process that makes ideas and the events that demonstrate the actuality of the idea in the world perceivable and able to be described. For scholars influenced by Foucault like Holton, the "archive has come to signify not only physical collections of documents and cultural artifacts, but also the repository of memories and knowledge, as well as the practice of remembering, forgetting, and cataloging memories and events of the past."[61] In this sense, Schomburg is reformulating "what can be said" about Africa and its people throughout the diaspora because his archive offers a collection to be surveyed against the dominant episteme/(empowered) historical a priori of his day. This is why Holton claims that Schomburg "worked to counter the ideological underpinnings of these European and U.S. collections interrogating the nature and species of the material fact thought to be explained by theory."[62] While it does seem obvious that "Schomburg's writings, as well as those of other black book collectors and archivists, exhibit an awareness of the relationship between power and the archive that Foucault identifies,"[63] Schomburg's work and thinking about history is not reducible to Foucault's abstractions and theorizations of historicity—the unveiling of Schomburg's project within history's (dialectical) ebbs and flows.

Schomburg is claiming, much like the system established by York Russell, that history, our ability to know the past, is decidedly created by our ability to assert necessary relationships between facts (in the world) and ideas (of our minds). In history, Schomburg's concern would be decidedly historiographic, since it recognizes history as a theoretical subject to any number of simultaneous and contradictory normative endeavors in its telling.[64] Philosophically, Schomburg could be read as having a concern about what is taken to be theory itself. Aijaz Ahmed's *In Theory: Class, Nations and Literatures* notes that "facts require explanations, and all explanations, even bad ones, presume a configuration of concepts, which we provisionally call 'theory.' In other words, theory is not simply a desirable but a necessary relation between facts and their explanations."[65]

Schomburg is attempting to address exactly this connection between the material event or entity made observable by historical research and our explanation of it—the idea it represents. Stated more simply, Schomburg is attempting to create observable facts that are presently unobservable because of the propaganda of white history. Schomburg, following Russell, would argue that specific facts (like proof of a Black Kmt) would necessitate specific ideas (like Black capacity for civilization or government). This is the scientism embraced by Schomburg—the scientific relation between fact and idea. This view holds that there is a necessary relationship between the fact and the idea it comes to represent, so that unearthing facts about the race offers already determined proofs or ideas about the race's nature. The searching for the fact—this process of looking for its existence—is quite distinct from the theory which only emerges from the union of the fact and its idea. The fact, its searching out and discovery, precedes theory—it is ante-theory.

Foucault begins his chapter on "The Historical *A Priori* and the Archive," in *The Archaeology of Knowledge* with a crucial point about the nature of the archive. "The positivity of a discourse ... characterizes its unity throughout time well beyond individual oeuvres, books, and texts."[66] The unity shared between works is not based on the books or texts possessing a shared truth or method, or a degree of scientific correctness about the world. Foucault understands this positivity of discourse to be an indication that thinkers "were talking about 'the same thing', by placing themselves at 'the same level' or at 'the same distance', by deploying 'the same conceptual field', by opposing one another on 'the same field of battle.'"[67] Positivity defines "a field in which formal identities, thematic continuities, translations of concepts, and polemical interchanges may be deployed."[68] On one hand we can understand Schomburg's engagement with history as proof of this unity of discourse, but we are left without a clear understanding of how positivity allows Schomburg access to the historical a priori. Foucault asserts that an historical a priori "is an a priori that is not a condition of validity for judgements, but a condition of reality for statements."[69] It is "An a priori not of truths that might never be said, or really given to experience; but the a priori of a history that is given, since it is that of things actually said."[70] The historical a priori is the repository of the meanings of statements, indeterminately shared in the world without debt to a predetermined law which gives rise to their existence. The historical a priori takes "account of the fact that discourse has not only a meaning or a truth, but a history."[71] This historicity of the a priori proposed by Foucault is important in grasping his system and clarifying the role of the archive. The historical a priori

> does not constitute, above events, and in an unmoving heaven, an atemporal structure; it is defined as the group of rules that characterize a discursive practice: but these rules are not imposed from the outside on the elements that they relate together; they are caught up in the very things that they connect; and if they are not modified with the least of them, they modify them, and are transformed with them into certain decisive thresholds. The a priori of positivities is not only the system of a temporal dispersion; it is itself a transformable group.[72]

The archive then emerges from the historical a priori operating in our discourse. "Instead of seeing, on the great mythical book of history, lines of words that translate in visible characters thoughts that were formed in some other time and place, we have in the density of discursive practices, systems that establish statements as events (with their own conditions and domain of appearance) and things (with their own possibility and field of use)."[73] Foucault names all these systems of statements as the archive. Does Schomburg engage-utilize-operate within these systems, specifically that of the archive? Does the statement "The Negro has a history," have meaning within the system and order of knowledge established by slavery which comes to define Blackness? Schomburg thinks not.

Schomburg asserts that Black history does not exist under the present order of knowledge and present regimes of power chronicling humanity's phylogenetic advance. The separation between what is Black, (non-human), not historical, and the white historical human is not a political assertion; the argument brings attention to the non-existence of the Negro. Schomburg argues, "For him [the Negro], a group tradition must supply compensation for persecution, and pride of race the anti-dote for prejudice. History must restore what slavery took away."[74] Civilization itself has created a unity of texts, books, and ideas that deny the existence of Black race. It defines Blackness singularly as the white race's slave, or the condition of being fit to be the slave. Schomburg believes such propaganda has ontological weight—it has defined Blackness as unperceivable, since any evidence of Black achievement and culture is by being "achievement" and "cultural" not (possible to be) Black. Schomburg is adamant that

> the bigotry of civilization which is the taproot of intellectual prejudice begins far back and must be corrected at its source. Fundamentally it has come about from that depreciation of Africa which has sprung up from ignorance of their true role and position in human history and the early development of culture. The Negro has been a man without a history because he has been considered a man without a worthy culture.[75]

This is why the Black historian is uniquely important. The Black historian has in fact created a background of civilization and discovered texts by 1925 that assert the cultural/racial presence of the Negro in history, but do these have meaning beyond the endeavors of the Black race? Can any historian simply find Black civilization whereby racism, or the racist order used to explain away the civilization of Blacks, simply re-organized when challenged by a demonstration of "facts" to the contrary? Can the racist observer, who denies humanity is a possibility of Blackness, in fact see the necessary connection between the fact/evidence/event and the explanation or ideas which follow? Because theory in fact establishes these connections between what is observed and what is explained abstractly beyond its particular time, anti-Blackness—the predilection of the white world founded upon the barbarism of slavery—resists the fullness of "fact" regarding Blackness.

There is something prior to theory, a position before the engagement with the fact only seen by the Black historian in Schomburg's thought. Before the facts in the world are given explanation, there is an origin of the fact captured as an event, or artifact that is not seen by the world at large. If Schomburg's work is an archive, it exists as such because of its difference and distinction with the historical a priori established within the discourses birthed by Europe and whiteness. For the "fact" to be connected to an "idea" there must be a positionality that sees such a connection as possible. This possibility is denied in a white supremacist world, so Schomburg's work in fact established a system of relations that is only possible (able to be real) within the purview of a Black history, not history more generally. Schomburg's indictment is not isolated to exclusion, it is an indictment of the philosophy used to link material events to the ideas they represent. He rejects the narrative of white civilization—its barbarism—occluding Blackness from realizing itself beyond the definition asserted by the racist schema of whites. The suggestion that there is a Black humanity, history, and civilization is ineffable under the white supremacist order. It has no possible meanings that correspond to events and relations in our present understanding. Even today, our understanding of Black humanity is imitative—a demand that Black humanity is truly just humanity; the one offered as a product of the West. Schomburg insists upon a different order where Blackness is not an accident considered by theory, but accounts for the materials accumulated for theory to engage.

Concluding by Exposing the Lingering Racism of Disciplinary Theory

Unlike our thoughts about the white supremacy of old—an incompatible imperial politics of conquest that exceeds our ability to articulate not only what an authentic existential "choosing" would look like, but our very imaginings of the petrified landscape under which our descriptions of deliberate historical growth becomes an ahistorical moral specter of agency—today, in the mind of the oppressed, white supremacy functions as the need, an insatiable desire; a revisionist yearning for the applicability of white thought and theory. "Theory," formulated upon the historical character and ideas of Europeans, is presented by disciplines as "actual knowledge;" the necessary connections between the development of entities and historical phenomena and the allegedly tested and true apparati determining how we should think about this world. The problem for the oppressed is that this world which serves as the ground of theoretical investigation is not presented as an untouched brute fact of our experience and perception. Instead, this world is imagined—phantasmal—and created by the thinker's internalization of the ontological commitments disciplines utilize to teach the scholar *their* theory is real and operates in reality.[76]

The characters, their aims and ends; the explanations for their existence and persistence throughout time, are defined by what we take to be given by the premises of the conceptual system(s) imposed upon the imaginative landscapes of reality. In this configuration, the oppressed are forced to discover themselves in the thought of their oppressors. The idea that the theories utilized by colonial thinkers to create racism, militarism, and anti-Blackness simultaneously exist as the solution to these creations is foundationally bankrupt. What is gained by utilizing an account of history and accepting the theories which explain the rise and fall of the ideas within that history, which is predicated on the assumed inferiority of Black peoples and nations? Is it enough of a corrective to simply suggest that the Black race is enough like the white race that white theory and history remain legitimate? This illusion that there nonetheless exists a theoretical account of humanity; a version of the human that is axiomatically sustained as a universal cultural possibility without regard to race—a pure humanity separate from the materiality of racist colonialism and imperial economics—is the allure of theory. It frees the Black mind from the stain of the Black body. Theory offers absolution. The relationship between ideas and facts in the world established by the perception of an observer, who is unraced, ungendered, unquestioned in its capacity for reason, is desired by the educated classes of a people who have been solely defined by their racial inferiority for centuries. However, it is this desire for the safety of theory which calls for our questioning of its function, or rather its distortion, of Blackness.

In our institutionalized activities of the philosopher, our scholarly inclination to make Black thoughts "converge" with the doctrines of white disciplines is an internalization of the Black scholar's inability to clearly articulate the limitations of white anthropology. Because we yearn for recognition, both of our own work and the figures we use to represent our endeavors, our philosophical practice inexorably divests our work of its transformative potential. As Black scholars, we happily extend the doctrines of white theory as evidence of our competence and desire to be accepted by the canons which initially excluded racial and ethnic peoples from its territories. Our work expands the reach of white theory to geographies, like Afro-Latin America, previously unsettled by white logics, and it is in this imperial intellectual endeavor that we demand recognition as a philosopher and scholar. This activity of thinking ourselves through the historical perspective of the colonialist presents an objective (material) contradiction, where on the one hand we claim the history of racism, colonialism, and imperial conquest to be socially constructed knowledge and mythologized categories of reality publicly announced as the concocted remnants of modernity, while simultaneously advancing the belief that this reality—its categories and knowledge—are in some way true and capable of extending beyond the contingency of white/European culture by bridging our races and establishing what is "our shared humanity."

It is in this regard that Schomburg challenges Africana peoples to construct culturalist paradigms to evaluate and study their own. He urges Black scholars to create theories rooted in the relationship between material facts/artifacts and the ideas one uses to explain their existence—Black theory, an anti/ante-theory of Black historical existence aiming to supersede the colonial confines of our present order. What Schomburg understood is that an Afrodiasporic unity is by its necessity a transgressive conceptual motivation. In telling history, Schomburg demands a philosophical origin story that deploys not simply reason or mechanistic schemes of profit and interest, but a culturally specific tale which presumes development of nations, peoples, and history is pushed forward by a racial interest. While there is disagreement with Adalaine Holton's account of Schomburg's archive, it is difficult to deny that his archival project does reflect "his belief that black history is an irreducible web of intersecting experience, languages, and cultural practices,"[77] or that his archive "allows for the comparison of Afrodiasporic communities across difference without discounting those differences. Such unity across difference, will give people of African descent the inspiration and intellectual foundation to liberate themselves from the continuing forces of white supremacy."[78] Rather than engaging in an archaeology, Schomburg offers Black scholars an ante-theory; a survey of the raw materials capable to be explained by ideas. By attempting to correct the substance-material thought uses to formulate theory, Schomburg attempts to adjust the possibilities and redraw the boundaries we assume constitute the "theoretical accounts" that can explain the condition and thinking of the

Black race. By changing the artifacts, events, and texts surveyed, Schomburg demands our present concepts be able to explain the necessary relation between what we urge in the abstract and what is apparent in the actual.

Notes

1. See J. Fred Ripley, "A Negro Colonization Project in Mexico, 1895," *The Journal of Negro History* 6.1 (1921): 66–73; and Robert E. May, "Invisible Men: Blacks and the U.S. Army in the Mexican War," *The Historian* 49.4 (1987): 463–477, which gives accounts of Black men fleeing to enemy lines to escape the racist order of America.

2. For a summary work of the attempts at an Afro-Latin historiography, see George Reid Andrews, *Afro-Latin America 1800–2000* (Oxford: Oxford University Press, 2004). Previous authoritative sources investigating an Afro-Latin history/culture were Pierre-Michel Fontaine, "The Political Economy of Afro-Latin America," *Latin American Research Review* 15.2 (1980): 111–141 and of course Anani Dzidzienyo "Activity and Inactivity in the Politics of Afro-Latin America," *SECO-LAS Annals* 9 (1978): 48–61.

3. Walter Mignolo, *The Idea of Latin America* (Malden: Blackwell Publishing, 2005), xi.

4. For outstanding histories in the Africanization of Mexico, see Marco Polo Hernandez Cuevas, *The Africanization of Mexico from the 16th Century Onward* (Lewiston: Edwin Mellon Press, 2010) and *African Mexicans and the Discourse of on Modern Nation* (Lanham: University Press of America, 2004).

5. Adalaine Holton, "Decolonizing History: Arthur Schomburg's Afrodiasporic Archive," *The Journal of African American History* (2007): 218–238

6. Christopher Bell, *East Harlem Remembered: Oral Histories of Community and Diversity* (Jefferson: McFarland and Co, 2013), 32.

7. Elinor Des Verney Sinnette, *Arthur Alfonso Schomburg, Black Bibliophile and Collector: A Biography* (Detroit: Wayne State University Press, 1989), 21.

8. Sinnette, *Arthur Alfonso Schomburg*, 21.

9. Schomburg Center for Research in Black Culture, Manuscripts, Archives and Rare Books Division, The New York Public Library. "Dos Antillas Political club page of contributions." New York Public Library Digital Collections. Accessed March 17, 2015. http://digitalcollections.nypl.org/items/86ce52a6-6d5a-554c-e040-e00a1806262b

10. Schomburg Center, "Dos Antillas Political club page of contributions."

11. Flor Piñeiro De Rivera, *Arthur A. Schomburg: A Puerto Rican's Quest for His Black Heritage* (San Juan: Centro de Estudios Avanzados de Puerto Rico y el Caribe, 1989), 9.

12. Winston James, *Holding Aloft the Banner of Ethiopia: Caribbean Radicalism in Early Twentieth-Century America* (London: Verso, 1998), 195.

13. James, *Holding Aloft the Banner of Ethiopia*, 198.

14. Jossianna Arroyo, "Technologies: Transculturations of Race, Gender, and Ethnicity in Arturo Schomburg's Masonic Writings," *Centro Journal* 17.1 (2005): 5–25.

15. Arroyo, "Technologies," 7.

16. Arroyo, "Technologies," 8.

17. Jossianna Arroyo, *Writing Secrecy in Caribbean Freemasonry* (New York: Palgrave Macmillan, 2013).

18. Arroyo, "Technologies," 9.

19. Jesse Hoffnung-Garskof, "The Migrations of Arturo Schomburg: On Being Antillano, Negro, and Puerto Rican in New York 1891–1938," *Journal of American Ethnic History* 21.1 (2001): 3–49, 3.

20. Hoffnung-Garskof, "The Migrations of Arturo Schomburg," 4.

21. Lisa Sánchez González, "Arturo Alfonso Schomburg: A Transamerican Intellectual," in *African Roots/American Cultures: Africa in the Creation of the Americas*, ed. Sheila S. Walker (Lanham: Rowman and Littlefield Publishers, Inc., 2001), 139–152, 140.

22. Lisa Sánchez González, "Arturo Alfonso Schomburg," 140.

23. See Anne McClintock, *Imperial Leather: Race, Gender, and Sexuality in the Colonial Contest* (New York: Routledge, 1995); Michele Mitchell, *Righteous Propagation: African Americans and the Politics of Racial Destiny after Reconstruction* (Chapel Hill: The University of North Carolina Press, 2004); and Kevin Gaines, *Uplifting the Race: Black Leadership, Politics, and Culture in the 20th Century* (Chapel Hill: University of North Carolina Press, 1996).

24. W.E.B. DuBois, *Black Reconstruction in America 1860–1880* (New York: The Free Press, 1998), 722.

25. DuBois, *Black Reconstruction*, 722

26. Arthur Schomburg, "Is Haiti Decadent," in Flor Piñeiro De Rivera, *Arthur A. Schomburg: A Puerto Rican's Quest for His Black Heritage* (San Juan: Centro de Estudios Avanzados de Puerto Rico y el Caribe, 1989), 51–58, 51.

27. Arthur Schomburg, "Is Haiti Decadent," 58.

28. Sinnette, *Arthur Alfonso Schomburg*, 38. William H. Ferris's *The African Abroad* (1913) however disagrees with Sinnette's date. In his text, the Negro Society for Historical Research is said to have been founded on April 18, 1911, at John E. Bruce's residence at Sunny Slope Farm in Yonkers, New York.

29. Alexander Crummell, "The Attitude of the American Mind Toward Negro Intellect," in *The American Negro Academy Occasional Papers*, ed. William Loren Katz (New York: Arno Press, 1969), 8–19, 17.

30. Crummell, "The Attitude of the American Mind Toward Negro Intellect," 17.

31. Sinnette, *Arthur Alfonso Schomburg*, 38.

32. William H. Ferris, *The African Abroad, or His Evolution in Western Civilization: Tracing His Development Under Caucasian Milieu Vol.2* (New Haven: The Tuttle, Morehouse, and Taylor Press, 1913), 863.

33. John Edward Bruce, "The Importance of Thinking Black," in *The Selected Writings of John Edward Bruce: Militant Black Journalist*, ed. Peter Gilbert (New York: Arno Press and the New York Times, 1971), 131–133, 131.

34. Bruce, "The Importance of Thinking Black," 132.
35. Carter G. Woodson, *The Mis-Education of the Negro* (Chicago: African American Images, 2000).
36. Woodson, *The Mis-Education of the Negro*, 5–6.
37. Woodson, 7.
38. Woodson, 149.
39. York Russell, *Historical Research* (New York: Negro Society for Historical Research, 1912).
40. York Russell, Historical Research, 1.
41. Russell, 1–2.
42. Russell, 2.
43. Russell.
44. Russell.
45. Russell, 5.
46. Russell.
47. Woodson, *The Mis-Education of the Negro*, 84–85.
48. Arthur A. Schomburg, *Racial Integrity: A Plea for the Establishment of a Chair of Negro History in our Schools and Colleges, etc.* (New York: August Valentine Bernier, 1913), 18.
49. Arthur Schomburg, *Racial Integrity*, 18.
50. Schomburg, *Racial Integrity*, 19.
51. Schomburg, *Racial Integrity*.
52. Schomburg, *Racial Integrity* 20–21.
53. Arthur A. Schomburg, "The Negro Digs Up His Past," *The Survey Graphic Harlem* 6.6 (1925): 670–672.
54. Arthur A. Schomburg, "The Negro Digs Up His Past," 670.
55. Schomburg, "The Negro Digs Up His Past."
56. Schomburg, "The Negro Digs Up His Past."
57. Adalaine Holton, "Decolonizing History: Arthur Schomburg's Afrodiasporic Archive," *The Journal of African American History* (2007): 218–238, 219.
58. Adalaine Holton, "Decolonizing History," 224.
59. Adalaine Holton, "Decolonizing History," 225.
60. Holton.
61. Holton.
62. Holton, 226.
63. Holton.
64. See Michael Bentley, "The Project of Historiography," in *Companion to Historiography*, ed. Michael Bentley (New York: Routledge, 1997), xi–xvii.
65. Aijaz Ahmed, *In Theory: Classes, Nations, Literatures* (New York: Verso Publishing, 1994), 34.
66. Michel Foucault, *The Archaeology of Knowledge* (New York: Pantheon Books, 1972), 126.
67. Foucault.
68. Foucault, 127.

69. Foucault.
70. Foucault.
71. Foucault.
72. Foucault.
73. Foucault.
74. Arthur A. Schomburg, "The Negro Digs Up His Past," 670.
75. Schomburg, "The Negro Digs Up His Past," 672.
76. Lewis Gordon has commented on this phenomenon in *Disciplinary Decadence: Living Thought in Trying Times* (Boulder: Paradigm Publishers, 2006).
77. Adalaine Holton, "Decolonizing History," 222.
78. Holton.

6
Chaos in the House of Reason: Positivism in the Americas, 1780–1900

Adriana Novoa

This essay starts with the question "What is the Enlightenment?" and ends with the one that consumed intellectuals at the end of the nineteenth century, "What is philosophy?" because these interrogations frame two of the main concerns about the government of the modern nation throughout the nineteenth century in Europe and the Americas. Three ideas guide the organization of the material. First, that there is a philosophical continuum in the Americas that explains the ideological commonalities among different nations. Second, while there were clear differences in racial politics and economic development between Europe and the Americas, an analysis of the philosophies that developed after colonial nation building provides a different picture. Over the nineteenth century philosophers confronted the same ideological challenges, originating a continental view of their field that needs to be considered. Finally, the known terms "modernity," "Enlightenment," and "positivism" need to be analyzed very carefully; a twenty-first century examination makes clear that while the intellectual goals of each might be similar, the various ways to achieve such goals led to constant debates. In opposition to the common association of the "era of Enlightenment" or "the era of positivism" with reason and certainty, this essay shows how the nineteenth century was consumed by intellectual chaos and instability, which explains why in this chapter positivism is not regarded as something clear and solid, an originator of clarity, but as an umbrella term used to emphasize the relationship between philosophy and science with socio-political development. While in the first half of the century philosophy and sciences were at the center of the republic's politics, by the end of the century it is not even clear what philosophy entailed, and what Enlightenment, *Ilustración, Iluminação,* or *Les Lumières* really meant.

According to Alfred I. Tauber, the term "positivism" "was coined by August Comte in the 1820s, although its complex history may be traced from Francis Bacon to David Hume, and most directly to the seventeenth century scientific revolution."[1] It is well known that the reception and adoption of positivism varies quite a bit from country to country, including periodization, readings, and leading intellectuals. For example, Michel Foucault explained that in France the sense of the Enlightenment was conveyed "via positivism and those . . . opposed to it," through a series of themes which include, "knowledge [*savoir*] and belief, the scientific form of knowledge [*connaissance*]," and the transition from the prescientific to the scientific.[2] Foucault also pointed out that the question "What is enlightenment?" had a different trajectory in the traditions of Germany and France. While German philosophy "shaped its answer into a historical and political reflection of society"; in France "it is the history of science in particular that has served as a medium for the philosophical question of historical Aufklärung, in a sense, the critiques of Claude Henri-Saint Simon, the positivism of Auguste Comte and his successors were in fact a way of resuming the inquiry of Mendelssohn and of Kant on the scale of a general history of societies."[3] While Foucault does not mention what happened in the Iberian case, Spain, Portugal, and their colonies also underwent a similar path in determining the meaning of the new ideas in the eighteenth century.

In the Spanish and Portuguese empires, members of the intellectual group that made up the Republic of Letters promoted the Enlightenment through "a network of the scholarly and scientific community of the sixteenth, seventeenth, and eighteenth centuries." The only requirement to belong to this association was to write letters; "those scholars who failed or refused to establish sustained lines of communication, could not be reckoned as citizens of this republic."[4] The networks created indicate important characteristics of this new culture: circulation, exchange, accumulation, and transmission of knowledge through a brotherhood devoted to find truth and certainty through reason. In principle, those who partake in these activities blurred other forms of colonial hierarchy related to economic, social, and cultural divisions because a "man of letters" was only concerned about communicating true knowledge in an impartial manner. By the seventeenth century, the natural and hard sciences led the development of inquiry through physics and mathematics, and their discoveries were tied to a repositioning of philosophy, questioning how effective Scholasticism was as the system that could be useful to understand the meaning of the new scientific thought and its teaching.

The two pillars of Iberian societies, monarchy and church, led the transition from Aristotelic Scholasticism to a thought that allowed scientific experimentation, which caused many debates and conflicts. For example, in 1746 the Portuguese philosopher Luis Antonio Verney (1713–1792) published a method of study that was very controversial but was adopted later by the Marquis of Pombal for his educational reforms.[5] It was published in Spanish translation in 1760 and supported an eclectic approach that promoted freedom to think outside the limits of a particular philosophy. In Verney's words, the "modern system is not to have a system: only in this way some truth has been discovered." A philosopher was then liberated from passion, and he could "propose the reasons for the things he observes." Those reasons that were clear were embraced and those doubtful were despised and rejected, and in this way "the body of the doctrine" was formed.[6]

This philosophy of experience aligned with advancements in physics and natural sciences, but "a physics that cannot be understood" had to be rejected, and things that were not proven "must not be admitted." Simplicity and clarity were the foundation of the new thought.[7] Politically, the intention was not revolutionary action, or any speculative form of government not based on known facts; Verney's book subtitle clarified that the method of study presented intended to be "useful to the Republic, and to the Church." In this Iberian enlightened culture, knowledge needed to be useful and applicable to the economic and social improvement of the empire through a government that ruled according to philosophical and scientific principles—the study of economics was a favorite subject among the Spanish illustrated elite. According to the Spanish dictionary of 1737, "republic" could mean the government of the public interests that at the time had started to imply "the government of many" to refer to "a government different from the monarchy." Accordingly, there were three ways to govern the *res publica*: monarchical, aristocratic, or democratic. This word could also mean the public cause, what was common or useful to the majority; the name of some peoples; and, finally, the group made by the men of wisdom and erudition.[8] Verney's use of the term republic was more related to the latter, and the book proposed a method to promote the education and culture of many under new philosophic and scientific ideas circulated by those who had true knowledge.

What Is the Enlightenment?

In 1747, Juan Bautista Corachán (1661–1741), a priest who was also professor of mathematics at the Spanish University of Valencia, explained that in "the Republic of Letters" laziness was forbidden and the erudite could not socialize with idle men. The enlightened [ilustrados] could only enjoy "an honest pastime that [will] strengthen the body to avoid the physical damage caused by a sedentary life among the literate community" (*comunidad letrada*).⁹ In the Spanish American colonies, this republic was also very important in the development of a new hierarchy based on intellectual bonds among its members. In a ceremony that took place in 1762 to celebrate the arrival of Don Manuel de Amat y Junient (1707–1782), former Captain General of Chile, as Viceroy of Peru, it was explained that this man had been sent by providence "to increase the society of letters of this republic." At this time "the sciences were shining more than in past centuries," but in the region the conditions for its development had not been fully developed.¹⁰ Science was indispensable for good government; "the Exact Sciences, even the Belle Lettres," were needed "for the person who hold[s] on his shoulders the enormous weight of the republic" because to reign was the "most difficult art of the arts." Using Plato's *Republic*, the absolute power of the monarch was here related to knowledge, monarchies would be happy "when the wise rule them, or the philosophers became kings."¹¹ The supremacy given to a governing erudite class based on their understanding of philosophical and scientific principles meant that blood lines alone were not enough to rule.

 The first scientific journal in the Spanish colonies appeared in 1768, edited and written by Jose Antonio Alzate y Ramírez (1737–1799) in Mexico. In the first issue, the editor clarified that he was following the newspapers (*periódicos*) and journals being published in Europe for an audience that was a mix of general public and scientific experts. Creating *Diario Literario de Mexico* would contribute "to the good of the Spanish nation" because agriculture, commerce, and mining needed scientific knowledge to improve. His critical approach would avoid dogmatic attacks, and, following the eclecticism that characterized the Iberian Enlightenment, the editor promised to be impartial and avoid "becoming a partisan to simply informing the opinions and doctrines proposed by all parties." He assured that he would only be critical of those ideas that were clearly wrong and not useful, a work that was "as needed as useful to the Republic of Letters."¹² The second issue was devoted to a thesis defended in Querétaro about theology and physics. Experimental physics is used to explain how God's creation had happened because sciences could support with the best evidence the actions of a rational creator that acted according to principles that were analyzed by writers of the classical Greek period, Buffon, Galileo, Descartes, Kepler, and other "modern physicists" (*físicos modernos*).¹³ Unlike other European traditions, this eclecticism was not at the service of a national philosophical or scientific tradition; intellectuals needed to consider local dynamics to create a useful thought.

 By the 1770s, the existence of this international republic of letters blurred some colonial hierarchies because the praising of freedom to think outside the oppression of dogma inspired many intellectuals in the colonies to create their own mix of ideas with an applied and useful objective, which by the end of the eighteenth century was mostly political and related to establishing a modern system of government based on a universal thought that was bringing humanity together with the aid of science. In the United States, the American Revolution reinforced the connection between the republic of letters and revolutionary action; at a ceremony that took place at Harvard College in April 1776 to honor George Washington, it was explained that academic degrees were originally instituted so that "men, eminent for knowledge, wisdom and virtue, who have highly merited of the republic of letters, should be rewarded with the honour of these laurels." Washington, known for his "knowledge and patriot ardour" by all those who supported the war, had earned this distinction.[14]

Revolution became then an emancipatory act of the mind, as much as Newton's research establishing physical laws had been, strengthening the links among philosophy, science, and politics. By the end of the eighteenth century, events that took place in the Americas helped to shape the universal perspective that understood revolutions as the entry of humanity into a new era through the creation of a political system that represented the popular will, which started to be considered the true modern political system among liberals. It was in the American continent where the most important revolutionary developments started to happen. First with the emergence of the United States in 1776, and, in 1804, the creation of the first Black nation in Haiti as the result of the Haitian Revolution. Shortly after, the movements of independence that helped to define liberal ideology during the nineteenth century started all over Latin America. In her fascinating account of the relationship between Hegel and Haiti, Susan Buck-Morss reminds us that the Independence of the latter surpassed "the metropole in actively realizing the Enlightenment goal of human liberty, seeming to give proof that the French Revolution was not simply a European phenomenon but world-historical in its implications."[15] Before Haitian independence, the French colony of St. Domingue was "the single richest and most productive colony in the world."[16] It was also "a major, if not the major center of organized and institutionalized science and medicine in the Western Hemisphere at the end of the eighteenth century."[17] The *Cercle des Philadelphes* was based there, and it was extremely active in communicating with other associations, scientists, and intellectuals on the continent and in Europe. It was affiliated with the American Philosophical Society in Philadelphia and had 160 international members, including Benjamin Franklin. The economic development of the colonies was tied up since the beginning of colonialism to science, technology, and philosophy, a process that continued in the nineteenth century with the dismantling of Scholasticism to replace it with another system that agreed with a new economic, social, and cultural order.

The Black leaders of the Haitian Revolution that ended colonialism in St. Domingue knew that they were creating a new path for the existing debates about freedom; the leader of the revolution, Toussaint de L'Overture (1743–1803), himself noticed how different the revolution he was leading was from the one that had happened in France in 1789. On November 18, 1801, L'Overture replied to a letter that Napoleon Bonaparte had sent him after his 1799 coup of 18th Brumaire, which had allowed him to gain power at the expense of the republican institutions. Affirming the desire of St. Domingue's population to become independent, Toussaint asked, "Why should it not? The United States of America did the same, and with the assistance of monarchical France they succeeded in establishing it." While the constitution passed in the ex-French colony was not perfect, he made clear that it challenged "the system" Napoleon had imposed upon the republic to "show a greater regard to personal and political liberty, to the freedom of speech, or the freedom of man" than what was created in France. Napoleon's kind of politics "would never be cordially received or cheerfully acquiesced in by the people of St. Domingo [sic]. Such changes, or such freedom, [were] far, very far from being desired even by us." The letter ended with L'Overture's clarification about the kind of ideological radicalism that predominated in Haiti, which was not materialist in nature, as it had been in France. Those like him were defenders of religion and spirituality, as was the "devoted" population of the island.[18] This tension between spiritualism and materialism in politics would continue throughout the nineteenth century, with a continuous oscillation between an understanding of new nations as the result of rationalist mechanical processes that were an affirmation of materialism, or as metaphysical entities that manifested a spiritual existence.

According to Marcus Rainford (1758–1817), a British officer who arrived at St. Domingue in 1799, Toussaint was an excellent leader because he was "surrounded by men of letters and science" who had "found little difficulty in the formation of a temporary constitution" based on "justice and equality (of right, not of property)". One of those extremely helpful in the process had been "Citizen Pascal," a descendant of the philosopher of the same name, who had married a local mixed-race officer's daughter, demonstrating how little racial prejudice influenced the French colony.[19] It turn, philosophy had enlarged "its horizon in the new world," and Rainford expected that thanks to this expansion, "absurd prejudices" would only be supported in the future by "a few inferior tyrants, who wish to perpetuate in America the reign of that despotism which has been abolished in France."[20] Obviously, this did not happen; ending slavery as an economic and social system posed a threat that tamed future emancipatory projects in the colonies. France quickly rescinded the emancipation of 1794 and by the beginning of the next century the trade of slaves continued as a foundation of the economy of its Caribbean colonies.

As a Spanish colony located in this region, Cuba was influenced by the ideological transformations happening in the neighboring islands. For example, Nicolás Calvo y O'Farril (1758–1800) proposed in 1794, at a meeting of the Economic Society of Havana, the creation of a position to teach chemistry to promote the development of Cuba.[21] In connection with philosophy, in 1797, a priest (*presbítero*), José Agustín Caballero (1762–1835), wrote his philosophical lectures, published as *Philosophia Electiva*, to introduce modern philosophical and scientific ideas to students. He supported moving away from Scholasticism in favor of the ideas of Gassendi, Descartes, and Newton that presented a model for scientific experimentation and reasoning accepted all over Europe.[22] His student, Félix Varela (1788–1853), also a member of the Catholic Church, continued his teacher's work, and his *Institutions of Eclectic Philosophy* (*Instituciones de Filosofía Ecléctica*) was published in 1812 in Latin, though the volumes that came out after 1814 were in Spanish. In the first volume, philosophy was defined as *"the knowledge of everything with certainty through the most fundamental causes and acquired with the light of reason. Therefore, everything comprehended in the universe, and even the creator of it according to reason,"* was the object of philosophy. This implied that "all the sciences (specifically the natural ones)" belonged to this discipline.[23] This volume on logic followed the work of Etienne Bonnot de Condillac (1714–1780), whose translated logic book was published in Caracas, also in 1812, following the reforms introduced by Baltasar Marrero (1752–1809). The Royal Academy of Spanish Language defined in 1817 the word *science* as the "knowledge of the human affairs" achieved by true principles, "such as those of the mathematics," but it was also a term used to identify knowledge "such as philosophy, jurisprudence, medicine, etc.," that was less certain though helpful to improve humanity.[24]

Varela favored the sensationalist philosophy of Locke, Condillac, and Antoine Destutt de Tracy (1754–1836), which by the 1820s implied an interest in sensation, sentiment, and their study through psychology. Unlike Descartes, Varela wrote that human existence was known because it was felt, which enhanced the role of perception.[25] The influence of Destutt de Tracy offers us an interesting case to verify the philosophical exchanges in the Americas. In 1809, this French philosopher sent his treatise on government to Thomas Jefferson (1743–1826), who liked it and published it in Philadelphia with a preface written by him.[26] Auguste Levasseur (1795–1878), who travelled with the Marquis de Lafayette to the United States from 1824 to 1825, mentioned in his book that "Mr. Salazar, Chargé d'affaires from the Republic of Colombia, for the

United States" proved himself a man "instructed in republican institutions, and entirely devoted to them." One night he "gained" everybody's hearts "giving a toast to Mr. Destutt de Tracy, and by proclaiming the happy influence produced by his writings in both hemispheres."[27] De Tracy was also in contact with Bernardino Rivadavia (1780–1845), who became president of the United Provinces of the River Plate (Argentina) from 1826 to 1827.

The idea of the Republic of Letters continued in early republicanism in the Americas. At a meeting of the American Philosophical Society in Philadelphia in 1823, the writer and politician Charles Jared Ingersoll (1782–1862) gave a speech mentioning that while "poetry, music, sculpture, and painting" were still lingering in the Italian culture, "philosophy, the sciences, and the useful arts, must establish their empire in the modern republic of letters."[28] According to this account, linking modernity with science and philosophy made the United States much more developed than Europe, since it was in this country where scientific and philosophical education were more effectively related to government and politics. For similar reasons, in a book about the history of the revolutionary war in Colombia, written in 1827 by José Manuel Restrepo (1781–1863), it was made clear that those who wanted to vote needed to demonstrate scientific knowledge besides owning property or a "useful business"; to vote for the state assembly, men needed to know "any science, or obtain a scientific degree."[29] Citizens needed to be connected to both Colombia and new knowledge.

This association, though, became problematic because of the difficulty to create a system that effectively synthesized philosophy, science, and politics. Philosophically, as explained by John Torrance, Descartes had separated his physics and his metaphysics, and from "the latter sprang the metaphysical systems of the seventeenth-century rationalists, Malebranch, Spinoza and Leibniz, eventually discredited and replaced in France by the empiricism of Locke and Condillac." At the same time, those who only followed Cartesian physics, mostly physicians, were anti-metaphysicists, which initiated "a decisive step away from philosophy towards science." This was viewed at the time as a mechanistic view of man, "which originated from the same circle as the distinction between science and metaphysics."[30] These divisions and their spin-offs troubled the linking of governing to philosophy and science because the different ideas about men also implied different types of society, which shaped the debates between materialists (mechanists) and spiritualists (those who defended metaphysics). By the 1820s, de Tracy was recognized as the thinker who had finished Condillac's philosophy by developing a transcendental materialism—which explains his influence years later over Karl Marx. This French philosopher's movement was known as *Idéologie* (Ideology) and it became popular partly because it connected philosophy, science, and politics since it was based on Cabanis' physiology.

De Tracy treated ideas "as sensations or impressions in the heads of individuals," and through their study the science of ideology "would ultimately become a branch of zoology." He revealed "the origin of ideas in universal human needs and desires," which allowed his followers to hope that this type of thought would be the foundation of rational morality and social order in new nations.[31] But the dominance of Ideology started to decline by the 1830s because it had deficiencies related to its methodology. At the same time, articles appeared in Cuba, and in the rest of the Americas, about the latest philosophical novelty, the eclecticism of Victor Cousin (1792–1867). These articles triggered a debate in Cuba when Félix Varela wrote against Cousin based on his interpretation of the new philosophy as a reduction of innatism or "spiritualism"; either the ideas were in the soul and were, then, innate; or the ideas were not previously in the soul and were formed without sensible images, which was materialism.[32] Following Vicente Medina's analysis of this debate we can say that this criticism was "primarily, although not exclusively, motivated by philosophical and pedagogical concerns about the impact of modern philosophy and modern science" in Cuba.[34] Materialist conceptions seemed more closely aligned with political radicalism and, importantly in Cuba, the abolition of slavery.[33]

Cousin's philosophy was known as Eclecticism, but it was different from the already mentioned eclectic ideas of the Spanish Enlightenment because it addressed what were by this time the failures of republicanism in France, and attempted a reconciliation of different philosophies, which was very relevant for those new republics in the Americas that were being roiled by political tensions. This eclecticism was linked to German ideas philosophically and scientifically through Natürphilosophie. In December of 1831, the *American Quarterly Review* published an article that praised Cousin and provided details about how his "influence" was "great and growing," so much so that "recently his name" had passed "the Atlantic and is beginning to be heard here, widely if not loudly."[34] In the 1830s several works of Cousin were published in the United States, one being the *Introduction to the History of Philosophy*, translated by Henning Gotfried Lindberg (1784–1836) and published in 1832.[35] Lindberg wrote in the preface how important Cousin was in Europe and, also, how French philosophy "may be said to be nearer neighbors to the inhabitants of America, than those of Great Britain." France also occupied "the high rank among civilized nations."[36] More importantly, Lindberg defined Cousin's work as characterized by "the genuine and enlightened love of humanity," a universalism that could be traced to his "firm belief in the truth of the Christian religion." But this faith did not stop him from thinking that the mysteries related to Christianity were accessible "to human understanding," which made them "proper subjects of philosophical inquiry and elucidation" in the work of his followers.[37]

Four years later, George Ripley (1802–1880), a member of the Transcendental Club, at this point embarked on a dispute with the Unitarian Church, to which he belonged as a minister, and edited a volume with the selected writings of Cousin, Théodore Jouffroy, and Benjamin Constant. This was part of a series that introduced French and German thinkers to the United States. In the introduction to Victor Cousin's writings, Ripley explained that this philosophy formed "an important epoch in the history of metaphysical science in France." It marked "the period of transition from the skeptical and sensual theories of the eighteenth century, to the more elevated and spiritual views of the nature of man," which was a focus of the philosophers at this time. Against the accusations of materialism and infidelity that characterized French philosophy in the United States because of sensationalism, or *sensualismo* in Spanish, Cousin's work was dedicated to placing philosophy "on a new path, and impressing it with a higher character. The design of his teachings, in fact, had been to restore philosophy to the eminence which it held in the golden days of English literature, and to revive the lofty spirit of Hooker, Cudworth, and Milton, in the midst of modern unbelief and selfishness."[38] Following Kant's unfinished project to reconcile "the holiest instincts of man with the rigid precision of science"; Cousin endeavored to "comprehend every element of human nature, in a broad and universal system," which was based on inquiry and induction.[39]

The same happened in Spanish America, where philosophy was used to solidify the foundation of a new society that lacked cohesion. For example, the introduction to the Spanish translation of Destutt de Tracy's logic book indicated that logic was the true "positive science" and "the art that teaches us humans to judge and reason," which made the understanding of the intellectual operations a crucial point to improve humanity.[40] The translation of Pierre François Toussaint de la Rivière's (1762–1829) logic book by Rafael Acevedo (1806–18640), published in Caracas in 1841, is another good example of this continuum. In it there is an explanation of a "new division" that had separated the physical and mathematical sciences from philosophy, limiting the scope of the latter. It was for this reason that the old understanding of philosophy as "a special science that was part of a universal scientific system" seemed to no longer apply.[41] Since the building of the civilized nation needed precision and exactitude to develop legislation, what had been done "in the science of law" was similar to what was attempted with the development of "natural history, physics, medicine and in general with everything that deserves the name of science: these are the ideas that we had named *philosophical* or *scientific*."[42] Due to the divergent paths that these two disciplines started to take, systems attempting to integrate both to improve society mostly failed by the mid-nineteenth century

Juan B. Alberdi (1810–1884), the liberal writer of the Argentine constitution of 1853, described the situation of philosophy in 1842 in terms that made clear the challenging multiplicity that was present in this field at the time. In the middle of excessive offerings, Alberdi explained that since the American continent practiced what Europe was teaching, its role was "completely positive and applied." The United States had proven that "it was not true that it was indispensable to have first a philosophical movement to achieve political and social change." It was for this reason that pure abstraction and metaphysics "would not grow roots in America."[43] Philosophy had to be "essentially political and social in its object, ardent and prophetic in its instincts, synthetic and organic in its method, positive and realist in the way it proceeded, republican in its spirit and destiny."[44] Contemporary philosophy resolved the problems of the present; American philosophy, for Alberdi, needed to solve American problems.

The growing uncertainty caused by conflicts between materialists and spiritualists partly explains why, by the 1840s, Cousin's main rival, the French Auguste Comte (1798–1857), started to get support from some intellectuals in the Americas, a trend that this philosopher himself tried to encourage to gain more disciples and funds outside France. He had published six volumes to explain his "positive philosophy" from 1830 to 1842, and while this work opposed metaphysical philosophies, his ideas were interesting to liberals supporting spiritualist positions in the Americas because of his take on moral and intellectual operations as social physics, which implied a scientific way to organize human societies that did not explicitly denied the existence of a Creator. John McClintock (1814–1870) became a supporter of the author of the *Positive Philosophy*, for example. He was editor of the *Methodist Quarterly Review*, and, in this position, he published articles to address this new philosophical system and its flaws and strengths. George Frederick Holmes (1820–1897) and Horace Binney Wallace (1817–1852) were some of the intellectuals that were behind McClintock's interest in French Positivism. The result was "the beginning of a five-year period during which the *Methodist Quarterly Review*, under the editorship of McClintock, gave a degree of attention to Comte that was unmatched by any theological journal in America."[45] The connection came originally through the Scottish publications that paid attention to Comte's work.

According to McClintock, Wallace believed in laws that were "implanted in the social nature of man" away from principles that had never been obeyed by man.[46] But Wallace also believed that Comte's positivism and Christianity could be reconciled, leading those who did not know the French philosopher well to misunderstand his true intentions, which resulted in a mixture of positivism and idealism that was characteristic of many blends that emerged at the time over the Americas. For example, a review of Wallace's *Scenery and Philosophy in Europe*, published in 1855, made clear that his work was "an additional proof that spiritual culture" was gradually attracting "the homage of the superior mind of the country, not in the study only, but in work also, and that the American intellect" was not "wholly fettered by gross and material interests."[47] In this understanding of philosophy, sciences were at the service of a higher goal related to knowing beauty and truth over capital accumulation, profits, and economic growth. It expressed the power that manifested "the invisible that gives to the visible its influence" over humans because matter was "penetrated by eternal laws of which it is the expression."[48] This meant that matter could not be separated from the spiritual, and science needed to pay attention to natural laws that were based on a spiritual continuity.

This naturalization of human societies as regulated by laws based on natural and observable phenomena increased the tensions that were crucial to the development of positivism in the Americas. In Latin America, the discussion of Comte's ideas had a different relationship with religion because the Catholic Church continued as the only representative of Christianity and closely associated itself with conservatives who fought some new ideas. In the Iberian world, as we saw, the replacement of Scholasticism had started in colonial times and through the same members of the Catholic Church, a process that was accelerated during the revolutionary period, but initially it did not imply that religion and science were incompatible. The wars between liberals and conservatives exacerbated debates about modern science because of the role of scientific thinking in the promotion of secularism. In 1851 the Mexican church economically supported the publication of Jean-Joseph Gaume's (1802–1879) analysis of the dangers of the recent philosophical rationalism.[49] Gaume was a French priest who published several well-known works in Europe defending the role of the Catholic Church in modern society. According to his book, originally published in 1844, individualism, progress, and emancipation were dangerous ideas that were introduced by French thinkers inspired by English and German readings, and they "totally and absolutely owned the new generations." The youth was into the adoration of a natural and rationalist religion expressed in the "modern constitutions that promoted secularism", which was the greatest danger to the success of the republic.[50]

The popularity of Comte's Positivism grew over the Americas in the 1860s in part because of the debates over materialism. For example, an article published in Boston's *Congregationalist* about Guizot's life mentioned that he had admitted that in France, "rationalism, positivism, pantheism, materialism and skepticism" were "spreading like imperceptible and impalpable miasmas, and affecting classes of the population to whom the very meaning of the words was unknown."[51] The same situation was happening in the United States, according to the article. A year later, in 1867, a letter to the editors of *Boston Investigator* affirmed that Comte, "though dead, was through his followers about to found a new sect." This article repudiated the "supernatural origin of religion, making man its source and object. Humanity is its deity, and eminent men who have contributed to the improvement of the race are the object of its worship." Henry Edger (1820–1880) was a disciple and correspondent of Comte identified as "the positivist Agent in the United States," in charge of furnishing "all desired information respecting the new doctrine."[52] As Gilles J. Harp has explained, Comte helped to renew liberal ideas in the United States during this decade, in part because Darwinism "alone undermined three long-held assumptions about the natural realm: a stable, created order now viewed as changing and highly competitive; fixed species were replaced by evolving species that could as easily become extinct as flourish;" and teleological assumptions "were discarded for a process of "natural selection" that was random" and was not based on morality.[53]

In Brazil the philosophical continuum that was sparked by eclecticism started, as it did in the American continent, by the 1830s.[54] *Compendio de philosophia*, written by the priest Francisco de Mont'Alverne (1784–1858) in 1833 but not published until after his death in 1859, reflected the influence of Cousin, but since it was published in the same year in which Darwin's *Origins* came out, it was received as a dated piece.[55] Silvio Romero (1851–1914) wrote in 1878 that this book was mostly ignored because Lyell's geology, Darwin's biology, and Comte's history were not included in the analysis.[56] Romero reflected that from the 1840s to 1870s there had been a great philosophical transformation expressed in historical studies, the popularization of the criticism of socialism and positivism, and "the definitive triumph of German religious science and the doctrine of Darwin."[57] This meant a synthesis of French Comtian philosophy with German evolutionary science impregnated by Romanticism.

Only in the 1870s there was a clearer recognition of how revolutionary this Darwinian evolutionism was, both scientifically and politically. At this critical juncture, and not coincidentally, belief in the possibility of a synthetic philosophical system was renewed in the Americas through the work of Herbert Spencer (1820–1903). In fact, this philosopher's reputation was largely made in the Americas. He was already known and influential through his ideas on education and defense of political liberalism but, after 1859, Spencer started to bridge his previous scientific views on biology, psychology, and morality with the new biological evolutionism to finalize his synthetic philosophical system.[58]

In the confusion related to the meaning of the Enlightenment after the Darwinian revolution, there was a need to create a philosophical umbrella that covered the contradictions arising from scientific, political, racial, economic, and social developments, and Spencer's philosophy was viewed as doing just that. In 1866 the already mentioned author of the 1853 Argentine constitution, Juan B. Alberdi, previously a rabid defender of the study of philosophy, wrote to a friend recommending him to tell his son to avoid the mistakes he had done dedicating his life to the study of this discipline. Unlike what had happened in his young years, the studies that were indispensable at the time were "modern languages (speaking and writing), economy, geography, and history (Modern America, at least)." Regarding religion, the youth should abstain "from studying what it is called *philosophy*." His skepticism was partly based on seeing what had happened in Europe with education, "on which there were not two opinions in agreement," tracing a torturous path for the ideological establishment of the republic.[59]

What Is Philosophy?

In 1867 an article appeared in the *Boston Investigator* about the "new philosophy," and "its ultimate evincing of God." In a letter from an unidentified reader, it is mentioned that the "works of Mr. Spencer are now deemed by scientific circles [as] transcending all other works on philosophical matters." The reader affirmed that they were "worthy of all the popularity they have gained, and should be read by all who have a taste for such reading." This new philosophy did not signify "any alteration in real science;" but had corrected many views that seemed right at the time, which gave "to the philosophy of the Sciences a new dress." While Darwin had not made any contribution in terms of creating a new philosophical system, Spencer presented to his readers "the first law of Nature:—Evolution, or Progression of matter by force" and integrated into a philosophy that he had started to develop before 1859. So, his readings were helpful to explain biological change and the resulting transformation of a society.[60]

Those who defended Christianity saw in the popularity of Spencer's work a new threat that made him part of a group to which Comte and Buckle also belonged, and now identified as "the whole school of Positivists" that was attempting to "displace Christianity by some form of Theism to be developed as the "Religion of the future." Some would see in Comte a philosophy that could integrate religion, even in a wrong form, with society. The article reported that "Mr. P. Baring-Gould has revived Comte's theory," in a book that "is to displace the effete Gospel of Humanity that is to displace the effete Gospel of Christ!"[61] A similar criticism about the displacement of Christian ideas by wrong philosophies is present in other countries. The Colombian Miguel Antonio Caro (1845–1909), for example, wrote in 1869 an extremely negative opinion on the work of Jeremy Bentham, which was used in combination with Spencer's by some positivists. Caro affirmed that there was nothing more opposite to Christianity than utilitarianism, a philosophy that was "the most dangerous for the youth."[62] He expressed his displeasure with schools that had been founded by Catholics for "the teaching of the sciences under the warmth of catholic virtue and the shadow of the cross" but were by then under the control of those who were teaching utilitarianism. Caro explained that after thirty years since the time in which this philosophy had been introduced, anybody who opposed it was called an agent of "fanaticism! Intolerance!" even when this was not true.[63] Anticipating an argument that José Enrique Rodó (1871–1917) would develop in *Ariel* by the beginning of the next century, Caro complained about the youth "being dragged into the arid regions of materialism."[64] The fear of having future leaders deprived of spiritualism was based on the nations' need to promote unity and love for each other at a time in which violence had destroyed many republics.

By the 1870s most of the nations of the American continent were recovering from traumatic civil wars that had wiped out their populations and economic resources. Ideologies that were identified with materialism and utilitarianism were viewed as too divisive at a time in which unity, altruism, self-sacrifice, and the reinforcement of a republican morality were in need. Caro does not include evolutionary ideas in his analysis, but they were in his mind when he emphasized that the "human lineage" was the "family of God," and that the real natural law was the one that came through revelation expressed through human instinct and not the sensual one. Instead, "a rational [instinct], a light that comes from above" was important.[65] Together with Spencer, Comte re-emerged as an important thinker in terms of his understanding of religion for those who did not want to openly embrace theology or accept the supremacy of evolutionary science. In Chile, for example, a translation of Comte's work was published in 1875, but it was a condensed version of his *Cours de philosophy positive* prepared in France for more popular audiences by his disciple Emile Littré (1801–1881) and published in 1868.[66]

This was a publication destined to an international audience that was starting to work together to promote Comte's positivism. The translator of the Chilean version, Jorge Lagarrigue (1854–1894), was a follower of Comte; he explained in the prologue that the importance of this work was that it was a solution to the "complete skepticism" that had affected the youth who had abandoned religious views only to find nothing to replace them. Positive philosophy was "the only one that could mend this grave illness that is affecting our nascent society."[67] Comte provided conviction in humankind's progress, and this was done through science, which was the head of civilization. His philosophy was directed to those who were searching for "a sure source of truth to understanding man's true position in the universe."[68] This reference was related to the changes that science and philosophy had experienced after Darwin, and the different meaning that "humanity" had after the introduction of natural law and the struggle for existence.

In the United States, Charles Hodge (1797–1878), the prominent leader of the Princeton Theological Seminar, expressed similar concerns.[69] Asking, "What is Darwinism?" he attempt to clarify all the different philosophical branches originated by Darwin's work, based both in the opinion of his enemies and followers. In his view, Darwinism was "a theory of the universe, at least so far as the living organisms on the earth are concerned."[70] Beyond this general definition, Hodge understood that many philosophers, such as Büchner and Spencer, had used Darwin to prove their previous ideas, which did not necessarily represent Darwin's intentions. The English scientist was "simply a naturalist, a careful and laborious observer;" but he was not a philosopher, nor has he interested in producing a system that synthetized all knowledge.[71] In fact Darwin was not responsible for the most extreme evolutionary positions that were being developed. He was not a Monist, because in admitting creation, he admitted "a dualism as between God and the world." Neither was he a "Materialist, inasmuch as he assumed a supernatural origin for the infinitesimal modicum of life and intelligence in the primordial animalcule, from which without divine purpose or agency, all living things in the whole history of our earth have descended."[72] But while Darwin had not been an extremist, he had not created a science supported by a philosophy and useful for politics, even when the new republics in the Americas assumed the natural existence of such links. By "design" those who objected to Darwinism meant "the intelligent and voluntary selection of an end, and the intelligent and voluntary choice, application, and control of the means appropriate to the accomplishment of that end." This type of design implied intelligence and was "involved" in its very nature.[73]

Hodge made clear that the denial of design in nature was "virtually the denial of God." This was the most extreme form of Atheism that had been seen at the time, and he recognized that Darwin himself believed in the Creator, but his work implied that this Creator, "millions on millions of ages ago, did something—called matter and a living germ into existence—and then abandoned the universe to itself to be controlled by chance and necessity, without any purpose on his part as to the result, or any intervention or guidance. He is virtually consigned, so far as we are concerned, to non-existence."[74] This was a radical departure from the previous belief in the perfecting power of knowledge, and it also changed in the same way the idea of civilization and progress as real historical forces that announced the certain arrival of a new era.

In 1878, a book with the writings of Raimundo Antônio da Rocha Lima (1855–1878), who had just died, was published in Brazil. This country's intellectuals followed the same ideas that were debated in the rest of the continent but, by the end of the nineteenth century, they would put the country under their own version of Comtean positivism, mixing Littré's interpretation with a variety of evolutionary views, including Darwin's and Spencer's.[75] Rocha de Lima was clear about the confusing path that philosophy and science had taken by the 1870s, and in his writings there is a clear rejection of materialism and its association to positivism, which had been defended by other writers. Rocha Lima wrote to one writer insisting that there was "a deep difference between positivism and materialism," but this was not clear and some had attributed atheism to positive philosophy and "despotism to its politics." According to the writer, the materialist school proclaimed that "organic matter was the substance and end of the universe;" meanwhile, positivism affirmed that these questions were impossible to know, abstaining from siding with any possibility.[76]

Rocha Lima made clear that positivists favored a conception of the world that was the result of the systematization of the sciences that "recognized in society other laws than the biological." They had "a conception of the world not a conception of man." This conception would arrive in the positivist era in which "the world takes its place among the stars (*astros*), and men in the gallery of all beings."[77] The present would emerge from the past, and prepare "the future through a law of filiation, unbreakable and eternal;" this true notion of law substituted "the gods of theology and the matter of metaphysics; the moral revealed becomes demonstrable; intuition turns to be deducted by scientific laws," which clearly shows how much Comte's philosophy is turned into an eclectic mixture of the ideas circulating at the time.[78] In addition, other forms of spirituality appeared as the result of these ideological problems. According to the Peruvian geologist Carlos Lisson (1868–1947), professor at the University of San Marcos, by 1891 "the religion question" in Peru implied that even when the constitution of the republic made Catholicism the religion of the state, this was only a consequence of the colonialism that had been "depurated by the ideas of the present century, and nobody pays attention to it." The reality was that side to side to Catholic temples "there were those of Buddha, the Reform, the Masonics, living all in peace, in a way in which religious tolerance is complete."[79] Obviously, Lisson was referring to the educated male minority that made the elite of the country, not to most of the population.

Positivist science, in both Spencer's and Comte's versions, offered different degrees of faith in universality, and the continuation of political purpose beyond natural law; involving biology, psychology and morals. It is for this reason that by the 1880s the term "positivism" did not offer a clear philosophical system beyond the connection between the scientific and the social areas of knowledge. A good example of this situation is in an article by Enrique Varona, published in 1880 in Cuba, still a Spanish colony supported by slavery despite the many revolutionary attempts that had ended in failure. In this essay he addressed the teaching of metaphysics, criticizing the inaugural speech given by Teófilo Martínez de Escobar (1833–1912) to open the academic year 1879–1880 at the University of Havana. De Escobar was a Spanish philosopher and professor of metaphysics at the university, and a follower of Karl Krause (1781–1932), who was influential in Spain's neo-Kantian movement. In a speech, de Escobar had criticized the supremacy that the sciences had acquired because the scientific thought of the time had enclosed knowledge "in the selfish sphere of the phenomenal and relative, distancing science from the infinite and absolute that was the center of universal harmony, and the foundation of the unity and internal relationships among the sciences."[80] This presentation was structured on three main themes that criticized positivism, empiricism, and, finally, inductive morality.

Varona questioned the teaching of metaphysics at the university because it was by then irreconcilable with scientific knowledge.[81] He expressed concern about the growing interest in idealism and the work of Kant and affirmed that Martínez de Escobar wanted "the unknown [to give] us the light over the known;" teaching that thought descended "from the dark peaks of abstraction to the firm ground of the concrete." This approach was "a mere anthropomorphic conception in which the notion of a primary and free cause and the idea of moral perfection were confused."[82] These differences, though, did not prevent both sides from being classified as "positivists," showing that this term gave coverage to a wide range of thinkers. Varona was a positivist because he defended Charles Darwin and his "cosmogenetic theory." Through the mechanisms of natural and sexual selection the "mysteries of the organic genesis of the world" were known. His essay ended with the praising of the "generation full of vigor and assertiveness" that was attempting to resolve the different interpretations of philosophy, science, and metaphysics. Even when it was not possible to predict the future results, "the study of phenomena, and only this study," was making this young generation progress. The path, then, was not speculative philosophy, but "experimenting in laboratories" in order to "dominate nature with their own arms; observing and inducing in the school of life and politics, avoiding speculating with mental entities." Even when men like himself would not "build theories" in the future they would improve society through science.[83]

We can observe the same unstable situation for philosophy in the United States. In 1879, the journal *Mind* published an article written by the future founder of the American Psychological Association, G. Stanley Hall (1844–1924), who had studied in Germany and knew Wilhelm Wundt (1832–1920), who was considered the leader in experimental psychology. Hall detailed the situation of philosophy, warning about the poor shape of philosophical instruction because there were "less than half a dozen colleges or universities in the United States where metaphysical thought was entirely freed from reference to theological formulae."[84] More importantly, philosophical instruction was determined "by the convictions of constituencies and trustees, while professors were to a great extent without independence or initiative in matters of speculative thought."[85] Outside of "schools and colleges, philosophical interests had taken on the whole wide range. Trendelenburg, Schleiermacher, Krause, Schelling, Fichte, Herbert and Lotze had all more or less found careful students and even disciples among men of partial leisure in the various professions, who have spent the last year or two of student-life in Germany." Above all this, the most influential philosopher was Georg Hegel, who "since 1867 has been represented by the quarterly *Journal of Speculative Philosophy*, edited by Wm. T. Harris of St. Louis," and secondly "Herbert Spencer and other English evolutionists," which had "been greatly extended by the *Popular Science Monthly*, edited by Dr. E. L. Youmans of New York."[86] St. Louis is mentioned as the city where the most interesting work was being written.

According to Hall's essay, while in Germany, Hegelianism was responsible for "the philosophical soil for the theories of evolution", those of Spencer, G. H. Lewes, and other English evolutionists had exerted "just an immense influence in the United States during the last decade." Evolutionism, though, was not represented by philosophers, but by scientists who "were not very interested in the history of speculation. If the worst side of the American college is the philosophical, its best is the scientific department."[87] Moreover, those who taught natural or physical sciences "tacitly" accepted or "openly" advocated evolutionary principles. In a country in which there had been such rapid development, "where the ploughboy was never allowed to forget that he might become a millionaire or even a President if he wills it earnestly enough, the catchwords of evolution often excite an enthusiasm which is inversely as the power to comprehend its scope and importance."[88] The main characteristic of the country's intellectual life was its heterogeneity, according to Hall.

Intellectual abundance also happened in the different religious denominations and in the semi-philosophical publications that included the philosophy of Swedenborg and Henry James Sr. The general "sect of spiritualists" was very large and had produced "a vast and dismal body of literature."[89] United States, in Hall's interpretation had a "very deeply rooted and persistent" patriotism that was "philanthropic, full of faith in human nature and in the future." He concluded by speculating that "if, according to a leading canon of the new psychology," the active part of human nature was "the essential element in cognition" and all possible truth was practical, then might it not "rationally hope that even those materialisms of faith and of business which we now deplore, are yet laying the foundations for a maturity of philosophical insight deep enough at some time to intellectualise and thus harmonise all the diverse strands in our national life?"[90] This question pointed to the tension existing in the materialism of the economic structure against the development of science and knowledge that were more important, according to Hall.

The perception that philosophy was getting behind science continued to be developed with the aid of scientific ideas, and the resulting malaise happened in most of the Americas simultaneously, so much so that Varona affirmed in one of his lectures published in 1880 that he was not teaching a course in philosophy because at the time it was not clear what philosophy was. While originally it was the "science of the sciences and embraced all human knowledge" this was not, anymore, the case. "In the divorce that emerged" among the diverse subjective activities, philosophy "was not anymore a system of nature" and had become "dogmatic speculation over subjective problems elevated to the highest degree of abstraction." It was for this reason that the renewal of the natural sciences indicated for some "the disappearance of philosophy." He negated this possibility because the problem was not in philosophy itself, but in the folly of philosophers. This discipline needed to continue because it represented the human desire to "possess a general synthesis that explained more or less completely the two worlds of reality, penetrating as possible in the enigma of its conjunction." The philosophical synthesis of the knowledge originated by the diverse aspects of reality, objective and subjective, was the result that Varona defended. At a time when so many systems "had crashed and fought" and while "the fight among different opinions" was each day more violent, the only conclusion that was possible was the acceptance that it was impossible to conclude anything, except for the method of scientific inquiry that allowed thinkers to make an objective decision about the abundant offerings that surrounded them.[91]

Around the same time, in the United States, William James (1842–1910), son of Henry James Sr., addressed the problems created by a weak philosophy. He started an essay with a simple question, "What is the task which philosophers set themselves to perform? And why do they philosophise at all?"[92] His reply is similar to Varona's, philosophers desired "to attain a conception of the frame of things which shall on the whole be more rational than the rather fragmentary and chaotic one which everyone by gift of nature carries about with him under his hat." The philosophy of evolution was represented by Spencer, and "notwithstanding the lacunae" in his system and the "vagueness of his terms," he was "bound to be, the most popular of all philosophers, because more than any other he seeks to appease our strongest theoretic craving. To undiscriminating minds his system will be a sop; to acute ones a programme full of suggestiveness." But in this passion for simplification also existed the passion for distinguishing, which was "the impulse to be acquainted with the parts rather than comprehend the whole."[93] The problem facing philosophy was a theoretical dilemma between Clearness versus Simplicity, and James' first conclusion was that there was not a system of philosophy that could hope "to be universally accepted among men," which "grossly" violated "the two greatest needs of our logical nature, the need of unity and the need of clearness," or entirely subordinated "the one to the other."[94] In front of his situation, James identified himself as a "phenomenist" who left "all metaphysical entities" to their fate contenting himself "with the irreversible datum of perception" that whatever was manifested was "the same, be it here or be it there." Toward the end, and returning to the original question, James described the intellectual populace of his day as one that prided itself "particularly on its love of Science and Facts and its contempt for all metaphysics." But metaphysics needed to be a part of philosophy. "The only alternative is between the good Metaphysics of clever-headed Philosophy and the trashy Metaphysics of vulgar Positivism."[95] Metaphysical knowledge needed to be renewed.

Conclusion

In 1882, in Boston, the philosopher and theologian Francis Ellingwood Abbot (1836–1903) wrote an article about the clash that was dividing philosophy and science. He attributed the source of the problem to the crumble of Scholasticism without any other system to replace it, and the development of a scientific method that had left philosophy behind.[96] This was even more clear when Spencer's reputation was destroyed by evolutionary biologist August Weismann (1834–1914), who proved Spencer's biology wrong after several exchanges in 1893.[97] The neo-Darwinians rejected neo-Lamarckian conceptions of use-inheritance that diminished the effects of natural selection, and this led to the rejection of the philosophies of Comte and Spencer because they contradicted evolutionary science. But elite-controlled countries that promoted modernization through a philosophy anchored in science, as was the case in Mexico, could not reject the same ideas that supported their politics. In 1895, a Mexican scientific journal rejected Darwinian science because "the only good thing that was acceptable in the work of Darwin and his followers was what they had taken from Lamarck."[98] Those who were Darwinists supported a metaphysical science and did not have evidence to support its claims. For example, they repeated that "the Indian race must disappear" ignoring that after centuries of European occupation they were still alive, which indicated the fallacy of considering certain men more apt to survive than others.[99]

Similar arguments were expressed in the United States by W. E. B. Du Bois (1869–1963), when he described in 1940 how he was educated as a graduate student at Harvard during the 1890s when William James was his philosophy professor. DuBois got a doctoral degree in history, although this field was at the time closely linked to sociology. As a Black man, he expressed dismay at the statistics that in 1890 showed "how quickly and certainly the Negro race was dying out in the United States" due to physical inferiority. He explained that he could "accept evolution and the survival of the fittest, provided the interval between advanced and backward races was not made too impossible." But as soon as he settled "into scientific security here, then the basis of race distinction was changed without explanation, without apology."[100] This use of science to justify racial views made possible interpretations that depended on who was the person recording the observation, negating the same scientific principles of objectivity and observation that were allegedly characteristic of modern science.

When Spencer died in 1903, he was very bitter about the philosophical chaos of the end of the nineteenth century. A year before he had published his last book in which he had rejected accusations that his philosophy was materialist, the "convenient weapon for theological and philosophical opponents."[101] Disappointed by the state of his country, he denounced "the political feeling now manifesting itself as Imperialism" that entailed some form of slavery as demonstrated by the Boer war that had just finished Africa.[102] He detested "that conception of social progress" that presented as "its aim, increase of population, growth of wealth, spread of commerce."[103] In his view, in numerous parts "appropriated" by the British, "the native races are being "improved" out of existence, so at home the progress of 'improvement' [was] yearly leaving less and less of the things which made the country attractive."[104] Surprisingly, the philosopher who was considered in the Americas the greatest defender of human progress wrote in the last year of his life that while "in some respects we may envy posterity, we may in one respect pity" those who would live in it.

The "disappearance of remnants and traces of earlier forms of life" would deprive them "of much poetry which now relieves the prose of life. Everywhere it is the same." This new civilization characterized by imperialism and oppression of others was praised for its economic growth, but it would be interesting for Spencer to know if what it would leave remains "as interesting as those which old times have bequeathed to us."[105] The failure of positivism meant that philosophy was at risk of becoming irrelevant as a field, but the roots of the modern republic depended on a greater balance between materialist and spiritualist conceptions to support the political system. As a result, philosophical renewal arrived in the Americas by the beginning of the twentieth century through pragmatism in the case of the United States, and a mixture of idealism and Bergson's philosophy in Latin American countries. In both cases there was a reconciliation of science with philosophy through metaphysical vitalism, which made it possible to renew the nations' ideology. The revolutionary path of emancipatory politics was also renewed with Marxism, a philosophy that had been present in the second half of the nineteenth century in the Americas as the formula to achieve emancipation scientifically. The triumph of science, though, did not last long. By the beginning of the twentieth century the question that started to reflect this era's concerns was "Is Darwinism Dead?"[106]

Notes

1. Alfred I. Tauber, "From Descartes' Dream to Husserl's Nightmare," in *The Elusive Synthesis: Aesthetics and Science*, (Springer Netherlands, 1996), 297.

2. Michel Foucault and James D. Faubion. *Aesthetics, Method, and Epistemology.* (New York: New Press, 1998), 468.

3. Foucault, 468.

4. Dirk Van Miert, "What was the Republic of Letters? A brief introduction to a long history." *Groniek. Historisch Tijdschrift.* N. 204/5 (2014): 269–287, 270.

5. Luís António Verney, *Verdadeiro Metodo de estudar para ser util à republica, e à Igreja.* (Naples, Italy: n/a, 1746).

6. Verney, *Verdadeiro Metodo de estudar,* 70.

7. Verney, *Verdadeiro Metodo de estudar,* 70. For historical analysis of the Spanish Enlightenment, see: Jorge Cañizares-Esguerra, *How to Write the History of the New World* (Palo Alto: Stanford University Press, 2001); Gabriel Paquette, *Enlightenment, Governance and Reform in Spain and its Empire, 1759–1808* (New York: Palgrave, 2008); Bianca Premo, *The Enlightenment on Trial: Ordinary Litigants and Colonialism in the Spanish Empire* (Oxford: Oxford University Press, 2017).

8. Real Academia Española. *Diccionario de la lengua castellana, en que se explica el verdadero de las voces . . . con las phrases o modos de hablar, los proverbios o refranes . . .* Vol. 5 (Madrid: Imprenta de Francisco del Hierro, 1737), 586.

9. Juan Bautista Corachan, *Avisos de Parnaso*. (Valencia, Spain: Academia Valenciana, 1747), 104.

10. Marques de Casaconcha, *Cartel del certamen El Nuevo Heroe de la fama. En el solemne triumphal recibimiento del Exmo. Sor. Don M. de Amat y Junient*. (Lima, Peru: Real Universidad de San Marcos, 1762), 2–3.

11. Marques de Casaconcha, *Cartel*, 36.

12. Joseph Antonio De Alzate y Ramírez, *Diario Literario de Mexico dispuesto para la utilidad pública, a quien se dedica*, n. 1, March 12, 1768. (Mexico: Imprenta de la Bibliotheca Mexicana, 1768), n/p/n.

13. De Alzate y Ramírez, *Diario Literario de Mexico*, n. 1, March 12, 1768.

14. De Alzate y Ramírez, *Diario Literario de Mexico*, n. 2, March 18, 1768.

15. Susan Buck-Morss, *Hegel, Haiti, and Universal History*. (Pittsburgh: University of Pittsburgh Press, 2009), 39.

16. James E McClellan III, *Colonialism and Science: Saint Domingue and the Old Regime*. (Chicago: University of Chicago Press, 2010), 2.

17. McClellan III, *Colonialism and Science*, 4.

18. "Toussaint Louverture to General Bonaparte." *Trewman's Exeter Flying Post*, 13 Jan. 1803, *British Library Newspapers*, https://link-gale-com.ezproxy.lib.usf.edu/apps/doc/Y3200648074/GDCS?u=tamp44898&sid=GDCS&xid=ee2b19f2. Accessed 19 Sept. 2019.

19. Marcus Rainsford, *An Historical Account of the Black Empire of Hayti: Comprehending a View of the Principal Transactions in the Revolution of Saint Domingo; with Its Ancient and Modern State*. (London: J. Cundee, 1805), 253.

20. Rainsford, *An Historical Account*, 374.

21. José Ignacio Rodríguez, *Vida del presbítero don Félix Varela*. (New York: O Novo Mundo, 1878), 34.

22. José Agustín, Caballero. *Philosophia Electiva*. (Spain: Linkgua, 2010), n/p/n. https://www.google.com/books/edition/Philosophia_Electiva/z_asDwAAQBAJ?hl=en&gbpv=0. Accessed December 10th, 2021.

23. Félix Varela y Morales, *Instituciones de Filosofía Ecléctica*, Vol. 1 *Lógica*. In *Obras*. Vol. 1. (La Habana: Editorial Cultura Popular, 1997), 18.

24. Real Academia Española, *Diccionario de la lengua castellana, por la Real academia Española*, 5th ed (Madrid, Ediciones de la Imprenta Real, 1817), 200.

25. Félix Varela y Morales, *Miscelánea Filosófica*, in, *Obras*. Vol. 1(La Habana: Editorial Cultura Popular, 1997), 321.

26. Thomas Jefferson, *A treatise on Political Economy* (Georgetown, 1817). Jefferson also translated another book by Destutt de Tracy, see: *Commentary and review of Montesquieu's Spirit of the Laws* (Philadelphia, 1811). The latter was also published in Spanish: Antoine Louis Claude Destutt de Tracy, *Comentario sobre el espíritu de las leyes de Montesquieu*. (Imp. de Fermín Villalpando, 1821). For Argentina, see: Mariano Di Pasquale, "La recepción de la Idéologie en la Universidad de Buenos Aires: El caso de Juan Manuel Fernández de Agüero (1821–1827)." *Prismas* 15, no. 1 (2011): 63–86; Klaus Gallo, "A la altura de las luces del siglo: el surgimiento de un

clima intelectual en la Buenos Aires posrevolucinaria," *Carlos Altamirano, Historia de los intelectuales en América Latina I* (Buenos Aires: Katz Editores, 2008): 184–185. For more information on the philosophical ideas in Argentina during this period, see the work of Klaus Gallo. For example: "El exilio forzado de un Ideologue Rioplatense. El pensamiento republicano de Lafinur y sus traumas." *Estudios de Teoría Literaria-Revista digital: artes, letras y humanidades* 3, no. 5 (2014): 187–200.

27. Auguste Levasseur, *Lafayette in America, in 1824 and 1825: Or, Journal of Travels, in the United States.* (New York: White, Gallaher & White, 1829), 7.

28. Charles Jared Ingersoll, A *Discourse Concerning the Influence of America on the Mind; Being the Annual Oration Delivered Before the American Philosophical Society, at the University in Philadelphia, on the 18th October, 1823.* (Philadelphia: Abraham Small, 1823), 11.

29. José Manuel Restrepo, *Historia de la Revolución de la República de Colombia.* Vol. 1. (Paris: Libreria americana, 1827), 137–138.

30. John Torrance, *Karl Marx's Theory of Ideas.* (Cambridge: Cambridge University Press, 1995), 30.

31. Torrance, *Karl Marx's Theory of Ideas*, 31. Destutt de Tracy divided the ways of knowing into Idéologie, the formation of ideas; Grammaire, the expression of ideas; and Logique, the combination of ideas. The Grammar was translated into Spanish in 1822. Antoine Louis Claude Destutt de Tracy, *Gramática general* (Madrid: Imprenta Callado, 1822).

32. José Manuel Mestre, Félix Varela, and José Zacarías González del Valle, *De la filosofía en La Habana* (La Habana: La Antilla, 1862), 94.

33. Vicente Medina, "The Philosophical Polemic in Havana Revisited," *Inter-American Journal of Philosophy* 4, no. 1(2013), 36.

34. "Cousin's Philosophy," *The American Quarterly Review* 10 (Sept-Dec. 1831), 292.

35. Victor Cousin, *Introduction to the History of Philosophy.* (Boston: Hilliard, Gray, Little, and Wilkins, 1832); *Elements of Psychology.* Translated by Caleb Sprague (Hartford: Cooke & Co., 1834).

36. Victor Cousin, *Introduction to the History of Philosophy*, v.

37. Cousin, *Introduction to the History of Philosophy*, vi.

38. George Ripley, Victor Cousin, Théodore Simon Jouffroy, and Benjamin Constant. *Philosophical Miscellanies.* Translated from the French of Cousin, Jouffroy, and B. Constant. With Introductory and Critical Notices by George Ripley (Boston: Hilliard, Gray & Co., 1838), 3.

39. Ripley et al., *Philosophical Miscellanies*, 4

40. Antoine Louis Claude Destutt de Tracy and Juan Justo García, *Elementos de verdadera lógica: Compendio ó sea estracto de los elementos de ideología del senador Destutt-Tracy.* (Madrid: Imprenta de Don Mateo Repullé, 1821), 6.

41. Pierre François Toussaint de la Rivière, *Nueva Lógica clásica*, trans. R. Acevedo (Caracas: Imprenta de V. Espinal, 1841), 60.

42. Toussaint de la Rivière, *Nueva Lógica*, 77.

43. Juan B Alberdi, "Ideas para presidir a la confección del curso de filosofía contemporánea," In *Escritos póstumos de J. B. Alberdi*, Vol. 15. (Buenos Aires: Imprenta Europea, 1900), 605.

44. Juan B Alberdi, "Ideas para presidir, 606.

45. Charles D. Cashdollar, *The Transformation of Theology, 1830–1890: Positivism and Protestant Thought in Britain and America*. (Princeton: Princeton University Press, 2014), 125.

46. J. M. McClintock, "Horace Binney Wallace." *Methodist Review* 36 (1854), 137.

47. Sidney G Fisher, "Art, Its Meaning and Method: Essays of Horace Binney Wallace." *The North American Review* 81, no. 1 (1855), 219. Also, see: Mary Pickering, *Auguste Comte: An Intellectual Biography*, Vol. 3 (Cambridge: Cambridge University Press, 2009).

48. Fisher, "Art, Its Meaning and Method," 222. The translation of Auguste Comte's *Positive Philosophy* by Harriet Martineau, who had travelled in the United States, was well known there, and was published in 1855 and 1858 in New York. See: *The Positive Philosophy of Auguste Comte*, trans. Harriet Martineau (New York: Blanchard, 1855); *The Positive Philosophy of Auguste Comte*, trans. Harriet Martineau (New York: William Gowans, 1858). This book had originally been published in 1853 in London.

49. Joseph Gaume, *Historia de la sociedad doméstica en todos los pueblos antiguos y modernos ó sea influencia del cristianismo en la familia*. (Mexico: Imp de Rafael y Vila, 1851). Translated from: *Histoire de la societe domestique chez tous les peuples anciens et moderne; ou, Influence du Christianisme sur la famille*, Volume 1 (Brussels: Gaume Freres, 1844).

50. Gaume, *Historia de la sociedad doméstica*, 170.

51. "Guizot on Christianity," *The Congregationalist* 36 (Boston, Massachusetts). September 7, 1866.

52. J. F.B. "Positivism." *Boston Investigator* (Boston, Massachusetts), Wednesday, August 28, 1867; pg. 133; Issue 17. These letters were later published under the direction of the Chilean Jorge Lagarrigue, who was the positivist apostle in Chile. See Auguste Comte, *Lettres d'Auguste Comte. Apostolat positiviste*, (Paris: Apostolat Positiviste, 1889), viii.

53. Gillis J. Harp, *Positivist Republic: Auguste Comte and the Reconstruction of American Liberalism, 1865–1920* (Penn State Press, 2010), 5.

54. See Paul Arbousse Bastide, "Sur le positivisme politique et religieux au Brésil." *Romantisme* 9, no. 23 (1979): 79–97.

55. Eduardo Ferreira. *Investigacões de Psychologia* (Bahia, 1854).

56. Sílvio Romero, *A philosophia no Brasil*. (Porto Alegre: Typographia da "Deustsche Zeitung": 1878), 4. See Charles Darwin, *On the origins of species by means of natural selection*. (London: Murray, 1859).

57. For Latin America, see Adriana Novoa and Alex Levine, "Darwinism," In *A companion to Latin American philosophy*, Susana Nuccetelli, Ofelia Schutte, and Otávio Bueno, eds. (New York: John Wiley & Sons, 2009), 95–109; Adriana Novoa and Alex Levine. *From Man to Ape: Darwinism in Argentina, 1870–1920*. (Chicago:

University of Chicago Press, 2010); Alex Levine and Adriana Novoa. ¡Darwinistas! The Construction of Evolutionary Thought in Nineteenth Century Argentina. (Leiden: Brill, 2012).

58. Carlos Tewksbury, "Herbert Spencer's Works," *Boston Investigator* (Boston, Massachusetts), Wednesday, March 6, 1867, Issue 44, 346.

59. Juan B. Alberdi, "Letter to St. André de Fontenay (Calvados). July 14, 1866. Juan Bautista Alberdi and Francisco Javier Villanueva. *Epistolario 1855–1881*. (Santiago de Chile: Andres Bello, 1967), 461.

60. Joseph P. Thompson, "Christianity Not a Development, but a Revelation." *The Congregationalist and Boston Recorder* (Boston, Massachusetts), December, 1869; Issue 49.

61. Joseph P. Thompson, "Christianity Not a Development, but a Revelation." *The Congregationalist and Boston Recorder* (Boston, Massachusetts), December 9th, 1869; Issue 49.

62. Miguel Antonio Caro, *Estudio sobre el utilitarismo*. (Bogotá: Impr. Mantilla, 1869), i.

63. Caro, *Estudio sobre el utilitarismo* ii.

64. Caro, *Estudio sobre el utilitarismo* v–vi. See José Enrique Rodó, *Ariel*, trans. Sayers Peden (Austin: University of Texas Press, 2010).

65. Rodó, *Ariel*, 53.

66. Auguste Comte and Emile Littré. *Principes de philosophie positive*. (Paris: Baillière, 1868).

67. Jorge Lagarrigue, "Introducción," In Auguste Comte, *Principios de Filosofía Positiva*, trans. Jorge Lagarrigue (Santiago de Chile: Imprenta de la Librería del Mercurio, 1875), viii.

68. Jorge Lagarrigue, "Introducción," ix.

69. See: Paul C. Gutjahr, *Charles Hodge: Guardian of American Orthodoxy* (New York: Oxford University Press, 2011).

70. Charles Hodge, *What is Darwinism?* (New York: Scribner, Armstrong & Co., 1874), 2.

71. Hodge, *What is Darwinism?*, 26. Ludwig Büchner (1824–1899) was a leader of philosophical and physiological materialism before Darwin's theory was known. His book *Kraft und Stoff* was published in 1855 and he later adjusted its ideas to fit the new evolutionary views. English translation: *Force and Matter: Empirico-philosophical Studies, Intelligibly Rendered*. (London: Trübner & Company, 1870).

72. Büchner, *Force and Matter*, 168.

73. Büchner, *Force and Matter*, 169.

74. Büchner, *Force and Matter*, 173–174.

75. Raimundo Antônio da Rocha Lima, *Crítica e litteratura* (Maranhão: V. de Campos, 1878), 36.

76. da Rocha Lima, *Crítica e litteratura*, 38.

77. da Rocha Lima, *Crítica e litteratura*, 40.

78. da Rocha Lima, *Crítica e litteratura*.

79. Carlos Lisson, *Breves apuntes sobre la sociología del Perú en 1886* (Lima: B. Gil, 1887), 28.

80. Teófilo Martínez de Escobar, "Oración Inaugural," *Revista El Museo Canario* 34 (May 23, 1880), 15. For more information about this speech, see: Sánchez-Gey Venegas, Juana. "Teófilo Martínez de Escobar: un krausista canario, catedrático de Metafísica en la Universidad de La Habana," *Tebeto: anuario del Archivo Histórico Insular de Fuerteventura* (Islas Canarias) 2, n. 5 (1992), 179–193. http://mdc.ulpgc.es/cdm/ref/collection/tebeto/id/126

81. José Enrique Varona, "La Metafísica en la Universidad de la Habana." *Revista de Cuba*, Vol. 7 (1880), 102.

82. Varona, "La Metafísica," 105.

83. Varona, "La Metafísica," 106.

84. Varona, "La Metafísica," 125.

85. G. Stanley Hall, "VI.—Philosophy in the United States." *Mind* 13 (1879): 90.

86. Hall, "VI.—Philosophy in the United States," 90.

87. Hall, "VI.—Philosophy in the United States," 100.

88. Hall, "VI.—Philosophy in the United States," 101.

89. Hall, "VI.—Philosophy in the United States," 101.

90. Hall, "VI.—Philosophy in the United States," 104.

91. Hall, "VI.—Philosophy in the United States," 105.

92. William James, "The sentiment of rationality," *Mind* 4, no. 15 (July 1879), 317.

93. Enrique José Varona, *Conferencias filosóficas* (Havana: M. de Villa, 1880), 26.

94. Varona, *Conferencias filosóficas*, 321–322.

95. Varona, *Conferencias filosóficas*, 322.

96. Varona, *Conferencias filosóficas*, 325.

97. Varona, *Conferencias filosóficas*, 340.

98. Francis Ellingwood Abbot, "Scientific Philosophy: A Theory of Human Knowledge." *Mind* 7, no. 28 (October 1882), 495. See the coverage of the debate: "The Spencer-Weismann Controversy." *Nature* (February 15, 1894), 373–374.

99. See the coverage of the debate: "The Spencer-Weismann Controversy," 373–374.

100. Agustín Aragón, "Apreciación positive de la lucha por la existencia," in *Memorias y Revista de la Sociedad Científica "Antonio Alzate."* Vol 9 (1895–96), n. 1–2: 145–162, 159.

101. Aragón, "Apreciación positive," 156.

102. William E. B. Du Bois, "The concept of race," in *Dusk of Dawn* (Oxford: Oxford University Press, 2007), 50.

103. Herbert Spencer, "Exaggerations and Mis-statements," In *Facts and Comments* (New York: D. Appleton, 1902), 153.

104. Herbert Spencer, "Imperialism and Slavery," In *Facts and Comments* (New York: D. Appleton, 1902): 157–171, 153.

105. Herbert Spencer, "Some regrets," in *Facts and Comments* (New York: D. Appleton, 1902): 6–12, 7.

106. For example, see: Arthur Keith, "Is Darwinism Dead?," *Nature* 119 (1927): 277; J. H. Robinson, "Is Darwinism Dead?," *Harper's Magazine* 145 (1922): 68–74.

PART IV
Current Trends and Future Possibilities

7
Latin American Philosophy Has No Quine, So What?

Susana Nuccetelli

In the twentieth century, many Latin American philosophers held skeptical positions about the very existence and quality of their own field of inquiry. Recently, a new skepticism has appeared in connection with the attempt by some Mexican philosophers to raise two "invisibility problems" for Latin American philosophy. Old and new skeptics in both halves of the Americas have wondered about the reasons for the absence of internationally recognized philosophers in Latin America—of the caliber of, for example, Willard van Orman Quine in North America. I acknowledge such an absence but argue that this fact need not be taken to support that there is something wrong with Latin American philosophy. After pointing out some deficits in recent attempts to substantiate that skeptical conclusion, I provide an alternative account that avoids normative conclusions about Latin American philosophy's quality.

Historical Background

It is undeniable that philosophy exists in Latin America as a discipline and profession autonomous from science, theology, literature, politics, education, and other disciplines or practices (hereafter, simply "disciplines"). And no one questions that Latin American philosophy meets current Western standards of proper representation in the Hispanic world's educational systems, learned societies, associations, journals, presses, etc. The only factual issue yet to be settled concerns its origins. When did it begin? Two apparently rival answers have been offered. Some maintain that its real origins are in the early twentieth century, since it was not until then that there was evidence of the existence of autonomous philosophy in Latin America, sometimes referred to as "philosophy as such" or "strict philosophy." Previously, it had not been practiced for its own sake but was subordinated to non-philosophical interests, chiefly in literature, politics, and education. On the other hand, according to others, its origins are in the sixteenth century with the introduction of Scholasticism by Iberian educators and theologians.[1]

But these positions are not really incompatible, since Latin American philosophy may have colonial origins when construed broadly, and contemporary origins when construed narrowly. Reasons for leaving colonial Scholasticism out of strict philosophy include this movement's main motivation, which was education, and the mostly imitative nature of its developments. The philosophy that came after independence from Spain and Portugal in the early nineteenth century also fails to qualify as "strict" because it was not practiced for its own sake, but rather subordinated to political and pedagogical interests. Between the 1910s and the 1940s, however, a generation of philosophers known as the *fundadores* or *forjadores* (hereafter "the Founders") began to practice it for its own sake, thereby turning it into an autonomous discipline within academia. They also created standard professional organizations and institutions devoted to philosophy and achieved recognition for it in the wider community. For all these achievements, they credited themselves with having brought *normalidad* (normalcy, understood as standardization) to philosophy in the region, by which they meant making its practice similar to that prevailing in academic philosophy in the West. At that point in recent history, there was no question that philosophy existed in Latin America. But was it any good?

A prominent skeptical view about this question emerged among those Founders who reflected on the quality of Latin American philosophy. By comparing its achievements with those of North American or European philosophy, they tended to agree with the following skeptical thesis:

SKEPTICISM (S1): Only a very small part of Latin American philosophy, if any part at all, is of value.

One of the first Latin American philosophers to endorse S1 was Brazilian Euryalo Cannabrava, who in 1927 arrived at this thesis by comparing the qualities of his local philosophy with those of North American philosophy. According to his view, Latin American philosophy was based on nothing more than sophistry and a kind of literary thinking far removed from the strict rules of reasoning followed so closely by North American philosophers. Consistent with this assessment is Cannabrava's explanation of the attractiveness of continental philosophy to Latin American philosophers, which at the time meant mostly contemporary offshoots of German idealism (construed broadly to include phenomenology and existentialism). Cannabrava believed that Latin

American philosophers were attracted to this philosophical tradition precisely because of its "lack of intelligibility," and "its metaphysical abuses and frequent violation of the rules of correct thinking."[2] Latin American philosophy was at its worst when addressing issues in philosophy of science. Here Cannabrava illustrates his claim by reference to Mexican Antonio Caso's writings on science, which in Cannabrava's view show an absence of any "real acquaintance with ... [its] development or technique."[3] All these shortcomings led Cannabrava to lament that "[i]n Latin America we do not have philosophers like Morris Cohen, Victor Lenze, Ernest Nagel, and F. S. C. Northrop, who have studied the sources of science and followed closely its development . . ."[4]

Let's assume that, at the time of Cannabrava's list, at least Nagel could perhaps somehow be equated with what I would call "a Quine." Cannabrava's conclusion, which is consistent with S1, combines the factual with the evaluative. For, to put it in our context, it doesn't simply state a matter of (putative) fact—viz., that Latin America does not have internationally recognized philosophers like Quine. It also has the normative connotation that there is something wrong with Latin American philosophy. In order to explain what is wrong with it, Cannabrava appeals to factors concerning the origins and history of the discipline in Latin America, which speak of its development in connection with literature and the arts, where precise reasoning and linguistic clarity are intentionally avoided. By contrast, in the English-speaking world, the development of philosophy connects it with the formal and the empirical sciences, where precise reasoning and clear language are important values. Call this explanation of Latin American philosophy's shortcomings "the genealogical explanation." I'll have more to say about it later.

Originalism

During the first half of the twentieth century, only a small number of philosophers in Latin America were, like Cannabrava, attracted to the analytic tradition. Partly because of this, those Founders who held the skeptical thesis S1 would give a different reason for their bleak conclusion. On their view, the main problem facing philosophy in the region was neither the lack of sound reasoning nor lack of linguistic clarity but lack of originality. In 1949, Argentinian Risieri Frondizi made an influential attempt at showing that this problem was indeed pervasive. On the evidence, Frondizi claimed, only 10% of strict philosophy in Latin America was original. The discipline had no significant history, theories, or methods. But most importantly, it had no really creative practitioners. Although, like Cannabrava, Frondizi was committed to S1, his reason for this thesis was then "originalism," the view that to be taken seriously, philosophical works must be original in some of the ways to be considered herein.

Given originalism, there is no Quine in Latin American philosophy simply because this discipline has not been sufficiently creative: It has not introduced innovative points of view. The lack of originality in Latin America philosophy, which entails the S1 thesis, has been a popular view among twentieth century Latin American philosophers—not only among philosophers and phenomenologists but also among Marxists and others. In fact, in 1925 (two years before Cannabrava's critique) Peruvian José Carlos Mariátegui expressed a similarly bleak view of Latin American philosophy grounded in Marxist reasoning.[5] He argued for S1 from a factual premise about the cultural and economic dependence of Latin America and the assumption that a region cannot have interesting philosophy unless it has achieved independence on both counts. In 1968, Peruvian Augusto Salazar Bondy offered a more sophisticated Marxist argument along the lines suggested by Mariátegui.[6] I have shown the vulnerability of this line of argument elsewhere.[7] But more needs to be said against its skeptical conclusion, S1, since at the end of the day it is undeniable that Latin American philosophy has not produced figures of Quine's caliber. What, if anything, is wrong with this discipline?

Originalists did of course think there was something wrong with it: its lack of sufficient originality. But, wary of simplistic explanations, they took pains to clarify what is meant by "originality." In 1968, Salazar Bondy's small but influential book devoted itself entirely to the question. It provides a meticulous analysis of the property of originality, which is distinguished from other properties such as authenticity and peculiarity, all considered relevant to the question at hand. This book was Bondy's contribution to the classic debate about Latin American philosophy's quality that took part in the second half of the twentieth century. In the course of this debate, participants have defined the relevant properties of a philosophy as follows:

(1) Original—a philosophy that is creative or novel;
(2) Authentic—a philosophy that is genuine or non-spurious; and
(3) Peculiar—a philosophy that is autochthonous in the sense of being related to a certain region.

Some anti-skeptics in that debate identified themselves with a tradition I call "distinctivism" according to which Latin America philosophy has property (3). Skeptics have replied that (3) is neither necessary nor sufficient for having (1) or (2). Other relationships that can be drawn among (1), (2), and (3) include that having (2) is necessary but not sufficient for having (1): a work that, by being genuine, has (2) may lack (1) if it fails to be creative, and also (3) if its author or topic is not related in some relevant sense to Latin America. Yet a philosophical work that lacks (2) by being imitative or results from, say, plagiarism would lack also (1) may nonetheless have (3), provided it shows some relation to Latin America. Having (1) is clearly neither necessary nor sufficient for having (3), but is sufficient for having (2).

More recently, Mexican Guillermo Hurtado and other Mexican philosophers of skeptical persuasion (hereafter, "the new skeptics") have added a fourth property to the list of good-making features a philosophy should have that Latin American philosophy allegedly lacks:

(4) Being tradition-generating—a philosophy that has generated a paradigm for subsequent philosophical work.

After arguing that Latin American philosophy lacks this property, new skeptics conclude that S1 is true.[8] They also think that it lacks properties (1) and (2). But what about (3)? Would its[9] possession by Latin American philosophy justify the dismissal of skeptical thesis S1, as the distinctivists believe?

Famously championed by Leopoldo Zea in a number of works, distinctivism is an anti-skeptical position popular also with other Mexican philosophers of his generation. Although distinctivists acknowledge that their discipline has been imitative, they argue that peculiarity is sufficient for (1) originality, which in turn does not require (2) authenticity.[10] Yet there is no good reason for thinking that peculiarity entails originality. After all, as defined above, "peculiarity" is a purely descriptive concept while "originality" is usually a term of praise used to express what's call in ethics a "thick" concept, partly descriptive, partly evaluative. When we say that a philosophy is original, we are not only saying that it is creative or novel but also that these features are something good. Since the same applies to properties (2) and (4), from the peculiarity of Latin American philosophy, nothing would follow about its being original, authentic, or tradition-generating. In this way, the new skeptics can resist the distinctivist reply. If they could also meet the non-distinctivist objection that raised here, they would have no difficulty in substantiating the skeptical argument, which invokes originalism to support the skeptical thesis S1 with the following argument:

Skeptical Argument SA:
1. Most, if not all, Latin American philosophy lacks good-making features such as property (4), being tradition-generating.
2. For any philosophy to be of value, it must have this feature.
3. Therefore, only a very small part of Latin American philosophy, if any part at all, is of value.

As we shall see next, given the new skepticism, a main reason for Latin American philosophy's deficit in property (4) is that it also lacks (1) and (2)—while (3) can be ignored because, as we have seen, it is too weak to support anti-skeptical conclusions. So both skeptics, the new and the old, agree on the basic charges to the quality of Latin American philosophy. But the new skeptics contribute to that debate something new: viz., a focus on its practitioners' incapability to generate philosophical dialog among themselves and with North American and European philosophers.

Two Invisibility Problems

Among the versions of SA's premise (1) put forward by new skeptics, the one offered by Carlos Pereda breaks Latin American philosophy's deficits on good-making feature (4) into two invisibility problems[11]:

> Problem 1: External Invisibility (EI)—Philosophers working in North America and other major centers of Western philosophy do not regularly and seriously consider contributions by their Latin American peers.
> Problem 2: Internal Invisibility (II)—Philosophers working in Latin America do not regularly and seriously consider contributions by their own Latin American peers.

Given II, Latin American philosophers' works have no impact on the works of their Latin American peers; and given EI, they have no impact on those of other Western peers. Evidence from II stems from facts such that, in Latin America, philosophical traditions are imported from major centers of Western philosophy, don't last very long, and those working on a certain tradition fail to establish philosophical dialog among themselves—let alone with their peers working on different traditions. Although new skeptics have made little effort to provide support for these claims beyond anecdotal evidence,[12] it is undeniable that Latin American philosophers don't make sufficient reference to their peers' work in their publications, papers presented at conferences, etc. Let's provisionally concede the II problem and turn to the support for EI, external invisibility. Here the evidence seems beyond dispute: No work by a Latin American philosopher has been tradition-originating in a way remotely analogous to the work of Quine.

Yet since II and EI point to factual problems, an anti-skeptic may reply that they cannot entail, either individually or jointly, skeptical conclusion S1, that there is something wrong with Latin American philosophy. There is room for accepting the existence of both problems while saying to the skeptic, "So what?" or "Why should Latin American philosophers care?" But this reply is in need of further support since even when the existence of problems II and EI does not entail the skeptics' conclusion, which is evaluative, it does provide non-deductive grounds for it. The argument now runs Normative Skepticism (NS): The two invisibility problems facing Latin American philosophy, II and EI, suggest that there is something wrong with it.

NS appears a plausible recast of SA above. Let's now consider how the new skeptics attempt to support its premise. Pereda charges that some vices of "arrogant reasoning" afflicting the work of Latin American philosophers are responsible for the II and EI problems.[13] Here we need to assume that Pereda is referring to most, but not all, Latin American philosophers as having such negative traits of intellectual character. The group should include neither Pereda nor other new skeptics who have similar views, since otherwise, their views would be self-defeating.[14] The vice-affected philosophers that Pereda has in mind are either distinctivists or universalists. Unlike the distinctivists, the universalists deny that philosophical theories, methods, and topics can be peculiar or relative to regions, persons, groups, or cultures. According to Pereda, their vices of arrogant reason consist of "subaltern fervor" and "craving for novelty," while the vice of distinctivists is "nationalist enthusiasm." On his prognosis, fixing the EI and II problems facing Latin American philosophy would require purging these traits of from its practitioners' intellectual character.

Another skeptic attempting to support the existence of at least the II problem for Latin American philosophy is Eduardo Rabossi, who charges that most of its practitioners fall into the category of "periphery philosophers." These have the self-image or attitude of "guachos," an Argentinian slang term used to designate anyone who is both an orphan and street urchin. Guacho philosophers not only fail to acknowledge their own "philosophical parents," they do not want to know about them at all. As Rabossi puts it, a guacho philosopher "doesn't take them [the philosophical parents] into account, he doesn't read them, he is not even interested in criticizing their defects or limitations; for him, his own philosophical past doesn't exist."[15] Lacking awareness of their own philosophical past and unwilling to establish dialogue with local peers, this philosopher can have neither philosophical traditions nor genuine philosophical communities. If Rabossi is right, then at the very least there is a serious impediment for Latin American philosophy to be tradition originating.

Hurtado makes his own attempt at substantiated both problems, the II and the EI, in the case of Mexican philosophy, but his reasoning also applies by extension to Latin American philosophy as a whole.[16] According to Hurtado, at the roots of problem II, internal invisibility, is the prevalent model for doing philosophy in Latin America, the "modernizing model." It creates bad traits of intellectual character among its followers, including a proclivity to form small groups and spend most of the time trying to learn some imported philosophy, to cite only foreign philosophers without paying much attention to regional peers, and to adopt the latest philosophical fashion with which they uncritically replace previous traditions. At the end of the day, in Latin American philosophy ". . . each modernizing movement got lost for the upcoming movement . . ." without creating either traditions or stable communities of dialogue.[17] "But the foreign philosophers," laments Hurtado, "even those who visit our countries to deliver talks, very rarely quote us in their work. There is therefore no genuine dialogue . . ."[18] In this way, Hurtado is acknowledging that there is EI for Latin American philosophy, but he thinks it will continue to exist "unless we create a genuine critical dialogue among ourselves and simultaneously exercise a constantly renewed memory of past dialogues."[19] Thus the II problem needs to be fixed first.

On this, Mexican new-skeptic Maite Ezcurdia disagrees: if it is true that most Latin American philosophers are driven by the modernizing model, reasons Ezcurdia, then it is rather the EI problem that must be fixed first.[20] Since she agrees with Hurtado that most Latin American philosophers do in fact work within the modernizing-model frame of mind, it follows that they would be motivated to consider their peers' works only after some of these works have acquired international recognition. So Ezcurdia contends that fixing the EI is bound to result eventually in correcting the II problem too. Be that as it may, Ezcurdia fully endorses the new skeptics' argument NS, which she thinks is also supported by the absence of certain kinds of originality in the works of Latin American philosophers. In her view, there are four kinds of originality corresponding to four non-overlapping properties that are desirable in philosophy anywhere: interpretative, argumentative, problem-making, and problem-solving originality. Latin American philosophers have on the whole been successful at interpreting the works of philosophers in major centers of the West, which counts as evidence of having interpretative originality. But she finds them lacking in originality of the other three kinds. Ezecurdia's brief diagnosis of these problems for Latin American philosophy quickly leads to a recommendation about how to fix its EI and II problems: namely, by means of fostering originality of the other three types. In particular, improvements in problem-solving originality are needed.

Pereda's recommendation for fixing the II and EI problems is less clear. He suggests Latin American philosophers should emulate the work of Latin American essayists, who have succeeded in establishing a dialogue among each other and with world culture. At the same time, he appears to draw a bright line between the philosophical essay, and strict philosophy, since he appears reluctant to count as philosophy the non-academic philosophical works produced by, for example, essayists such as Octavio Paz and Carlos Fuentes.

In any case, like Ezcurdia and Pereda, other new skeptics make explicit or implicit recommendations to solve the II and EI problems, from which we can infer that their skepticism about Latin American philosophy is not as radical as the skepticism of Cannabrava and Frondizi. Whether for modesty or common sense, neither of them made such recommendations—leaving us wondering whether they thought a solution was possible at all.

Against Normative Skepticism

There are, however, reasons to think that, if new skepticism is true, any recommendations about how to fix the II and EI problems for Latin American philosophy are futile. For one thing, by all counts, universalism is a widely held and probably majority view in Latin American philosophy.[21] If Pereda is right about universalism's vices, since it is a widely held view, the intellectual character of most Latin American philosophers have the bad traits of subaltern fervor and craving for novelty. As a result, they per force devote considerable time and effort to assimilating the latest fads coming from the United States and Europe (something about which Pereda agrees with other new skeptics). It is hopeless to think that these philosophers can devote themselves to reform their intellectual characters and produce work that is original to a significant degree. Such activities would require a considerable amount of motivation, time, and effort that the universalists lack. They are already too busy learning and abandoning traditions, replacing them with new fads that they try to assimilate, only to abandon them in short order and begin all over again. (Someone once told me that there is a new philosophical fad every ten years!) Thus there seems to be an empirical constraint for the universalists to follow the Pereda/Hurtado/Ezcurdia recommendations for improving the Latin American philosophers' intellectual character or their critical thinking skills.[22] Furthermore, the new skepticism is vulnerable to several strong ad hominem, all focused on the fact that the new-skeptics' recommendations fall into the very problem they are designed to fix—namely, the lack of dialogue between philosophers inside Latin America and between these and their peers in North America and Europe. Here are the objections:

Ad hominem against the new skeptics' claim that Latin American philosophy faces the internal invisibility (II) problem.

Case #1: The new skeptics themselves never engage with, or at any rate acknowledge, the arguments and subtle conceptual distinctions of Latin American philosophers within the same skeptical tradition. Notoriously absent in their work is philosophical dialog with the old skepticism. As suggested at the beginning of this chapter, this tradition originated in the work of philosophers of different persuasions who have produced a rich set of arguments questioning the quality of Latin American philosophy. Cannabrava's and Frondizi's views considered above are merely the tip of the iceberg. When the new skeptics address the same issue, their references, if present at all, are only to the work of other new skeptics. A notable absence in their discussions is Salazar Bondy's subtle analysis of originality as a concept and as a property of Latin American philosophy—even when his discussion is especially relevant, for example, to Ezcurdia's four types of originality.

Case #2: On the issue of how to improve the quality of Latin American philosophy: Although there is a great deal of overlap among the new skeptics' own recommendations, with a few exceptions they neither acknowledge each other's works nor join forces to bust their capacity of being tradition-generating. Once again, the new skeptics' attitudes illustrate the very problem they are trying to fix.

Ad hominem against the new skeptics' claim that Latin American philosophy faces the external invisibility (EI) problem.

The new skeptics invariably ignore the arguments their peers in North America are having about the same subject matter—namely, the quality of Latin American philosophy. To cite but one example, consider Jorge Gracia's 2003 charge that originalism amounts to an unreasonable demand on any philosophy.[23] If the charge is right, then at the very least Ezcurdia's proposal collapses. Or take Gracia's argument for construing Latin American philosophy as an ethnic philosophy, which, if sound, would undermine new skepticism as a whole by relaxing the quality requirement that Latin American philosophy be tradition-generating. Although these and other arguments by peers in North America bear directly on the quality of Latin American philosophy, they are ignored by the new skeptics, whose argumentative strategies systematically fall into the very problems they are designed to fix.

I submit that these are strong ad hominem against the new skeptical argument that there is something wrong with Latin American philosophy from the premise that it faces the II and EI problems. The new skeptics' own approach to the debate about this discipline's quality is undermined by their failing to establish the sort of internal and external dialog they consider indicative of having any philosophical value.

Conclusion

There is abundant textual evidence that the quality of Latin American philosophy debate has generated intense debate among its practitioners. As a result, there are significant skeptical and anti-skeptical traditions about that discipline. The attempts to substantiate new skepticism (Pereda's, Rabossi's, Hurtado's, and Ezcurdia's) are proof of the currency of an old skeptical tradition among Latin American philosophers regarding the quality of their field. This by itself amounts to a counterexample to the claim that Latin American philosophy lacks the property of being tradition-generating. It follows that Latin American philosophy does after all have some stable philosophical traditions and communities of the sort commonly found in, for example, North American philosophy. In light of the evidence provided here, II is false.

The EI thesis, however, points to a fact made vivid by Cannabrava's concern about the absence of internationally recognized philosophers in Latin America. True, Latin American philosophy has no Quine. While in graduate school in the United States, my fellow students asked me, on more than one occasion, Why? Cannabrava offered a genealogical explanation that amounts to a Kuhnean answer (of course years before T. S. Kuhn's 1962 book).[24] It invokes external factors concerning the history of philosophy in Latin America. Although his answer was quick and superficial, it pointed in the right direction. In my view, it is ultimately for historians and sociologists of philosophy to determine the exact factors that made it possible for North America to have many internationally recognized philosophers and scientists, and Latin America to have only a few—and none as influential as Quine. Note that Cannabrava's explanation is consistent with the Founders' view of Latin American philosophy: before the twentieth century, it developed subordinated to others' interests, chiefly literature and the arts. Positivism did not have the same impact in all the regions that adopted that philosophy. While in North America and the United Kingdom it secured for philosophy some long-established methodological connections with the sciences, both formal and natural, in Latin America it was often put at the service of failed dictatorial adventures, with disastrous consequences for some countries. That only fostered resentment towards science among intellectuals of the region, which in turn accounts for the rapid spread of the anti-positivist view known as "Arielism" among the youth in the early 1900s.[25] In the meantime, the lingering influence of positivism in North America and the United Kingdom, together with Moore and Russell's rejection of idealism in the early twentieth century, laid the foundations of contemporary analytic philosophy by fostering developments such as logical positivism and logical atomism during the early days of philosophy of language and symbolic logic.

More, of course, needs to be said. Any complete account should also factor in economic and cultural elements. Among the former is the fact that the greater wealth of private and public universities in North America enables access to libraries and other research resources unavailable in Latin America.

Furthermore, through an accident of history, the North has come to hold a linguistic advantage. English has become the lingua franca of the philosophical community, as well as a barrier for many Latin American philosophers who wish to publish in the best journals and with the publishers who can best promote their work in an international forum. At the end of the day, then, the question of why there is no Quine in Latin American philosophy turns out to be of no philosophical interest. If I am right, it has a solely factual answer that can be found only by historical and sociological research. When intended as normative, it is a fallacious complex question presupposing that there is something wrong with Latin American philosophy. This cannot be assumed without argument. And of several arguments for that conclusion examined here, only those pointing to the lack of international recognition for Latin American philosophy are supported by the evidence. But again, far from being normative, their conclusion refers to facts to be accounted for by the social sciences.

Notes

1. The first view can be found in, for example, Francisco Romero, "Sobre la filosofía en Iberoamérica," in *Filosofía de la persona y otros ensayos* (Buenos Aires: Losada, 1944), 147–157; Risieri Frondizi, "Is There an Ibero-American Philosophy?" *Philosophy and Phenomenological Research*, 9 (1949): 345–355; Francisco Miró Quesada, *Despertar y proyecto del filosofar latinoamericano* (Mexico City: Fondo de Cultura Económica 1974). For the second view, see Jorge J.E. Gracia, et al., "Latin American Philosophy," in *The Oxford Companion to Philosophy*, ed. T. Honderich (Oxford: Oxford University Press 1995); and Guillermo Hurtado, *El búho y la serpiente: ensayos sobre la filosofía en México en el siglo XX* (Mexico City: UNAM, 2007.

2. Euryalo Cannabrava, "Present Tendencies in Latin American Philosophy," *Journal of Philosophy*, 5: 113–119 at 114.

3. Cannabrava, "Present Tendencies in Latin American Philosophy," 117.

4. Cannabrava, "Present Tendencies in Latin American Philosophy," 117

5. José Carlos Mariátegui, "Existe un pensamiento hispano-americano?" *Repertorio Americano*, 17 (1925): 113–15, http://inif.ucr.ac.cr/recursos/docs/Revista%20 de%20Filosof%C3%ADa%20UCR/Vol.%20XIV/ No.%2038/Existe%20un%20 pensamiento%20hispano-americano.pdf (accessed 10/1/2012).

6. Augusto Salazar Bondy,¿*Existe una filosofía de nuestra América?* (Mexico City: Siglo XXI, 1968).

7. Susana Nuccetelli, "Is 'Latin American Thought' Philosophy?" *Metaphilosophy* 4 (2003): 524–537

8. Guillermo Hurtado, *Routledge Encyclopedia of Philosophy*, Dianoia XLV, 45, 1999: 227–234, http://dianoia.filosoficas.unam.mx/files/6813/6960/3472/DIA99 _Resenas_Hurtado.pdf (accessed September 16, 2014).

9. For textual evidence, see Susana Nuccetelli, "Latin American Philosophy: Metaphilosophical Foundations," In *Stanford Encyclopedia of Philosophy*, ed. Edward N. Zalta, http://plato.stanford.edu/entries/latin-american-metaphilosophy/.

10. Distinctivists argue that Latin American philosophy has peculiarity because its philosophers mostly come from a Latin American context and this context "permeates" their works. But then they make the doubtful claim that its peculiarity will lead to its originality, which Latin American philosophy is bound to develop por añadidura (i.e., in addition). See for example Leopoldo Zea, *La filosofía como compromiso de liberación*, L. Weinberg de Magis and M. Magallon (eds.) (Caracas: Biblioteca Ayacucho, 1991) and my objections to his argument in Nuccetelli, "Is 'Latin American Thought' Philosophy?."

11. Carlos Pereda, "Latin American Philosophy: Some Vices," *Journal of Speculative Philosophy*, 3 (2006): 192–203

12. Pereda is an exception, since he appeals to data from the *Enciclopedia iberoamericana de filosofía*, a multivolume, ongoing publication that began in 1987 in Spain, where almost no reference to works of Latin American philosophers can be found in the volumes devoted to general subjects. See Carlos Pereda, "Latin American Philosophy: Some Vices."

13. Carlos Pereda, "Latin American Philosophy: Some Vices."

14. Pereda needs to restrict the scope of his skepticism about Latin American philosophy to avoid making self-defeating claims. After all, if all Latin American philosophers have bad traits of intellectual character, as a Latin American philosopher himself, Pereda will have them too. Therefore, if he is right, we should reject his claims (as well as the claims of other new skeptics).

15. Eduardo Rabossi, *En el comienzo Dios creo el Canon*. Biblia berolinensis. Ensayos sobre la condición de la filosofía (Buenos Aires: Gedisa, 2008), 103, my translation.

16. Guillermo Hurtado, "Two Models of Latin American Philosophy," *Journal of Speculative Philosophy* 3 (2006): 204–213 at 206; Guillermo Hurtado, *El búho y la serpiente: ensayos sobre la filosofía en México en el siglo XX* (Mexico City: UNAM 2007), 24.

17. Guillermo Hurtado, "Two Models of Latin American Philosophy," 206.

18. Hurtado, 205.

19. Hurtado, 210.

20. Maite Ezcurdia, "Originalidad y Presencia," in *La filosofía en América Latina como problema*, ed. Cruz Revueltas (Mexico City: Publicaciones Cruz, 2003), 196–202.

21. Augusto Salazar Bondy,*¿Existe una filosofía de nuestra América?* (Mexico City: Siglo XXI, 1968); Francisco Miró Quesada, "Posibilidad y límites de una filosofía lationamericana," *Revista de Filosofía de la Universidad de Costa Rica* XVI, 43 (1978): 76.

22. To my knowledge, Rabossi made no such recommendation. If so, his claims about the prevalence of guacho philosophers in Latin America seem to support radical skepticism about the quality of Latin American philosophy.

23. Jorge J. E. Gracia, "Ethnic Labels and Philosophy: The Case of Latin American Philosophy," in *Latin American Philosophy: Currents, Issues, Debates*, ed. E. Mendieta (Bloomington, IN: Indiana University Press 2003), 57–67.

24. Thomas S. Kuhn, *The Structure of Scientific Revolutions* (Chicago: The University of Chicago Press, 1962).

25. The Arielists' plain hostility toward the sciences sprang of Uruguayan José Enrique Rodó's *Ariel*, a neo-romantic narrative closer to literature than philosophy. The book pitches aesthetic values against the scientific values of North America, which are misrepresented as part of "utilitarianism."

Bibliography

Cannabrava, Euryalo. "Present Tendencies in Latin American Philosophy." *Journal of Philosophy* 5 (1927): 113–119.

Ezcurdia, Maite. "Originalidad y Presencia," In *La filosofía en América Latina como problema*. Edited by Cruz Revueltas. Mexico City: Publicaciones Cruz, 2003.

Frondizi, Risieri. "Is There an Ibero-American Philosophy?." *Philosophy and Phenomenological Research* 9 (1949): 345–355.

Gracia, Jorge J. E. et al. "Latin American philosophy." In *The Oxford Companion to Philosophy*, Edited by T. Honderich. Oxford, Oxford University Press, 1995.

———. "Ethnic Labels and Philosophy: The Case of Latin American Philosophy." In *Latin American Philosophy: Currents, Issues, Debates*, Edited by E. Mendieta, 57–67. Bloomington, IN: Indiana University Press, 2003.

Hurtado, Guillermo. *Routledge Encyclopedia of Philosophy*, Dianoia XLV, 45, 1999: 227–234, http://dianoia.filosoficas.unam.mx/files/6813/6960/3472/DIA99_Resenas _Hurtado.pdf (accessed September 16, 2014).

———. "Two Models of Latin American Philosophy." *Journal of Speculative Philosophy* 3 (2006): 204–213.

———. *El búho y la serpiente: ensayos sobre la filosofía en México en el siglo XX*. Mexico City: UNAM, 2007.

Kuhn, Thomas S. *The Structure of Scientific Revolutions*. Chicago: The University of Chicago Press, 1962.

Mariátegui, José Carlos. "Existe un pensamiento hispano-americano?" *Repertorio Americano* 17 (1925): 113–15, http://inif.ucr.ac.cr/recursos/docs/Revista%20de%20 Filosof%C3%ADa%20UCR/Vol.%20XIV/ No.%2038/Existe%20un%20pensamiento %20hispano-americano.pdf (accessed October 1, 2012).

Miró Quesada, Francisco, "Posibilidad y límites de una filosofía lationamericana," *Revista de Filosofía de la Universidad de Costa Rica* XVI, 43 (1978): 75–82.

———. *Despertar y proyecto del filosofar latinoamericano*. Mexico City: Fondo de Cultura Económica, 1974.

Nuccetelli, Susana. "Latin American Philosophy: Metaphilosophical Foundations." In *Stanford Encyclopedia of Philosophy*, ed. Edward N. Zalta, http://plato.stanford .edu/entries/latin-american-metaphilosophy/.

———. "Is 'Latin American Thought' Philosophy?" *Metaphilosophy* 4 (2003): 524–537.
Pereda, Carlos. "Latin American Philosophy: Some Vices." *Journal of Speculative Philosophy* 3 (2006): 192–203.
Rabossi, Eduardo. *En el comienzo Dios creo el Canon. Biblia berolinensis. Ensayos sobre la condición de la filosofía*. Buenos Aires: Gedisa, 2008.
Romero, F. "Sobre la filosofia en Iberoamérica," in *Filosofía de la persona y otros ensayos*, 147–157. Buenos Aires: Losada, 1944.
Salazar Bondy. Augusto. *¿Existe una filosofía de nuestra América?* Mexico City: Siglo XXI, 1968.
Zea, Leopoldo. *La filosofía como compromiso de liberación*. Edited by L. Weinberg de Magis and M. Magallon. Caracas: Biblioteca Ayacucho, 1991.

8
Latin American Thought as a Path toward Philosophizing from Radical Exteriority

Alejandro A. Vallega

Introducción / Introduction

The title of this volume, *Philosophizing the Americas*, and the theme of this chapter, "Current Trends, Future Possibilities," invite a meditation on the situation as well as the very possibility of speaking of philosophy in light of the unfathomable contexts, experiences, lives, and ways of being that are often gathered under the term Latin America. Indeed, to speak of "philosophizing the Americas" one must wonder whence and how this philosophizing occurs in the Americas as inter-American experiences. In my case I will focus on Latin America, and from specific moments in Latin American philosophy I will open the path of thinking in radical exteriority that may resonate with the possible development of inter-American philosophies. My discussion develops a narrative, which step-by-step exposes a path toward the recognition of opening trends and possibilities in Latin American philosophies throughout the Americas, as well as the possibility of rethinking the sense of philosophy and modernity in light of these philosophies. As the reader will find, such a path will lead to thinkers who sustain a border thinking in which Latin America, the Caribbean, and Latino/a thinkers begin to interplay and contribute to a broad sense of philosophy as thought that cannot be reduced to the traditional history of philosophy and its protagonist, as told in the Western European/North American traditions. At the same time, this opening does not mean the exclusion of Western traditions, but rather the transformative appropriation that accompanies the affirmation of thought and humanity beyond the traditional determination of such terms. The point is a radicalizing and intensifying of philosophical thought by recognizing thinking, ways of being, and configuration of knowledge that remain buried and excluded, obscured and misrepresented. In listening to those voices, in letting philosophy turn to the oppressed and excluded, one finds possibilities opened by experiences figured by border thinking, intersectional and decolonial thought, deconstruction, and hermeneutics (rethought from Latin American distinct contexts, as it occurs for example in the exemplary work of Colombian philosopher Santiago Castro-Gómez). These ways of thinking are paths toward thinking in radical exteriority, in that they always occur with a sense of alterity that may sustain thought: never letting difference become the other of a centralized identity or system of power, never becoming a comfortable other to those traditional claims of identity that become enclosed in themselves and idealized to the point of seeing themselves as the only and original or essential time-space and sense of being human. We are speaking of ways of thinking that remain beyond the dominating rationalism or ideology that sees itself as holding a word that may speak for all, naming all, measuring, determining, and ultimately making of all difference accessible objects of knowledge and production in terms of one history and canon of knowledge and existence. As this essay shows, Latin American thought presents a radical option to and departure from such closed systems (closed systems even in their self-criticism, which is itself a further affirmation of their closure.) I should add that, as the reader will see, to philosophize the Americas does not mean to ask the old traditional question about the possibility and identity of "American" or "Latin American" philosophy as if there was an essence or historical destiny behind these ways of philosophizing. At the same time, as the discussion will show, neither can one take for granted what philosophy means, as if one could find the language and way of articulating existence that guarantees a universal sense for philosophizing and of ascribing identity.

The following discussion aims to thrust one forward toward philosophy in the sense of philosophizing, and this thinking is something that I would say is alive in distinct ways in the Americas. However, to philosophize the Americas must mean to think with as well as beyond the separation of Western philosophy over its genitive "other" (the imaginary, exotic, "orientalized," Latin America, Africa, Asia). I take philosophizing to be the engagement of the distinct situations of peoples by them, in an articulate critical conceptual manner born of the concrete practices and culture of those peoples. In other words, I take any philosophizing to be born of living culture, of the distinct lives that are the earth from which philosophy in its originary and not merely descriptive or analytical sense may occur. The sense of originary will become evident through the discussion in the following pages: I can preface the discussion by saying that by this term I mean to indicate that philosophizing, when it happens, when there is the connection with the distinct ground from which it may spring, philosophizing composes the articulation of senses of being in which actors, communities, and beings come to take their place and to find identities. Thus, the following pages move from an ambiguous sense of alterity and openings toward this that appears as inseparable from an exclusive and excluding sense of philosophy understood as the task of identifying the origin and essence of what is Latin American, and proper to Latin America, to ways of thinking that figure radical diversity and diversifying spaces, border experiences, hybrid unfolding of lived senses of being, ultimately articulating in distinct ways being in and beyond the Americas. In asking then about the currents trends and future possibilities of philosophizing the Americas, I will turn to the very question of the situation from which philosophizing may arise, i.e., within the limits of the connection between distinct lives and ways of being, and philosophical, conceptual, and critical articulations of these, and to the future trends that become apparent today as utopian ways of thinking. By utopian, I mean the way contemporary philosophers constitute narratives that open a horizon for conceptual determinations of being in the Americas, and, again, in my case particularly in Latin America.[1]

La vida ante el progreso / *Life Before Progress*: On the Radical Side of Latin American Philosophy of Liberation

> "It appears possible to philosophize in the periphery . . . only if the discourse of the philosophy of the center is not imitated, only if another discourse is discovered. To be different, this discourse must have another point of departure, must think other themes, must come to distinctive conclusions by a different method."
> (ENRIQUE DUSSEL, *PHILOSOPHY OF LIBERATION*)[2]

1. Latin American Philosophy

Enrique Dussel's words present a challenge that orients Latin American philosophy today. In order to grasp this challenge in terms of its conceptual historical lineages, and in order to engage the situation from which Latin American philosophy arises today, one may begin by taking a few steps back. In 1942, at the very beginning of World War II, the Mexican philosopher Leopoldo Zea, one of the major figures in the very shaping of Latin American philosophy in the twentieth century, writes in "Concerning an American Philosophy" (*En torno a una filosofía americana*):

To be a Latin American was until very recently a great misfortune, because this did not allow us to be European. Today it is just the opposite: the inability to become European, in spite of our great efforts, allows us to have a personality; it allows us to learn, in this moment of crisis in European culture, that there is something of our own [*algo que nos es propio*] that can give us support. What this something is should be one of the issues that a Latin American philosophy must investigate.[3]

In this work, as well as throughout his career, Zea gives a point of departure for the future of Latin American philosophy. He does this by recognizing the existence of a Latin American philosophy as a tradition with its own characteristics and drives. The continuity between this initiative and Dussel's words above is evident. In both cases Latin American philosophers must turn to their concrete situations in order to develop a philosophy that will contribute to philosophical thought in general. In Zea's case this is a turn toward "*lo propio*," that which is our own. This turn toward our own Latin American situation and issues is complicated in Zea's case by the inseparability of Latin America from Europe. In the same essay Zea explains the sense of "our own": "What makes us lean toward Europe and at the same time resist being European is what is properly ours, what is American."[4] Clearly, Latin American philosophy is understood here in a narrow sense. Zea is speaking of a tradition that remains wedded mainly to Europe and this points to the intellectual middle class. Moreover, although Zea echoes Simón Bolívar's claim about the American's being a species between European and Indigenous,[5] in the case of Zea, indigenous thought and culture are seen as a matter of the past, and not part of the Latin American reality of the time. In the same essay Zea writes: "We do not feel, as Asia, the heirs of our own culture . . . we Latin Americans do not view the world as the Aztecs or the Mayans did. . . . A Mayan temple is as alien and meaningless to us as a Hindu temple."[6] In part by virtue of Zea's reductive view, as well as as the result of his clear view concerning the majority of the intellectual middle classes, Zea is led to conclude that what is Latin America's "own" (what constitutes a Latin American sense of identity, this being in between being European and American) is a sense of inferiority fed by unwavering desire to be Westerners while realizing that desire into self-hate as one sees that one's reality is not anywhere near Western values. "Americans feel European by origin but inferior to this origin in their circumstance . . . [The American] feels disgust for what is American and resentment against what is European."[7] Thus an asymmetry becomes explicit, in which Latin American life and its ways of engaging European philosophy are always seen as secondary to Western thought and experience. As Zea sees it, this is the result of a relationship that begins with the violence between the conqueror and the conquered, which eventually turns into an internal existential sense of being.

The asymmetry makes it impossible to recognize the original creative appropriation (rather than mere repetition) of the Western tradition that happens in the Americas. This lack of vision in terms of what is characteristically American begins to be undone by Zea's work. For Zea, World War II in Europe marks an interruption in the existential pattern of self-deprecation and of the Latin American tendency to look toward Europe (and North America) for the philosophical thought that might articulate one's identity. With the failure of European thought/values made obvious by the war,[8] Latin America experiences a moment of opportunity to look into its own philosophical issues and values.

For Zea, the response must be a creative one; it is a question of originary creativity (*originalidad*). This *creatividad* depends on rethinking universal issues and Western thought out of Latin American experience.[9] Thus, philosophy in Latin American must appropriate traditional articulations and make them their own. This figures a transformative appropriation: in putting Western thought through a Latin American existential and historical lens, philosophy is made new. Indeed, Latin American philosophers must "select, adapt, the expression of Western philosophy that may best suit our needs, our reality."[10] However, in recognizing and seeking what is proper to the Latin American situation, Zea insists that Latin American identity is inseparable from European identity: ". . . whether we want it or not, we are the children of European culture. From Europe we have received our cultural framework, what could be called our structure: language, religion, customs; in a word our conception of life and world is European."[11]

One finds then in Zea's own thought a struggle between finding an originary sense of identity and always remaining, even in that struggle under a Westernized way of thinking. Ultimately Zea turns to a concept of history that remains well wedded to Western philosophy. In the preface to *Discurso desde la marginación y la barbarie* (*Discourse from Marginalization and Barbarism*), written in 1988, Leopoldo Zea recalls the aim behind his 1957 work *America en la historia* (*America in History*): "In *America in History* my aim was to situate the history of Latin America within the context of universal history in relation to the order and planetary power of the center designated as the Western world."[12] Alas, Zea opens a path for a thinking rooted in Latin American experiences, for the recognition of Latin American thought in its historical appropriation of Western philosophy, while turning to this creative task in the name of a Westernized sense of history and universal concepts. It is as a result of Zea's recognition of this inseparability from Western thought that his question must remain with the issue of a historical universal Latin American identity, and yet, the question of a Latin American philosophy is now an issue and reality that marks an opening for the thinkers to come.

2. The Situation of Latin American Philosophy

A major controversial response to Zea's complex turn in his interpretation of the identity of Latin American philosophy appears in 1968. This response would announce a fundamental shift in Latin American philosophy, a turn toward what thereafter will arise as Latin American Philosophy of Liberation. The critical and controversial response and challenge comes from the Peruvian philosopher Augusto Salazar Bondy's exemplary and seminal critical essay, "The Meaning and Problem of Hispanic American Philosophic Thought."[13] To the question of the very existence of a Latin American philosophy, Salazar Bondy's response is negative. Speaking of that very history Zea finds as evidence of Latin America's philosophical identity, the Peruvian writes, "Our balance cannot fail to be negative, as has been that of practically all historians and interpreters of ideas in Hispanic America. In fact, it is impossible to extract clearly from this process an articulation of ideas, a well-structured dialectic of reflection and expositions, and of concepts and solutions nurtured by its historical and cultural circumstance. On the contrary, what we find in all of our countries is a succession of imported doctrines, a procession of systems, which follow European, or, in general, foreign unrest. It is almost a succession of intellectual fashions without roots in our spiritual life, and for this reason, lacking the virtue of fertility."[14]

Bondy and Zea begin from different places, which end up configuring different ways of engaging the very sense of a Latin American situation. Salazar Bondy does not turn to history but to the concrete social, political, and economic circumstances which figure the very possibility of interpreting the sense of history, and of identity and universality within it, that Zea (following the Western tradition) takes as a given. For Salazar Bondy, philosophy is not a matter of engaging experience in a creative way that may allow Latin America to participate in Western universal history but is born of its concrete circumstances, and it is only possible in an originary sense if concrete reality is given conceptual articulation. With this turn Salazar Bondy will expose the colonialism that informs and underlies the complex of inferiority Zea sees as characteristic of Latin American consciousness.

For Salazar Bondy, a genuine or originary philosophy arises as the rational articulation of a distinct living culture/community: "it [philosophy] cannot fail to be the manifestation of the rational conscience of a community."[15] Indeed, for him philosophy is "the conception that expresses the mode in which the community reacts before the whole of reality and the course of existence, and [the community's] peculiar manner of illuminating and interpreting the being in which it finds itself installed."[16] And culture[17] is "the organic articulation of the original and differentiating manifestation of a community."[18] Thus, philosophy is born through a culture and lives only for as long as that growth continues to occur. In the case of Latin American philosophy, Salazar Bondy sees a break between the organic articulation of communities and philosophy. Given his understanding of the very possibility and unfolding of philosophy out of the organic lives of Latin American communities, Salazar Bondy concludes: "It is not strange that a community which is disintegrated and lacking in potential should produce a mystified philosophic awareness [. . .]. Our thought is defective and inauthentic owing to our society and our culture."[19] With this analysis of culture and philosophy by Salazar Bondy, the "history" of philosophy Zea wants to recognize as characteristically Latin American is exposed as a series of borrowed and copied forms of thought, a critical vision that ultimately shows an economy of dependency subtending Latin American philosophy and consciousness.

Before moving on to his introduction of colonialism, and in terms of Salazar Bondy's understanding of what is "authentic" and Latin American, at least two characteristics must be underlined. First of all, at the beginning of the essay, Salazar Bondy excludes Pre-Columbian indigenous thought and its lineages and traditions by taking it as a thinking that offers nothing to philosophy. "This essay assumes that Hispanic American philosophical thought began with the discovery of America and Spanish Conquest; and that it is now possible to trace its development . . . The assumption arbitrarily casts aside the rich pre-Columbian cultural past for a variety of reasons. First, there are no data sufficiently precise and trustworthy concerning the thought of the indigenous peoples. Second, there was no integration, nor even sufficient sociopolitical and cultural interaction among the pre-Conquest peoples."[20] Again, as in the case of Zea, indigenous thought is excluded because it is thought of as lost in the past and gone. At the same time, one must note that the Peruvian thinker does not ignore indigenous culture but assumes the absence of evidence for philosophical thought. For Salazar Bondy, philosophy is a matter of rational analysis of concepts that sustain a system of values. Therefore, the rich culture of the indigenous peoples is not sufficient material or evidence for investigating or engaging them in a way appropriate to philosophy.[21] And yet, Salazar Bondy's analysis will open a crucial path for thinkers who will be able to turn toward indigenous, African, Asian, and other ways of thinking and lineages in Latin America; one that opens out of a critical exposure of a world-system still structured by the lineages of colonialism.

As Salazar Bondy sees it, the difficulty faced by Latin America is one shared by the Americas, as well as by all "third world" countries, today known as "developing" or "emerging" nations. The asymmetry exposed by Zea, as well as the complex of inferiority behind Latin American thought, result from the pernicious appropriation of Latin America and other peripheral peoples and cultures around the world by a group of central powerful nations which compose the world's economic, political, and conceptual dominating center of power. Behind the so-called mother countries appears not only great industrial and economic power but also a "culture of domination" over Latin America.[22] It is due to this domination that authentic culture and its philosophy remain impossible: "The dominated countries live with a view to the outside, depending in their existence upon the decisions of the dominant powers, that cover all fields of expression . . . This trait is not alien to the receptive and the imitative character of philosophy [. . .] that is typical of Hispanic America."[23] Thus, Salazar Bondy's analysis exposes not only a break in cultural development in the Americas, but also points to a geopolitical world context by virtue of which this happens. Indeed, one may say that Salazar Bondy's response to Zea's call and claim for a Latin American philosophy leads deep into the movement of history in its concrete eventuation and to the exposure of the situation of Latin American philosophy as inseparable from politics, economy, and issues of power. Thus, the Peruvian philosopher announces the very beginning of the arising of Latin American philosophy of liberation as well as the inception of decolonial thought as a central part of the first. These are the two last moments I want to introduce as background before moving on to some of the principal current trends and opening paths in Latin American philosophy.

3. Latin American Philosophy of Liberation

The first moments of Latin American philosophy of liberation occur as a series of encounters between mostly Argentine philosophers in 1968 and 1969. The group of young philosophers met in Santa Rosa de Calamuchita, in Cordoba, Argentina, and then, in 1970, during the First Semana Académica of the Universidad del Salvador, Buenos Aires, Argentina.[24] At these first meetings the theme was dedicated to "Argentine thought." However, the papers presented at the latter meeting would have a definitive impact at the Primer Congreso Argentino de Filosofía in March of 1971. In 1971, at the Second Semana Académica of the Universidad del Salvador, the topic becomes broader: "Latin-American liberation."[25] Some of the major figures involved in the arising of philosophy of liberation were: Osvaldo Ardiles, Alberto Parisi, Juan Carlos Escannone, Mario Casalla, Carlos Cullen, Rodolfo Kusch, Horacio Cerutti

Guldberg, H. Assmann, Arturo Roig, and Enrique Dussel.[26] Two of the figures that remain points of references for the later development of Latin American philosophy are Enrique Dussel, who publishes his *Filosofía de la Liberación* in 1977, and Hector Cerutti Guldberg who also in the same year publishes his *Filosofía de la liberación latinoamericana* (Philosophy of Latin American Liberation).[27]

Dussel's understanding of his thought as "anadialectical" may introduce the idea behind philosophy of liberation. *"Ana"* means from exteriority, *"dia"* unfolding, and *"logos"* figures the comprehension of a new articulate horizon.[28] As the opening quote of this section indicates, a philosophy of liberation aims to give articulation (*logos*) to a new horizon from the specific situation of the excluded and oppressed. Given the Latin American situation, as already exposed by Salazar Bondy, this would mean thinking not from the centers of power and in light of their hegemonies, but out of the periphery. This would mean thinking out of the very asymmetrical situation already indicated by Zea, but doing so not in terms of Westernizing history and values. The place from which thought may arise may be made more explicit by considering the way philosophy of liberation takes on the thought developed by the Argentine economist Raul Prebisch and by the American Jewish sociologist Immanuel Wallerstein, "world-system-theory."[29] This theory makes explicit how the world economy works in terms of predominant centers of economic, political, and sociological (hence also, cultural) powers, and their periphery. Prebisch uses this theory to show that underdevelopment in Latin America results from a world system that gathers wealth at the center while using peripheral nations and peoples to produce it. While this figures the domination of the center over the "third world," it also produces the dependency that is already clear to Zea when he speaks of Latin American philosophy always looking to Europe.[30] The Latin American situation then must be thought through a contrast between center-periphery, dominator-dominated, capital-work, totality-exteriority.[31]

Given this situation, Salazar Bondy, Dussel, and the philosophers of liberation set on a double task. On the one hand to expose and undo the domination and dependency at every level. On the other hand, liberation is ultimately a matter of finding new ways of articulating those oppressed and excluded lives and histories of the periphery.[32] Indeed, as Dussel dramatically states, for the philosophers of liberation philosophy only begins from the periphery: "The philosophy that has emerged from the periphery has always done so in response to a need to situate itself with regard to a center and a total exteriority (*ante el centro y ante la exterioridad total*)."[33] Even in its "Western" beginnings philosophy arises as a thinking over-against the violence of the center but from a periphery, from a total exteriority.[34] This last expression "total exteriority" becomes central here, since it indicates a radical situation distinct to those in the periphery: to speak of "total" here does not mean severing Latin American philosophy from the modern Western and westernizing traditions. The sense of a totality indicates a way of relocating the originary movement of philosophical thinking to a periphery that is always already at play in the unfolding of Western modernity and yet excluded and obscured. Thus nothing excluded by philosophy is to be rethought from the other, the oppressed, and excluded, the indigenous, African, Muslim, Jewish ways of thinking that are part of and yet undermined by Westernizing rationalism/capitalism. Moreover, this is a turn that is phenomenological and existential (although Dussel himself will turn to theory, pragmatism, and the logic of rationalism); thus the figure of the worker/slave, the woman, and the orphan, in their lived experiences come to populate and sustain Dussel's theory. Indeed, for Dussel the universal material principle behind philosophy of liberation is life.[35] This fundamental universal material principle Dussel finds also in his new reading of Marx.[36]

Before moving on to the way current philosophers have taken up this task and taken it beyond the philosophy of liberation, and in order to engage the sense of what follows the thinkers already discussed, I would like to deepen the sense of the turn to a thinking from the periphery as a thinking from radical exteriority by underlining the work on "decolonial" thought by the Peruvian sociologist Aníbal Quijano.

4. The Decolonial Turn

Aníbal Quijano's work focuses on what he calls "the coloniality of power and knowledge."[37] With this concept of "coloniality," he exposes the development of a racial system that underlies the world order today. This system develops as the dark side of modernity, as the conquest of the Americas becomes the site for the invention of a rational European self or the "I" (*ego cogito*) and its inferior "other," while the lives and ways of being of the conquered are appropriated and thereby discarded, excluded, and oppressed. Only what is of use for the conqueror is put to the service of the developing system of power and knowledge.[38] One finds two fundamental pillars in the development of this system: the idea for the first time in human history of one worldwide economic system that would subsume all previous ones (capitalism) and the division of humans into natural racial difference, a division that constitutes peoples' identities by identifying their "natural" capacities, functions, potential, and role in society and the world.[39] In his work Quijano identifies the very roots of the system of domination, dependency, and exclusion (of the periphery) we have been discussing. The division between European rational being and the other is produced through the normalization of the conquered (as well as of the conqueror into its position of rational being par excellence), as a result of which peoples of color, those who are descendants of Europeans, and the Europeans themselves each come to have a specific place/function in the newly constituted hierarchy. Each "racial" group is defined by a physical place in the city which in turn is determined by their work functions and by their wage assignments (servant, slave, etc.). From these economic allocations also appears a social placement (worker, manager, owner, ruler . . .), and the social placement situates peoples under their supposedly "natural" epistemic characteristics. Finally, as a result, Europeans, peoples of European descent, and those considered other races are identified in terms of a supposed mental capacity, as well as physical and affective inclinations. Thus, peoples of African descent, indigenous peoples, Asian people, and people of the Middle East become the other of reason and of the project of white and mestizo modernity in Latin America. Once the other of Western rationalism, European and later North American, has been constituted, the conquerors recognize themselves by contrast as the origin and inheritors of reason, as the messengers who bear on their shoulders the insight for a project of universal human freedom, equality, and justice (the enlightenment's ideals) led by a single path: calculative instrumental reasoning in the name of the development of capitalism and under the racial difference between the developed and underdeveloped peoples of the earth. This project is sustained by the development of a distinct idea of temporality.

The narrative of the superiority of Western experience and ways of being to its genitive other leads to a kind of egocentrism, a self-referential view of existence, and in turn this way of seeing experience situates all possibilities of knowledge under a single temporal line. It is the rationalism of the European/North American world that orients all sense of existence as the most developed form of humanity/knowledge. As a result, the Western "now" becomes the epitome and only potential horizon of possible human existence, leaving all other past and present lineages, histories, and ways of articulating existence in the past, and, at best, understanding them as ever lagging behind. As Quijano points out, "the Europeans generated a new temporal perspective of history and relocated colonized populations, along with their respective histories and cultures, in the past of a historical trajectory whose culmination was European."[40] Here appears a single linear historical account of existence, in which the now and the future belong to Western rationalism/capitalism, while all other ways of being become underdeveloped parts of realities that are partially valuable in terms of their application to the westernized way of seeing the present and projecting the only possible future for humanity. As Quijano indicates, this single way of seeing reality through history is clearly manifested by a series of epistemic prejudices that orient philosophy as well as the sciences and humanism today, namely, the binary logic between: Eastern-Western, primitive-civilized, magical/mythic-scientific, irrational-rational, traditional-modern ...[41] Inseparable and essential as an invisible undercurrent that sustains the development and perpetuation of the coloniality of power and knowledge in its various transmutations appears this hegemonic sense of temporality, a temporality that ultimately limits the very imaginaries and dispositions in light of which possible paths for being may be articulated. Having exposed such a system, one must wonder if and how there may be a second moment to liberatory thought, that is, as one must move from the critical exposure of the normative system to the positive articulation of those lineages, histories and ways of being that are excluded, oppressed, and erased by the coloniality of power and knowledge.

Quijano's work takes temporality in Latin American experience to be distinct from the Westernized sense of temporality just discussed:

> One of the many meanings that is beginning to form Latin American identity is that here, because of the 'metamorphosis' of our modernity, the relationship between history and time is completely different than in Europe or the United States. In Latin America what is a sequence in other countries is a simultaneity. It is also a sequence. But in the first place, it is a simultaneity.[42]

Temporality in Latin American experience and thought occurs as the simultaneous overlapping of ways of being that in westernized terms are supposed to be in the past. Quijano takes a classic example of this sense of reality from José Carlos Mariátegui, when he points out that in Latin America the various ways of economic exchange that supposedly lead to capitalism and are left behind in a dialectic movement (bartering, slavery, feudalism . . .) are all operative at the same time and serve to configure the economy in the South. In the same manner one may see that this simultaneity also constitutes Latin American experience, and its many distinct ways of constituting a sense of being. This is clearly captured in Quijano's further inquiry into simultaneous temporality, where he recognizes that it is not in the social sciences but in literature, in the form of a mythic articulation of reality, that figures like José Maria Arguedas and Gabriel García Márquez manage to expose the distinct Latin America's distinct senses of being.[43]

Quijano writes, "It is a question of a different history of time, and of a time different from history."[44] In general, what makes this temporality distinct is not a formal issue; simultaneous temporality may occur anywhere. The point is that this temporality is experience in an explicit and configurative manner at play in the very configuration of consciousness and underlying the senses of identities in Latin America. Thus, the claim is not ontological but dynamic and attentive to living practices and singularity, rather than to some essential structure that is "Latin America," or the proper way of being "Latin American." In fact as the rest of the discussion shows, this is a moment in which the "identity" question becomes plural, decentralized, and originary or monstrous beyond the idea of an origin: This occurs as existence in its distinct configurations begins to appear as a palimpsest of living histories, memories, lineages, practices, and unfathomable possibilities. But to say this is to go too fast. First of all, this indicates that if one turns to Latin American experience, one finds directionalities and dispositions that cannot be reduced to Westernized ways of delimiting existence. This conclusion leads to a series of radical openings for philosophy both in Latin America and worldwide. The different history of time points to the necessary rethinking of modernity in terms of the excluded experiences and thoughts that are constitutive and yet repressed and erased from Western modernity. Thus, one finds an opening for rethinking modernity, now as a pluriversal experience. Moreover, this is an eruptive moment in which distinct ways of thought appear at the center of figures of identity traditionally conceived as autonomous and essential, or at least historically necessary in the single line of westernizing development. Thus, the exposure of philosophy to what remains constitutive and yet beyond it figures a point of dissemination in which neither content nor form remain impermeable or to be taken as givens: philosophical thought is inceptively renewed (for example by Afro-Caribbean, Islamic, Asian, and Indigenous and popular thought, written as well as oral). At the same time, within Latin American philosophy, the issue of dependency comes undone as one must turn to the concrete lives, histories, lineages, and ways of articulating existence that have been excluded. Such a conclusion certainly reaches back to Zea, and Salazar Bondy, as well as Dussel, but it also takes one further. This is because now the issue is to engage in a thought that must listen to the configurations of senses of being that arise throughout Latin American life. This is not an appeal to life in the name of theory, but it may only be accomplished by speaking in light of and out of the distinct experiences of the excluded; that is, not in the name of giving voice and including what has been excluded into a rationalism and history already in play, but by engaging in the interruptions, encroachments, and fecund openings that occur as one turns to think with Latin American experiences in their superposition and simultaneity of meanings and traditions. Finally, in turning to such simultaneity of senses of beings, and in being found at the heart of modernity's dark side, Latin American philosophy may occur as a thinking in radical exteriority, that is as a thinking that from within and from beyond westernized modernity gives new wings to philosophy. In the next section I introduce some of the figures that I see engaging with this challenge today as they make openings for the thinkers of tomorrow.

Utopias vivas / *Living Utopias*

Speaking of Latin America's simultaneous temporality, Quijano concludes that, "With these resistances, a new utopia is beginning to be formed, a new historical meaning, a proposal of an alternative rationality."[45] Quijano is speaking here of simultaneous ideals that in their interaction or overlapping come to figure new openings for society. In the case of philosophy one may speak of new openings for thought, alternative rationalities, both in form and content. (One must turn to literature, to García Márquez, to find the articulation of Latin American temporality; in the same way, one must turn to indigenous belief in order to understand Latin American political and mythical thought, a foundation of politics today.) Indeed, the term "utopian" here refers us to the Peruvian historian Alberto Flores Galindo, who recognizes in his work the way simultaneous imaginary utopian configurations of the senses of existence operate in the very unfolding of Latin American history and consciousness.[46] The following figures engage the disseminating experience of simultaneous temporalities and narratives of existence, each in a distinct way born from remaining with the concrete situation in which the thought arises, in resistances, reconfigurations, interruptions, and overlapping densely populated by histories, lineages, memories, violence, loss, as well as by the originary force found within each situation as intensely and relentlessly engaged.

1. Deconstruction's Concrete Expression (Out of Latin American Experience): Santiago Castro-Gómez

One of the seminal works found in contemporary Latin American philosophy is Santiago Castro-Gómez's *Crítica de la Razón Latinoamericana* (*The Critique of Latin American Reason*) from 1996. In this work Castro-Gómez characterizes his thought in the following manner: "The critique of Latin American reason becomes a critique of the discourses that postulate a supposed 'Latin American reason.'"[47] To say it in another way from the same work, Latin American philosophy turns into a critique of its presuppositions about identity, what is Latin America's "own," the idea of authenticity, and the transcendental ascription of philosophy to the liberation of "a people." Castro-Gómez writes that this critical thought operates as "a deconstruction of the narratives, which on the basis of homogeneous identities, insist on representing Latin America as 'the absolute other of modernity."[48] Indeed in his work from 1996, he recovers deconstruction by re-appropriating in order to give his critique of previous Latin American philosophies of identity. In his work the Colombian philosopher contrasts "meta-narrative" and the beginning or opening for "other types of legitimate narratives."[49] If the meta-narratives no longer function in relation to Latin American experience, the other narratives operate at the small and singular level of living experience. Given the histories and lineages gathered under the term "Latin America," he turns to a hybrid thinking that engages the concrete and distinct overlapping of cultures and ways of being that constitute Latin American experience and the possible ground for philosophical thought. Castro-Gómez turns in his work to other major contemporary Latin American thinkers, such as Joaquín Brunner, Néstor García Canclini, and Nelly Richard. What holds these figures together for him is the fact that each engages life as a reality constituted by "fragmented identities, historical discontinuity, the heterogeneity of cultures, the consumption of symbolical goods, and the proliferation of divergent meanings."[50] Here the critique turns into affirmation of the hybrid and dynamic in Latin American experience, a way of thinking that, rather than closing Latin America in as the other of modernity, reinscribes philosophy and modernity into a hybrid global movement. "My aim is to show in what way the 'critical ontology of the present' has become fruitful for a philosophical reconceptualization of 'the Latin American' in the times of globalization."[51] Thus, Castro-Gómez turns from a critique of past philosophers to encounters in distinct experiences of Latin American reality in a hybrid global context. At the same time, one should also keep in mind that in turning to deconstruction, to a figure like Foucault, Santiago Castro-Gómez overcomes the divide between Western and Latin American thought, and through his thought shows that there is a basic point of encounter between deconstruction and Latin American thought: two figures of decolonial thought that bring forth spaces of distinctness and hybridity in which philosophy may be rethought.

2. Walter Mignolo and the "Colonial Difference"

If there is a major critical bridging between Castro-Gómez in his critique of previous Latin American philosophies of identity and in his appropriation of deconstruction in a Latin American and global context, the Argentine philosopher and critical theorist Walter Mignolo finds a way of bringing these two ways of articulating Latin American reality together. For Mignolo, modernity occurs as a time-space of "decolonial difference," in which many ways of articulating existence coexist, including those exposed by the philosophy of liberation as westernizing discourse from the center as well as the metanarratives Castro-Gómez finds behind the call for an authentic creative Latin American thought and a recognition of identity.

In the preface to *Local Histories/Global Designs*, Mignolo writes: "The colonial difference is the space where coloniality of power is enacted." In other words, Mignolo seeks a thinking that arises from within the dynamic space in which the coloniality of power and knowledge occurs. Following early thinkers such as Dussel, Mignolo engages knowledge in light of geopolitical spatiality. In situating conceptual knowledge in this way he makes evident the overlapping and borders that configure Latin American thought and experience simultaneously in a local as well as global situation—discourses and narrative that would otherwise seem totally separate realities appear now as alternatives at play in the configuration of meanings and knowledge.[52] In such a space of overlapping and often conflicting meanings one finds that concrete experience and practices along with discourses serve as distinct and disseminating elements in the configuration of limits and possibilities for knowledge. This occurs as epistemic spaces become pluralized in terms of central globalizing discourses as well as local distinct discourses that have been until now considered behind or inappropriate as forms of knowledge. Theses inappropriate or subjugated forms of knowledge constitute the dark side of modernity, and in opening thought to it, as does Quijano in fact, one finds alternatives to how the world and senses of the human may be articulated and in that articulation be given leeway for inclusiveness and pluriversal (rather than universal) dialogues. As the Argentine thinker explains: "The colonial difference creates the conditions for dialogic situations in which a fractured enunciation is enacted from the subaltern perspective as a response to the hegemonic discourse and perspective. Thus, border thinking is more than a hybrid enunciation. It is a fractured enunciation in dialogue with the territorial and hegemonic cosmology (e.g., ideology, perspective)."[53] This fracture is the result of the coloniality of knowledge, which now Mignolo recognizes in an assertive positive manner by exposing the presence and originary character of the narratives and practices once excluded and oppressed by a central hegemonic modern discourse. This affirmation of the excluded occurs, as Mignolo understands the colonial difference, as a locus of broken enunciation, that is, as a living site that affords thought the alternative of other discourses, practices, and ways of unfolding a dialogical space in the present and toward the future.[54]

The locus of broken enunciation is never freed from its history of colonialism (hence the "broken" element), but at the same time, with the understanding (standing under, withstanding, undergoing) of the colonial difference, lineages that sustain colonial economies and the resistance to them become active constitutive parts of a much more broad and rich modernity that now remains to be unfolded in disseminating and alternative movements. The colonial alternative is best found for Mignolo in a kind of thinking in between narratives and practices.[55] Mignolo understands thinking in the colonial difference as "border thinking" or "border gnosis."[56] As he explains, in his view, "At the end of the twentieth century, border thinking can no longer be controlled and it offers new critical horizons to the limitations of critical discourses within hegemonic cosmologies (such as Marxism, deconstruction, world system analysis, or post-modern theories)."[57] In other words, again from Mignolo, border thinking figures, "the moment in which the imaginary of the modern world system cracks."[58] In recognizing the alternative narratives and practices operative in modernity and beyond hegemonic determinations of modernity, one finds a decentering movement and the opening of the decolonial alternative; here the alternative is crucial, since with the decolonial option there is never a sense of a central necessary discourse that must orient all other articulations of existence and the human.[59]

3. A Living Decolonial Philosophy: Nelson Maldonado-Torres

In his work on "the coloniality of being" Nelson Maldonado-Torres explores a border thinking figured by the concrete histories and lives of the excluded. As the Caribbean philosopher explains, "coloniality of being would make primary reference to the lived experience of colonization and its impact on language [. . .]; the 'coloniality of being' responds to the need to thematize the question of the effect of coloniality in lived experience and not only in the mind."[60] Thus, the excluded, the oppressed, the experiences of the periphery, occur not as part of the general category of being, or of a periphery in general. Rather it is in engaging the distinct experiences that constitute the coloniality of knowledge (Quijano) that one finds a sub-ontological level of experience. "The sub-ontological difference relates to what Walter Mignolo has referred to as the colonial difference. But while his notion of colonial difference is primarily epistemic, sub-ontological difference refers primarily to being."[61] The sub-ontological emerges then as a new category that with its specific phenomena extends the traditional conceptions of being in philosophy, while in doing so giving articulation to what has been excluded by Westernizing traditional understandings of onto-logy. First one finds a negative critique: "The barbarian was a racialized self, and what characterized this racialization was a radical question or permanent suspicion regarding the humanity of the self in question."[62] Thus appear races that are in their very being always already held in question from the arising of the coloniality of power and knowledge and the

Western *ego cogito*. As a result one finds a traditional ontology grounded not in wonder but in a "racist/imperial Manichean misanthropic skepticism."[63] This being in question appears in its full pernicious character when one realizes that the races "in question" as to their humanity and value by virtue of the doubt are also made available for war. That is, the bodies of slaves and women, of children and the stranger, are by definition taken as available to suffer what for the *ego cogito* would be unthinkable and unacceptable: slavery, rape, degradation, silencing . . . [64] In this way a system of "natural" exploitation and degradation sets in,[65] in which the "lower races" and the weak are defined phenomenologically and essentially in a way that "'killability' and 'rapeability' are part of their essence understood in a phenomenological way."[66]

In his analysis and exposition of the coloniality of being, Maldonado-Torres reaches directly through and out of the experiences of suffering of the damned (the *damnés*) of the earth. As a result new voices are heard, voices that are not merely theoretical but that call into question philosophy out of living embodied experience. "Why go on is preceded only by one expression, which becomes the first instance that reveals the coloniality of Being, that is the cry. The cry, not a word, but an interjection, is a call of attention to one's own existence. The cry is the pretheoretical of the question . . . it is the cry that animates the birth of theory and critical thought. And the cry points to a peculiar existential condition: that of the condemned."[67] This cry exposes philosophy to a trans-ontological experience, the call before the theoretical, a call that in its sounding out gives to thought an almost lost ethical possibility. In a rethinking of the "the gift," a figure of the other and a thought to come developed by Derrida and Levinas, Maldonado-Torres explains that given their existential embodied experience, the lives of the *damnés* are reduced/exploited/destroyed systematically to the point that they are bereft of their capacity to give (*donner*). The result of the coloniality of power and knowledge is "a subject from whom the capacity to have and to give have been taken away from her or him. The coloniality of being is thus [. . .] gift-giving and generous reception as a fundamental character of being-in-the-world."[68] With the cry an ethical possibility returns from the lives of those traditionally handed over for death. "The ontological thus carries with it the marks of both positive achievement and betrayal of the trans-ontological relation, a relation of radical givenness and reception."[69] Thus, Maldonado-Torres's thought has a second moment beyond negative critique; it opens a path for thinking in terms of that radical givenness and reception possible and necessary for being human in an ethical sense. It is in this radical spacing that for the Caribbean philosopher a new way of thinking beyond the coloniality of power and knowledge may arise. "Without giving to an Other there would be no self just as without receiving from the

Other there would be no reason. In short, without a trans-ontological moment there would be no self, no reason, no being. The trans-ontological is the foundation of the ontological."[70] In a turn that interpolates the cry of the excluded into traditional Western philosophy one finds the task for the setting of new institutions and social-political spaces. "The decolonial turn marks the definitive entry of enslaved and colonized subjectivities into the realm of thought at before unknown institutional levels."[71]

4. María Lugone's Feminist Decolonial Thinking

In her seminal essay "Toward a Decolonial Feminism," Argentine feminist philosopher María Lugones begins an intimate reflection from the broken locus of enunciation; more specifically, she studies the internal resistance to the coloniality of power and knowledge that occurs in people's intimate and communal lives. As Lugones explains at the beginning of her essay, she wants to figure out "how to think about intimate, everyday resistant interactions to the colonial differences. When I think of intimacy here, I am not thinking exclusively or mainly about sexual relations. I am thinking of the interwoven social life among people who are not acting as representatives or officials."[72] Lugones begins her work by focusing on the very experience of the excluded, particularly in terms of the construction of a racialized gendered existence. As she shows, the gender difference between men and women is inseparable from the distinction between man and savage. Thus, men and women are the agents of civilization, while native males and females remain not human, as subject to exclusion, oppression, and elimination.[73] Under this coloniality of gender, men appear as agents and logical locus and therefore the compasses of existence, the "heterosexual, Christian, a being with mind and reason."[74] Women appear in an asymmetrical relation to them, as the ones who serve as "someone who reproduced race and capital through her sexual purity, passivity, and being homebound in the service of the white, European, bourgeois man."[75] But beyond this troubled gender difference remain the others, the indigenous and dark races under civilized men and women. "This distinction became a mark of the human and a mark of civilization. Only the civilized are men or women. Indigenous peoples of the Americas and enslaved Africans were classified as not human species—as animals, uncontrollably sexual and wild."[76] Lugones is clear in that this system or existential *taxis* is not without profound violence, as indigenous traditions and cultures in the Americas are destroyed, not for the sake of salvation but in order to develop the normative system of power.[77] But Lugones finds in this moment of oppression and exclusion also a counter movement. She points out that, "In our colonized, racially gendered, oppressed existences we are also other than what the hegemon makes us be."[78] Thus her work focuses on the resistance that occurs with every move to oppress and exclude. "I suggest we focus on the beings that resist the coloniality of gender from 'the colonial difference'."[79]

As Lugones understands it, resistance is a tension between being turned into normalized (racialized gender) subjects and an active subjectivity. As the philosopher explains, "Resistance is the tension between subjectification (the forming/informing of the subject) and active subjectivity, that minimal sense of agency required for the oppressing resisting relation being an active one, without the appeal to the maximal sense of agency of the modern subject."[80] From recognizing this double movement within the colonial difference, one sees a subjectivity and way of being appear otherwise than in terms of the rational subject defined by the established system of power, knowledge, and practices. Thus, Lugones goes beyond the negative analysis of the coloniality of power and knowledge as she turns to everyday life and the way these seemingly minimal experiences/intimate moments constitute spaces of fecund resistance and transformation.[81] "The production of the everyday within which one exists produces one's self as it provides particular, meaningful clothing, food, economies, and ecologies, gestures, rhythms, habitats, and senses of space and time. But it is important that these ways are not just different. They include affirmation of life over profit, communality over individualism, 'estar' over enterprise, being in relation rather than dichotomously split over in hierarchically and violently ordered fragments."[82] Here the struggle for liberation remains central but it occurs at the seemingly simplest and minutest levels of existence. Moreover, the issue is always one of self in community and not individual subjects. "The fractured locus includes the hierarchical dichotomy that constitutes the subjectification of the colonized. But the locus is fractured by the resistant presence, the active subjectivity of the colonized against the colonial invasion of self in community from the inhabitation of that self."[83] For this reason, Lugones concludes, "Communities rather than individuals enable the doing; one does [something] with someone else, not in individual isolation."[84] This primacy of community and life over individualism aims to recognize a logic of existence that does not merely react to a capitalist economy but offers decolonial alternatives, not in the ideal sense but as concrete ways of life that are recognized in their singular and present eventuation. "The logic they follow is not countenanced by the logic of power. The movement of these bodies and relations does not repeat itself. It does not become static and ossified. Everything and everyone continues to respond to power and responds much of the time resistingly—which is not to say in open defiance, though some of the time there is open defiance—in ways that may or may not be beneficial to capital, but that are not part of its logic."[85] With this introduction of the intimate and minute in peoples' lives as the site for decolonial struggle, Lugones is able to make concrete and show that liberatory practices are not only possible but already occurring in peoples' lives; lives that are understood well in terms not of being (*ser*) but of dwelling and remaining with experience in community and in lives concrete and fecund movements (*estar*).[86]

5. Temporalizing Cultural and Social Critique: Nelly Richard

Nelly Richard first emigrated from France in 1970 to become part of Salvador Allende's Popular Front (*unidad popular*), the first socialist government democratically elected in the world. Three years later, in 1973, a *coup d'état* violently interrupted the democratic process. In spite of the savage persecution of intellectuals perpetuated by the military regime, Richard chose to remain in Chile and became a significant figure in the movements of resistance and critique against the narrative and actions of the military government. Her work, which during the dictatorship was first circulated in mimeographed copies and passed among students by word-of-mouth, is now acknowledged as some of the most interesting and spurring thought in Latin American philosophy in the form of social critique. Richard's early writing focused on the work of artists of the resistance such as CADA (*Colectivo de Acción de Arte*, the artists' action collective). As was the case then, her present work still engages the fragmented character of history, consciousness, trauma, and the temporality experienced under such overlapping of experiences. By focusing on the return of discarded histories, memories, and repressed and excluded aspects of history and public consciousness, Richard has created a body of work that effectively unsettles and figures the undoing of official narratives focused on identity, nationalism, economic progress, and the erasure of trauma in the name of prosperity understood as progress.[87] Engaging critically and through emphasis on experience through works of art and public culture, fabricated meanings, values, and formulations of life ordered and appeased by the rhetoric of democracy and neoliberalism, Richard exposes the insufficiency of the official rhetoric and narratives. She does this in a manner that ultimately is able to recover or introduce in an inceptive originary way the discarded memories and histories of distinct and excluded peoples. Her work, like that of Garcia Canclini, and Maria Pia Lara[88] is interdisciplinary and hybrid in character, as she crosses the boundaries of the modern/colonial system. As she explains in one of her works: "Once one has discarded 'the amnesiac smoothing out of history, which is among other things, an offence to the present,' the work of memory may be reimagined."[89] Through this process, the normalized consciousness of peoples under the colonial difference and its single temporality find themselves exposed to other time-spaces in which other senses of existence may be found. The subject who experiences passively objectified recollection becomes a dynamic memory-subject "charged with the possibility of a creative engagement of the relations of past and present."[90] This occurs in a way analogous to what Benjamin introduces in his "Thesis on History": In this case the subject does not find him/her-self through an objective engagement of a chronological order with a fixed past and certain present. Rather one finds oneself exposed to "ties between past and present, in order to make explode that now-time (Benjamin's *Jetzeit*) retained and compressed within the historical particles of many discrepant recollections, previously silenced by an official memory."[91] Richard's work exemplifies a philosophy fed by a social and cultural critique that is no longer theoretical but that instead engages in the very transformation of the fabric of consciousness by engaging the radical temporality distinctive to Latin American experience. Richard's work, as is the case with Chilean philosopher Willie Thayre,[92] is rooted in Benjamin's work, social critique, and critical theory as well as in Marxism, yet her turn to the trauma and destruction of social consciousness in Chile makes her work unique and a seminal source for engaging Latin America's difficult social consciousness.

6. The Struggle for Latino/Latina Philosophies

In tracing Latin American thought from the philosophy of liberation through decolonial issues, I have wanted to set the background for introducing the contemporary side of Latin American philosophy that takes further the questions of liberation and decoloniality. At the same time, if in 1996 Flores Galindo already could state fittingly that dependence theory was no longer sufficient to understand Latin American experience, this is precisely why I have discussed here the four thinkers I have chosen out of many others. My aim has been to begin to show the possibilities that are opening today in Latin American philosophy. Such an opening would not be fittingly introduced, as limited as a presentation as this is, if one did not consider some of the figures that relate and overlap directly with Latin American philosophy while developing a decolonial border philosophy in the United States.

The main thrust in the United States occurs under the development of Latino/Latina philosophies, movements deeply engaged in questions of power, race, and gender. Among the many figures in the field appear Jorge E. Gracia, Eduardo Mendieta, and Linda Alcoff.[93] The three have produced works that are seminal to Latino/Latina/Latinx philosophy and identity, and they occupy an important space in the overlapping of Latino/Latina and Latin American philosophy: Walter Mignolo, Maria Lugones, and Nelson Maldona-Torres.[94]

Having noted this important difference, there are a number of other crucial issues that relate to thinking in radical exteriority and that remain beyond the scope of the present work. With the questioning of the coloniality of power and knowledge arises the task of the epistemic reconfigurations of philosophy and our expectations of what counts for rationality and knowledge in general. This work in terms of race and gender issues and Latino/Latina thought and experiences, has been developed by Linda Martín Alcoff, Ofelia Schutte,[95] Chela Sandoval, and Maria Lugones.[96] Issues of race and exclusion in the Americas in the Latin American, Caribbean, and Latino/Latina experiences also have been made powerfully clear by the work of the Caribbean Philosophical Association, Nelson Maldonado-Torres, Ramón Grosfoguel, and Lewis Gordon, among others. Dina V. Picotti from Argentina exposes in her work the history of racism concerning Afro cultures and their destruction in South America.[97]

Jardínes de caminos que se bifurcan / Gardens of Forking Paths

Memory brings one to encounter some of the limits of one's conceptual imagination. What we remember gathers one into a place from which futures become possible. Through our discussion, philosophizing, spurred by the philosophy of liberation, may now reach toward the gardens of Cordoba, the age of philosophy in Al'Andalu, toward Africa, Asia, and toward the Indigenous thought of old as well as today's living traditions and political movements. With this seemingly anachronistic step one ends up "philosophizing" beyond Western delimitations, while exposing modernity to its unbridled and distinct elements (rather than the comfortable genitive other of Western rationalist). Other beginnings, other modernities, and hence other possibilities become apparent, and with them choices unsuspected by the traditional discourses on modernity, the end of history, globalization under quantitative calculative rationalism, and the death of God (to name a few of the major themes that orient Western and Westernizing thought). A literal "*krisis*," a time-space, a series of decisive breaks that become apparent in engaging the concrete histories, lineages, and temporalities, and the living articulations of ways of being found in Latin America as the very ground for philosophizing. With Latin American philosophy one finds possibilities, interruptions, encroachments, and choices to be made. At the same time in the simultaneous overlapping one finds a hybrid spacing, a lightness and dispersing, a playfulness and irreverence in Latin American philosophy that, although often inseparable from violence, misery, and suffering, may very well serve to bring forth anew those questions, issues, and ways of understanding and articulating existence that have already been formulated, reformulated, and reaffirmed at their limit by negative critiques (in a reactive rather than originary movement.) In light of the all-too-brief introduction of figures and ways of articulating beings that I have touched on, in engaging the concrete situation in which philosophizing may or may not occur, in following these movements and dynamics opened through this engagement with Latin American thought, perhaps one may speak of "Americanizing" philosophy; rather than only of "philosophizing" the Americas, since the dynamics and forces, the inspired and fecund movements that may give form and content to thought may very well be found anew in light of the lives and times of the Americas, in one's exposure to America's utopian memories. This task of "Americanizing philosophy" is what already claims us and at the same time remains ahead for us.

Notes

1. I am alluding to the work on utopian thought in indigenous political movements in Peru, that outstanding work by Alberto Flores-Galindo, *In Search of an Inca: Identity and Utopia in the Andes*. eds. and trans. Carlos Aguirre, Charles F. Walker, and Willie Hiatt (New York: Cambridge University Press, 2010); Alberto Flores Galindo, *Buscando un Inca: Identidad y utopía en los Andes* (Mexico, D.F.: Grijalbo, 1993).

2. Enrique Dussel, *Philosophy of Liberation*, trans. Aquilina Martinez and Christine Morkovsky (Eugene, Oregon: Wipf & Stock, 1985), 173. From here on I refer to the work as PL.

3. Leopoldo Zea, "En torno a una filosofía americana." *Filosofía de lo americano*. (México: Nueva Imagen, 1984), 34–49 (primera publicación en *Cuadernos americanos* 3 (1942): 63–78), *En torno a una filosofía americana* (México: El Colegio de México, 1945); translated as "The Actual Function of Philosophy in Latin America," *Latin American Philosophy in the Twentieth Century* (New York: Prometheus Books, 1986), 223. The actual title of the essay is Concerning (en torno a) *Latin American Philosophy*. I will use CLAP to indicate the text. Unless indicated otherwise with the words "my translation," I will use the available English translation (LAP). LAP, 223.

4. "Lo que nos inclina hacia Europa y al mismo tiempo se resiste a ser Europa, es lo propio nuestro, lo americano." CLAP, 3. My translation.

5. Simón Bolívar, "Jamaica Letter: Reply of a South American to a Gentleman of this Island (Jamaica)," *Latin American Philosophy for the 21st Century*. eds. Jorge J. E. Gracia and Elizabeth Millán (New York: Prometheus Books, 2004), 63–66.

6. LAP, 360. Zea's position will broaden and become open in light of his encounter with the development of the Latin American philosophy of liberation in the late 1960s and 1970s, a movement I discuss below.

7. "El americano se siente europeo por su origen, pero inferior a éste por su circunstancia . . . Siente desprecio por lo americano y resentimiento contra lo europeo." CLAP, 4. My translation.

8. ". . . nuestra época se ha caracterizado por la ruptura entre las Ideas y la realidad. La cultura europea se encuentra en crisis debido a tal ruptura." ". . . our epoch is characterized by the rupture between ideas and reality. European culture is in crisis because of such rupture." Ibid, 8.

9. ". . . the themes we have called universal and the themes proper to the American circumstance are closely linked. In treating one we need to treat the other." CLAP, 365.

10. *Latin American Philosophy as Philosophy and Nothing More*, Leopoldo Zea, *La Filosofía Americana como Filosofía Sin Más* (Mexico: Siglo XXI Editores, 2010), 39. From here on indicated as FASM. All English texts are my translation.

11. CLAP, 364.

12. Leopoldo Zea, *Discurso desde la marginación y la barbarie* (España: Anthopos, 1988), 11.

13. Augusto Salazar Bondy, "The Meaning and Problem of Hispanic American Philosophic Thought," *Latin American Philosophy for the 21st Century*, eds. Jorge E. Gracia and Elizabeth Millan-Zaibert (New York: Prometheus Books, 2004); *¿Existe una filosofía de nuestra América?* (Mexico: Siglo XXI, 1988) (first published by Siglo XXI in 1968). An abridged version was published as *Sentido y problema del pensamiento filosófico hispanoamericano*, with an English translation in 1969. This was a lecture given by Salazar Bondy at the University of Kansas. *Sentido y problema del pensamiento filosófico hispanoamericano (with an English translation)* (Lawrence, Kansas: Center of Latin American Studies, 1969). Hereafter I refer to the essay as it appears in *Latin American Philosophy for the 21st Century* as M & P.

14. M & P, 387.

15. M & P, 390.

16. M & P, 390.

17. Under culture one must include the people's frustrations, alienation, mystification, and authenticity. M & P, 391–392.

18. M & P, 391.

19. M & P, 395–396.

20. M&P, 381.

21. This is a complicated issue I take up in Chapter Two of *Latin American Philosophy: from Identity to Radical Exteriority*. The difficulty comes from the fact that Salazar Bondy's thought ultimately proves to be neither historical/cultural nor analytical. In other words, his way of understanding philosophy is beyond the Nor American divide between analytical and continental schools.

22. M & P, 395.

23. M & P, 396.

24. *Revista de Filosofía Latinoamericana*, Liberación y Cultura, Tomo 1—enero-junio, 1975—N. 1 (San Antonio de Padua, Buenos Aires, Argentina: Ediciones Castañeda).

Revista de Filosofía Latinoamericana, Liberación y Cultura, Tomo 1—julio-diciembre, 1975—N. 2 (San Antonio de Padua, Buenos Aires, Argentina: Ediciones Castañeda); *Cultura Popular y filosofía de la liberación*, ed. Fernando García Cambeiro (Buenos Aires, Argentina: Colección Estudios Latinoamericanos, Vol. 15, 1975); *Hacia Una Filosofía de la Liberación Latinoamericana*, Enfoques Latinoamericanos número 2. (Buenos Aires: Bonum, 1973).

25. *El pensamiento filosófico latinoamericano, del Caribe y "latino" [1300–2000]* eds. Enrique Dussel, Eduardo Mendieta, Carmen Bohórquez (D.F., Mexico: Siglo XXI Editores, 2009), 400–401.

26. Leopoldo Zea and Arturo Ardao also contribute eventually to one of the editions of the first journals to introduce philosophy of liberation. *Revista de Filosofía Latinoamericana*, Liberación y Cultura, Tomo 1—julio-diciembre, 1975—N. 2 (San Antonio de Padua, Buenos Aires, Argentina: Ediciones Castañeda), 175–181.

27. Horacio Cerutti Guldberg *Filosofía de la liberación latinoamericana* 3rd Ed. (México: Fondo de Cultura Económica, 2006). From here on cited as FLL, followed by the page number. See also Ofelia Schutte, *Cultural Identity and Social Liberation in Latin American Thought* (Albany: SUNY Press, 1993), 175–181.

28. PL, 170.

29. On the Dussel–Wallerstein dialogue, see for example Dussel's "World-System and Transmodernity, *Nepantla: Views from the South* (Durham), Volume 3, Issue 2 (2002), 221–244. Also see Dussel's "Debate on the Geoculture of the World-System," in *The World We are Entering 2000–2050*, eds. I. Wallerstein and A. Clesse. (Netherland: Dutch University Press, 2002), 239–246.

30. Hence, as Dussel puts it, we encounter an economy of "domination and exploitation." Enrique Dussel, *Filosofía de la Cultura y la Liberacion* (México, D.F.: Universidad Autónoma de México, 2006), 29.

31. PL, 173.

32. Near the end of the book Dussel states that the praxis of philosophy of liberation occurs with a proto-philosophical discourse which moves as the political introduces the ethical, and the latter philosophy. PL, 173.

33. PL, 3.

34. PL, 3–4.

35. Life/experience is the fundamental moment, the universal material principle (*Ethics of Liberation*, 140), that guides and constitutes the end or goal for philosophy of liberation both in Dussel's *Ethics of Liberation* (Enrique Dussel, *Filosofía de la Liberación en la edad de la globalización y de la exclusión*, Quinta Edición (Madrid: Editorial Trotta, 2005), and in *Politics of Liberation*. *Politics* is divided into three volumes: The first part is titled *Politics of Liberation: A Critical World History* (Enrique Dussel, *Politics of Liberation: A Critical World History* trans. Cooper (SCM Press, 2010). Originally published as *Política de la liberación: historia mundial y crítica*. (Madrid: Trotta, 2007).) The second volume is titled *Política de la Liberación: arquitectónica* (Enrique Dussel, *Política de la liberación: arquitectónica* (Madrid: Trotta, 2009).)

36. Dussel finds the logic of exteriority by reading Marx anew in his works on Marx through the 1980s: In 1985, Enrique Dussel, *La producción teorética de Marx. Un comentario a los Grundrisse* (México: Siglo XXI, 1985); in 1988, Enrique Dussel, *Hacia un Marx Desconocido. Un comentario a los Manuscritos del 61–63* (México: Siglo XXI UAM-I, 1988); in 1990, Enrique Dussel, *El último Marx (1863–1882)* (México: Siglo XXI UAM-I, 1990). These works culminate in the 1994 work, Enrique Dussel, *Las metáforas teológicas de Marx* (Caracas, Venezuela: El perro y la rana, 2007). Several essays have also been published in English: "Marx's Economic Manuscripts of 1861–63 and the 'Concept' of Dependency, *Latin American Perspectives* 17, no. 2 (Spring 1990); "Post–Marxism, the Left, and Democracy," 62–101; "Four Drafts of Capital," *Rethinking Marxism* 13, no. 1, (Spring 2001); "Marx, Schelling, and Surplus Value," *International Studies in Philosophy* XXXVIII, no. 4 (2006).

37. Anibal Quijano, "Coloniality of Power, Eurocentrism, and Social Classification," *Coloniality at Large: Latin America and the Postcolonial Debate*, eds. Mabel Moraña, Enrique Dussel, and Carlos A. Jáuregui (London: Duke University Press, 2008), 181. I will refer to this article as CP followed by the page number.

38. As Quijano explains, "In effect, all of the experiences, histories, resources, and cultural products ended up in one global cultural order revolving around European or Western hegemony." CP, 189.

39. "[. . .] a supposedly different biological structure that placed some in a natural situation of inferiority to the others." CP, 182.

40. CP, 190. See also Walter Mignolo *The Darker Side of the Renaissance* (University of Michigan, 2003) and *The Idea of Latin America* (London: Blackwell, 2005).

41. CP, 190.

42. Aníbal Quijano, "Modernity, Identity and Utopia in Latin America," *Boundary 2* 20 no. 3 (1993). Reprinted in Aníbal Quijano, "Modernity, Identity, and Utopia in Latin America." *The Postmodern Debate in Latin America* (Durham: Duke University Press, 1995). Original version in Spanish: *Modernindad, Identidad y Utopia en América Latina* (Quito, Eucador: Editorial El Conejo, 1990); MIU, 149–150. The numeration and reference will be from the original English version of the article, here after referred to as MIU.

43. "For many of us this was the most genuine meaning of our search and confusion during the period of the agitated debates over dependency theory. It is also true, however, that we were able to get at the question of our identity only intermittently. It was no accident that is was not a sociologist but a novelist, Gabriel Garcia Márquez, who by good fortune or coincidence, found the road to this revelation, for which he won the Nobel Prize. For by what mode, if not the aesthetic-mythic, can an account be given of the simultaneity of all historical times in the same time? And what but mythic time can be this time of all times? Paradoxically, this strange way of revealing the untranslatable identity of a history proves to be a kind of rationality, which makes the specificity of that universe intelligible."(MIU, 150)

44. MIU, 150.

45. MIU, 152. Quijano's argument for a utopian Latin American modernity is not about a promise beyond the present. Utopian thought indicates for Quijano what

must be done now, in light of the present situation. In this sense utopian thinking arises from life and toward life.

46. Alberto Flores Galindo, *In Search of an Inca: Identity and Utopia in the Andes*. Eds. and Tr. Carlos Aguirre, Charles F. Walker, and Willie Hiatt (New York: Cambridge University Press, 2010). Alberto Flores Galindo, *Buscando un inca: Identidad y utopía en los Andes* (Mexico, D.F.: Grijalbo, 1993).

47. Santiago Castro-Gómez, *Crítica de la Razón Latinoamericana*. Segunda edición (Bogotá, Colombia: Pontifica Universidad Javeriana, 2011); CRL 12.

48. CRL, 12. What comes into question is the idea of the proper, the other, historically determined identity, the ideas held in different ways by Zea, Bondy, and Dussel.

49. CRL, 33.

50. Santiago Castro-Gómez, "La filosofía latinoamericana como ontología crítica del presente: Temas y motivos para una ´Critica del al razón latinoamericana." *Revista Dissens*, no. 4, http://www.javeriana.edu.co/pensar/Disens41.html.

This article is in Spanish, all English translations are mine. Henceforth cited as FLO followed by the paragraph number: FLO, 3.

51. FLO, 4.

52. Walter Mignolo, *Local Histories/Global Designs: Coloniality, Subaltern Knowledges, and Border Thinking* (Princeton: Princeton University Press, 2000), ix. Henceforth cited as LH followed by the page number.

53. LH, x.

54. In "Semiosis Colonial: la dialéctia entre representaciones fracturadas y hermenéuticas pluritópicas" ("Colonial Semiosis: the Dialectic Between Fractured Representations and Pluritopical Hermeneutics"), Mignolo explains that: "the fracture of the object or subject that attempts to understand and the implied fracture of the discourse and the position of the subject of understanding." Walter Mignolo. "Semiosis Colonial: la dialéctia entre representaciones fracturadas y hermenéuticas pluritópicas," *De la Hermenéutica y la Semiosis Colonial al Pensar Descolonial*. (Quito, Ecuador: Abya-yala, Universidad Politécnica Salesiana, 2011), 136. The article was first published in *Foro Hispánico: Revista hispánica de los países bajos* n.4 (1992): 11–27.

55. Mignolo writes: "'Nepantla' a word coined by Nahuatl speakers in the second half of the sixteenth century, is another example. 'To be or feel in between,' as the word could be translated into English, was possible in the mouth of an Amerindian, not of a Spaniard." LH, x.

56. LH, x.

57. LH, x.

58. LH, 23.

59. Mignolo associates the way this break occurs with Foucault's sense of the "insurrection of subjugated modes of knowledge," which the French philosopher introduces in his lectures at the College de France in 1976. Michel Foucault, *"Society Must Be Defended": Lectures at the College de France, 1975–1976* (U.S.: Picador, St. Martin's Press, 2003).

60. Nelson Maldonado-Torres, "On the Coloniality of Being: Contributions to the Development of a Concept," *Cultural Studies* 21, nos. 2–3 (March/May 2007): 242. Hereafter cited as CB followed by the page number.

61. CB, 254.
62. CB, 245.
63. CB, 245.
64. CB, 248.
65. CB, 253–254.
66. CB, 255.
67. CB, 256.
68. CB, 258.
69. CB, 258.
70. CB, 258.
71. CB, 262.
72. María Lugones, "Toward a Decolonial Feminism," *Hypatia* 25, no. 4 (Fall, 2010). From here on sited as TDF followed by the page number.
73. TDF, 743.
74. TDF, 743
75. TDF, 743.
76. TDF, 743
77. "Turning the colonized into human beings was not a colonial goal. . . . The civilizing transformation justified the colonization of memory, and thus of people's sense of self, of intersubjective relation, of their relation to the spirit world, to land, to the very fabric of their conception of reality, identity, and social, ecological, and cosmological organization. Thus, the Christian became the most powerful instrument in the mission of transformation, the normativity that connected gender and civilization became intent on erasing community, ecological practices, knowledge of planting, of weaving, of the cosmos, and not only on changing and controlling reproductive and sexual practices." TDF, 744–745.
78. TDF, 746.
79. TDF, 746.
80. TDF, 746.
81. ". . . instead of thinking of the global, capitalist, colonial system as in every way successful in its destruction of peoples, forms of knowledge, relations, and economies, I want to think of the process as continually resisted, and being resisted today." TDF, 748.
82. TDF, 754.
83. TDF, 749.
84. TDF, 754.
85. TDF, 754.
86. Here one may turn back to one of the founders of Latin American philosophy of liberation, a figure that has remained not acknowledge for the most part, with the exception of few philosophers, among them Mignolo, Lugones, and Günther

Rodolfo Kusch (1922–1979). Kusch develops his work through a profound engagement with indigenous and popular thinking in the Americas, and sets a path yet untapped in Latin American philosophy. Kusch is able to articulate the aesthetic experience of the being (*estar*) of indigenous peoples, and in light of this insight, he begins a path for the interpretation of the distinct experiences that underlie popular experience in Latin America, thereby offering a possible fulcrum for rethinking philosophy and its basic concepts out of a situated Latin American thought. See among other works: Günther Rodolfo Kusch, *Indigenous and Popular Thinking in América*, trans. María Lugones (Ann Arbor: Duke University Press, 2010). *La seducción de la barbarie-Análisis herético de un continente mestizo* ed. Fundación Ross, with Prólogos for the 1st and 2nd Ed. by F. J. Solero and C. Cullen, (Rosario, Argentina: 1983); *El pensamiento indígena y popular en América* 3rd Ed. (Buenos Aires: Hachette, 1977); *La negación en el pensamiento popular* (Buenos Aires: Cimarrón, 1975); *Geocultura del hombre americano*, (Buenos Aires: F. García Cambeiro, 1976); *Indios, porteños y dioses* 1st Ed. (Buenos Aires: Stilcograff, 1966; 2nd Ed., 1994); and, *Esbozo de una antropología filosófica americana* (S. Antonio de Padua: Castañeda, 1978). His complete works are collected in four volumes under the title *Obras Completas* (Rosario, Argentina: Editorial Fundación Ross, 1998–2003).

87. See Nelly Richard, *Márgenes e instituciones: Arte en Chile desde 1973* (Santiago, Chile, Metales Pesados, 2007.)

88. Maria Pia Lara, *Narrating Evil* (New York: Columbia University Press, 2007).

89. *The Insubordination of Signs: Political Change, Cultural Transformation, and Poetics of the Crisis*, trans. Alice A. Nelson and Silvia R. Tanderciarz (Durham: Duke University Press, 2004), 19. Hereafter cited as IS, followed by the page number.

90. IS.

91. IS.

92. Willie Thayre, *El Fragmento Repetido* (Santiago, Chile: Metales Pesados, 2007).

93. Eduardo Mendieta and Linda Martín Alcoff, *Identities: Race, Class, Gender, and Nationality* (Hong Kong: Blackwell, 2003); Ada María Isasi-Díaz and Eduardo Mendieta, *Decolonizing Epistemologies: Latina/o Theology and Philosophy* (New York: Fordahm University Press, 2011); Mariana Ortega and Linda Martín Alcoff, *Constructing the Nation: A Race and Nationalism Reader* (New York: SUNY Press, 2009); Jorge J. E. Gracia, *Hispanic/Latino Identity: A Philosophical Perspective* (Massachusetts: Wiley-Blackwell, 1999); Jorge J. E. Gracia, *Race or Ethnicity?: On Black and Latino Identity* (New York: Cornell University Press, 2007); Jorge J. E. Gracia, *Forging People: Race, Ethnicity, and nationality in Hispanic American and Latino/a Thought* (University of Notre Dame Press, 2011).

94. The first two are from the Southern Cone, the latter is a Puerto Rican/Caribbean philosopher; all of them reside in the United States and are deeply aware and engaged with Latino/Latina issues, while sustaining a continuous exchange between Latino/Latina philosophies and Latin American philosophies without neglecting their distinct characters.

95. Ofelia Schutte's work on feminist philosophy and Latin America has inspired new generations of philosophers who are presently contributing to such studies. See also Raúl Fornet-Betancourt, *Mujer y filosofía en el pensamiento iberoamericano: Momentos de una relación difícil* (Barcelona: Anthropos, 2009).

96. Linda Martín Alcoff, *Epistemology: The Big Questions* (Massachusetts: Blackwell, 1998); Linda Martín Alcoff, *Visible Identities: Race, Gender and the Self* (Oxford: Oxford University Press, 2006). Particularly in relation to decoloniality see, Chela Sandoval, *Methodology of the Oppressed* (Minneapolis: University of Minnesota Press, 2000); María Lugones, *Pilgrimages/Peregrinajes: Theorizing Coalition Against Multiple Oppressions* (Feminist Constructions) (New York: Roman and Littlefield, 2003).

97. Dina V. Picotti, *La Presencia Africana en Nuestra Identidad* (Buenos Aires: Ediciones Del Sol, 1998). On the issue of how to understand the contemporary situation see also Dina V. Picotti, "La Utopía Americana de la Propia Emergencia Civilizadora," in *Agora Philosophica. Revista Marplatense de Filosofía* X, nos. 19–20 (2009), www.agoraphilosophica.com.ar.

9
Afro-American Writing: Motifs of Place

James B. Haile, III

Without a geographical basis, the people, the makers of history, seem to be walking on air . . .

—JULES MICHELET, *HISTORY OF FRANCE*

[t]he lived fact that human being always necessarily involves human-being-in-place suggests that any emotional bond between people and environment requires a descriptive language arising from and accurately portraying this lived emplacement.

—DAVID SEAMON, "PLACE ATTACHMENT AND PHENOMENOLOGY: THE SYNERGISTIC DYNAMISM OF PLACE"

Introduction

With the first inaugural conference, "Shifting the Geography of Reason"[1] and the essay, "African American Philosophy, Race, and the Geography of Reason,"[2] Africana philosopher Lewis Gordon introduced the concept of "the geography of reason" to Africana Philosophy.[3] Few Africana philosophers, though, have fully accepted the challenge of such a concept—thinking "the geography of reason";[4] rather, they have been content that the concept plays a metaphorical or symbolic role—one that suggests the colonial acquisition of knowledge, and the power of naming that knowledge as the marking of the modern Western world.[5] There is, though, tremendous potential in thinking the fullness of "the geography of reason," specifically as it relates to Africana philosophy in terms of how we come to understand, research, and raise and answer questions concerning Africana people, their histories, and their identities.[6] This chapter, in accepting the challenge of the concept, will argue that thinking the fullness of "the geography of reason" quite simply means thinking the concept beyond metaphor or symbolism to the living-meaning of geography as spatial-location for philosophical enquiry. In other words, thinking "the geography of reason" in its fullness means thinking it terms of the concept of place.

The concept of place, then, not only helps us to raise and answer new questions concerning Africana peoples, but it also helps us to both locate new sources within Africana intellectual history, and to (re)read traditional Africana resources in a new light. For the purposes of this chapter, I will be examining the resource of "Afro"-American writing and literature through the lens of place to offer new accounts of texts and authorial intent of a people to think themselves, their living conditions, and their own history (as well as that of world history). The works of writers Richard Wright, George Lamming, and Dorothy E. Mosby help us situate ourselves upon this new ground: the living-meaning of the geographic spatial-location of the "Americas," situating their work (and themselves as authors) as Afro-"American" writers and literatures of place.[7]

The chapter is divided into four parts. The first part will discuss the significance of place in Africana philosophy. The second part will discuss the philosophy of place, the significance of place for [doing] philosophy, and irony of philosophy of place for/in "Afro"-American writing and literature. The third part will be a discussion of spatial imagination within Afro-"American" writing and literature. And, the fourth and final part will be a discussion of the phenomenal experience of geographical space within "Afro"-American writing and literature.

The Significance of Place in Africana Philosophy

There are radical possibilities in reading Africana literature, in general, through a robust concept of place—in what environment-behavior researcher David Seamon terms "place attachment"[8]—and for philosophizing that radicality as its own methodological foundation. Why philosophy of place? What can it offer to contemporary Africana philosophy, especially to contemporary Africana existentialism and phenomenology? What can it capture that has, so far, been under-mined and under-excavated from the tradition of Africana philosophical expression? And, what is revealed about/in "Afro"-American literature and writing?

For Gordon, the central concern of Africana philosophy is the question concerning experience. Not only the question, what is the experience of Africana persons or, what is the experience of being an Africana person in a modern, Western, anti-black world? But, and more fundamentally, how do we come to constitute the concept of "experience" to consciousness itself, such that "experience" can be understood within an Africana context, applied to Africana persons, and understood to be operating within Africana literary, philosophical, or political texts and contexts?[9] This question is remarked upon by Paget Henry in the opening of his essay, "Africana Phenomenology: Its Philosophical Implications" where he writes,

> Given some of the exclusive claims on reason that the West has made, it has been difficult to see clearly the rationality of non-Western peoples. This eclipsing of the rationality of non-Western peoples, particularly people of African descent, has made problematic the status of theory in fields such as Africana Studies.[10]

In other words, within the modern Western world that has denied "reason" or the capacity to interpret the social, political, and economic worlds—that is, to create, determine, and contribute to History—to "persons of African descent," theorizing from an Africana position is increasingly necessary, but also increasingly difficult. What is meant by "reason" where "reason" has been denied? How do we assess "reason" when it is ontologically set as the limit of Africana persons (and other persons of color)? The challenge of Africana philosophy, then, is not only to theorize about Africana persons and from Africana persons, but to create the conditions for the possibility of theory itself—to create what we mean by "theory." If Africana philosophy does not, what happens then is, "Colored folks offer experience that white folks interpret."[11] Persons of color are reduced to having experiences, but not theorizing about those experiences. Gordon writes,

> [i]t is very important what both the one who experiences and those who interpret the experience draw on for the development of their interpretation. If the one with experience plays no role in the interpretation of the experience, then a form of epistemic colonization emerges, as we have seen, where there is dependence on the interpretations from another's or others' experience as the condition of interpreting experience. The more concrete manifestation of this relationship is familiar to many black intellectuals . . . The task, then, is to avoid reductionistic experience—that is, to avoid reducing people of color only to their experiences and, worse, to the epitome of experience itself.[12]

What happens, then, when Africana persons are reduced to their experiences—or reduced to only experience—and Africana philosophy does not provide a robust methodological praxis for thinking the myriad of Africana experiences? What Gordon and Henry argue for is a methodological structure for thinking these Africana experiences, with the central concern for the meaning of living in the world—the meaning of "experience" or the human life-world. Yet, what is often overlooked in formulating an answer to this question and in addressing methodological praxis is the role that place plays as the foundation for who peoples or communities are: how they understand their world and locate themselves within the temporal-spatial reality of past, present, and future. "The idea of philosophical topology, or 'topography,'" Martin Heidegger writes, "takes the idea of place or topos as the focus for the understanding of the human, the understanding of world, and the understanding of the philosophical."[13] This is the idea we will explore in this chapter.

In what remains of this section, I will need to say something more about what is meant by the "Americas" and those inhabitants of "America"; and, what, specifically, is meant by "Afro"-American writing and literature.

Within the context of discussing "Afro"-American writing and literature, it must be specifically noted as to what exactly is meant by the "Americas" and who exactly is being counted as the inhabitants of the "Americas." By the "Americas" I mean the annunciation of a metaphorical, symbolic, spatio-temporal-geographic space-place in which and through which the inhabitants experienced themselves transformed into new types of men: the European turned "American" explorer; the African turned enslaved; and the indigenous turned native. In her essay, "1492: A New World View"[14] theorist Sylvia Wynter argues that Columbus' voyage represented this transformation.[15] She writes,

> This formulation is the basis of my proposed view of 1492. This view is that both the undoubted 'glorious achievement' of the process that led up to Columbus' realization of his long dreamed-of voyage and the equally undoubted horrors that were inflicted by the Spanish conquistadores and settlers upon the indigenous peoples of the Caribbean and the Americas, as well as upon the African-descended Middle Passages and substitute slave labor force, are to be seen as the effects of Western Europe's epochal shift.[16]

The "New World," then, was not just the "discovery"—that is, in the phenomenological sense of "revealing" or "uncovering"—of a new land mass, but a "discovery" of a new logic to understand the world at large, the self, and social order. That is, with the "discovery" of the "New World" there was also the "discovery" of "new men." Without going into too much detail of her argument, what is important to note is that for Wynter, this experience gave rise to a new logic-order, one that was not dependent on the metaphysical transcendence of the church (and the church order of the Old World), but was led by reason and the transcendent absolutism of the state and law itself.[17] The importance of this shift, for our sake, is that it set forth a new definition of "humanity," new sets of relations between "humanity" and the "land"—both in the sense of space and of place—and a new social order.[18]

This new identity was not merely that of "Europe, Part Two," but a new identity rising out of the new landscape (geographic terrain) and a new sense of place within the world-logical-order, culminated in the break from Europe and the Old World logic-order—for examples, in the Declaration of Independence in 1776 and with the Monroe Doctrine of 1823, each instituting an entire New World logic-order.[19] This New World logic-order was not only a foreign policy, but also a place-based identity policy wherein the Western Hemisphere became both a spatial-geographic terrain and the "place" (the "New World") for/of this "New Man" (in contradistinction to Europe and the Old World).[20] This "New World" and new "American" identity, though, came to be for those from the African continent—the new Diaspora—not so much an exploratory experience or the formation of sovereign jurisdiction, but an experience of enslavement. The question of the meaning of the "New World" remains: Where do Africans, considered to be proto or sub-human, fit within the modernizing world?[21] The question of place for those enslaved Africans, though, has not been as pronounced as the question of the problem of their existence.[22] Yet, the question of place has remained central to "Afro"-American experiences and self-recognition. As Katherine McKittrick notes in her text, *Demonic Grounds: Black Women and the Cartographies of Struggle*,

> The relationship between black populations and geography—and here I am referring to geography as space, place, and location in their physical materiality and imaginative configurations—allows us to engage with a narrative that locates black histories and black subjects in order to make visible social lives which are often displaced, rendered ungeographic. Black histories where, for example, progress, voyaging, and rationality meet violence and enslavement are worked out in geography, in space and place, in the physical world.[23]

I take up the fundamental question posed within place literature concerning the "Afro" experience, a question inherent in McKittrick's text, and specifically stated by Michael Keith and Steve Pile in their text, *Place and Politics of Identity*: "can concrete geographical and historical circumstances ... be understood as expressions of abstract social relations?"[24] That is, can we think of geography as the abstract framework—or logic-order—that organizes our understanding of and behavior within certain sets of relations? I ask this question, though with a twist: rather than merely looking through the lens of problems—that is, in terms of the "politics" of oppression and resistance—surrounding "Afro" peoples within the Americas to answer this question, this chapter seeks to answer this question by looking to place as productive of "abstract social relations" (logic-order), rather than as a site of resistance or contestation. Looking through the lens of "production" we are able to address place in relation to the inner lives of people, such that when one thinks of the "Americas" as it is being used herein, one must think not only of this history of "New World" exploration and expansionism—the break from Europe terrestrially and theoretically; and, the rise of the specific domain of the "Western Hemisphere" as the "place" of/for this new Western man—or the experiences of those enslaved Africans and their descendants within this New World exploration/expansionism, but also as the creation of a new "American" "Afro" identity, one that is created as "Afro" peoples navigate and produce their own sense of "place" within this new Western hemispheric logic-order.[25]

It is here, within the latter question of the meaning of "place" for "Afro" peoples within the "Americas" (New World logic-order) that I take to be Gordon's central focus in the "geography of reason." With the development of Gordon's concept in the direction of geo-spatial reasoning we are able to (re)think, that is, (re)frame our understanding of the "Americas," specifically from "Afro" perspective(s).[26] While this chapter is not exhaustive in terms of the ways in which the "Afro" experiences are shaped by and shape particular understandings of the "Americas" as a place—in the broadest of terms—what is offered here is a methodology to (re)frame our discussion/analysis of the "Americas," and of "Afro"-American existential and phenomenological realities—within the conceptual and living experiences of the matrices of the "New World"—that can, hopefully, open up new ways of reading traditional texts and offer new texts to the canon of "American" and "Afro"-American philosophies.[27]

Motifs of Place

Place is generally understood by philosophers, human geographers, and social scientists in the following way. In his "Place," human geographer Tim Cresswell writes,

> Place is a meaningful site that combines location, locale, and sense of place. Location refers to an absolute point in space with a specific set of coordinates and measurable distances from other locations. Location refers to the "where" of place. Locale refers to the material setting for social relations—the way a place looks. Locale includes the buildings,

streets, parks, and other visible and tangible aspects of a place. Sense of place refers to the more nebulous meanings associated with a place: the feelings and emotions a place evokes.[28]

What is important to note is the relationship Cresswell sets up between location, locale, and a sense of place. For Cresswell, location and locale—aspects of a geographical or spatial location—are, themselves, only understandable in/by virtue of our feelings and emotions in relation to a particular space. That is to say, our feelings and emotions order and organize a particular space such that it can be experienced as a place. It is our attachment that allows for an experience: a location as a set of spatial relations—near or far, next to or besides, etc.; and, a locale as the setting of/for the spatial relations—a park, for example, is the tangible, material proof of our ordering and organizing of a particular space, for without our organizing there is but a "forest" or "wilderness"—disorganized, bare space.[29] Creswell further clarifies this point when he writes,

> Consider the location 33.3251 44.4221. This location in abstract space marks the city of Baghdad in Iraq. While its location tells us where Baghdad is and enables us to locate it on a map or program it into a Global Positioning System, it does not really tell us much else. Baghdad is also a locale. It has mosques, homes, markets, barricades, and the Green Zone. It has a material structure that, in part, makes it a place . . .
> . . . The idea of meaning has been central to notions of place since the 1970s in Human Geography. Location became place when it became meaningful. Meaning marks the most obvious difference between 33.3251 44.4221 (a mere location) and "Baghdad"—the place that occupies that location. Cruise missiles can be loaded with information like 33.3251 44.4221 but not with "Baghdad" and all the meanings that that place implies.[30]

One can read Cresswell to be arguing that it is through our emotional attachment that we make possible and disclose our "experience" of a place. That is to say, our experience of place is total: it is a location and a locale revealed through the meanings and feelings associated with that particular space. It is in this way that our feelings and emotions transform a particular geographical space into a place. Place, then, is the phenomenal result/product of existential (or meaningful) relatedness.

David Seamon further clarifies place as phenomenal product, focusing on the intentional structure of subjects actively engaged in a particular geographical space. For him, it is the intentionality or intentional state of actors that draw spaces together into active sets of relations, and produces out of those relations, places. He writes,

> Phenomenologically, place can be defined as any environmental locus in and through which individual or group actions, experiences, intentions, and meanings are drawn together spatially. In research relevant to place attachment, a place can range in scale from a furnishing or some other environmental feature to a room, building, neighborhood, city, landscape, or region. Phenomenologically, place is not the physical environment separate from people associated with it but, rather, the indivisible, normally unnoticed phenomenon of person-or-people-experiencing place. This phenomenon is typically multivalent, complex, and dynamic.[31]

Seamon's addition of the intentional structure of place further emphasizes the relational aspect of place. Place sets forth fundamental relations: 1) it sets the relation of space to itself (as in location); 2) it sets things within space in relation to one another (locale); 3) it sets us in relation to one another in space (social organization, or a sense of place); 4) it sets us in relation to geographic space and to sets of relations within space (us in relation to geographical space through the intentional structure of its organization); and, 5) it sets us in relation to ourselves (we are the disclosive possibility of 1–4). Place, then, reveals us as the foundation of place and sets place out as the phenomenal reality of ourselves. That is, place is the organization of space and that through which we come to experience space as organized. As such, place, as a phenomenal relatedness (of 1–5) speaks to and beyond itself: As fundamental relationality it suggests a further concern. If understood as 1–5, place is, then, a phenomenal grounding and the product of phenomenal grounding—and question—"what does it mean to organize and put things within active sets of relation as a grounding that is also an essential grounding?"

These phenomenological (disclosive) aspects of place are critical, according to Jeff Malpas, because it is through these aspects that we, as human beings, begin to think and to philosophize. Malpas writes, "[T]he attempt to think place, and to think in accord with place, is at the heart of philosophy as such."[32] What does Malpas mean that "to think place" is at the "heart of philosophy"? Part of what he means is disclosed when he writes of the relation of place to thinking the following:

> To ask after the origin of thinking is itself already to place oneself within the ambit of the topological . . . Here, the connection of 'origin'" with 'ground,' and both of these with place, also becomes

apparent. The question of origin is thus not a question about the temporal or historical starting point for thinking, nor is it a question about the cause of thinking . . . To ask after origin in a genuinely philosophical sense . . . is to ask after that on and in which thinking finds its footing and support, from which it takes its orientation and direction.[33]

According to Malpas, our very presence as humans organizes the spaces surrounding us into meaningful (and meaning-filled) place; it is only after their organization that we, then, begin to think or become self-consciously aware of place itself. Place provides an orientation, a direction from which to begin thinking itself. This is what was hinted at in the disclosive nature of place as an "essential grounding": that which both grounds (location and locale) and is grounded in its grounding (of location and locale). For Malpas, then, place is not intentionally created, as Seamon suggests; place allows or creates the conditions of/for intentionality. What concept, then, of place is Malpas working from? He writes,

It is only appropriate that the exploration of the place of thinking should begin where thinking itself begins and so take as its starting point the placed origins of thinking. Here origin is itself to be understood not as some temporal starting point, but rather as that out of which something comes to appearance. Origin is thus already topological—to begin is to begin in and from out of place.[34]

Malpas' notion of place can be understood in the idea of topos or the topological. Topos refers to the very human activity of setting-forth; it is that which creates limits and draws boundaries. This activity, for Malpas, is rudimentary in that it does not provide content, per se, but allows for the possibility of a context in which content can be present. Again, revisiting our park example from earlier: "park" is the organization of a particular space so that certain things are set in relation to one another—trees to other trees, trees to a stream, etc. This setting of relations is due to human activity—it is us who create the sense of relation between the trees and the trees to a stream; it us who carve a path between the trees and to the stream, etc. But, before the "park" is established, there is only the unknown—that about which nothing is known. What is more, it is that about nothing can be known, for its boundaries have not been established, and it is a broad continuum of possibility. In the drawing of boundaries and limits, a place is established. As such, then, "park" is both an issue of knowledge (and the possibility of knowledge) and an existential phenomenal reality. In addressing the origin of our knowledge and experience of a "park," we engage in topological thinking, for we are not only asking what a "park" is—that is, how it has been organized—but we are also asking after the source of the organization: we are asking after that which can only be known after it has already been established. "What is a park?" can only be answered after it already is a "park." Our relation, then, to place is both as the constructors and experiencers.

Earlier, we discussed Lewis Gordon's concept of "experience" and its pivotal role in Africana philosophy. "[I]t is very important" Gordon writes, "what both the one who experiences and those who interpret the experience draw on for the development of their interpretation." Here, Gordon is referring to what we are calling the topological—that which is itself the limit, a limit that can be drawn upon in the development of an interpretation of the world. What is the context in which the content of experience can be produced? Place, then, for Gordon, as for Cresswell and Malpas, comes to be the existential reality of people and what is produced phenomenally (by those people). A discussion of place, then, is a discussion of the context of that place as well as the content. It is, essentially, a topological concern. Seamon suggests this in his usage of "life-world" to describe the context/content of experienced reality when he writes,

> As a phenomenological concept, place is powerful both theoretically and practically because it offers a way to articulate more precisely the experienced wholeness of people-in-world, which phenomenologists call the lifeworld—the everyday world of taken-for-grantedness normally unnoticed and thus concealed as a phenomenon. As a phenomenon integral to human life, place holds lifeworlds together spatially and environmentally, marking out centers of human meaning, intention, and comportment that, in turn, help make place.[35]

The significance, then, of Gordon's introduction of "the geography of reason" and "shifting the geography of reason" cannot be understated. Its radical potential is inherent to its suggestion that reason itself is a living engagement of people with their environment; but, what is more, that "reason" as a contested term, and as the foundation for philosophical investigation, emerges from the origin of place.[36] Gordon's concept, then, suggests: 1) philosophy itself is a spatial product—or the product of an existential phenomenal reality; and, 2) understanding the "reason" or philosophy of a people necessitates understanding their relation to the life-world, and to their place reality. What this means for Africana philosophy is that "reason" itself is shifted from an abstract universal into a place-based product.

What, then, is an Africana philosophy of place? And, how is an Africana philosophy of place related to Africana literature, generally, and to Afro-" "American" writing specifically?

Place has played and continues to play a significant formative role in "Afro"-American writing/literature. The concept of "place" within the "Afro" context expands the existential and phenomenological concepts of Cresswell, Seamon, and Malpas to encompass a broad range of human reality from encounters between nature and technology, rural and urban, mobility/movement and fixity/permanence and contingency.[37] It is in this way that "Afro"-American writing/literature encompasses many of the elements discussed in the previous section, but offers new ways of understanding traditional philosophical treatments of place.[38] While in philosophical treatments the concept of place is often the juxtaposition of these elements in the experience of a place, within "Afro"-American writing and literature there is a simultaneity of presence within this range—for example, in much "Afro"-American writing and literature, the presence of elements of the rural and elements of the urban are not juxtaposed, but are co-extensive in the urban problems present in a rural setting, creating an rural-urbanity.[39] "Afro"-American writing and literature, though, is not centrally concerned with demonstrating the ways in which these aspects are actually complementary, the ways in which the contradictions are not real contradictions, but part of a larger synthesized whole, or the ways in which tensions are to be fixed or mitigated through direct action. "Afro"-American writing and literature allows the presence of conflict within these elements, and allows it as a condition for the possibility of experiencing particular places. As such, place is often read as "conflict," yet operates as a source of remembrance—if not nostalgia.

In the presence of these conflicting elements, though, there is often one constancy: the presence of the concept of "land." "Land" appears as part of the specific grounding/founding of the world and of the self within "Afro"-American writing and literature. This concept is not exclusively that of material space; the concept also engages an "imaginative landscape" (one that can be and is often disconnected from any direct experience with material space), which produces notions of "home," "belonging," and "dwelling."[40] As the experience of material reality and/or that of an imaginative landscape, "Afro"-American writing and literature has a certain feel of urgency: for in the discussions of the experience of place in remembrance, material presence, or imagination are also discussions of separation, abandonment, alienation, and dislocation of an "old" or "original" place—specifically, through internal displacement, statelessness, colonial appropriation of space, all problems considered to be symptoms of the shifting realities of consumerism and capital exploration/expansion (gentrification, etc.).[41] Our modern moment situates "place" as the critical praxis for understanding the human person.[42] "Afro"-American writing and literature, then, reflects this complex notion of place and the need for place-thinking.

Heretofore Africana phenomenology has, to a large extent, been the historization of the flesh. That is, Africana phenomenology has almost exclusively focused on embodiment—locating the concept of "place" in the body; blackness within the historical embodiment of "black" persons trapped in and reduced to their bodies—to the exclusion of other more expansive understandings or aspects of our living engagements.[43] Gordon's introduction of the concept of "the geography of reason" and the notion of "shifting the geography of reason" means expansion beyond the metaphorical or analytical to an engagement with place as the beginning of thinking of the Africana itself. This is particularly important for Africana philosophy for it reveals the philosophic positions of Western Europe and the Americas as not merely "ideas" or "the history of ideas," but as the "hermeneutical situatedness" of ideas themselves. It is a reminder that "[p]hilosophy begins, then, in that same place that is the place for the emergence of world."[44]

Gordon's "geography of reason," though, is ironic for and within Africana philosophy, as "reason" itself, as noted earlier, plays an ironic role in Africana philosophy. As such, "place" in Africana philosophy is ironic, especially within "Afro"-American writing and literature.[45] We recognize that within the European and American Western intellectual traditions, the role of place is formative not to what the world is, but to what the world is not. Specifically, place has been a way of marking what belongs to the "new values" of civilization and which values (and persons who hold such values) do not belong or are the outliers of the civilized world.[46] What is ironic, here, then is to forward a theory of "place" from those discounted from having "place" at all. It is in this way that the chapter will be contextualized within the Western episteme and ontos; it will be from within the perspective of the irony of the task itself, yet the results of the task—Africana senses and expressions of place—are not themselves ironic or contextualized within a European episteme and ontos, but within a constituted multiplicity of Africana ethos.[47] Such an irony, though, is the challenge of "place" within the Africana reality.[48]

Place in the Africana context, then, is a taking-back, a self-naming, a proclamation of disinvestment of the "land" from the colonial, dislocated, or alienated context. As Europeans ironically created the context to think the "Americas" as a place distinct from the mother continent, so, too, in the works of Richard Wright, George Lamming, and Dorothy E. Mosby, do we get the emergence of a new settlement of resistance and existence, bringing in and settling together the North, South, Central, and Caribbean "American" experiences in the process of land-making, land-masking.[49]

The "Americas" in this context, can be understood as a burgeoning newness directly facing an old past which haunts and taunts, and reminds one that where one is supposed to come from is the source of one's own alienation: an alienation of roots, of origin. It also reminds that place can never be given, nor imposed, but is the accomplishment of consciousness becoming self-conscious of its own existence and its own identity; it is a reminder of the possibilities that place offers to re-new itself. Nowhere is this more pronounced than in Afro-"American" writing and literature: whether it concerns a village, an urban city, natural landscapes, geographies, imaginary spaces, or futurist valleys.[50]

Historical, Platial Imagination

George Lamming, in his collection of critical essays, *The Pleasures of Exile*, describes himself and his project as writer—that is, as an examiner of his experiences—topologically. He writes in an essay entitled, "The Occasion for Speaking," the following:

> In order to take you inside of what I know, I shall have to draw on what an older man would justly call his *reminiscences*. I would like to suggest the *psychological origins* of such a migration so that we may be able to reflect on how his journey towards each writer's expectation may have been responsible for his development both as a man and as a writer.[51]

And, in another essay entitled, "A Way of Seeing," he writes the following:

> I shall have failed to communicate my meaning if I leave the impression that I am constructing theories. I haven't got the kind of equipment which is required of men who engineer ideas; but I do believe that what a person thinks is very much determined by the way that person sees. This book [*The Pleasures of Exile*] is really no more than a report on one man's way of seeing, using certain facts of experience as evidence and a guide.[52]

Lamming, in these two essays, echoes what both Lewis Gordon—in his notion of "experience"—and Paget Henry—in his concern for theory in Africana studies—claim: Africana persons need to (re)claim the meanings of their own experiences through the conscious activity of writing those experiences, even in the face of all the problems and ironies therein. For Lamming, as for Gordon and Henry, this reporting of "one man's way of seeing" is itself a sort of theory, yet not the "abstract" sort in which ideas precondition the meaning of experience. Rather, what Lamming (Gordon and Henry) is referencing, is a sort of meta-theory set upon the phenomenology of embodied experience-consciousness. In this way Lamming's "way of seeing," one that is "responsible for his development both as a man and as a writer" is not going to be that generation of theories by those who "engineer ideas." To engineer an idea implies an artifice to be created—in the sense of manufacturing. What Lamming, Gordon, and Henry are suggesting, though, is a phenomenological disclosure of one's own world—that is, the activity of the drawing of boundaries—through a telling of their own experiences.

This is an important note for Africana philosophy—and for "Afro"-American writing and literature—for the generation of ideas in ways that are similar to the ways in which "place" itself is generated: both in simultaneity and contradistinction; both with contradiction as with resolution. For Lamming, the "facts of experience," then, serve as both evidence and a guide—that which grounds is also grounded. It is this creative tension of phenomenal experience-consciousness that generates Lamming's notion of "home" as well as that of the "exile." The questions left to ask of Lamming (et al.) are, "What is reported, then, if it is not theory, nor the generation of theory?" "What does Lamming mean by reporting a way of seeing using 'certain facts of experience as evidence and a guide?'" It is here that the topological aspects of Lamming's word choice are significant and telling as to what his writing concerns.

In his essay, "The Negro Writer and His World," Lamming offers the framework for his discussion in *The Pleasures of Exile*—"the psychological origins" of "the way a person sees"—within that of writing, within language itself.[53] Lamming notes that,

> The Negro is a men [sic] whom the Other regards as a Negro; and the dichotomy, the split, as it were, which may exist at the very centre [sic] of this consciousness, shall have been created by that old, and it would seem eternal conflict between naming of a thing and a knowledge of it.[54]

He continues,

> We attribute to any class of objects (stones, leaves, birds, insects) these names, and we have immediately found a way of avoiding the mystery which clothed these objects in their original state of silence and anonymity.[55]

That "original state" is what is remembered and is at the heart of the irony of "Afro"-American writing and literature. The issue of language and of naming goes to the heart of the irony of "reason" and of "philosophy" posed earlier;

and, the irony of "Afro" experiences within the New World logic-order of exploration, expansionism, as well as exploitation and colonialism. The language of the "New World" is a language which has been used to rob and reduce, to "locate" one a Negro—that is, to create a world and the meaning of a world in which there are such things as Negroes—and, is that through which one is to recall or "what an older man would justly call his reminiscences, the psychological origins of a migration" such "that we may be able to reflect on how his journey towards each writer's expectation may have been responsible for his development both as a man and as a writer." It is important to note that, for Lamming, this journey is one of silence and a certain sort of anonymity of his private world, but also "a moral law which demands that he address himself to his social world," one that attends to the brooding reality that language is not merely embarked for critical reflection—or the generation of abstract second-order theory—but operates as a marker for and in remembering who or what you were; it is a manner of shaping or reshaping the world.

This is what Lamming means when he writes,

> To speak of his [the Negro's] situation is to speak of a general need to find a centre [sic] as well as a circumference which embraces some reality whose meaning satisfies his intellect and may prove pleasing to his senses. But a man's life assumes meaning first in revelation with other men, and his experience which is what the writer is trying always to share with the reader, is made up not only of things which happen to him, in his encounter with others, but also of the different meanings and values which he chooses to place on what has happened. What happens to him depends to a great extent on the particular world he happens to be living in, and the way he chooses to deal with his own experience is determined by the kind of person he considers himself to be. In other words, he is continually being shaped by the particular world which accommodates him, or refuses to do so; and at the same time he is shaping, through his own desires, needs and idiosyncrasies, a world of his own.[56]

It is in this way that language is at once a mode of reminiscence and that of reshaping the world by the reframing of the individual's world. What, though, is a Negro world within the Caribbean? What does it mean for a Negro to name and reclaim the world? And, what is his/her "world"?

His world was that of the Caribbean, which for him, echoed and mirrored the "Americas," not only in terms of the "Afro"-experience of exploitation and colonialism, but also in terms of the creative process of self-naming that is the "Afro"-experience within the Western hemisphere. The "world" of the Negro writer, though, was not that of merely oppression, but one that is "[f]rom the point of view of imaginative literature,"[57] in which place is not understood as a spatial location, but an imaginative location historically set and existentially reminiscent.

> [T]he West Indian novel, particularly in the aspect of idiom, cannot be understood unless you take a good look at the American nineteenth century, a good look at [Herman] Melville, [Walt] Whitman, and Mark Twain.[58]

Lamming's discussion of Herman Melville and Moby Dick in his essay, "Ishmael at Home" offers further, stunning insight—through the relationship between Melville and C. L. R. James—into what Lamming has in mind both about place and about the "Americas," and that of Negro writing. In the essay, Lamming explores different Americas—that of the United States as well as the idea of the Americas more generally.[59] The relationship between the Caribbean and the United States is ironically illuminating. He writes,

> The West Indies are lucky to be where they are: next door to America, not the America of the Mason-Dixon line or the colonising [sic] policies in the guise of freedom and self-defence [sic] . . . It's a different America that the West Indies can explore. It's the America that started in the womb of promise, the America that started as an alternative to the old and privileged Prospero, too old and too privileged to pay attention to the needs of his own native Calibans. In the Caribbean we are no more than island peaks; but our human content bears a striking parallel with that exploration upon which America was launched in the result, if not the method, of its early settlements.[60]

This Caribbean, though, not U.S. America, is part of the Americas not only by its proximity—geographically (that is, spatially) and meaningfully (that is, by place-attachment)—but it is also part of European exploration and expansionism by way of the Caliban, and a reworked, re-newed Prospero.[61] Here, Caliban is both a linguistic being in search of his own language to speak his own, new world; but, he is also a creation of the historical forces in which he finds himself, forces that call forth the creative self-invention necessary to bring out of nothing a "new world." This is the "American" Caliban of the Caribbean. By linking the narrative of Prospero and Caliban—the narrative of colonization of both culture and language—with that of the "American" foundation in exploration and "new" self and world building, Lamming is saying something about the meaning of language as the foundation for the "Americas," and his prospects as a Negro writer to create a world of his own from these early settlements. In this way, Lamming's usage of Melville's Redburn unites the entire Western hemisphere into a kind of "America"—as an orientation or "way of seeing"—through the figure of Caliban—that of C. L. R. James. Lamming uses James as a figure through which to think the "Americas," through which to write the "American" experience uniting the disparate histories. He writes,

> Settled by the people of all nations, all nations may claim her [the' Americas'] for their own. You cannot spill a drop of American blood without spilling the blood of the whole world . . . Our blood is as the flood of the Amazon, made up of a thousand noble currents all pouring into one . . . We are not a nation so much as a world.[62]

Similarly, Dorothy E. Mosby in her text, *Place, Language, and Identity in Afro-Costa Rican Literature* employs Lamming's theory to the realities of literature within "place" and Afro-"American" writing to "Afro"-Costa Rican writing and literature in particular, but to "Afro"-Hispanic writing and literature more broadly construed. Such an approach critically highlights an important facet of place and the function of the novel in "Afro"-American writing and literature, particularly amongst "Afro"-Costa Rican and "Afro"-Hispanic writers. Namely, the role of the novel, that of story-telling and the story-teller reflects our earlier point concerning the naming function of language and the crafting of one's "experiences" toward self and world formation. Unfortunately, though Lamming's Caliban-turned-James must be given voice, he finds himself excluded from the dominant narratives of "America" and "American" history.

Mosby, too, notes the exclusion of Afro-"American" experiences from the realities of the Americas. She writes,

> Afro-Hispanic literature has been increasingly recognized as a rich body of work that deals powerfully with the multiperspective realities of the Americas. Nevertheless, Afro Hispanic writers are overlooked or socially excluded by the traditional Hispanic literary canon because their writing is considered too specific in its themes on the black experience . . . Therefore, the issue is not only inclusion in civil society, but inclusion within the canon of Hispanic literature.[63]

In other words, "Afro"-Hispanic literature is thought strictly in terms of 'race"—that is, of telling the "Americas" strictly in terms of the "Afro," a racial designation—rather than in terms of the articulation of place—that is, the telling of the "Americas" and of the "Afro" in terms of place formation, as opposed to "race" formation. The flattening out of the topological aspects of "Afro"-Hispanic writing denies the possibility of complex theories of existence, and complex relations to notions of place. "Afro"-Hispanic writing, though, is topological in that it offers a way of framing meaningful articulations of itself within their world. Mosby highlights this point when she writes,

> The majority of the contemporary Afro-Costa Rican population can be traced to the West Indies when migrant laborers were contracted in the late nineteenth century to construct a transcontinental railroad from San Jose to Puerto Limon ... The workers were required to fulfill the terms of their agreement with the British-and North American-owned Northern Railway Company, which in turn guaranteed the workers return passage to their places of origin. However, for lack of compliance on the part of the company and economic problems that plagued the venture, a significant portion of the population remained in Costa Rica. The Afro-West Indians generally maintained their ethnolinguistic and cultural difference from the Hispanic culture of Costa Rica until it became apparent after several generations and historical changes that the return "home" was impossible and that this "new" land was home.[64]

Here Mosby is offering an historical view of the "Afro" presence within the Western hemisphere and the dislocation of the "Afro" from its roots in the West Indies—a result of European expansion and exploitation, a theme familiar to the "Afro"-American tradition.[65] Additionally, Mosby is highlighting the ways in which a new "home," a new place was constructed out of the new place of natal alienation. This historical view reveals the spatial aspects of 1) the distance or closeness to one's home "land" helps to shape and influence identity; and 2) the distance or closeness one feels within their "new" home, no longer that of the "old" world. For Mosby—as for much of "Afro"-American writing—terrestrial space helps to shape and navigate phenomenal senses of time with respect to "new" and the "old" worlds—"it became apparent after several generations and historical changes that return 'home' was impossible and that this 'new' land was 'home.'" In this sense, the spatial shapes and organizes the "temporal," or how time is understood and experienced. She further writes,

> The experience of exile in this context becomes the distance and cultural separation from the point of origin—whether real or imagined—and the subject's location. The space of Jamaica, for example, is real for the first generation, but for the fourth generation the island occupies space in the imagination. The disconnect and the inability to return home force a change in identity, regardless of the unifying historical common ground or the essential "oneness" of the West Indian cultural identity.[66]

The topological, then, comes to shape the historical, and underpin the development of an identity, which Mosby, borrowing from cultural critic Stuart Hall cites as not "an already accomplished fact," but a "production, which is never complete, always in process, and always constituted within, not outside, representation."[67] This becomes an important line of emergence of identity because if identity is to be thought as that which is produced and not given, then writing—and the novel—stands central—within the framework of language and that of representation—to the production of identity and the expression of identity in terms of a life-world. As such, literature can, then, offers a phenomenological underpinning to meaning and process not only of identity, but also history and what we term 'historical' and their interrelation to notions of place—as the marker of past, present, and future. Writing—and the novel—here, then, serves a pivotal role in locating the "location" or "where" we are. She writes,

> The literature written by the Afro-Costa Ricans of West Indian descent is no mere reflection of a social reality, but helps us to understand how an identity is textually constructed and represented. In the configuration of the Afro-Costa Rican identity, attitudes toward the islands of family origin assume different positions depending on the subject's generation and the external-internal historical forces.[68]

Citing Dorothy E. Mosby's work, Kwame Dixon argues with Mosby that, "identity 'in process' is best understood through the examination of literature."[69] For Dixon, while Mosby's work explicitly concerns "Afro"-Costa Ricans and the "Afro"-Costa Rican experience, it is also expressive of that which is beyond the "Afro"-Costa Rican experience to a more foundational "Afro"-Latin experience "to cover all of the culture affected by the imperial process from the moment of colonization to the present."[70] Quoting Mosby at length, Dixon argues, specifically, this "Afro"-Latin experience—through the "Afro"-Costa Rican experience—can be understood as follows:

> Afro-Costa Rican writing reveals this struggle to be Costa Rican and black, which is characterized by a difficult negotiation of difference and identity. Afro-Costa Rican identity emerges as the results of migrations of a colonized population who were once the ethnic majority at "home" to a situation as neo-colonized, ethnic minority population in a country with a distinct cultural identity. These multiple dispersals constitute and inform the expression of this identity in literature.[71]

As Lamming and Mosby remind us, in the philosophical thought of Gordon and Henry, the significance of writing is the significance of language, of speaking. Speaking a language is speaking a world—writing a world into an existence wider than the individual, private existence. It is to disclose the phenomenal experience of existence, and the world emergent from that existence. "Afro"-American writing, then, is the disclosure of the phenomenal experience of the Afro-"Americas."

Phenomenological Experience of Geographic Space

The question opening Richard Wright's *Haiku: This Other World*,[72] a question that is reflected in his early writings—and throughout his corpus of fiction for that matter—haunts and hangs over Lamming's work on Negro writing and that of Mosby's analysis of "Afro"-Hispanic literature. This question, in the introductory remarks of Wright's collection of nature poetry, is posed by his daughter and executor of his estate, Julia Wright. She asks, "how the creator of the inarticulate, frightened, and enraged Bigger Thomas ended up leaving us some of the most tender, unassuming, and gentle lines in African-American poetry."[73] This, she claims, is Wright's "biographical enigma."[74] Here, in Julia's question, we see portrayed some of the seeming contradictions spoken of earlier in our discussion of Africana literary senses of "place": specifically, the juxtaposition between the natural world of beauty and tenderness, and the social human world of toughness and fear. She is really asking, in a less direct way, "What is the relationship between Wright's racial-realism and his nature thinking and writing?" and, "What could connect these two, seemingly disparate and contradictory elements?"[75]

What makes this relationship even more enigmatic is that, throughout Wright's fictional realism, there were always elements of the natural, elements which were usually followed, preceded by or existing within some human event.[76] Specifically, we can see this theme throughout his early works: in the opening pages of *Black Boy* (1945), where the protagonist's setting fire to his house is followed by his beating, but also his reflections of the "coded meanings" of nature[77]; we can see this in the juxtaposition of nature (in fields of grass and a pond) and social reality (the presence of a white woman, who prefigured the death of black boys) in "Big Boy Leaves Home" (1938);[78] we can see this in Wright's first novel, *Native Son* (1940) in the presence of urban nature—a rat—within an urban setting[79] and, perhaps, most significantly in one of his earliest poems, in collaboration with Langston Hughes, "Red Clay Blues"(1939).[80]

In much Wright scholarship, the address of this enigma has usually been to acknowledge the presence of "nature" within Wright's oeuvre without a full accounting of its meaning for the larger project[81] that is, to acknowledge its presence without acknowledgment of its significance for how we are to read his oeuvre—in particular, his early works in relation to his later works.[82] Wright biographer, Michel Fabre, like many other readers takes this more traditional approach to the reading of Wright's oeuvre. While he acknowledges that "[i]n some of his experimental phrases of the 1930s he was unwittingly already composing haiku,"[83] he, nevertheless, chronologically orders Wright's work, with his haiku as "the final stage of his evolution."[84]

Meta L. Schettler in, "Healing and Loss: Richard Wright's Haiku and the Southern Landscape" goes in a different direction from Fabre's claim, while maintaining a traditional interpretation. Schettler, rather than chronologically ordering Wright's oeuvre, situates it psychologically, arguing that Wright's haiku were his

> [a]ttempts to reclaim this [Southern identity] essential part of his life. Although Wright famously wrote, "Tradition is no longer a guide. The world has grown huge and cold," many of his haiku do affirm a distinctly African American tradition of remembrance. In the landscapes of his haiku, the world is no longer "huge and cold," but deeply personal and intimate.[85]

Shettler understands Wright's haiku as his attempt to reclaim "the world of his childhood," a world from which he was separated, spatially, in France during his self-imposed exile. In addition to a psychological project, for Shettler, Wright's haiku represent a restorative "journey," a journey within himself to merge the South of violence with the South that could, possibly, be his "place." She writes,

> Here Wright proposes that the violence of racism creates a break within nature itself . . . [T]he whole body of Wright's haiku can perhaps be seen in this light, as part of a long journey in writing to overcome, resist, and combat the damage inflicted by racism and racial violence and also part of a new journey to reclaim his connection to the earth and the Southern landscape.[86]

Shettler's "remembrance" is part of what Keneth Kinnamon refers to as Wright's "pastoral thinking.' For Kinnanom,

> [t]his nostalgic pastoral impulse is a common theme in urban Negro folklore, and it has been given memorable literary expression by Richard Wright . . . In Wright's work the pastoral motif recurs frequently, particularly in the early fiction. The word "pastoral" is here used somewhat loosely to indicate a retrospective rural nostalgia from the vantage point of the author's urban present . . . [87]

For Shettler and for Kinnamon, Wright's haiku stands in-between Wright the writer from the History of Wright's experiences. In a sense, it operates as a bridge between these two selves, making sense of the past and the possibility of the future.[88] Neither Shettler nor Kinnamon can accept that the South as the space in which violence occurred could, itself, have been both rejected and accepted at the same time; a space in which one feels alienated, and yet situates it as "home," as their own place. This, too, is perhaps the source of Julia Wright's "literary enigma," and traditional scholarship's desire to think Wright's chronologically.

Yet, if one looks to Wright's earliest works, in particular, "Red Clay Blues," one finds continuities rather than contradiction. In this poem, Wright mentions needing the South, its clay soil, even its inherent inequalities; he situates this as a "blues" refrain, but not necessarily one of nostalgia: his remembrance exceeds ideas of the South. He remembers and yearns for the place of the South.

> I miss that red clay, Lawd, I
> Need to feel it on my shoes.
> Says miss that red clay, Lawd, I
> Need to feel it on my shoes.
> I want to see Georgia cause I
> Got them red clay blues.
>
> Pavement's hard on my feet, I'm
> Tired o' this concrete street.
> Pavement's hard on my feet, I'm
> Tired o' this city street.
> Goin' back to Georgia where
> That red clay can't be beat.
>
> I want to tramp in the red mud, Lawd, and
> Feel the red clay round my toes.
> I want to wade in that red mud,
> Feel that red clay suckin' at my toes.
> I want my little farm back and I
> Don't care where that landlord goes.[89]

Wright, in a sense, is answering the "enigma": the question of the Great Migration, the question on many lips regarding the South generally, but Mississippi specifically: "how could one harken back to the South, to Mississippi, to remember and to hold it in remembrance?" and, "How could one find within exploitation a sense of "home," a sense of one's "place"?"[90] One can find what amounts to an answer to these questions at the end of *Black Boy* when he writes of his migration North. He writes,

> I was leaving the South to fling myself into the unknown, to meet other situations that would perhaps elicit from me other responses . . . I was not leaving the South to forget the South, but so that some day I might understand it . . .
> . . . Yet deep down, I knew that I could never really leave the South, for my feelings had already been formed by the South, for there had been slowly instilled into my personality and consciousness, black though I was, the culture of the South.[91]

Neither the chronological nor the psychological explanation answers the enigma of why his haiku scenes were present from the very beginning, before his self-imposed exile: What was he reclaiming in those moments? This enigma, though, is critical in understanding Wright's oeuvre. Understood not as chronology, nor as the sequential development of "idea," nor as the bridging of contraries, Wright's nature writing displays, from the very beginning, the role that nature played in and the importance of the development of his notion of the American South as his "place." It is not merely space to which Wright refers, but the meaning of that space phenomenologically. What occurs for traditional explanations of Wright, but of Africana writing more broadly, is the forgetting of the phenomenological aspects of writing itself.

Wright's haiku and his nature writing not only capture the relationship between the natural world and the human world through remembrance; for Wright, these works also capture his understanding of "America" as a place—the mystery of its spatiality. Wright, like Lamming, theorized the "Americas" as a place imaginatively, but also spatially and geographically. Bruce Janz's discussion of both the development of indigenous culture as well as its clash with modernity and modernization is apropos. He writes,

> Pre-modern maps tended to be maps of place, heavily governed by human concerns and settlements. They represented what mattered, and ignored what did not . . . As soon as the world was regarded spatially instead of platially, maps changed. They began with an abstract grid, lines of longitude and latitude, into which the details of geography fit. Anything which happened to be there was included. Abstract space, rather than experienced place, becomes the operative geographical mode. This shift makes possible the control and domination of the

world—all places are in principle knowable a priori, in the terms set by those who constructed the grid. All places are assumed to be like the places of the mapmakers . . . Spatiality brings new implications to land ownership. This shift in imagining the physical world makes exploration possible—new lands are no longer out of bounds . . . but are accessible to anyone who can find their way there and plant a flag. And spatiality inclines us to think in terms of a mosaic of juxtaposed nations on a map, bits of real estate owned and controlled by different interests.[92]

What Janz is demonstrating here is the effect of how we think can have on how we actually imagine and experience the world, specifically in terms of how the world itself is carved up into what is "real." The shift from place to bare space is one that Sylvia Wynter refers to in her phenomenological description of Columbus' expedition creating a New World—one of exploration and exploitation in which the world became an empty space of conquest and of naming. For Wynter, and for our purposes, this shift from place to bare space (on maps, etc.) was also the shift from pre-modern to modern. The modern shift effected how we think of and experience place and offered a unique challenge. The challenge of modernity, then, is the challenge of thinking the world disjunctively between bare space and lived place—a disjunctive that we are still encountering in the tension still present in Wright's enigma, Lamming's—via Gordon and Henry's "experiences"—challenge of Negro writing, and in Mosby challenge of the juxtaposition between blackness and Hispanic writing. Homi Bhaba offers us some insight into the modern problem. In his essay, "Race, Time, and the Revision of Modernity," he writes,

> The challenge to modernity comes in redefining the signifying relation to a disjunctive "present": staging the past as symbol, myth, memory, history, the ancestral—but a past whose iterative value as sign reinscribes the "lessons of the past" into the very textuality of the present that determines both the identification with, and the interrogation of, modernity: what is the "we" that defines the prerogative of my present?[93]

This disjunctive element is critical to understanding the constant reference of natural landscapes in relation to personal and political formation, not only at the level of language, but within the boundary of the "land" itself—as spatial location, but also as signifier of "world."

In *Black Boy*, Wright notes that nature is not only a mystery that surrounded us, but that we were also a part of this mystery. He notes,

> Each event spoke with a cryptic tongue. And the moments of living slowly revealed their coded meanings. There was the wonder I felt

when I first saw a brace of mountainlike, spotted, black-and-white horses clopping down a dusty road through clouds of powdered clay.

There was the delight I caught in seeing long straight rows of red and green vegetables stretching away in the sun to the bright horizon . . .

. . . There was a vague sense of the infinite as I looked down upon the yellow, dreaming waters of the Mississippi River from the verdant bluffs of Natchez . . .

. . . There was the yearning for identification loosed in me by the sight of a solitary ant carrying a burden upon a mysterious journey . . .

. . . There was the incomprehensible secret embodied in a whitish toadstool hiding in the dark shade of a rotting log . . .

. . . There was the thirst I had when I watched clear, sweet juice trickle from sugar cane being crushed.

There was the hot panic that welled up in my throat and swept through my blood when I first saw the lazy, limp coils of a blue-skinned snake sleeping in the sun. . . .

. . . There was the cloudy notion of hunger when I breathed the odor of new-cut grass.

And there was the quiet terror that suffused my senses when vast hazes of gold washed earthward from star-heavy skies on silent nights . . . [94]

The language between man and nature, though a mystery, also revealed something about us: how we related to one another, and what, in our dealings with nature we are missing. Also, in *Black Boy* he notes,

> Having grown taller and older, I now associated with older boys and I had to pay for my admittance into their company by subscribing to certain racial sentiments. The touchstone of fraternity was my feeling toward white people, how much hostility I held toward them, what degrees of value and honor I assign to race. None of this was premeditated, but sprang spontaneously out of the talk of black boys who met at the crossroads . . .
>
> . . . And the talk would weave, roll, and surge, spurt, veer, swell, having no specific aim or direction, touching vast areas of life, expressing the tentative impulses of childhood, Money, God, race, sex, color, war, planes, machines, trains, swimming, boxing, anything . . . The culture of one black household, and folk tradition was handed from group to group. Our attitudes were made, defined, set, or corrected; our ideas were discovered, discarded, enlarged, torn apart, and accepted. Night would fall. Bats would zip through the air. Crickets would cry from the grass. Frogs would croak. The stars would come out. Dew

would dampen the earth. Yellow squares of light would glow in the distance as kerosene lamps were lit in our homes. Finally from across the fields or down the road a long slow yell would come:
"Youuuuuuuu, Daaaaaaaavee!"[95]

What is significant here is that the call of the boys was within the same space as the call of crickets and frogs; the movement of the boys is paralleled by that of bats . . . the decisions made, the ideas developed were done right alongside the presence of a present natural world; the light of the stars shone alongside that of kerosene lamps, which "were lit in our homes."

Lamming, in his description of the Caribbean islands resembles that of Wright's description of Mississippi and the red-clay, as well as the relationship between the boys, their language and communication with one another. Lamming also captures the mysteries in relation to human identity; but, he also captures the ways in which these mysteries can leave open the possibility of re-interpretation, of a new sense of place.[96] To answer the question, perhaps seminal to *The Pleasures of Exile*, "How and where is the Caribbean?"—a question similar to the one posed in Wright's *Black Boy* about the meaning of the South—Lamming writes,

> Islands of the Caribbean are evidence of some ancient mountain range that rode one without a flaw between the extreme points of North and South America. None but geologists can now conceive the years, lost by the millions, before that huge, continuous family of mountains broke and fell beneath the sea. Long submerged, it has left an archipelago of peaks like a swarm of green children patiently waiting its return.
> These islands are scattered in a curve of dots and distances continuing for nearly two thousand miles from the coast of Florida to the Northern tip of South America. Coaxed by winds and water, these volcanic peaks display strange and familiar shapes . . . Their history has been similar, a sad and hopeful epic of discovery and migration.
> . . . Today their descendants exist in an unpredictable and infinite range of custom and endeavor, people in the most haphazard combinations, surrounded by memories of splendor and misery, the sad and dying kingdom of Sugar, a future full of promises. And always the sea![97]

The cartographical map for Lamming, as for Wright, continue to be those maps "governed by human concerns" as one can see in their language and their description as human reality rather than abstract space; one can see the personality of the people emergent from within the geographical region—this, for Wright and for Lamming is what is implied within Gordon's "geography of reason." The shift from platial to spatial thinking is critical, especially for Wright as well as for Lamming, for their attachment to "land" and to the memory of "land" is critical, not only in how they understand the "Americas" and the place of the "Americas," but also in their criticism in the de-placialization of "land" in commodification.[98]

For Lamming as for Wright, platial coordinates are phenomenological; it is the core of their topographical and topological thinking. Lamming's remembrance of these islands, and their history, and the sea is the reclamation of the time when "only the sun get permission to say the time," of "a faith in the immortality of the land," when "their hands hold the land,"[99] what Wright referred to as the mystery of nature.

Similarly, Dorothy E. Mosby explains her relation to Costa Rica in the following eco-phenomenal terms:

> There is a Creole saying in Limon, Costa Rica, that speaks to the history, identity, and culture of the Afro-Costa Ricans. To say "me navel-string bury dere" is an affirmation of "belonging" to a place and a challenge to those who deny the cultural contributions of the descendants of West Indian immigrants born in Costa Rica who helped to form its modern state. To bury your "navel-string" or umbilical cord in a place is, in effect, to plant the self in a particular space or territory. The expression refers to the folk practice of "burying an infant's umbilical cord in its parents' home ground ... or in some place of symbolic significance." It is to literally take a piece of the developing self and to intern it so that it becomes part of the land and, in doing so, represents an indelible bond between the self and place. To bury the "navel-string" of the descendants of Afro-West Indian immigrants in Costa Rica is to root the self to a location—to affirm that this place is a home, even if home neglects, denies, or renders invisible the black presence.[100]

This explanation frames the text in its entirety as it also frames our earlier discussion of topological thinking. Her framing of the text in terms of an umbilical cord between the self and the "land" offers a robust philosophical conception of "place," echoing both Wright and Lamming's conceptions of place being phenomenally set within geographical space. What is, perhaps, more significant and more interesting than the phrase itself—"me navel-string bury dere"—is that she uses it to describe her text on "Afro"-Costa Rican literature. In this sense, she connects the very real experience of being "land-tied" with both language and story-telling/story-teller. It is here that Lamming, Wright, and Mosby are all connected: the literature itself is the writing of "place," which is but a physical, psychological, phenomenological and existential expression of being human, and of human being. It reveals that "Afro"-intellectual traditions are created expressions of "Afro" meanings of world, and of "Afro" world-making.

Conclusion

Lewis Gordon's concept sets loose, or perhaps free, not only Afro-"American" experiences—from the confines of the forces of bare material history, suggesting an alternate historiography, one that includes the clay of Georgia, the verdant bluffs of Mississippi, the islands and the sea of the Caribbean, and the umbilical relations of home ground—but also frees thinking itself to reflect on the nature of human consciousness and what constitutes human "experience," and critical intellectual reflection (philosophy) of that "experience." In such a setting loose, "place" comes to reshape our understandings of Africana persons, the meaning and significance of the "Americas," and of Afro-"American" experiences. Within this chapter a question has been concretely posed, a question that is set to affirm a methodological investigation in Africana philosophy, and to "Afro"-American literature, a question which challenges multiple assumptions of the meaning of each; a question for us to (re)think the meaning and the fullness of "place."

Notes

1. "Shifting the Geography of Reason" has been the theme for the now twelve-year old annual conference for the Caribbean Philosophical Association (http://caribphil.org/). The organization and the theme are meant to capture the Caribbean "not solely as a geopolitical region, but more generally as a trope to investigate certain dimensions of the multiple undersides of modernity." What is of interest here is not the Caribbean or "the geography of reason" as a trope, but the notion of understanding the Caribbean as a geopolitical region—what does it mean to capture the Caribbean, its thought, and its people in terms of a region—in terms of a region of thought.

2. Lewis Gordon, "African-American Philosophy, Race, and the Geography of Reason," in *Not Only the Master's Tools: African-American Studies in Theory and Practice*, eds. Lewis R. Gordon and Jane Anna Gordon (Boulder, CO: Paradigm Publishers, 2006), 3–50.

3. I say, "introduced to Africana Philosophy" with the latter term in italics to mean that he introduced the concept to the field, not that he himself generated the idea. The idea of "the geography of reason" was present in European philosophy in philosophers such as Martin Heidegger and Maurice Merleau-Ponty, (in the early and middle 20th century) and in Latin American philosophy in scholars such as

Enrique Dussel (in the mid-twentieth century) and has long been a prominent theme in Afro-American literature in writers such as Richard Wright (from the early part of the 19th century, more prominently in the early 20th century). "Introduced" merely means was picked up in the lexicon in contemporary Africana philosophy. This essay, though, contends that the concept has not been as fully developed or utilized in Africana philosophy as it has been in the earlier practices—a point that will be made throughout the essay.

4. Gordon, himself, alludes to the role that spatial location has in generating concepts. This is significant, because, for Gordon, one's location in relation to "power" or spheres of influence affects one's theorizing in and about the world. This influence is not merely metaphorical, but also a spatially-located reality. Gordon writes,

> African-American thought should take seriously the critique of the rural–urban divide in Africana thought. We should recognize that thought is affected by the exigencies of space. For example, much political thought is prejudiced by its etymological foundations—namely, in the Greek Polîs or Greek city-state. Barbarians stood outside such walls. Cities, however, required ways of organizing people that increasingly created distances between them. The implication here is that we should not presume a symmetric understanding of political life when we move from urban to rural, because the values of politics is more conducive to the former than the latter. The historic relation of the world outside the city to those inside was one of war. The rural aim is the elimination of politics. I bring this up because of the ongoing problem in black politics of black nationhood. In many ways, white supremacy and antiblack racism function as those encircling walls that necessitate an internal political relationship to those inside the city. What this means, then, is that the search for an internal necessity in black politics and black life is a mistaken understanding of what such relationships are. The internal opposition is a fundamentally political one because of that external necessity, which means, then, that dissent and opposition versus unanimity . . . [that is] a primary feature of black life . . . All this brings us finally to the transformation of the geography of reason. (emphasis added)

Gordon, then, links the spatial locatedness of persons to the generation of theory itself. He writes of African-Americans, or New World thinkers the following: "An insight from such production is the call to be epistemologically imaginative. By resisting in-advance rejections of such terms as 'binaries' and 'dualism,' New World black thought can work through such categories when they are most relevant" (55). Their locatedness as outside—metaphorically and spatially—the sources of power (often in Black Belts, etc.), has, for Gordon, generated what he terms "creolization and racialized thought." This theme—the role of spatial-location to the cultivation of ideas—is not a theme that he picks up later in greater depth when discussing Africana philosophy.

5. There is, though, the notable exception of philosopher Bruce B. Janz ("The Territory Is Not the Map: Place, Deleuze, Guattari, and African Philosophy," *Philosophia*

Africana 5, no. 1 [2002]:1–17; "Philosophy as if Place Mattered: The Situation of African Philosophy," in *What Philosophy Is*, eds. Havi Carel and David Gomez [London: Continuum Publishers, 2004], 103–115; *Philosophy in an African Place* [Lanham, MD: Lexington Books, 2009]; paperback 2011; "African philosophy: Some Basic Questions," in *Atuolu Omalu: Some Unanswered Questions in Contemporary African Philosophy*, ed. Jonathan O. Chimakonam [Lanham, MD: Rowman & Littlefield, 2014]). *Philosophy in an African Place* seeks to not only ground the practice of philosophy-in-place; but what is more, it seeks to originate the concepts of a philosophy from within place. He writes,

> My purpose at this point is somewhat different than what I hope others will use this book for. I hope that others will take this book as a call to identify the place of concept, and to create new concepts appropriate to the place, which can then also serve to transform the place. (Janz, Philosophy, 217)

For Janz, concepts are not transcendental, but emerge from within a particular place. As such, philosophy is platial or place-based in that its questions, which generate its concepts, are generated from within a particular place. This becomes, for Janz, important as a way of claiming the necessity of/for African philosophy, rather than the mere export of ideas to Africa, or responses to the questions about the reality of African philosophy. "Questions," he writes, "come from places. They are not transcendental, but rather are rooted in ways of reflectively existing that occur throughout the world." He, then, asks the seminal question, "How is it that the concepts that are central to African philosophy not only can be thought platially, but they also contribute to a renewed and more robust understanding of place?" (Janz, *Philosophy*, 217). And, while Janz's work is instructive to the question of place in African philosophy, it is, for the most part meta-philosophical in that it is seeking the ground in which new concepts of African philosophy may emerge, or what he calls "the place of African philosophy," but does not, on the whole show the ways in which place, as we are thinking here, are operative—in particular, he does not discuss the physical places examined in African literature, which is significant for our thinking here.

6. Bruce Janz highlights this point through a series of questions. In his essay, "Philosophy as if Place Mattered: The Situation of African Philosophy," in *What Philosophy Is*, eds. Havi Carel and David Gamez (London: Continuum Publishers, 2004): 103–115, Janz offers eight questions concerning philosophy and the place of philosophy to answer the seminal Derridian question to the discipline itself: "where does the question of the right to philosophy take place?," which can be immediately translated by "where ought it take place?" Where does it find today its most appropriate place?" (Janz, 103) Janz's questions highlight in Gordon's concept, "the geography of reason," the unspoken: what is the place of questioning itself, the place of thinking, of philosophizing?

7. As such, when I refer to "Afro"-American writing, I am referring to those written expressions of "Afro" peoples in the "Americas" that constitute their own self-perception of identity, space, time, and place. When I refer to "Afro"-American

literature, I am referring to that canonized collection of "Afro"-American writings. And, when I refer to Africana philosophy, I am referring to this second-order reflections of "Afro" peoples and their expression, in this case writing and literature.

8. David Seamons, "Place Attachment and Phenomenology: The Synergistic Dynamism of Place," in *Place Attachment: Advances in Theory, Methods and Research*. Lynne Manzo and Patrick Devine-Wright, eds. (New York: Routledge/Francis & Taylor, 2013)

9. While these are not verbatim quotations, they do reflect the general tone and worries of Gordon, "African-American Philosophy," 19–25; and Lewis Gordon, "Africana Philosophy and Philosophy in Black," *The Black Scholar* (Winter 2013): 46–51.

10. Paget Henry, "Africana Phenomenology: Its Philosophical Implications," *Worlds & Knowledges Otherwise* (Fall 2006): 1–23.

11. Gordon, "African American Philosophy," 37.

12. Gordon, "African American Philosophy," 37.

13. Jeff Malpas, *Heidegger and the Thinking of Place: Explorations in the Topology of Being* (Boston: MIT Press, 2012), 43.

14. Sylvia Wynter, "1492: A New World View," in *Race, Discourse, and the Origin of the Americas: A New World View*, Vera Lawrence Hyatt and Rex Nettleford, eds. (New York: Smithsonian, 1995).

15. This claim was also echoed in Sylvia Wynter's essay "Ethno or Socio Poetics," *Alcheringa/Ethnopoetics* 2, no. 2 (1976): 78–94.

16. Wynter, "1492," 13.

17. It is important to note that for Wynter, the Old World logic-order understood human relations and the relations with the land in terms of Church order and religious metaphysics wherein the world and our place within it (our cosmogenesis) was entirely predicated upon a belief in God, and the triadic order of knowledge—man, God, angels; sin and innocence; Heaven and Earth. But, with the emergence of the post-Old World logic-order, what determined human relations and the relations with the land was the State—a secular logic-order—and the law of the State. Wherein the priests, and/or clergymen may have carried out the Divine ordinance, it is now carried out by operators of the State and its law (Wynter, "1492," 13–15).

18. In her essay, "Ethno or Socio Poetics" Wynter claims that this new definition of 'humanity' and new set of relations with 'humanity' and the land was an economic one rather than a religious one. She terms this new man, homo economicus and this new set of relations with the land as "an alien frontier Nature" (Wynter, "Ethno or Socio Poetics," 81).

19. While these two moments do not constitute the new logic-order of the New World, they are indicative of the European exploration and expansionism that encapsulated the break from the Old World and the birth of the New World. As such, one can find similar historic moments in Central and Southern "Americas" in the interactions between those Europeans born on the "American" continent and those Europeans born on continental Europe; as well as the social order between those African descended persons, indigenous persons, and Europeans

(both continental "American" and continental European); and in the Caribbean between those of indigenous origin, those of African origin, and those of mixed-raced origin.

20. What is being claimed here, and within Wynter's work, is not saying that these two moments specifically came to define the "Americas" and frame the "American" experience. Rather, it is to say that the constitution of the "Americas" and the "American" experience emerged from a certain shift within Europe with the developing travel and exploration of foreign lands; the disintegration of the Old monarchical logic-order; the rise of the Enlightenment and empiricism with regards to truth; and, that these shifts are captured in these two moments, which are indicative of the sea-change. Throughout the Central and Southern regions of the hemisphere as well as what is now called the Caribbean there are specific moments that signify and capture this shift and the New World logic-order.

21. Along with the en-placement of the indigenous peoples and their culture, that is, the question of what happened to the Old World for the indigenous peoples—what happened to their world logic-order in the presence of this New World logic-order? If space were permitting, this question could be explored alongside the question of Africans within the New World logic-order, for these two questions are intertwined.

22. This can be noted in the myriad of references to W.E.B. Du Bois' double-consciousness and Frantz Fanon's notion of alienation to the almost exclusion of regional or geographic identities of "Afro"-identities—this is especially true of Africana philosophy.

23. Katherine McKittrick, *Demonic Grounds: Black Women and the Cartographies of Struggle* (Minneapolis, MN: University of Minnesota Press, 2006), x.

24. *Place and the Politics of Identity*, Michael Keith and Steve Pile, eds. (New York: Routledge, 1993), 1.

25. I am equally concerned with how "Afro" peoples responded to this new Western logic-order, as to how they created, in the midst of this dis-placement, their own logic-order of place. What is being suggested within this chapter is not an exhaustive analysis of the different ways in which place is made by African persons within the Americas, but a challenge to scholars of the African diaspora to take seriously the role that "place" plays in the self-constitution of those persons we call African and of the Diaspora itself.

26. "Afro" American is an ironic displacement of context and content wherein the "place" of displacement becomes the conceptual and living spaces of "Afro" persons. That is, "Afro" persons of the Americas operate outside of the "American" context of European expansionism and exploration, as that which is necessary and peripheral to, but critical for the execution of the project of the "New Man" in the "New World." As such, the term "Inter-America" carries within itself this tension and this irony of context and content, meaning and creation for it includes the "New Man" and the "New World" as well as the "other" worlds—Old and New—of indigenous peoples and the newly arrived Afro peoples.

27. It must be noted here that there is no central or singular "Afro" perspective of the "Americas." Rather, the perspectives are plural—from North to Central to Southern Americas as well as the Caribbean; meaning, there are many ways in which 'America' has been interpreted, and many different senses of "place" and identity construction within and along-side these perspectives.

28. Tim Cresswell, "Place," *Elsevier, Inc.* (2009) https://booksite.elsevier.com/brochures/hugy/SampleContent/Place.pdf

29. Similarly, existential philosopher Jean-Paul Sartre argues in *Being and Nothingness* that it is in virtue of embodied consciousness (or existential phenomenology) that the material world comes to have an order of a set of spatial relations that shape/determine, and a social meaning of those material relations. He offers the example of a park. He writes,

> I am in a public park. Not far away there is a lawn and along the edge of that lawn there are benches. A man passes by those benches. I see this man; I apprehend him as an object and at the same time as a man. What does this signify? What do I mean when I assert that this object is a man?
>
> If I were to think of him as being only a puppet, I should apply to him the categories which I ordinarily use to group temporal-spatial "things." That is, I should apprehend him as being "beside" the benches, two yards and twenty inches from the lawn, as exercising a certain pressure on the ground, etc. His relation with other objects would be of the purely additive type; this means that I could have him disappear without the relations of the other objects around him being perceptibly changed. In short, no new relation would appear through him 'between those things in my universe: grouped and synthesized from my point of view into instrumental complexes, they would from his disintegrate into multiplicities of indifferent relations. Perceiving him as a man, on the other hand, is not to apprehend an additive relation between the chair and him; it is to register an organization without distance of the things in my universe around that privileged object. To be sure, the lawn remains two yards and twenty inches away from him, but it is also as a lawn bound to him in a relation which at once both transcends distance and contains it. Instead of the two terms of the distance being indifferent, interchangeable, and in a reciprocal relation, the distance is unfolded starting from the man whom I see and extending up to the lawn as the synthetic upsurge of a univocal relation. We are dealing with a relation which is without parts, given at one stroke, inside of which there unfolds a spatiality, which is not my spatiality; for instead of a grouping toward me of the objects, there is now an orientation which flees from me. (Jean-Paul Sartre, *Being and Nothingness*, 341)

Sartre, here, is arguing, as is Cresswell, that it is by virtue of embodied consciousness that the material world comes to have spatial relations—spatial relations are the ordering and organizing of bare space into meaningful sets of relations; the material world is ordered because we are ordering it. The manner in which we order it is the significance that it has, and becomes our place: or, what Cresswell notes as the "feelings and emotions" tied to a particular material space.

30. Tim Cresswell, "Place," 1.
31. David Seamon, "Place Attachment and Phenomenology."
32. Malpas, *Heidegger and the Thinking of Place*, 43.
33. Malpas, *Heidegger and the Thinking of Place*, 44.
34. Malpas, *Heidegger and the Thinking of Place*, 14.
35. Seamon, "Place Attachment and Phenomenology."
36. Making "American Philosophy" a philosophy of the "Americas" as a place.
37. It must be noted, though, that these aspects of "place" are not exclusive to Africana persons, nor that these authors have not spoken about these aspects of "place"—specifically, Cresswell discusses the aspect of "movement" and "mobility" in his understanding of "place," see for example, Tim Cresswell, *On the Move: Mobility in the Modern Western World*—rather, it is say that these aspects are not fundamental to these authors' writings on "place" in the same way they are in Africana literatures. There are various existential and phenomenological, along with historical reasons, as to why Africana persons think of "place" in these broader terms. Going further into the distinctions between Africana senses of place and those of European and Anglo-Americans might take us too far adrift from the major point about place, for making such distinctions would inevitably lead us to make distinctions within the ideas of the human, of nature or the environment—those aspects that help to constitute "place"—etc.

38. See Edward Casey, *Getting Back Into Place: Toward a Renewed Understanding of the Place-World* (Bloomington: Indiana University Press, 1993); Yi-Fu Tuan, *Space and Place: The Perspectives of* Experience (Minneapolis: University of Minnesota Press, 1977); Tim Cresswell, *Place: An Introduction* (Oxford: Wiley Blackwell, 2015).

39. In the work of Richard Wright, this rural-urbanity is present in his experience of many cities throughout the South from Memphis, Tennessee to Jackson, Mississippi; and, even in his understanding of treatment of the great migration landscape of Chicago—a city that is urbanized and industrialized, but still experienced by black people as having the same problems of rural living. For more on this, see Richard Wright's *12 Million Black Voices*.

40. For examples, see Lucille Clifton's *Black Nature: Black Writing*; Dianne D. Glave's *Rooted in the Earth: Reclaiming the African American Environmental Heritage*; Thylias Moss' *Black Nature*; Judith A. Carney's *In the Shadow of Slavery: Africa's Botanical Legacy in the Atlantic World*; Kimberly N. Ruffin's *Black on Earth: African American Ecoliterary Traditions*; Richard Westmacott's *African-American Gardens: Yards in the Rule South*; Vaughn Sills' *Place for the Spirit: Traditional African American Gardens*; Grey Gundaker's *Keep Your Head to the Sky: Interpreting African American Home Ground*; Dudley Edmondson's *The Black & Brown Faces in America's Wild Places: African Americans Making Nature and the Environment a Part of the*

Everyday Lives; Carolyn Finney, *Black Faces, White Spaces: Reimagining the Relations of African Americans to the Great Outdoors*; Kimberly K. Smith's *African American Environmental Thought: Foundations*; Alison H. Deming's *The Colors of Nature: Culture, Identity, and the Natural Worlds*.

41. Within the specific history of Africana peoples, battles over land, land-rights and land-ownership has been pronounced either through enslavement or colonization. As such, the specific relation of Africana peoples to "land" is more than a generic accounting of historic or cultural meaning. "Land" represents the totality of the human experience of rootedness and rootlessness, or permanence and migration, of peoplehood and the nation-state and statelessness. But what is more, as a methodological principle, place reveals the myriad of complex ways in which we can and must come to understand the study and understanding of persons.

42. That is, how do we project out the meaning and the experience of existence within the world? This, perhaps, in addition to the question of how we are to understand existence and the world itself may the most pressing questions of philosophy generally, and are especially pressing within and for Africana philosophy, a field for whom identity has been termed a central concern. What is at stake, here, is the meaning of philosophy itself and practice of philosophy. That is, what is stake here is the internal working of not just what we term Africana, but how this term practices itself/and is practiced (within the world). Methodologically explore the thematic content. Which necessitates not starting with problems as "problems," but with the set of living conditions out of which the world itself becomes what it is in its interpretable form. That is, we cannot begin with the set of problems as traditionally presented, but must begin with people existing in the world; a world, which nevertheless, may contain those elements later deemed problematic. Nevertheless, the "problems" themselves or the elements do not present themselves as problematic, but are interpreted as so. We are doing a sort of proto-phenomenological project, clearing the ground for an existential analysis.

43. That is, black phenomenology is almost exclusively related to the body and embodied experience—or what has been termed facticity—and psychological effect of black embodiment. Black phenomenology, though, does not extend beyond embodiment to discuss other theories of place. One can do a simple search for black phenomenology to realize that much of the search results in discussions of Frantz Fanon and W.E.B. Du Bois.

44. Jeff Malpas, *Heidegger and the Thinking of Place*, 14.

45. What does it mean for a "black" to think when thinking has been the exclusive domain of whites? For a black, then, to assert itself as a thinking thing as a way of rejecting European or white hegemony over "reason" (and, thus, humanity), the product of a black philosophical is ironic.

46. Philip Erchinger, "Moving Things into Certain Places: Nature, Culture and Art as Practice in Victorian Writing," *Literature Compass. Special Issue: Literature and Philosophy in Nineteen Century Britain* Vol. 9, Issue 11 (2012): 786–800, more directly, and more indirectly, Gaston Bachelard's *The Poetics of Space* (Boston: Beacon Press,

1958), in which senses of space and place are predicated within an already existing ethos wherein the individual is experiencing place as that which appears before, but is not disclosed through the effort of irony itself. Also, see Katherine McKittrick's edited collection, *Sylvia Wynter: On Being Human as Praxis* (Durham: Duke University Press, 2015), especially chapters 7 and 8 for a discussion of the ways in which "land" or what is termed, "territory" comes to shape our understanding of the "person" in the form of "native" and "colonizer."

47. We are, in a sense, following Bruce Janz's claim of African philosophy that "the core question of African philosophy should shift from the spatial question 'What is African philosophy?' to the platial question, 'What is it to do philosophy in this place?'" (Janz, *Philosophy*, 217) to address Gordon's concept, "the geography of reason" we are shifting the question of what it means to do philosophy—that is, to pose and answer certain questions. "African philosophy," writes Janz, "has, by and large, not thought carefully enough about its own questions, but has allowed its questions to be defined by a skeptical and dismissive West" (Janz, *Philosophy*, 219). This, for Janz, is problematic because, for him, "[q]uestions come from place. They are not transcendental, but rather are rooted in ways of reflectively existing . . ." (Janz, *Philosophy*, 219). I am, here, not as interested in verifying the truthfulness of the claim concerning "African philosophy, by and large" as "the goal of African philosophy should be to generate and create its questions" (Janz, *Philosophy*, 219). And while Janz's concern is African philosophy, his concern of place and its role in philosophizing is germane to our concern here about Africana philosophy and its relation to place. In a sense, we are asking Gordon's "geography of reason" question, but more directly.

48. The concept of "place" has been used by much of modern Western philosophy not so much as an identifying claim as a limit-concept: that is, it is a concept that creates boundaries, and in the creation of those boundaries has made a determination of inside/outside, who philosophy does and does not include. The dominant issue of the limit or boundary of philosophy, of the inside/outside is notion of the "human" or the "person/people." Place has been determined humanity and personhood, rights and obligations; it has been used to deny the humanity or personhood of those inhabiting certain geographical locations, in particular those on the African continent. The denial of the personhood of those "outside" is a denial of their "worlds" and the existence of their "internal" life, such as thinking, reason, contemplation, or soul. Much has been written concerning the denial of African and African descended "worlds" and the existence of African and African descended persons internal life. Much of this has been written from an existentialist perspective, one in which the "black," "African," or "Negre" is reduced to their body, or to the pure exteriority of embodiment without a dual internal component. But such a denial is also the denial of place. For example, Hegel's critique of Africa—"What we properly understand by Africa, is the Unhistorical, Undeveloped Spirit, still involved in the conditions of mere nature"—is a critique of personhood; but, what is overlooked, though, is that the denial of personhood is ultimately a

denial of "place"—without "place" there can be no history, for place is the condition upon which consciousness can exist for-itself as self-recognizing. Within the African context, for Hegel, this is no "place," rather there is but "the conditions of mere nature." The assertion, here, then of place of formative and the methodological illumination of Africana theories of place becomes germane to doing Africana philosophy.

49. George Lamming, "In the Beginning," in *The Pleasures of Exile* (Ann Arbor: University of Michigan Press, 1960), 16.

50. Here, the emphasis has shifted from "Afro"-American to Afro-"American," signifying a shift in emphasis from the meaning of the "Afro" experience, to how that experience has come to define and redefine the meaning of the "Americas." An example of this is in the ways in which George Lamming traces the ironic relationship between the British Caribbean and United States Afro-American identity, an irony that is not only historical, but spatial in the sense of historic imagination. He writes of his relation to not only Richard Wright and James Baldwin, but to Melville and Whitman and Twain:

> [t]he West Indian novel, particularly in the aspect of idiom, cannot be understood unless you take a good look at the American nineteenth century, a good look at Melville, Whitman, and Mark Twain (George Lamming, "The Occasion for Speaking," 29).

One must ask, what is occurring in Lamming's assessment of the necessary inner relation between the Caribbean writer and the "American" writer; between the British Caribbean writer and the Afro-American writer. The Afro-American writer and the British Caribbean writer are tied by myth: the myth of Europe; the myth of culture; the myth of the center of "reality" against which one must and always judges oneself. But it is also a myth that exposes a particular perspective on the part of the Afro-American and the British Caribbean subject: a perspective that relates to the construction of the "world," a perspective that offers, phenomenologically, a source of its resistance in the human (reference consciousness always mounts its own resistance). An irony of being part of a world that is post-colonial—post-British colonial; post-European history one in which "Kierkegaard-Nietzsche-Shaw line-up and hysterical aversion to contemporary British philosophy" has all but redefined the meaning of the English tradition, and the English novel, which "now lies in the hands of the non-English, accompanying the claim with side-swipes at the incompetence of the English to write English poetry." The world has moved passed this view of itself and still denies those in whom this view most naturally is suited: it is this irony that links the Afro-American and the British Caribbean subject; and irony that is post-colonial. Such an irony unites and disunites the Caribbean to that of the rest of the Americas, "[t]he West Indies [thus] occupy a strategic position between North and South America." Each shares in this irony. It is this irony that draws Lamming and Walcott close to Wright. But it is also this irony that draws each closer to the earth, to the land, to notions of place-creation as the source for identity formation.

51. George Lamming, "The Occasion for Speaking," 24; emphasis added.
52. Lamming, "A Way of Seeing," *The Pleasures of Exile*, 56.
53. "The Negro Writer and His World" (*Cross Currents* 6, no. 2 (1956): 156–162) was given at the 1st International Conference of Negro Writers and Artist at the Sorbonne in Paris in 1956 (published later that year in *Presence Africaine*). His collection of essays, *The Pleasures of Exile* was published four years later, in 1960. Many of the themes in his talk were echoed and elaborated in his writings, in particular, what he meant by "home" and the process of writing "home."
54. Lamming, "The Negro Writer and His World," *The Pleasures of Exile*, 328.
55. Lamming, "The Negro Writer and His World," 328.
56. Lamming, "The Negro Writer and His World," 329.
57. Lamming, "The Negro Writer and His World," 331.
58. Lamming, "The Occasion for Speaking," 29.
59. Lamming, "Ishmael at Home," *The Pleasures of Exile*, 152.
60. Lamming, "Ishmael at Home," 152.
61. Lamming is here speaking of Gordon's spatial proximity to power; but also speaking other to that notion, at times beyond it to the contemplation of the meaning of what has been constructed: the Caribbean, the Americas, and the two subjects, neither Ishmael, neither the whale.
62. Herman Melville, *Redburn: His First Voyage*, 1848; reprinted in Lamming, "Ishmael at Home," 153.
63. Dorothy E. Mosby, *Place, Language and Identity in Afro-Costa Rican Literature* (Columbia, MO: University of Missouri Press, 2003).
64. Mosby, *Place, Language and Identity*, 2; emphasis added.
65. It must not be overlooked here that economic exploitation framed the social reality of the West Indian peoples, in both choosing labor and also being displaced from their homeland because of the labor they "chose."
66. Mosby, *Place, Language, and Identity*, 3; emphasis added.
67. Stuart Hall, "Cultural Identity and Cinematic Representation," *Framework: The Journal of Cinema and Media* No. 36 (1989): 68–81. Cited in Dorothy E. Mosby, *Place, Language and Identity*, 4.
68. Dorothy E. Mosby, *Place, Language and Identity*, 3.
69. Kwame Dixon. "Review of Dorothy E. Mosby, Place, Language and Identity in Afro-Costa Rican Literature," *A Contra corriente: A Journal on Social History and Literature in Latin America* (2004), 97.
70. Kwame Dixon, "Review of Dorothy E. Mosby," 97. For examples of such literary works see Richard Jackson's *Black Writers in Latin America*; Miriam Jiminez Roman's edited text, *The AfroLatin@Reader: History and Culture in the United States*, and most famously, Junot Diaz.
71. Dorothy E. Mosby, *Place, Language and Identity*, 234. Cited in Dixon, 104.
72. Richard Wright, *Haiku: This Other World* (New York: Arcade, 2012).
73. Wright, *Haiku*, vii.
74. Wright, *Haiku*, vii.

75. Julia's question reflects much of the confusion and the tension concerning blackness and black literature spoken of which Mosby spoke in terms of being "considered too specific in its themes on the black experience." Rather than taking blackness—the "Afro"—as the foundation for/of an experience, it is taken as juxtaposed to genuine experience.

76. One of Wright's contributions to Africana literature is a challenge to biographical narrative explanation. Wright's oeuvre challenges the view of his own "development" as a writer; a development of ideas, of sentiment, of theory—in the sense of an existential bildungsroman wherein he plays the lead character within his own unfolding life, a life where he doesn't quite know where it is headed and discovers along-the-way certain truths evident at the beginning, but self-reflectively unknown until the end. Whereas Wright has been read chronologically—e.g., his political poetry preceding his novel form, and his novel form preceding his haiku writing—it is unclear what such an approach may reveal. What, though, is more and more clear, is what such an approach may actually conceal.

77. Richard Wright, *Black Boy*, 10–13.

78. Richard Wright, "Big Boy Leaves Home," in *Uncle Tom's Children* (New York: Harper Perennial, 1938/2023). Published two years before *Native Son* (1940), the story served as a primer for his later novel, *Native Son*. For more on the relationship between the natural world and the social world in "Big Boys Leaves Home," see Keneth Kinnamon's "The Pastoral Impulse of Richard Wright," (*Midcontinent American Studies Journal* 10, no. 1 (Spring 1969): 44. Also, for more examples of relation of the natural world to the social world in Wright's early work, see "The Man Who Saw a Flood" in *Eight Men*, and "Down by the Riverside," in *Uncle Tom's Children*.

79. Richard Wright, *Native Son*, 1–5.

80. In "Red Clay Blues," one of Wright's earliest poems (in collaboration with Langston Hughes) directly links political action, liberation, protest, and nature/natural world, natural thinking.

81. See Michel Fabre, *The World of Richard Wright* (Jackson, MS: University of Mississippi, 1985); *The Other World of Richard Wright: Perspectives on His Haiku*, ed. Jianqing Zheng (Jackson, MS: University of Mississippi Press, 2011).

82. For example, questions such as, "What would our reading of Wright look like if we located haiku at the beginning of his oeuvre?"; "What would that mean for his writing, for his ideas of identity, consciousness, personality and his thinking on place more generally, and specifically on 'America'?" appear with much more urgency and in need of much more explanation to develop a more fully rounded picture of Wright as a thinker and his works as place-oriented.

83. Michel Fabre, *The World of Richard Wright*, 53. As evidence, he offers identical lines from *Black Boy* (1945) and his haiku (1960). From *Black Boy*: "There were echoes of nostalgia I heard in the crying strings of wild geese winging south against the bleak autumn sky." An identical haiku can be found in *Haiku: This Other World*. This is but one of many examples in direct correlation between his

early fiction and his haiku writing. I am, though, not arguing that Wright was intentionally composing haiku in his early writings, just that the content of his haiku were always present in his thinking, which needs to be addressed in terms of its relation to his fiction.

84. Michel Fabre, *The World of Richard Wright*, 53.

85. Fabre, *The Other World of Richard Wright*, 43.

86. Meta L. Schettler, "Wright's Haiku and the Southern Landscape," in *The Other World of Richard Wright*, 48.

87. Keneth Kinnamon, "The Pastoral Impulse in Richard Wright," 42.

88. This, perhaps, is what Shettler's aim is when he situates Wright's haiku as follows: "Like Toni Morrison, bell hooks calls for 'ritual reenactment' to 'conquer terror' for 'it is the retelling of our history that enables self-recovery.' For Wright the haiku begin this process of ritual reenactment, healing, reconciliation and self-recovery" (45).

89. Richard Wright and Langston Hughes, "Red Clay Blues," *The New Masses* (August 1, 1939).

90. This theme of tension between exploitation and place-making is one that runs throughout Wright's work. See "The Man Who Saw a Flood" in *Eight Men*; and, "Down By the Riverside."

91. Richard Wright, *Black Boy: A Record of Childhood and Youth*, 284; Bruce Janz, "Philosophy as if Place Mattered," 106–7.

92. Homi K. Bhabha, "Race, Time, and the Revision of Modernity" in Atlas of Transformation, http://monumenttotransformation.org/atlas-of-transformation/html/r/revision-of-modernity/race-time-and-the-revision-of-modernity-homi-k-bhabha.html.

93. Richard Wright, *Black Boy: A Record of Childhood and Youth*, 15.

94. Wright, *Black Boy*, 92.

95. Compare Wright's *Black Boy* and *Haiku* to Lamming's *In the Castle of My Skin* and "In the Beginning, Lamming," 16–17.

96. George Lamming, "In the Beginning," 16–17.

97. This was a dominant theme in Wright's own work, from "Down By the Riverside" and "The Man Who Saw a Flood" as well as in Lamming's "In the Beginning." It also a dominant theme in the history of Afro-American literature.

98. George Lamming, "In the Beginning," 19–21.

99. Dorothy E. Mosby, *Place, Language and Identity*, ix; emphasis added.

PART V
Inter-American Philosophy of Race

10
Alain Locke, José Vasconcelos, and José Martí, on Race, Nationality, and Cosmopolitanism

Jacoby Adeshei Carter

Introduction

Alain Locke holds a social constructionist view of race. Race, for him, is a matter of distinctive variations within culture transmitted across generations. Locke held that race was in point of fact a social and cultural category, rather than a biological one. For this reason, he developed the notion of ethnic race or culture group. By ethnic race, Locke means a peculiar set of psychological and affective responsive dispositions, expressed or manifested as cultural traits, socially inherited and able to be attributed through historical contextualization to a specifiable group of people. The concept of ethnic race is a way of preserving the demonstrated distinctiveness of various groupings of human beings in terms of characteristic traits, lifestyles, and forms of expression without resulting to the scientifically invalidated notion of biological race.

In *The Cosmic Race*[1] José Vasconcelos presents his vision of a "cosmic race" as a uniformitarian form of cosmopolitanism. Vasconcelos is a racial realist, who also believes that race is biological, as well as social. However, he is not a racial purist—quite the contrary. He, like Locke, recognizes races as historically composite even if biologically distinct populations. The cosmic race is the projected result of cultural and biological amalgamation. Vasconcelos develops this notion as a response to the problem of how to forge a genuine Mexican and Pan-Latin American identity, one that ameliorates conflict over racial difference and can move the country and the continent forward.

José Martí is a racial eliminativist and a racial anti-realist. Martí argued that race was neither a biological nor a social kind. Moreover, he astutely pointed out that racism is a double-edged sword. Racism is the belief that human beings can be sorted into distinctive racial types, whether those types are biological or socially determined. Martí was keenly aware that racialism served to both perpetuate racial chauvinism and strife, but that it also functioned as a means of cultural correction and advancement. Martí cautioned, however, that racialism in itself was divisive and contrary to the success of an independent nation.

All three of these thinkers radically reconceived the concept of race and argued, for different reasons, in favor of the radical transformation, if not elimination, of races. I argue that Martí's position poses serious challenges to the racialism of Vasconcelos and Locke. Against Vasconcelos, Martí argues that the supposed superiority of the cosmic race is false, that the notion of racial amalgamation itself reifies racial difference, and that all forms of racialism obstruct the success of an independent nation. I consider possible responses to these arguments by Vasconcelos, and conclude that although their various positions are not at odds in ways that the two philosophers may have envisioned, a number of Martí's challenges are unanswerable by Vasconcelos. Against Locke, Martí argues that even racialism aimed at social uplift for an oppressed group perpetuates racism, and that racial identification impedes individuals' abilities to form more meaningful associations. I then consider Locke's likely response to the challenges posed by Martí. I argue that Locke's and Martí's positions are not as opposed as either may have thought, and that in fact they are complementary; given that Locke's speciously pragmatist racial realism does not commit him to the continued existence of races into an indefinite future, he may well come to accept the racial eliminativism of Martí. I further argue that something like Locke's reconstructionist view of race is likely required by Martí's position in the interim as one works towards elimination.

In the end, I argue that this inter-American philosophical approach to race has theoretical, practical, and historical advantages. It has the theoretical advantage of broadening our racial perspective to fit various contexts, offering multiple critical perspectives, and yielding in the end a more accurate and useful racial perspective. Additionally, there is the practical advantage of diverse philosophical traditions coming to better understand what they have in common, and perhaps deriving renewed support from that discovery. Finally, there is the historical benefit of better understanding various contexts and knowledge of prior inter-American exchanges that can serve as a theoretical foundation for future investigations.

Between Eliminativism and Cosmopolitanism: Alain Locke's Philosophy of Race

One can identify in the work of Alain Locke two unreconciled strivings, or perhaps better, clusters of strivings which constitute a paradoxical paradigm for philosophical understandings of race, particularly as they bear on the prospects for cosmopolitanism and world citizenship. Most generally these strivings could be expressed as the reality of race, and of particular races, for instance Black or Asian on the one hand, and the non-reality of race on the other. More specifically it poses an existential question concerning, if, and why, persons ought to continue to self-identify as members of a race. The tension is as difficult as it is longstanding in the philosophy of race, and, as I hope to show, has been a salient feature of racial thinking by various American thinkers, even some outside the racial context of the United States. Locke articulates the tension thus:

> The proposition that race is an essential factor in the growth and development of culture, and expresses culturally that phenomenon of variation and progressive differentiation so apparently vital on the plane of the development of organic nature, faces the pacifists and internationalists with a terrific dilemma, and a consequently difficult choice. Even so, granted that race has been such a factor in human history, would you today deliberately help perpetuate its idioms at the cost of so much more inevitable sectarianism, chauvinistic prejudice, schism, and strife? It amounts to this, then, can we have the advantages of cultural differences without their obvious historical disadvantages? For we must remember that national and racial prejudices have been all through history concurrent with such traditional differences, and have grown up from the roots of the engendered feelings of proprietorship and pride.[2]

For Locke the perpetuation of racial idioms runs the risk of continuing racism, provincialism, oppressive race practices, and social stratification and division. In claiming this, he does not dismiss the possibility that there may be beneficial aspects of racial identification in some contexts. Locke formulates the problem as one of particular concern for those with cosmopolitan sensibilities and value commitments. If race has an important bearing on cultural progress and distinctiveness, are those consequences of racialism sufficient to outweigh the negative consequences of racialism in terms of prejudice, chauvinism, pernicious race creeds, and negative race practices?

More than that, as Locke notes, there are important practical implications:

> The political crimes of nations are perpetuated and justified in the name of race; whereas in many instances the cultural virtues of race are falsely appropriated by nationalities. So that in the resultant confusion, if we argue for raciality as a desirable thing, we seem to argue for the present practice of nations and to sanction the pride and prejudice of past history. Whereas, if we condemn these things, we seem too close to a rejection of race as something useful in human life and desirable to perpetuate.[3]

Racialism can be put to good or bad uses. An endorsement of racialism as it currently exists and the practices and attitudes that presently accompany it is ipso facto an endorsement of existing race creeds and the present racial order. However, if the consequences of racialism are not only negative, if racialism can be useful for beneficent social purposes, then it seems that it ought to be endorsed. The troubling thing for Locke is the possibility of eliminating undesirable racial practices and preserving the desirable practices. Locke thinks that, at least on the practical side, this tension can be resolved. In fact, the resolution of this tension is the driving focus of his social and political philosophy.[4] Locke's

> answer to this dilemma . . . lies behind one very elemental historical fact, long ignored and oft-forgotten. There is and always has been an almost limitless natural reciprocity between cultures. Civilization, for all its claims of distinctiveness, is a vast amalgam of cultures. The difficulties of our social creeds and practices have arisen in great measure from our refusal to recognize this fact. In other words it has been the sense and practice of the vested ownership of culture goods which has been responsible for the tragedies of history and for the paradoxes of scholarship in this matter. It is not the facts of the existence of race, which are wrong, but our attitude towards those facts.[5]

By race creed, Locke means an action-guiding set of beliefs or aims concerning racial differentiation and practice held and taught by a social group, typically a dominant one. Race creeds originate, motivate, and reinforce race practices.[6] Locke contends that race creeds are a modern invention, and speculates that older forms of racialism differ from contemporary conceptions in that the former were often instinctual practices that were not informed by a "doctrine of race," whereas the latter are characterized by a malevolent and specious justification of irrational practices and beliefs.[7] Race practices for Locke are quite literally the way people in a given society act practically on their racial creeds and institutionalize the racial practices of that society. Race creeds and practices also embody the racial attitudes and beliefs of a particular society.

So, what we get then from Locke by way of addressing the unreconciled tension between abolishing our racial categories as pernicious and unreal, and maintaining them out of a sense of self-identification and liberating struggle is a judgment in favor of a radical reconstruction of our race creeds, race practices, racial attitudes, and racial sensibilities in light of the fact that races, if anything, are composite amalgamations of various cultures and cultural elements, they are transitory and ephemeral, not permanent and static. A great deal more is to be gained by a pluralistic, relativist, and cosmopolitan orientation toward human distinctiveness understood as primarily cultural and ethnic, than from the continuation of racial categorization. Individual human persons and the various social entities comprised of them are all dynamically complex centers of intersection. The transformation of our racial categories and methods of racial stratification and systematization is, if not inevitable, at least to be expected. More than that, it is requisite for the liberation of the many populations, and release of the full capacities for flourishing of individual members of the populations, that have been the victims of pernicious race creeds, practices of stratification, and systematization.

I turn now to a consideration of two other American thinkers on race and nationalism as it relates to the prospects of world citizenship and cosmopolitanism. I look first at the idea of the cosmic race (*la raza cósmica*) in the work of José Vasconcelos as well as his rejection of a narrow nationalism as antithetical to a cosmopolitan worldview. I end with a consideration of the Cuban revolutionary writer and activist José Martí. Martí sees racial identity as an obstacle to national identity, and as such as an obstacle to a more cosmopolitan picture of world citizenship.

La Raza Cósmica: Cultural and Physical Amalgamation in José Vasconcelos's Philosophy of Race

Race thinking in the United States is characterized in large part by the notion of racial purity. This idea served to make race a permanent social, economic, and cultural barrier. Conceptions of race in Latin America differ in some marked ways from those in other parts of the Americas, particularly the United States. An important feature of the phenomenon of race in Latin America is the issue of racial synthesis; that is, the amalgamation of various races through miscegenation into a single hybrid racial identity. As one contemporary political theorist, Diego von Vocano, has observed, racial thinking in Latin American is often characterized by a *synthetic paradigm*; that is, "a mode of thinking about the phenomenon of race and its tributaries in a way that eludes fixed, rigid notions and tends to incorporate those which are mixed and fluid."[8] Von Vocano claims that the synthetic conception of race is "the philosophical comprehension—and transcendence—of the idea of *mestizaje*."[9] Historically, one of the leading proponents of the synthetic paradigm of racial thinking in Latin America was Mexican philosopher José Vasconcelos, who "is known as one of the major exponents of this idea of *mestizaje* and its conceptualization within the ideological context of early twentieth century."[10]

Spanish and Portuguese colonists created the category of the *mestizo* along with the other twenty or so racial categories known as *castas*, which enabled the categorization of more or less distinct ethnoracial types, the myriad amalgamations that formed throughout the parts of the Americas under their imperial control. *Mestizo* was "a racial category designed to place the 'hybrid' within the racialized caste system imposed by the colonizers in Latin America."[11] More than that, the related concept of *mestizaje*—roughly the process of forming the mestizo identity—is both a biologically determined and socially constructed racial identity. Some have argued that *mestizaje* is "predominantly a politico-nationalist project with a heavy ideological charge."[12] *Mestizaje* functioned in some Latin American countries, particularly those vying for independence or in the midst of revolution, as an answer to the problem or racial plurality and division. The idea being that Latin American nations or republics are racially homogeneous, or at least ought, where possible, to be conceived of in that way to avoid the possibility of racial discord undermining the emerging nations while still in an incipient state. This concern in Latin America goes back at least as far as Simon Bolivar. Mestizo/a is both a political and racial conception. As Amado observes: "The notion that widespread miscegenation during the colonial era had given rise to a predominantly mixed population south of the Rio Grande was used as a unifying ideology in the deeply divided, unequal, disjointed, independent republics."[13]

Mestizaje is both biological and cultural for Vasconcelos even if it is more strongly biological than cultural. Vasconcelos, contrary to Locke, understands race as productive of culture; that is, in his view race determines culture. Vasconcelos thinks that the *mestizo* race will create a culture and civilization distinct from, and superior to, those of which it is composed. Moreover, Vasconcelos's philosophy of race is one that asserts the superiority of the *mestizo*, the cosmic race:

> Vasconcelos's philosophy subverted the view of the supremacy of "pure races," but proclaimed the higher status of the *mestizo* by virtue of the natural selection of the best characteristics of each in the crossbreed. Moreover, Vasconcelos's theory assumes an essentialist view of race, as biological, rather than socially constructed, whereby the white epitomize civilization and Indians and blacks are characterized by lower intellectual and aesthetic qualities.[14]

Vasconcelos's aesthetic theory is important to his philosophy of race. Vasconcelos seems to understand many social ills: poverty, lack of education, misery, and calamity, as failures to instantiate beauty.[15] As civilization progresses toward ever more beautiful types it must jettison those qualities and features that degrade beauty. Vasconcelos's philosophy of race is not nearly as inclusive as it might on the surface seem. While he advocates the phenotypical disappearance or erasure of all previously existing racial types, he seems to regard certain racial types as further removed from the ideal "cosmic" or *mestizo/a* type. Moreover, he does not view all races as contributing equally to *la raza cosmica* either in terms of cultural or physical contribution. In the case of people racialized as Black, for example, he sees their contribution to *mestizaje* as a predominantly physical one; Black people literally color or darken *mestizos/as* without adding much if anything in the way of culture.

Vasconcelos is sometimes read as advocating a "selective," contrasted with an "inclusive" philosophy of race. Vasconcelos argues that "superior" qualities and values will emerge from the process of *mestizaje*, which also eliminates "lower" or "inferior" types. He writes:

> The lower types of the species will be absorbed by the superior type. In this manner, for example, the Black could be redeemed, and step by step, by voluntary extinction, the uglier stocks will give way to the more handsome. Inferior races, upon being educated, would become less prolific, and the better specimens would go on ascending a scale of ethnic improvement, whose maximum type is not precisely the White, but that new race [mestizo/a] to which the White himself will have to aspire with the object of conquering the synthesis. The Indian, by grafting onto the related race, would take the jump of millions of years that separate Atlantis from our times, and in a few decades of aesthetic eugenics, the Black may disappear, together with the types that a free instinct of beauty may go on signaling as fundamentally recessive and undeserving, for that reason of perpetuation[16]

On Vasconcelos's account, "[t]he *mestizo* category was supposed to subsume all others, thus becoming the 'cosmic' race—totalizing, hegemonic, and superior".[17] If "the mestizo category is supposed to subsume all others," then at least in some Latin American countries the category had to include people of African descent. If *mestizaje* did not include African descendant peoples, then they would have to remain permanently outside the racial constitution of the nation, and the category could not be claimed to include the full plurality of races present in many Latin American countries. Vasconcelos certainly intended for the mestizo/a category to include peoples of African descent, though for that supposed race "aesthetic eugenics" was a process of purification and betterment more than it was for other races.

Vasconcelos highlights the essentially ephemeral nature of races. But unlike Locke, rather than simply observing that racial existences are often of diverse origins and lead inevitably into newer historical forms, Vasconcelos observes that the transformation from one historical form to another is not always a matter of progress, being sometimes instead a case of regression or degeneration.

As a cosmopolitan project, Vasconcelos's view is one that seeks to transcend the constraints of racial identity and overcome the limitations of a nationalist orientation. The cosmic race is for Vasconcelos the idealized historical outcome of current processes of interaction, miscegenation, and integration, leading him to claim ultimately that "[a] mixture of races accomplished according to the laws of social well-being, sympathy, and beauty, will lead to the creation of a type infinitely superior to all that have previously existed."[18] As he understood it, "[c]ivilization . . . always derives from a long, secular preparation and purification of elements that are transmitted and combined from the beginning of History."[19] Civilization is rarely, if ever, the product of any one racial group, and its greatest historical forms have all been the result of a diverse amalgamation of peoples from various places.

"No contemporary race," as Vasconcelos sees them, "can present itself alone as the finished model that all the others should imitate" though some have and may still wish to present themselves in that way.[20] The parochialism and chauvinism of some races that have occupied positions of power and privilege relative to others is fundamentally misguided on this account, as the system fails to recognize an important and salient fact; namely, that nowhere in history do we have a "race capable of forging civilization by itself. The most illustrious epochs of humanity have been, precisely, those in which several different peoples have come into contact and mixed with each other."[21] It is in this mixing that Vasconcelos hopes that the pernicious forms of racial identification that stand as obstacles to a more cosmopolitan orientation and comportment can be overcome. To be sure, he sees the mestizo race as already headed down this path being as it is an inextricably mixed racial type. "The so-called Latins," he observes, "insist on not taking the ethnic factor too much into account in their sexual relations, perhaps because from the beginning they are not, properly speaking, Latins, but a conglomeration of different types and races. Whatever opinion one may express in this respect, and whatever repugnance caused by prejudice one may harbor, the truth," Vasconcelos sees and insists upon, "is that the mixture of races has taken place and continues to be consummated. It is in this fusion of stocks that we should look for the fundamental characteristics of the Ibero-American idiosyncrasy" as a particularly fecund source of the sentiments and practices of cosmopolitanism.[22]

Racial chauvinism is not however for Vasconcelos the only impediment to the desired cosmopolitan outlook, there is also the restrictive influence of patriotism and nationalism. Human communities often find themselves "proud of a patriotism [that is] exclusively national," and fail to notice in that "the dangers that

[can] threaten a race as a whole."[23] The suggestion here being of course that the more expansive cosmic racial understanding is a way of freeing ourselves of the restrictions and limitations of national identity. "If patriotism does not identify with the diverse stages of" its historical development, "it shall never overcome a regionalism lacking in universal breadth and courage," and will likely "degenerate into a narrow and provincial shortsightedness."[24]

Race and Revolution: José Martí's Racial Eliminativism

Another Latin American thinker, José Martí, understands racial and national identification differently. For Martí, race is an irreconcilable obstacle to national identity as well as to cosmopolitanism. Martí argued that, "[m]en have no special rights simply because they belong to one race or another. When you say 'men,' you have already imbued them with all their rights."[25] Much like Vasconcelos, Martí understood racial chauvinism on the part of both racialized whites and Blacks as fundamentally invidious and antithetical to a humanistic and cosmopolitan worldview. "To insist on racial divisions, on racial differences, in an already divided people," Martí argued, "is to place obstacles in the way of public and individual happiness, which can only be obtained by bringing people together as a nation."[26]

> "Racist" is a confusing word, and it should be clarified. Men have no special rights simply because they belong to one race or another. When you say "men," you have already imbued them with all their rights. Negroes, because they are black, are not inferior or superior to any other men.... Everything that divides men, everything that specifies, separates or hems them in, is a sin against humanity.... To insist on the racial divisions and racial differences of a people naturally divided is to obstruct both individual and public happiness, which lies in greater closeness among the elements that must live in common.[27]

Racial membership for Martí does not bestow or deny rights. All human beings are possessed of exactly the same natural rights. Martí claims that being racialized as Black does not make a person superior or inferior to any other. This might be a consequence of the belief that racial membership does not bestow inferiority or superiority on its members. And it might be that Martí thinks races cannot be hierarchically ranked because no persons are members of races, and so there is no hierarchical ranking to be done. Martí later claims that Negroes are not inherently precluded from cultivating their human potential, nor are their innate capacities limited by what happens to them.

Professions of one's race are for Martí superfluous. Racial identification does not add to our understanding of a person. Racial identities are merely extravagant and excessive. In one sense, Martí's claim that race does not add to our understanding of a person seems mistaken. As racial constructionists are quick to point out, the phenomenon of race has many practical consequences for people's lives. Knowing or failing to know about the phenomenon of race, including how one is racially identified in a given context can have very significant actual consequences in one's life. In that sense, race does add to our understanding of how certain people will likely function in some social settings. Now, if the question is, "what does race add to our understanding of the person *qua* person; that is, the person as such?" things may be a bit different. Given that racial membership is not associated with superiority or inferiority, possession of rights, or innate capacities or incapacities of any kind for Martí, it is not obvious that race tells you anything of consequence about persons as such. The way a person is racialized may tell you a great deal about her likelihood of encountering certain economic, social, or political advantages or disadvantages, without conveying anything of individual significance about her. The negative consequences of racialism—that it divides, subjugates, and deprives people of freedom, to name but a few—are all in Martí's estimation "sins against humanity". That is, they diminish individual personhood and autonomy in one's own person or that of another, rather than allow it to flourish. It is the divisiveness inherent in racialism that he finds objectionable.

Where a people are already divided, racialism, Martí argues, is antithetical to public and individual happiness that can only come from free and voluntary association of like-minded people, as in the forming of a nation. It ought to be stated and demonstrated, Martí argues, that people racialized as Black are not inherently incapable of fulfilling its human potential and capacity. Martí points out that the world is not short on injustice. He adds that ignorance often passes for wisdom. By way of example, Martí notes the commonly held belief at the time that the Negro is inherently inferior to whites in intellect and sentiment. The fact that racialized Blacks are not innately inferior coupled with the false wisdom of those who believe that they are, necessitates a "defense of nature," that is, a demonstration of the fact that people racialized as Black are fully human and on a par with all other races. It does not matter, Martí contends, if this is called racism. It is a matter of natural respect and honesty, the desire for peace and the nation's well-being. He writes:

> And what does it matter if this truth, this defense of nature, is called racism, because it is no more than natural respect, the voice that clamors from man's bosom for the life and the peace of the nation. To

state that the condition of slavery does not indicate any inferiority in
the enslaved race—for white Gauls with blue eyes and golden hair
were sold as slaves with fetters around their necks in the markets of
Rome—is good racism, because it is pure justice and helps the
ignorant white to shed his prejudices. But that is the limit of just
racism, which is the right of the black man to maintain and demonstrate that his color does not deprive him of any of the capacities and
rights of the human race.[28]

Martí articulates a notion of "good racism." To claim that enslavement does not entail the inferior humanity of the enslaved is an example of good racism. The claim is supported by the fact that past enslavements of racialized white populations is not taken to indicate white inferiority—not even in those cases where racialized white populations were subjugated by racialized Black populations. Good racism, according to Martí, is pure justice. It is an assertion motivated by self-respect, against pernicious claims of racial inferiority. He seems to think that the shedding of prejudice by those racialized as white is aided by good racism. The right of racialized Black people to prove and maintain their humanity, potential, capacity, and rights is the limiting condition of just racism.

Martí asks,

What right do white racists, who believe their race is superior, have for
complaining about black racists, who see something special in their
own race? What right do black racists, who see a special character in
their race, have for complaining about white racists? White men who
think their race makes them superior to black men admit the idea of
racial difference and authorize and initiate black racists. Black men
who proclaim their race-when what they are really proclaiming is the
spiritual identity that distinguishes one ethnic group from another-
authorize and incite white racists. Peace demands of Nature the
recognition of human rights; discrimination is contrary to Nature and
is the enemy of peace. Whites who isolate themselves also isolate
Negroes. Negroes who isolate themselves incite and isolate whites.[29]

Martí argues with some rhetorical force that the racialism of racialized whites and Blacks negates the right of both to object to the counterclaims of the other. The trouble is that both, in being racialists, agree to a kind of realism about race. Whether one assigns superiority and special traits to one race or denies them to another, both believe that different populations of human beings constitute races. Martí contends that the differing racial conceptions of Black and white racialists are equally provocative to the other and so neither is in a position to complain. This may seem a bit curious given his earlier claims concerning good racism. But there it was the demonstration that certain pernicious racist beliefs are false that met with Martí's approval. Good racism can be understood as merely a position of counter-assertion devoid of racialism.

An important concern in the historical and political context of Latin America, which Martí is acutely attuned to as it relates to the Cuban revolution, is the ethnoracial and class divisions imposed by Spanish colonial rule. The concern dates back at least as far as Simón Bolivar, who recognized the racial diversity of nearly all Latin American countries, and the presence in some of relatively large populations of enslaved indigenous and African descendant peoples, as a potentially serious problem for the countries he wished to liberate from Spanish colonial rule. Bolivar "did indeed fear some of the political and social consequences of racial diversity, and in this sense he contributes to the effort of trying to understand how to deal with racial pluralism in a postcolonial society."[30] An important dimension of the problem posed by racial diversity for Bolivar concerned the role of various racial and racially mixed populations in the quest for independence, as his "greatest fear" was "that of *pardocracia*, the idea that only *pardos* should rule Venezuela and turn it into a sort of Haiti."[31] Bolivar recognized that "[c]*riollos*, *pardos*, mestizos, mulattos, *negros*, and *indios* . . . were often pitted against each other, sometimes in ways that approached race wars."[32] It has been observed that "for Bolivar, the root of these conflicts was political, not racial, that is, not grounded on irreconcilable racial identities."[33] And for his part, Martí would agree, though for different reasons than Bolivar's, that the underlying problem is not recalcitrant racial identities. However, this still puts Martí in the rhetorical position of having to address in his justification and promotion of Cuban independence the racial differences and disparities that existed in Cuba, which at the time was still a slave-holding country. To this end Martí maintains that,

> In Cuba, there is no fear of a race war. Men are more than whites, mulattos or Negroes. Cubans are more than whites, mulattos or Negroes. On the field of battle, dying for Cuba, the souls of whites and Negroes have risen together into the air. In the daily life of defense, loyalty, brotherhood and shrewdness, Negroes have always been there, alongside whites. Negroes, like whites, are divided by their character—timid or brave, self-sacrificing or selfish—into the diverse parties in which men group themselves. Political parties form around common concerns, aspirations, interests and characters.[34]

Nationalism, for Martí, is a way to join the interest of superficially diverse peoples in a way that forges between them those points of contact requisite for seeing beyond difference to a common humanity. "Political parties form around common concerns, aspirations, interests and characters. . . . similarities are sought and found beneath superficial differences; the common purpose is the fusion of that which is basic in the analogous characters, even though they may differ in incidentals."[35] Nationalism depends upon "the similarity of characters, which is a superior uniting factor, [and] outweighs the inner frictions between men of varying color and the difficulties that, at times, result."[36] Martí suggests that "[a]ffinity of character is more powerful than the affinity of color. So-called Negroes, consigned to the unequal or hostile pursuits of the human spirit, will never be able to join, nor will they want to join, against so-called whites in like position."[37] Persons possessed of the nationalist sentiment as Martí understands it, whether "black [or] white, will treat one another with loyalty and tenderness, out of a sense of merit and the pride of everyone who honors the land in which [they] were born, black and white alike" will work "together to develop men's minds, to spread virtue and to promote the triumph of creative work and sublime charity."[38]

Martí argues that "[p]atriotism should be censured when it is invoked to prevent friendship among all men of good will, in the entire world, all who can see the growth of unnecessary wrongs and are honestly trying to alleviate them."[39] He regarded "patriotism as a sacred duty" to fight "to make ones country a happy place in which to live," but a place in which one does not insist on one's own rights while refusing to fight for the rights of others.[40] Each individual nationalist effort, affirming as it does those universally human points of contact between compatriots, instills in the patriotic individual those sentiments and habits that enable a more cosmopolitan outlook.

In Martí's view, then, while racial identities are provincial and unduly truncate human personhood, national identities and political associations break down barriers and free human capacities. Whereas racial labels tenuously mark inferiority or superiority, national identities convey more fully the humanity and character of people. Martí believes that as members of such social groups, peoples of African descent will have less cause to use the word "racist," recognizing instead that justification of racism is merely a specious argument, valid only among people of deficient character, for denying the rights of African descendant people. Designating things racist, even in good faith, will cease to be useful.

A key aspect of Martí's understanding of race, one that he shares significantly with racial eliminativists, is that a significant part of the harm racialism does is to limit racialized people's humanity, autonomy, and individuality to a single identity conception, and to one not freely chosen. Martí seems to think that no person is justifiably reducible to a racial identity. To designate a person as white, mulatto, or Negro, for example, is always to leave some important aspect of that person's identity and personhood unstated. Things become a bit more paradoxical; however, when Martí says immediately following this that Cubans are more than whites, mulattos, or Negroes. Why should constructed national labels take precedence over constructed racial labels? Is there something about national labels that allows them to speak to the identity and personhood of an individual in a way that racial labels cannot? If so, what is it?

Martí's answer to these queries is multifaceted. First, national identities are freely chosen in his view, not forcibly imposed. Second, national identities are determined by a similarity and affinity of character. The actions and traits of character required to form an independent nation naturally unite persons of different putative racial descriptions. Those racialized as white as well as Black, he maintains, can be grouped according to their similarity of character. Those who possess virtuous dispositions will form one group, and those possessed of a vicious character will form another. To be sure, Martí has in mind particular virtuous traits and vicious traits but the underlying principle may well be true for a different set of dispositions than those Martí has specifically in mind. The underlying claim is that similarity of character forms group bonds across racial, ethnic, religious, cultural, and class boundaries. Third, political parties unite people on the basis of shared concerns, interests, and aspirations, in addition to similar character traits they share despite the minor differences in detail and varying incidental characteristics and motivations. That is, they conjoin not only like characters, but common concerns and purposes. Finally, the bases for solidarity in national identities and political parties join people more strongly than does mere association on the basis of phenotypical similarity.

Martí's Eliminativist Challenge to Vasconcelos and Locke

It may prove interesting to consider Vasconcelos's and Locke's philosophies of race from the critical vantage point of Martí's racial eliminativism. First, regarding Vasconcelos, Martí would likely argue that the biological racialism on which his view of *mestizaje* depends is scientifically false and fundamentally misguided. It is false for the same reasons that other forms of classical racialism are false; specifically, that the belief that races are genetically discernible populations is scientifically dubious, that biological populations even if scientifically determined need not correspond to putative racial categories, and that genetic characteristics do not cause or influence cultural aptitude or traits. While the concept of *mestizaje* has the specious advantage of abandoning ideas of racial purity, in Vasconcelos's conception it still relies on an understanding of races as biologically real entities, and a close, perhaps causal, relationship between those entities and specific cultural traits and characteristics.

Another aspect of Vasconcelos's philosophy of race to which Martí might take exception is the claim that the mestizo is a racially superior type. Martí explicitly rejects the notion of racial superiority and inferiority. He does so because a careful examination of the many putative racial categories yields an understanding that the sorts of political and social successes that are typically taken to characterize superior races have been experienced by various racialized populations, even those that have been considered inferior. On the other hand, the lack of political and cultural success that has typically been associated with racial inferiority has likewise been the plight of racialized populations commonly regarded as superior. Martí's argumentative strategy in this regard is to look at various instances throughout human history when such reversals of fate have been the case. His own example is the enslavement of the Gauls, but other historical examples such as the Moorish occupation of the Iberian Peninsula serve also to make the point.

Martí might well express some sympathy with the spirit of Vasconcelos's position insofar as it is aimed in part at a rejection of the traditional racial hierarchy, but as Martí explicitly rejects the idea of racial superiority or inferiority he must ultimately stand in opposition to this feature of Vasconcelos's position. Martí argues that because races are not real, racial difference is merely illusory, as is the idea of racial hierarchy. That is, even under the presupposition that ideas of superiority and inferiority are attributable to different populations, it does not follow that such status is attributable to race, and if biological racial differences are merely illusory, then notions of superiority and inferiority are not attributable to such differences.

A major aspect of Martí's racial eliminativism is his rejection of racialism; that is, the belief that the human species is naturally divisible into genetically distinct subspecies, and that those subspecies correspond to a set of phenotypic, demographic, individual or cultural traits. Vasconcelos's view of *mestizaje* is one of a hybrid or amalgamated racial type, one that results from the social and physical intercourse of supposedly pure racial types. The resultant mestizo race is understood by Vasconcelos as itself a distinct racial type, and to that specific type he attributes superior status on the basis of the belief that the mestizo would embody the best characteristics, and be devoid of the worst characteristics, of each of the biological racial kinds out of which it is constituted, where those characteristics are understood to be cultural traits caused by the unique biological features of the various races that make up the mestizo.

The implications of Vasconcelos's view to which Martí is acutely attuned are that the view of the mestizo as a composite racial type forged out of various pure racial types, reifies the notion that African, Anglo-Saxon, Latin, and Antillean are distinct racial types. In order to merge distinct racial types into a new cosmic racial type, one must first presuppose a racial difference between the original unmerged types. More than that, Vasconcelos's view is that the resulting mestizo race is itself a distinct racial kind. Recall that for Martí any assertion of racial distinctiveness is divisive. What is more, Vasconcelos does not even seem to want to deny that racial distinctiveness is divisive. After all, he means to point to the distinctiveness of the mestizo as the source of its superiority. And he could not possibly avoid that position given his views. So it turns out that the mere fact that the mestizo is an essentially hybrid racial kind does nothing at all to address Martí's worries about the divisiveness of racialism. Even the idea of an amalgamated hybrid race, the idea of *mestizaje*, is one that promotes racialism.

Finally, against Vasconcelos Martí would likely press the argument that all forms of racialism impede the success of national independence and the formation of free republican states in Latin America. Martí and Vasconcelos shared the belief that Latin American nations were unique in their ethnoracial constitutions in that nearly all were ethnoracially diverse. As such, American nations were forced to confront the difficulties of racial difference and stratification in their efforts to achieve independence and form functioning liberal democratic states. Moreover, both men believed that the system of racial differentiation that American nations inherited from their colonizers was a formidable structural obstacle, among others, to the formation of independent functioning states. And while both advocated different proposals for dealing with the racial reality of American nations, they were agreed in the belief that the colonial system of racial stratification was untenable in free and independent American states. So, if the implied criticism of Vasconcelos's racial outlook by Martí holds sway, then insofar as the former's racial understanding retains exactly the features of the colonial system of racial domination that have proved so problematic for Latin American states; namely, a commitment to scientifically invalidated conceptions of biological racialism, false notions of racial superiority, and an inherently divisive racialism that confounds reasonable attempts at constructing free and independent Latin American nation-states, then that racial philosophy must fall victim to the same criticisms as the colonial model of racial domination.

In the case of Locke, there appear to be more similarities in their racial views than between Martí and Vasconcelos, but that is not to suggest that Martí's views are without applicable criticisms to Locke's philosophy of race. To begin, Martí might well press the claim against Locke that even the revised notion of social or ethnic race is a form of racialism that reifies racial difference.

The principal difference between Locke and Martí, and the primary thrust of the latter's possible criticism of the former, is the belief that all forms of racialism lead ultimately to pernicious social division. Locke's account of race is in some important respects the opposite of Vasconcelos's view, as race for Locke is a product of culture, not the other way around, as it is for Vasconcelos. Yet, even though racial differences do not reduce to genetic differences on Locke's account, racial populations for him are still distinctive populations, even if only culturally distinct. Martí recognizes that there will likely exist social and individual differences within any society. What he takes issue with as essentially divisive is the racialization of that difference; that is, treating said difference as a biological racial difference.

This ties into another possible criticism of Locke by Martí; specifically, that Locke's advocacy of racialism for social justice is still a form of racism to which Martí would object. The issue here is a bit more nuanced because Martí's conception of "good racism" would seem to permit the use of racialism for purposes of social justice. The trouble as Martí sees it is that such invocations of racialism seem to presuppose a belief in racial distinctiveness even if such a belief is not held by one who advocates racialism as a form of "good racism." Racialism in such situations is contextual, but even in being contextual presupposes a racial division within the human species. That is, even granted that Locke's use of racialism for social justice is an instance of "good racism," it seems one must assume the racialism of the bad racist to argue that the attribution of inferiority or superiority is mistaken.

Finally, against Locke, Martí is likely to press his claim that racial identification is an impediment to realizing better identities. Racial identification does not structure identity around the shared personality, character, and values around which Martí thinks political associations are built and which are essential to the positive features of political party associations.

Vasconcelos's and Locke's Responses to Martí

Having specified the probable criticisms of Vasconcelos and Locke on Martí's behalf, it remains to be seen how each might respond to those criticisms. In the case of Vasconcelos, whose biological racialism is unmistakable, he would be forced to concede Martí's critique. In fact, Vasconcelos later in life does in fact recant the notion of *la raza cosmica*. However, despite making such a concession to Martí's position, Vasconcelos loses his claims only concerning the biological aspects of his view. He cannot successfully maintain the claim that *mestizaje* is a biologically distinct racial kind that results from the physical intermingling of distinct racial kinds that exist in the Americas. However, he very well could maintain that even if the notion of physical miscegenation is mistaken because there are no distinctive biological racial populations, there could nevertheless be social intercourse between the various cultural elements found in the Americas. That is, though Vasconcelos may be forced to concede that *mestizaje* is not a process of mixing biological races, it is nonetheless a process of mixing definite cultural elements. This view would be akin to that articulated by Locke, and in that regard subject to the same criticism levelled against Locke.

In response to the second criticism, namely, that belief in mestizo racial superiority is itself a commitment to the misguided idea of racial superiority and inferiority, Vasconcelos could argue that attributing superiority to a hybrid racial type is a preferable alternative to such attributions to supposedly pure racial types. Moreover, the fact that the superiority of the mestizo race depends on its being a combination of racial types is meant by Vasconcelos to highlight the fact that no putatively pure race is superior to all others. On his account all of the commonly understood racial groupings are lacking in some important features that contribute to the realization of an ideal civilization. The racial superiority of the mestizo then is in part a demonstration that none of the recognized racial populations that exist in the Americas is in a position to claim superiority outright. Mestizo racial superiority might be intended to exert a humbling influence. What is more, this might qualify Vasconcelos's position as an instance of "good racism."

Vasconcelos's response to Martí's criticism that racial amalgamation reifies the belief in racial differences might well be that *mestizaje* represents an appreciation and respect for plurality as part of a larger whole. Vasconcelos's view of race does not celebrate racial difference; instead it venerates racial plurality and hybridity. The aim is to emphasize what people in the Americas have in common and the ways in which they are able to realize the advantages of intermingling.

Finally, Vasconcelos might defend against Martí's claim that racialism is an impediment to national independence by countering that *mestizaje* unites national elements in a manner that facilitates independent state formation. *La raza cosmica* was conceived as a way to conjoin the disparate racial elements of Mexican society and enable the pursuit of a progressive social agenda. Vasconcelos faced a problem common to American nations; namely, how best to ameliorate the social strife caused by racial division. His answer was to advocate a form of racialism that understood every member of the state as caught up in a process of racially conjoining into a single racial identity that would characterize the nation.

In the case of Locke, he could reply to Martí's first criticism that the proper understanding and attitude toward race need not be divisive. A crucial aspect of Locke's philosophy of race is his commitment to cultural pluralism. For Locke, the revised notion of ethnic race, devoid of biological racialism, makes possible a mutual appreciation of, and across, difference. Locke's and Martí's philosophies of race share a rejection of racial superiority and inferiority. For Martí this is because there are no races. For Locke this is because he draws a distinction between the existence of race and our attitudes towards them. Supposed racial superiority and inferiority is the historical result of political, economic and cultural factors that allow some populations to exert dominance over others. Racial superiority is little more than a false narrative politically and economically fortunate nations tell about themselves. Racial inferiority is nothing other than the story they tell about others for their own advantage. The existence of social races does not entail, in Locke's account, any racial hierarchy. The recognition that race is a product of culture, and a belief in reciprocity across cultures, means for Locke that insofar as racial differences are ultimately cultural, and mutual respect and reciprocity across cultures is possible, that such reciprocity is at least possible in regard to racial difference. For all three thinkers a major aspect of their racial views is navigating the complex racial plurality of the Americas. Locke's prescription, contrary to Martí, is to recognize racial diversity as a positive feature of American nations, one that understood in the proper way makes cooperation through difference possible.

In reply to Martí's potential worry that racialism in pursuit of social justice is still likely to be divisive, Locke might likely begin his defense by pointing out some agreements between his own view and Martí's. Martí was concerned that racism and racialism of any kind lead almost inevitably to social division of the sort that is inimical to the interests of an emerging American nation. The notion of "good racism," by which he means the invocation of racialism as a means of disproving pernicious race creeds and curtailing prejudicial race practices, is a point of agreement between Martí and Locke.[41] Take for example the claim that a past history of enslavement does not entail the inferior humanity of the enslaved population. Support for this claim is to be found in the fact that past enslavements of portions of the white race does not indicate white inferiority, not even in those cases where the white race was subjugated by the Black race. This is an example of Martí's notion of good racism or racialism. Martí argues that good racism is pure justice.[42] Such implementations of good racialism are motivated by self-respect against claims of racial inferiority. Martí contends that the shedding of prejudice by whites is aided by good racism.[43] The right of members of the black race to prove and maintain their humanity, potential, capacity and rights is the limiting condition of just racism. Locke and Martí are in substantial agreement on these points.

Locke's answer to this dilemma lies in what he sees as the "almost limitless natural reciprocity between cultures."[44] Civilizations, Locke notes, despite their many claims to distinctiveness, are vast amalgamations of cultures. That is, civilizations are constituted by the multiplicity of cultural contributions made by members of many populations, some even by cultural groups that constitute a race, what Locke calls social or ethnic races. Racialism, in Locke's view, can be put to good or bad uses. An endorsement of racialism as it currently exists and the practices and attitudes that presently accompany it is ipso facto an endorsement of existing race creeds and the present racial order. However, if the consequences of racialism are not only negative, if racialism can be useful for beneficent social purposes, as Locke contends it can be, then it seems that it ought in those limited circumstances to be endorsed. The troubling thing for Locke is the possibility of eliminating undesirable racial practices and preserving the desirable practices. If all political conceptions of race are scientifically false, then invocations of race meant to correct their theoretical inaccuracies are instances of good racialism. If reactions to political conceptions of race are instances of good racialism, then good racialism is appropriate in a larger range of circumstances than Martí seems to acknowledge.

In response to the last criticism on Martí's behalf, Locke could argue that while parochial racial identification is in fact problematic in the way Martí suggests, the pluralistic and cosmopolitan form of racial identification he advocates does not restrict one arbitrarily to a single identity. An important aspect of Locke's view is that it urges a change in attitude toward both one's own racial membership and that of others. One crucial aspect of this changed perspective is the recognition that one's racial identity is just one among many, and one that need not be held provincially or chauvinistically.

Locke's Challenge to Martí

It is perhaps worthwhile in the case of Locke to consider how he might go beyond merely defending against the potential criticisms of Martí, but might well articulate a few criticisms of his own of Martí's racial eliminativism. Much of what Martí says about national identities and membership in political parties, Locke could argue, could be true of races too. Racial solidarity can be a means of joining together similar characters, and surely can unite persons with common interests, concerns, and purposes. Moreover, while races themselves are provincial, their interests and aims, as well as their political organizations, need not be. More to the point, Locke's own thinking in regard to the phenomena of race contact is that war is perfectly capable of uniting otherwise antagonistic racial groups. In situations where otherwise antagonistic racial groups find that they have a common enemy and similar interests, the barriers of race can be broken down.

Martí at times seems to assume a greater uniformity among the Cuban people in terms of values, dispositions, projects, and aspirations than may have in fact been the case. However, even if one grants Martí that before, during, and for a time following the revolution, the Cuban people will be similar in these respects, they are not likely to remain so uniform long after the revolution. Eventually, newer, dissimilar characters, projects, and values would arise around which various people would unite and ipso facto differentiate.

Locke here challenges Martí to see the other side of the issue he has posed. Martí contends that political parties unite analogous characters. Locke challenges him to consider that in uniting those analogous characters, what unites them to one another also distinguishes them from dissimilar characters. Unless one assumes a homogeneous Cuban people in terms of their values, dispositions, aims, and projects, Locke's point is relevant here. If the Cuban people are heterogeneous in regard to these factors, then the very recognition of similarities that enable the formation of analogous groupings of people show how that same group differs in the salient respect from other people or groups in the society. It must be noted that in Locke's view, while difference is often a precondition of group antagonism, the mere fact of difference is insufficient for conflict between groups.

Toward an Inter-American Philosophy of Race

The task of articulating an inter-American philosophy requires that one take a bit of intellectual license. This creates a situation in which contemporary scholars must exercise some creativity. Locke, Vasconcelos, and Martí all reflected explicitly on the countries of their births, but they were all intellectually concerned beyond their own national confines. One finds in thinkers like them material for an incipient inter-American philosophical perspective. Part of the task is to explicate the considered and stated views of such thinkers on subjects that extend throughout the Americas. This involves an innovative exegesis that draws on multiple aspects of their overall thought on a plurality of subjects across multiple contexts. The potential rewards are proportionate to the challenge of such an endeavor. Such a task may yield a clear articulation of positions consistent with, in the very least, but perhaps, it is to be hoped, even implied with some non-negligible degree of force by Locke's, Vasconcelos's, and Martí's philosophic worldviews. Conceptual resources pertinent to matters of contemporary concern can be found as readily in pondering over what intellectuals neglected to say, and accounting for the seeming dereliction, as in concerning ourselves with what they did say.

Various American regions share common historical threads but many also diverge at important and interesting points. Locke, Vasconcelos, and Martí were keenly aware and critical of the predilection toward focusing on North America to produce at best a myopic view of all of the Americas, or at worst a complete blindness to large portions of the Americas. Systematic thinking about the Americas need not establish a superficial unity across the continents. There is, however, the possibility of discovering theoretical, cultural, and intellectual cognates that resonant with/in the plurality of cultures which comprise the Americas.

One could approach theorizing the Americas through the experiences of those of African heritage in various American contexts or use the perhaps narrower conceptual framework of race. This approach evidences the variety of perspectives of and about peoples of African descent variably racialized as Black in the Americas, all the while serving as a coordinating thread with which to weave together the ostensibly disparate strands of Black life. Through this lens one is able to see the larger effects of historical and social processes, even as they are varied to fit specific contexts, across time and place.

There are several benefits that accrue to any serious and sustained attempt at philosophizing in an inter-American context—even when that exploration is circumscribed by a single racialized population—not least of which is the potential for increased cross-cultural understanding. A broader philosophical framework can serve not only to bring out the relative distinctiveness but also the plurality of American cultures. Viewed in comparative relation to one another, the various cultures of the Americas could become better understood internally and externally to whatever extent a comparative and functional understanding makes that possible. With regard to the more circumspect project of looking at the American portions of the African diaspora, this larger framework obviates a more heterogeneous, and thereby accurate picture of Black life, and the variety of forms of living, ethnic variation, religious practice, and artistic expression to be found within peoples of African descent. In looking at the varied existence of people of African descent in the Americas, as well as the myriad responses to their existence in different contexts, one reveals for philosophical investigation a more wide-ranging set of phenomena than Black people as such.

Next, an inter-American approach has the potential to deepen the philosophical enterprise by exposing the arguments and positions of philosophers to a diversity of critical perspectives. A theoretical point of view that extends beyond the specious claims to universality of Anglo American philosophy will help philosophers escape the narrow confines of ethnically or racially delimited American philosophies. An environment in which persons are regularly brought into theoretical and practical contact with critical perspectives of groups of which they are not members (provided they are oriented toward such difference in a manner that makes them receptive to it) is one that holds out the possibility of greater—perhaps ever-increasing plurality and critical insight provided the necessary orientation is maintained over time.

Practical advantages emanate from a more expansive view of the Americas, principal among which is that the knowledge of others' effort at ameliorating similar problems in different contexts can strengthen one's own resolve and resources for solving problems. So, too, as we come to greater realization of the multiplicity of successful adaptive responses by different ethnic, racial, and cultural groups in the Americas to global and historical forces that bear on us all in varying degrees, do these groups stand to gain the wisdom of not only our own, but of other's experiences.

Furthermore, there is historical precedence to support not only the interconnectedness, but also the theoretical salience of scholarship generated in one part of the Americas being applicable to other American contexts. Moreover, scholarly focus on all of the Americas as they interrelate will help obviate the superficial isolation of American cultures and the artificial divisions across culture-groups, or manifest the deeply entrenched nature of cultural and ethnoracial divisions across the Americas. Inter-American philosophy provides a framework from which to consider these issues without arbitrarily privileging any one perspective.

What, then, are we asking of theorists such as Locke, Vasconcelos, and Martí? Presumably, they cannot solve practical or theoretical issues of contemporary concern, unless they are little more than the mere persistence of problems of their own day. Locke, Vasconcelos, and Martí offer instead a stable point of departure in the form of a philosophical springboard from which to launch our own ameliorative efforts, as well as a sound philosophical framework suited to facilitate a proper determination of the nature of a given social problem and the likely prospects for its successful resolution.

Notes

1. José Vasconcelos, *La Raza Cósmica/The Cosmic Race*, trans. Didier T. Jaén. (Baltimore: Johns Hopkins University Press, 1997).

2. Alain Locke, "The Contribution of Race to Culture," in *The Philosophy of Alain Locke: Harlem Renaissance and Beyond*, ed. Leonard Harris. (Philadelphia, PA: Temple University Press, 1989), 202.

3. Alain Locke, "The Contribution of Race to Culture," 202.
4. Alain Locke, "The Contribution of Race to Culture," 202–206.
5. Alain Locke, "The Contribution of Race to Culture," 202–203.
6. Alain Locke, *Race Contacts and Interracial Relations: Lectures on the Theory and Practice of Race*, ed. Jeffrey C. Stewart. (Washington, D.C.: Howard University Press, 1992), 63.
7. Alain Locke, *Race Contacts and Interracial Relations*, 63–64.
8. Diego A. Von Vocano, *The Color of Citizenship: Race, Modernity, and Latin American /Hispanic Political Thought*. (New York: Oxford University Press, 2012), 16; Javier Sanjinés, *Mestizaje Upside Down* (Pittsburg: University of Pittsburg Press, 2004); Carrie C. Chorba, *Mexico, from Mestizo to Multicultural* (Nashville: Vanderbilt University Press, 2007).
9. Von Vocano, *The Color of Citizenship*, 16.
10. Maria L. Amado, "The 'New *Mestiza*,' the Old *Mestizos*: Contrasting Discourses on *Mestizaje, Sociological Inquiry* 82, no. 3 (August 2012): 446–59. doi:10.1111/j.1475-682X.2012.00411.x., 448; Ada Ferrer, "The Silence of Patriots: Race and Nationalism in Martí's Cuba," in *José Martí's "Our America": From National to Hemispheric Cultural Studies*, eds. Jeffrey Belnap and Raúl Fernández (Durham, NC: Duke University Press, 1998), 228–49; Jorge L. A. Gracia, ed. *Forging People: Race, Ethnicity, and Nationality in Hispanic American and Latino/a Thought* (Notre Dame: University of Notre Dame Press, 2011).
11. Amado, "The 'New *Mestiza*,' the Old *Mestizos*," 447.
12. Von Vocano, *The Color of Citizenship*, 16; Ofelia Schutte, "'Undoing Race': Martí's Historical Predicament," in *Forging People: Race, Ethnicity, and Nationality in Hispanic American and Latino/a Thought*, ed. Jorge J. E. Gracia. Notre Dame: University of Notre Dame Press, 2011); Gracia, *Forging People*.
13. Amado, 448.
14. Amado, 448.
15. Andrea J. Pitts, "Toward an Aesthetics of Race: Bridging the Writings of Gloria Anzaldúa and José Vasconcelos," *Inter-American Journal of Philosophy* 5, no. 1 (2014): 80–100.
16. José Vasconcelos, *The Cosmic Race*, 32.
17. Amado, 448.
18. José Vasconcelos, *The Cosmic Race*, 31.
19. Vasconcelos, 11.
20. Vasconcelos.
21. Vasconcelos, 32.
22. Vasconcelos, 19.
23. Vasconcelos, 10.
24. Vasconcelos, 12.
25. José Martí, *José Martí: Selected Writings*, ed. and trans. Esther Allen (New York: Penguin Books, 2002), 172; See also José Martí, *José Martí Reader: Writings on the Americas*, edited by Deborah Shnookal and Mirta Muñiz (New York: Ocean Press, 2007).

26. José Martí, *José Martí: Selected Writings*, 172; See also L. Guerra, *The Myth of José Martí: Conflicting Nationalisms in Early Twentieth Century Cuba*, (Chapel Hill: University of North Carolina Press, 2005).
27. Martí, 318.
28. José Martí, *José Martí: Selected Writings*, 319.
29. Martí, 319.
30. Von Vocano, 71.
31. Von Vocano, 71.
32. Von Vocano, 60.
33. Von Vocano, 60.
34. José Martí, *José Martí: Selected Writings*, 319.
35. Martí, 174.
36. Martí, 174.
37. Martí, 174.
38. Martí, 174.
39. Martí, 162.
40. Martí, 162.
41. Martí, 318–321; Locke, *Race Contacts and Interracial Relations*, 20–38.
42. Martí, 319.
43. Martí, 319.
44. Locke, "The Contribution of Race to Culture," 202–203.

Bibliography

Amado, María L. "The 'New *Mestiza*,' the Old *Mestizos*: Contrasting Discourses on Mestizaje" *Sociological Inquiry* 82, no. 3 (2012): 446–59. doi:10.1111/j.1475-682X.2012.00411.x.

Chorba, Carrie C. *Mexico, from Mestizo to Multicultural*. Nashville: Vanderbilt University Press, 2007.

Ferrer, A. "The Silence of Patriots: Race and Nationalism in Martí's Cuba," in *José Martí's "Our America": From National to Hemispheric Cultural Studies*. Edited by Jeffrey Belnap and Raúl Fernández. Durham, NC: Duke University Press, 1998, 228–49.

Gracia, J. L. A, ed. *Forging People: Race, Ethnicity, and Nationality in Hispanic American and Latino/a Thought*, Notre Dame: University of Notre Dame Press, 2011.

Guerra, L. *The Myth of José Martí: Conflicting Nationalisms in Early Twentieth Century Cuba*, Chapel Hill: The University of North Carolina Press, 2005.

Locke, Alain L. *Race Contacts and Interracial Relations: Lectures on the Theory and Practice of Race*. Edited by Jeffrey C. Stewart. Washington, D. C.: Howard University Press, 1992.

———. "The Contribution of Race to Culture," in *The Philosophy of Alain Locke: Harlem Renaissance and Beyond*. Edited by Leonard Harris. Philadelphia, PA: Temple University Press, 1989.

Martí, J. *José Martí Reader: Writings on the Americas*. Edited by Deborah Shnookal and Mirta Muñiz. New York: Ocean Press, 2007.
———. *José Martí: Selected Writings*. Edited and translated by Esther Allen. New York: Penguin Books, 2002.
Pitts, A. "Toward an Aesthetics of Race: Bridging the Writings of Gloria Anzaldúa and José Vasconcelos," *Inter-American Journal of Philosophy*, 5:1(2014): 80–100.
Sanjinés, Javier. *Mestizaje Upside Down*. Pittsburg: University of Pittsburg Press, 2004.
Schutte, Ofelia. "'Undoing Race': Martí's Historical Predicament," in *Forging People: Race, Ethnicity, and Nationality in Hispanic American and Latino/a Thought*, edited by Jorge J. E. Gracia. Notre Dame: University of Notre Dame Press, 2011.
Vasconcelos, José. *The Cosmic Race (La Raza Cósmica)*. Translated by Didier T. Jaén. Baltimore: The Johns Hopkins University Press, 1997.
Von Vocano, Diego. *The Color of Citizenship: Race, Modernity, and Latin American / Hispanic Political Thought*. New York: Oxford University Press, 2012.

11
Reason, Race, and the Human Project: Sylvia Wynter, Sociogenesis, and Philosophy in the Americas

Michael Monahan

When one considers the history and contemporary condition of the Americas in a philosophical context, the typical shelters of abstraction and disengagement to which most philosophers retreat become impossible (in good faith, at least) to maintain. Deliberately and conscientiously placing the timeless and universal concepts of Being, Truth, or Beauty in the specific context of the Americas demands that we attend to ways in which the very claims to timelessness and universality on behalf of these concepts has been maintained and legitimated through their violent imposition on the global stage. That is, the way in which cultural practices and ideas of European origin came to dominate, to a greater or lesser extent, the entirety of the Western Hemisphere has far more to do with conquest, slavery, and genocide than with the appeal of the culture or the power of the ideas. Taking seriously the place and context of *our* philosophizing, in other words, brings the critical encounter with the *particularity* of philosophical practice to the foreground, and raises very serious questions about the notion that there ever has been any such thing as philosophy *simpliciter*.

Indeed, the *idea* of the Americas is born out of a violent imposition. In the moment of the *colonial* encounter, "The Americas" emerged as a resource-rich *terra nullius* waiting to be conquered and exploited. An expedition intended to open trade with "the Orient" quickly became an expedition to conquer and colonize.[1] As well, and of significant importance in the context of philosophy, the colonial encounter marked a seismic shift in the way that the peoples of the emerging European nation states thought of themselves and their place in the political, spiritual, and natural order of things. Taking seriously (and philosophically) the specificity of the Americas therefore demands that one come to grips with violence, exploitation, slavery, environmental degradation, and the general colonial *ethos* of domination, conquest, and *manifest destiny*, along with the way in which this context shaped the ways we think about philosophy and philosophers. To ignore, bracket, or abstract away from this violent moment of encounter and its centuries-long legacy is to commit oneself to a *misunderstanding* of the reality not only of the Americas, but also of Europe. Indeed, part of what this reveals is that the *normal* study of "modern philosophy," which is in fact the study of the philosophy emerging out of Europe in this same period, in ignoring or disavowing the colonial encounter, is not only engaging in exactly this sort of misunderstanding of the very history it purports to study, but in a significant way is a perpetuation of that disavowed or bracketed colonialism.

Furthermore, while the colonial encounter is central to the idea of the Americas, this moment of encounter is also essential to the emergence of the idea of Europe as well. That is, the Portuguese, Spanish, English, French, and Dutch came to think of themselves *as European* through these moments of colonial encounter with Africa and the Americas. What this means is that the fifteenth- and sixteenth-century advent of the intellectual and political manifestations of European modernity (the Enlightenment) and the beginning of the colonial enterprises of the major European powers of the time, as has been frequently noted, were not merely chronologically coincidental, but deeply conceptually (and some have argued, causally) linked. Starting from the critical insight of this link between Enlightenment Modernity and Colonialism, this chapter will take up two tasks. First, building on the work of Sylvia Wynter, I will argue that a particular account of reason was central to the philosophical aspect of the encounter and the ideas of Europe and the Americas that emerged from it; an account that is in turn constitutive of a particular account of personhood in need of further elaboration and philosophical critique. Of special significance is the role that the developing concept of *race* played in the articulation and utilization of the modern conception of the person as *rational man*. Second, I will take up the following crucial question: if the critique of these notions of reason and personhood is to be taken seriously, then with what, if anything, should they be replaced? Drawing upon the work of Lewis Gordon and José Medina, I will argue that a more viable account of these two crucial concepts, and one most appropriate to the history and present reality of the Americas, will emphasize dynamism, openness, and *resistance* as central both to reason and to a more genuinely universal and liberatory concept of the human.

Colonialism, Modernity, and the Man of Reason

The dominant approach to the relationship between Enlightenment Modernity and European Colonialism is to see the latter as simply a failure to live up to the ideals of the former. The notions of universal human rights and the foregrounding of individual liberty and religious toleration are political and intellectual ideals, and like any ideal, there can be a wide variety of failures to live up to them. Of course, those on the receiving end of the colonial bayonet have long recognized this deep inconsistency between Enlightenment political ideals and Colonial political realities, but more recently thinkers have been raising questions about the ideals themselves, not just their implementation. Aimé Césaire, Frantz Fanon, Sylvia Wynter, Enrique Dussel, Walter Mignolo, and Maria Lugones, just to name a few, have argued in various ways that colonialism is intimately tied to the ideals of European modernity, such that the ideals are themselves *infected*, so to speak, with what, following Anibal Quijano, has come to be referred to as *coloniality*. Walter Mignolo explains that while colonization is meant to refer to the physical and geographic occupation of a place and people, coloniality is the way in which this occupation is extended into the cultural, epistemic, and psychological realms. Thus, "whereas decolonization refers mainly to specific moments of political struggles to send the invaders back home, decoloniality opens up the domain of the epistemic and the hermeneutical, explanation and understanding, political and ethical processes delegitimating the colonial matrix of power and building a world that is nonimperial and noncapitalist."[2] Most significantly for present purposes, Mignolo makes the further claim that "coloniality is constitutive of modernity," such that "there is no modernity without coloniality."[3] If this view is correct, it follows that, contrary to the approach characteristic of mainstream political philosophy, colonialism is not a deviation from or failure of the ideals of European modernity, but rather a *realization* or *expression* of them. Clearly, this is a significant and controversial claim in need of further elaboration, and toward that end, I turn now to the work of Sylvia Wynter.

Over the past two decades, Wynter has written a series of articles exploring the seismic shifts in the intellectual and political landscape of Europe from the ninth through the nineteenth centuries, and their relation to colonialism. She captures the central theme of her engagement with these questions in the opening of a 2003 article as follows: ". . . the struggle of our new millennium will be one between the ongoing imperative of securing the well-being of our present ethnoclass (i.e., Western bourgeois) conception of the human, Man, which overrepresents itself as if it were the human itself, and that of securing the well-being, and therefore the full cognitive and behavioral autonomy of the human species itself/ourselves."[4] The problem, in other words, is that "Man", a particular *genre* of humanity, as Wynter puts it, articulated in and through European modernity, and with a particular conception of what it means to be essentially and universally human, has convinced itself, and most of the world, that *it* is the fullest realization of that universal and essential concept.[5] Crucially, not only the well-being, but also the very existence, of this particular genre *Man* is fundamentally parasitic upon the well-being and existence of the rest of the species—*Man* needs, in short, other human beings who, though still members of the same species, are not truly or fully realized manifestations of *Man*. They stand, in Wynter's terms, as the "human Other to *Man*."[6] Such human others were cast by representatives of the genre *Man* not simply as a different way of being human, "but rather as the Lack of what they themselves were; as such, as the 'vile Race' Other to *their* 'true' humanness, the evil nature as opposed to their 'good natures.'"[7]

Key to Wynter's argument here is this relation of *lack*. It is one thing to recognize significant differences between different populations and cultures, and another thing entirely to view one's own culture and population group as the highest and see all others as incomplete or corrupt manifestations, or as pale reflections of the *real* thing. Non-European peoples lacked some vital element: reason, virtue, autonomy, self-discipline, etc., and this crucial *lack* placed them outside of or beyond the norms governing *full* human beings.[8] Property rights, cultural autonomy, liberty, and even life itself were denied on the grounds that only European culture and European persons were fit to govern (and profit from) the world's resources. In considering philosophy in the Americas, every effort must be made to reveal and subject to critique the processes whereby this relation of lack was created, maintained, and legitimated.[9]

Key to understanding how this came to be requires an exploration of Wynter's appropriation of Frantz Fanon's conception of *sociogeny*. In his seminal *Black Skin, White Masks*, Fanon argues that "alongside phylogeny and ontogeny, there is also sociogeny," and, dubbing this "the sociogenetic principle," Wynter argues that it is a constitutive element of human subjectivity.[10] The sociogenetic principle, put simply, claims that we are the kinds of things that we are (both as individuals and as a species) as a result not only of the biological processes that produce us, but also as a result of the *social* processes and conditions in which that biology functions and through which we are produced.

Taking up recent work on the philosophy of mind, especially that of David Chalmers and Thomas Nagel, Wynter argues that sociogeny is inescapable, given the way that human consciousness works. According to her reading, what Fanon is revealing in his use of the concept sociogenesis is:

> that there are subjectively experienced processes taking place, whose functioning cannot be explained in the terms of *only* the natural sciences, of only physical laws . . . the transformation of subjective experience is, in the case of humans, culturally and thereby

socio-situationally determined, with these determinations in turn, serving to activate their physicalistic correlates. In consequence, if the mind is what the brain *does*, *what* the brain *does*, is itself culturally determined through the mediation of the socialized *sense of self*, as well as of the 'social' situation in which the self is placed.[11]

Wynter's argument is that complex biological organisms (like us) have sophisticated neurochemical systems for signaling both reward (pleasure) and punishment (pain) that are both a result of (on the species level), and a motive for (on the individual level), adaptive behaviors. But as human beings, our experience of pleasure and pain, and thus what counts as *normal* behavior (or more specifically, our *subjective experience* of our behavior and that of our fellows as *normal*), is conditioned not merely by biology, but also by our specific cultural situatedness. As Wynter makes the point: "although born as biological humans (as human *skins*), we can *experience ourselves as human* only through the mediation of the processes of socialization effected by the invented *tekhne* or cultural technology to which we give the name *culture*."[12] Being human is thus a matter of sociogeny, in addition to ontogeny and phylogeny. Taking this into account opens up a crucial series of questions about the ways and means of sociogenesis as a historical process, and sets the stage for her inquiry into the relation between European modernity, as a *sense of self*, and colonialism/coloniality.

Before further elaborating Wynter's argument, it is important to say a bit more about the idea of sociogenesis and how it is understood to function. Fanon's particular usage of the term appears quite early in *Black Skin, White Masks*, and is deployed in part as a rebuke to overly reductionistic accounts of human existence. That is, Fanon is distancing his own analysis from the tendency to see human behavior as either strictly determined by biology (both individual, ontogeny; and species-wide, phylogeny), or strictly determined by the individual's *psyche* (in the broad sense of ratiocination as well as subconscious motivations). *Sociogeny* is thus meant to pick out the way in which the particular socially constituted networks of norms, meanings, symbols, modes of bodily comportment, and so on, shape us as agents both *biologically* and *psychically*.

In part, this means that what we might, for the sake of simplicity, call *culture* can shape us as individuals and as a species in ways that need to be taken into account if we are to come anywhere near an adequate understanding of human beings. "An impact of social reality," as Lewis Gordon states in his discussion of sociogenesis, "is ontological; it transforms concepts—knowledge claims—into lived concepts, forms of being, forms of life."[13] In the context of racism and coloniality that was Fanon's focus, the implications of this move are monumental. Racism and coloniality are not simply a set of dispositions or beliefs that one acquires in the course of one's life, and that one can, if one is so inclined, subject to rational scrutiny and accept or reject. Rather, racism and coloniality *shape* the subjectivity of all those who fall within its purview such that what counts as *reasonable*, *normal*, and *intelligible*, for example, is inextricably conditioned by the colonial/racist *milieu*. To truly address racism, therefore, requires not simply changing individual minds or particular laws and policies, but rather reshaping cultures so that they, in turn, can reshape those subjects who are *subject* to it.

A central theme of Fanon's work, in light of the centrality of sociogenesis, was an elaboration of the tremendous impact that colonial racism had and continues to have on subjects in both the (former) colonies and the Mother/Fatherland. In particular, Fanon draws attention to the way in which French culture has positioned itself as the paradigmatic *norm* of reason, of music, of literature, and indeed of culture as such (civilization), against which the benighted denizens of the colonies could only ever compare in terms of *lack*. For the child growing up in Martinique, this meant coming to understand oneself as striving toward an end that one can never reach—there is only one destiny Fanon says of the colonial context, and it is *white*.[14] The resonances with DuBoisian "double consciousness" here are clear—a racist culture generates the conditions whereby those who are posited as *lacking* full humanity will see themselves through the eyes of their oppressors, with the result that they *become* a problem that the white society must face.[15]

The myriad responses to this sense of oneself as placed *by birth* at a distance from the fullest realization of the human are the theme of Fanon's text, and one might read it as a catalog of some of the common responses to this condition and their limitations: from attempting to take on the language and culture of the colonizer, to seeking a kind of proximate whiteness through romantic engagement with white lovers, to attempts to rationally confront racist representation, to lashing out in anger at those who would call your humanity into question, to the embrace of colonial representations of the colonized in an effort to give it a positive valence (one interpretation of the *négritude* movement). What Fanon's analysis reveals so brilliantly is the way in which each of these strategies, in effect, turns back on those who deploy them, and far from elevating them in their own eyes or those of others, only serves in the end to reinscribe their inferiority in relation to the white. As Lewis Gordon has noted, this creates a world in which the pathological is *normal*, and efforts to be normal become pathological.[16]

Of course, for both Fanon and Wynter, while sociogenesis *conditions* human behavior in ways that must be taken seriously, it does not *determine* it. That is, sociogenesis shapes our subjectivity, but insofar as we remain subjects, we can push back against that conditioning. Their work itself stands as testimony to this. Even in the face of an anti-Black world denying their full humanity, to produce work that reveals the mechanisms of racism and calls on the re-articulation of humanity in the face of its systematic degradation is a clear proof that it is possible to struggle, not to overcome or end sociogenesis, since both Fanon and Wynter see it as an inescapable reality of human subject formation, but rather to shape the processes of sociogenesis in ways that are more conducive to liberatory expressions of the human. With this in mind, I want to return to Wynter's analysis of the genesis of the *genre Man*.

The intellectual and cultural upheavals that marked the development of European modernity can thus be understood as shifts in the cultural *tekhne* that condition the European sense of self (and indeed, bring forth the very idea of *Europe* as such).[17] The first of these shifts in the fundamental account of the fullest or highest manifestation of the human, according to the historical portrait Wynter offers, was from *Christian* to *rational political subject*. This was a shift from a view in which the church offered redemption from original sin through proper behavioral subordination to its dictates, to one in which the increasingly secular state offered redemption from our irrational and affective aspects through subordination to the rational state.[18] In terms of the normative ideal of what it meant to be human, it was a transition from the *True Christian Self*, to the rational *Man*.[19]

Later developments in the natural sciences, and especially biology, led to a further fundamental shift to a *biologistic* conception of humanity, in which the fullest or highest realization of the human was not *only* the most rational, but also the most *evolved*.[20] European domination in this moment became proof not only of Europe's cultural superiority, but also of the genetic/biological superiority of European Man. This shift developed hand-in-glove with the then-emerging concepts of *race*, and in this way the rationality of European *Man*, as realized first and foremost in European political and economic institutions, can thus be read as a consequence or, even better, an *expression* of their superior biological fitness—their *whiteness*. Wynter sums up this point as follows:

> Seeing that because all modes of human conscious experience, and thereby, of *consciousness*, can now be seen to be, in all cases, the expression of the culturally constructed mode of subjective experience specific to the functioning of each culture's sociogenic *sense of self*, the same recognition can now be analogically extrapolated to the species-specific *sense of self* expressing the genomic principle defining of all forms of organic life.[21]

Central to Wynter's argument, then, is the idea that European modernity built itself around the formulation (or rather, modification), of a notion of the highest, or put differently, the *purest*, manifestation of the human.[22] In other words, European *Man* is the most pure realization of humanity, and all others are impure or corrupted manifestations of the species.

This development of Europe's *sense of self* took place within a fundamentally binary framework that, according to Wynter, positioned the European *propter nos* always in *relation* to some Other that embodied (and this fact of embodiment would become increasingly crucial at the height of the Enlightenment and the development of the biologistic conception of *Man*) a central *lack* of the essential feature(s) of that self-described highest realization of *Man*. In the earliest stages it was the Christian versus the pagan/heathen, then the rational and civilized versus the irrational and savage, and finally the fully developed and "highest" (purest) form of the species versus the degraded or stunted (corrupted/mongrel) forms. Significantly, it was the encounters first with western Africa, and then with the "new world", that provided the contrasting forms of the human Other to European *Man*. As Wynter makes the point, "It was therefore to be the peoples of the Americas and the Caribbean who—after being conquered, Christianized, and enserfed in the imposed *encomienda* labor system, with their lands and sovereignty forcibly expropriated—were now to be made discursively and institutionally into, as [Jacob] Pandian points out, the embodiment of an ostensibly 'savage and irrational humanity,' and, as such, the Human Other to *Man*, defined as the rational political subject or citizen of the state."[23] The processes of colonialism as practiced first by the Portuguese after they rounded Cape Bojador, then by the Spanish in their transatlantic adventures, who were joined soon thereafter by the English, French, and Dutch, made possible, according to Wynter, the development of the ideal of the rational, self-sufficient *Man* in *contrast* to the irrational, dependent *native* of the colonies in Africa, the Americas, and Asia. Drawing on Fanon's discussion of the colonial condition, Wynter sums up the idea as follows: "While the black man must experience himself as the *effect* of the white man—as must the black woman vis a vis the white woman—neither the white man or woman can experience himself/herself *in relation to the* black man/black woman in any way but as that fullness and genericity of being human, yet a genericity that must be verified by the clear evidence of the latter's *lack* of this fullness, of this genericity."[24] At the heart of Wynter's argument, therefore, is the idea that the alleged universality of Enlightenment humanism is not only surreptitiously quite particular (white/male/bourgeois), but importantly feeds parasitically from the contrast with those who *lack* the full realization of (the Enlightenment ideal of) humanity.

At the core of this conception of the human that drives European modernity, and central to the argument I will advance in this chapter, is a particular account of reason. What separated *Man* from beasts was rationality—that ability to *master* internally one's drives and passions, and master externally the forces of nature, bending them both to one's rationally chosen ends. That is, the fully rational, and thus fully *human* agent will manifest that rationality by controlling his passions and drives, exercising an internally directed domination and control over those unruly and bestial elements of the psyche that are contrary to a life of reason and autonomy.[25] At the same time such a fully rational agent will impose a rational order on the unruly chaos of the social and natural world, asserting the same domination externally as he must internally, to maintain and demonstrate his status as fully rational. One can see this manifest as well at the political level, where the rational state will direct its coercive and controlling efforts to those sections of the populace understood to be the least rational and most unruly.[26]

This has significant implications for the understanding of colonialism. The understanding of reason was such that its proper exercise was the highest expression of our essential humanity, to control and bend the material world to our ends via science and industry (one may think of Locke here). Fully rational, independent, and autonomous agents controlled their environment, not the other way around. Likewise, it was the proper expression of rationality to dominate and control those "human others" who *lacked* full or proper reason. Rational *Man* expressed and demonstrated *his* rationality by taking on the burden of paternalistic stewardship of those unfortunates incapable of full rationality, independence, and autonomy on their own. If we think of this notion of the *Man* as manifesting the *purest* realization of reason, and in this way as the purest manifestation of the human (*Man*), then this process of domination and control can be thought on the model of a process of purification. This purification has "internal" and "external" processes that operate both at the individual and at the social/political levels.

The purification of reason, and thus the purification of the human, takes place on an individual level internally when we purge our *selves* of irrational/external influences. The *mastery* of one's desires, instincts, and emotions, along with the characteristic enlightenment principle of rejecting tradition and establishing one's beliefs by the light of one's own rationality, are all ways in which impurities and corrupting influences are purged (rendered "external" to the self) and reason is purified within the agent. Likewise, there is a purification process directed externally, when the rational agent exercises control over the external world and forges it into a more rational (typically understood as useful or profitable) order. Furthermore, at the social level, purification also manifests internally, when the body politic places the levers of power in the hands of only the highest (i.e., "purest") manifestations of human reason in order to control those unruly and irrational elements whose only function is to serve as human resources (labor both productive and reproductive), and externally, when the rational state sets out to identify, conquer, and exploit those portions of the globe and its population that fail to live up to the standards set by reason. Indeed, if rationality is made manifest only through these processes of purification, then to fail to dominate and control the irrational is a failure to *be* fully rational. Thus there is a kind of *imperative* to engage in such processes of purification—failure to do so renders one's status as rational suspect. In short, given this understanding of reason, colonialism was not just an expression of European opportunism, but a rationally determined *imperative* to purify the globe and subject it (as is right, proper, and part of the rational order of things) to the will of only the most rational of agents, whose rationality was itself demonstrated through that act of subjugation.

Thus, colonialism is not an unfortunate process that just happens to coincide with the development of European modernity, but each is intimately bound up with the other. Does this mean that we should abandon modernity altogether, along with any universal notion of the human as such? Wynter certainly does not advocate such an approach, and dedicates her work to the articulation a new understanding of humanity. If we are to attempt to meet Wynter's challenge to realize "the Human Project" (Wynter 2006, 163), then we will need to meet this concept of reason as domination head on.[27] And it is crucial to emphasize that, for Wynter, this does not mean simply the negation of reason and the valorization of the irrational or a-rational, nor does it mean a turn to the anti-modern or the post-modern. For she holds that there was a glimpse of something important in the development of European modernity, and the legacy of 1492. Her own words here are provocative, and worth quoting at length.

> Because the mutation by which we have gradually come to secure the autonomy of the mode of cognition specific to our species in the wake of the voyage of 1492 has been only partial, and its true victory therefore remains incomplete, the completion of that first true victory is necessarily the *only* possible commemoration of 1492. Such a completion would call therefore for another such conceptual move into a 'realm beyond reason'—one able to take our present mode of reason itself, and its system of symbolic representation and mode of subjective understanding that orient the perceptual matrices that in turn orient our behaviors—as the object of a new mode of inquiry.[28]

The challenge is thus to subject the notion of reason inherited from the "incomplete victory" of European modernity to critical scrutiny, by taking seriously the way in which the function of reason, as manifest in and through human beings, is conditioned by and realized through *sociogeny*. It is, in other words, not simply about biology, or pure scientific laws, but also about *meaning* and the ways in which different (social) systems of meaning condition biological processes. Thus, it is as much a matter of *poetics* as it is a matter of logic. We must, she tells us, close the "dangerous gap that now exists between our increasing human autonomy with respect to our knowledge of physical and organic levels of reality, and our lack of any such autonomy with respect to knowledge of our specifically human [sociogenetic] level of reality (1995, 49).[29]" I turn now to the question of how best to close this "dangerous gap."

Sociogeny and Epistemic Poetics—Resistance and the Creolization of Reason

There are two important and interconnected ideas at work so far that need to be drawn out and made more explicit. The first is that the account Wynter offers is not simply about various changes and developments in the *sense of self* of Europeans, but also and significantly about the development of Europeans *as such*. The "invention" of Africa, or of Latin America through the course of the colonial era was also at the same time the invention of Europe. That is, just as the idea of Africa as a place, inhabited by a particular *type* of people, was a *consequence* of the colonial encounter with Portuguese, Spanish, English, Dutch, and French colonizers, so too does the idea that all of those colonizers were *European* result from that encounter. Colonialism, in other words, is deeply implicated in the very genesis of Europe as a place, and Europeans as a people. As Nelson Maldonado-Torres has pointed out, 1492 marked not only the "discovery" of the lands and peoples of what would come to be known as the Americas, but also the expulsion of the Moors from the Iberian Peninsula. "Modern anti-Semitism, modern antiblack racism, and modern colonialism," Maldonado-Torres states, "find a common historical referent in the end of the Spanish *reconquista* and the beginning of a new form of conquest in the Americas."[30] It was a year, in other words, that marked a significant milestone in the "purification" of the continent internally, and inaugurated the project of purifying the globe externally. It is a moment in which it becomes possible, despite the ongoing and deeply entrenched rivalries and enmities between the European nation states that would carry on into the twentieth century and beyond, to still recognize each other as similarly *European*, a fact which was most salient *in the context of and in relation to* the colonized.

The second crucial idea here has to do with Wynter's emphasis on the ways in which human thought and reason both shape and are shaped by the specific background ideologies and cultural norms in which we develop and mature as individuals and as collectives. This just *is* Fanon's "sociogenic principle", and as with his own formulation, informed as it is by his background in psychiatry, Wynter affirms that sociogeny is an *aspect*, and not the whole, of human consciousness. Within the colonial context, the *sense of self* of both the colonizer and the "native" are deeply shaped by that context and its articulation of what is *normal* for participants in that system. At the same time, by taking up and acting out these prescriptions of normalcy, they legitimate and perpetuate that colonial context. We are thus possessed of "uniquely hybrid nature/culture modes of being human, of human identity."[31] Sociogeny, therefore, does not simply reduce human consciousness to culture, as if nature/culture were an all-or-nothing dichotomy. Rather, it takes seriously the ongoing dialectic between these two modes. What it points to, ultimately, is the failure of seeing humanity as *purely* one or the other, or expecting explanations of human behavior or phenomenon to fit neatly into one category or the other.

These two crucial ideas—that the history of colonialism is also the history of the emergence of the *idea* of Europe and of Europeans, and that it is such ideas and cultural practices that inevitably shape our consciousness, conditioning what counts as *normal* and, ultimately, as *rational*—point toward the way in which what is at stake here is the perennial question of the relation between the individual and the collective. Again, Wynter is explicit about this point: "[Fanon's] new definition of the human being as a hybrid mode of, so to speak, 'nature-culture' or 'ontogeny-sociogeny,' implies that the processes by which we produce our societies in order to live are the same auto-instituting processes by which we at the same time produce ourselves as this or that modality of an always already socialized, and therefore sociogenic, *kind/genre* of being human; and, as such, an always already inter-altruistically bonded and thereby kin-recognizing mode of the *I* and the *we*."[32] The true force of Wynter's argument over the course of these articles is this very powerful idea that, for any given epistemic agent, what counts as a successful and reasonable account of the world is conditioned by the particular *we* in which that agent is enmeshed.

This is the reason why the way in which European modernity advanced its particular notion of the human *we* as if it were the universal has been and in many ways continues to be so terribly destructive. It is more than simply a kind of normative or cultural imperialism (though that is certainly bad enough)—it is also a crucial epistemic failure. It is a failure to recognize the way in which sociogeny always conditions one's (epistemic) agency in ineluctable ways. A genuine commitment to truth and reason would thus face the particularity of that conditioning, not disavow or ignore it. Furthermore, as an epistemic endeavor directed toward an attempt to understand human beings, this failure can have disastrous consequences. To use Wynter's terminology, the hegemony of the concept *Man*, as the universal ideal of European modernity, was dependent upon a concept of the "Human Other to *Man*."[33] What is more, since what made one a representative of this highest and *purest* manifestation of humanity (*Man*) was the exercise of reason, understood in part as the domination and control of that which was *external* to itself, then we can also see that the generation of the concept *Man* in European modernity in effect *prescribed* colonialism. The "discovery" of the Human-Other as the savage, the irrational, the benighted, and the corrupted effectively *demanded* domination and control by those who, through the act of dominating, demonstrated their status as rational, civilized, and pure—and thus simultaneously demonstrated their right to dominate.

This is why, as Lewis Gordon has pointed out, philosophers coming from *outside* of European (including Euro-American) traditions have been so concerned with the metacritique of reason.[34] The dilemma for those philosophers thinking from the underside of modernity is the following. If reason is meant to define us in our humanity, but "we" (non-Europeans) are *a priori* understood to be beyond the bounds of reason despite all evidence to the contrary, then reason itself has failed from the start. It has never been a search for truth, but a rigged game serving colonial and white supremacist interests. How then can we subject European reason to rational critique, given that it has already defined itself as a universal that admits of no outside *from which* it would be susceptible to critique? Much of the fifth chapter of Fanon's *Black Skin, White Masks*, is about precisely this problem. How can we the colonized set about a rational critique of a conception of reason that functions as a closed system with us clearly on the outside (underside)?

The problem, emerging from that "dangerous gap" between our conception of the natural world and our understanding of sociogeny (and thus ourselves), is that of a kind of "epistemic closure"—an epistemic attitude that views itself as impervious to "external" challenge or critique.[35] In this particular case, the closure is a result of the insistence that there *is* nothing external to the system in question. Thus, it might be better to say that the dangerous gap is one between our understanding of the natural world and our *disavowal* of sociogeny. If reason is understood fundamentally as an effort to gain *control* over the world, then it will tend toward closed and mechanistic (thus controllable) systems of explanation, and where it cannot find them, it will either attempt to impose them, or declare them utterly irrational and chaotic. This is true whether the domain in question is one of physical objects and resources, or human populations, both of which are in need of cataloging (enclosing) and ordering (both in the sense of imposing order upon, and in the sense of commanding), so that they can be properly controlled. The various critiques of this ideal of reason are myriad, but what is central to this chapter is the way in which it is incapable of accounting for the sociogenic principle. If the way in which epistemic agents reason, and indeed the way in which the agents themselves are shaped, is a matter of sociogeny, then reason, as a project of control, is doomed to a kind of circularity. For in attempting to enclose everything into a single rational system, it is no longer the epistemic agents who are in control, but rather the hidden and disavowed sociogenetic forces that have shaped those agents. To be sure, the European *Man* of Reason might well shape non-European cultures (and thus bring them to at least *approximate* proper civilization), but Wynter's point is that he cannot see *himself* as a product of sociogenesis. He is what he is by virtue of his biology (race) and his autonomous (dominating) will, it is the lot of others (the human Other to *Man*) to be held back by their inferior nature, which significantly includes an incapacity for full autonomy. To subject his own rationality to rational scrutiny would be to admit that his understanding of reason (and thus, of himself as fully rational) is incomplete, and that cannot be tolerated.

This means that the conception of reason inherited from European modernity has maintained its claim to universality by disavowing, excluding, or erasing any evidence of "external" or alternative conceptions, and by ignoring its own sociogenetic specificity (its particular *European-ness*). In the context of philosophy in the Americas this has meant that *proper* philosophy (understood as philosophy *simpliciter*) was always clearly working within the European tradition (taken to include the United Kingdom, of course) and ignored the very possibility of worthwhile subject matter emerging from indigenous American or African sources.[36] But as Wynter argues, and as I have attempted to stress, maintaining this attitude and this view of reason and philosophy is ultimately a *failure* to be reasonable. It thus raises an interesting question about the viability of a universal *concept* of reason capable of offering a critical perspective of the Enlightenment *conception* of reason. It is, in a certain way, a question of resolving the tension between the modern and the postmodern. If taking seriously the colonial roots of European modernity causes us to question the view that reason is a universal and closed system yielding fixed, stable, and mind-independent truths, then are we left only with an open field of groundless interpretations? That is, do we abandon reason as inherently colonial, and turn instead to culturally based hermeneutics, or do we instead attempt to articulate an alternative idea of reason? Gordon accounts for this dilemma in terms of what he calls "neopositivism" and "postmodern hermeneutics," and points toward a possible solution as follows:

> The neopositivist believes that all truth beyond what is gained by the methods of the exact sciences is trivial and therefore inconsequentially dropped. The Postmodern hermeneuticist takes the position that truth can never meet tests of permanence and exactitude, which means that it should be subordinated to processes of interpretation. A question that is raised in response to both, however, is that of the dynamism of truth. Why can't truth be dynamic?[37]

The idea that truth might be "dynamic" suggests that an entirely different approach to reason and epistemology might be necessary. If truth is dynamic, then epistemic success cannot be understood as the arrival at (or proximity to) some fixed and stable endpoint, and reason cannot be simply the formal procedures conducive to that arrival.

By way of an alternative, I will turn to José Medina's recent work *The Epistemology of Resistance*. One of Medina's many concerns in this extraordinary text is with the ways in which our cultural milieu, especially under conditions of oppression, can make it difficult for agents to recognize their own epistemic limits, a phenomenon he refers to as *meta-blindness*.[38] In effect, meta-blindness points toward the way in which sociogenesis conditions agency such that our own epistemic lacunae, far from being sources or motives for seeking knowledge, can be altogether hidden from us. In the specific context of oppression that is Medina's focus, this means that we can be insensitive to the ways in which we are insensitive to the injustices suffered by others (or even ourselves). The prescription for this *meta-blindness* is to have our mental processes disturbed by means of *resistance* and what he refers to as "epistemic friction."[39] Epistemic friction occurs when the "normal" function of our ways and means of interpreting ourselves, the world, and our place within it encounters something uncanny or at odds, generating resistance and *friction* within that interpretive/epistemic system. This is, furthermore, a fundamentally social process requiring interaction with precisely those individuals, groups, and contexts that are in important ways "outside" of one's own epistemic framework, and thus most likely to generate friction through that interaction.[40] Meta-blindness, in other words, is an epistemic limitation or failure that results in large part from an excess of homogeneity. Just as ecological systems fail as diversity is reduced and monoculture takes over, epistemic systems fail as they exclude, disavow, or marginalize those understood to be outside in some significant sense. To combat meta-blindness and promote *meta-lucidity*, one must therefore cultivate the kind of diversity that presents the resistance to one's meta-blindness necessary to generate epistemic friction in oneself and others.[41]

In terms of our understanding of reason, and the persistent question of how we can rationally critique the conception of reason inherited from European modernity, Medina's work offers some promising avenues to pursue. Now, if it were the case that we could arrive at the universal perspective or "God's eye view" in which there were no epistemic lacunae or moments of meta-blindness in need of correction, then perhaps aiming toward *that* monoculture might be worth pursuing. But the lessons of the colonial encounter, and the principle of sociogenesis, make clear that striving toward such a perspective is not only futile, but can be terribly dangerous and damaging *even on strictly epistemic grounds*. If our epistemic ideal cannot, therefore, be the arrival at some final and static set of claims or principles that settle all questions, then our aim, and the conception of reason that informs it, must be one that takes pluralism, resistance, and *friction* into account. Medina's metaphor of friction is particularly productive in this context, because it points not only to the idea that there must be at least two interacting elements that generate the friction, but also, that it must take place over time. As a physical phenomenon, in other words, friction entails movement (and thus change over time)—it is a *dynamic* process, not a static endpoint.[42] Returning to Gordon's point about truth as dynamic, we might thus claim that a dynamic account of truth will require an equally dynamic account of reason as a process, not of arriving at some destination (a static notion of truth), but rather one of facilitating and enriching the never-ending process of seeking out more and more productive moments of epistemic *friction*.[43]

The failure of European modernity's understanding of reason is that it treated (and continues to treat) alternative understandings of the world either as simply lesser and *lacking* versions of itself, or as so totally alien as to be irreconcilable. In either event, it had no need to enter into productive engagement with them (to facilitate productive *friction*), and sought instead to incorporate all alleged diversity into its own monolithic system (like an invasive species taking over an ecosystem and driving it inexorably towards monoculture). From the alternative perspective of reason and truth toward which I have been gesturing here, it was in this way an epistemic failure, despite its technological sophistication. Indeed, this points toward precisely the "dangerous gap" that Wynter saw so clearly—European modernity was able to make tremendous progress (for some value of "progress") in its mastery of the natural world, but at the expense of utterly failing to grasp the significance of sociogenesis, and thus its own glaring epistemic lacunae and meta-blindness.

What is needed, as Wynter points out, is for human beings to exercise their "ability, without any change in their physiology, to transform their behaviors, their social realities, and their genre-specific Ideologies," by "reinventing their genres or kinds of being human and, therefore, their modes of knowing, feeling, behaving in new modalities."[44] Wynter's suggestion that *Man* must be separated from the notion of the *human*, points toward a reconceptualization of the *Human* as being *necessarily* diverse in its expression.[45] That is, what is *essential* to humanity is precisely the way in which our fullest (and in this way, most *universal*) expression requires that a variety of "genres" of the human be interacting in ways that are conducive to processes of epistemic (and cultural, and theoretical, and so forth) *friction*.

The history of European modernity is one of the disavowal of the different *genres* of the human, and Wynter's call to action is one that invites us to refuse to allow that disavowal, but rather to take up and explore the many genres of the human, their particular self-concepts, and their particular (corresponding) understandings of reason. The friction that might emerge from this project can help advance what Wynter calls "the Human Project." By way of example, take Miguel León-Portilla's account of the Pre-Columbian Nahuatl concept of *neltiliztli*. Often translated as "truth" in English, León-Portilla points out that its "stem syllable *nel* has the original connotation of solid firmness or deeply rooted," which he stresses is of great significance given what he describes as the Nahuatl emphasis on the transient nature of existence.[46] Roots may provide stability, but they are also growing, living, changing things. A notion of truth as "rootedness", would thus offer an interesting way to approach understanding reason as a search for truth that contrasts with that of the European modernity described by Wynter. Or, for another example, one could see glimpses of alternative understandings of reason emerging from the Haitian revolution.[47] The possible "genres" to be explored here are far too many to enumerate, let alone describe in a way that would remotely do them justice. The crucial point is that they exist, and it is only a sustained self-deception that enables their invisibility to the *philosophical* eye (or perhaps better, the philosophical *I*).

The effort to bring together these different genres of the human and their corresponding notions of reason is not simply to "celebrate diversity" for its own sake, but ultimately is part of a project that Wynter understands to be more genuinely *universal* than Enlightenment modernity ever was. Her project is ultimately a deeply *humanistic* one. She aims at a notion of humanism that points not toward some monolithic and ultimately *dehumanizing* ideal like that of European *Man*, but rather toward a dynamic, and polyvalent (or, as Medina suggests, "polyphonic") ideal. It is thus in *resisting* efforts to assimilate the diverse genres of humanity into *Man* that the possibility for a genuine humanism lies. Likewise, as reason has played such a crucial role in the centuries-long effort toward that assimilation, it, too, must be reconceived as *requiring* resistance, friction, and diversity.

This emphasis on a more dynamic understanding of reason as a process requiring the diversity necessary to generate productive friction and encounters with resistance, as opposed to a closed and totalizing system, can now be used to help illuminate Wynter's call for a furthering of "the Human Project." The sociogenetic principle dictates that one thing that *is* universal about human beings is that our *sense of self*, our understanding of what is *normal* and rational, is going to be inescapably conditioned by the cultural milieu in which our sense of self comes to maturity. From a subjective perspective, then, the effort to understand the world demands that I come to grips with these sociogenetic processes, which in turn requires that I place myself in a position conducive to epistemic resistance and friction. Our shared humanity, in other words, lies precisely in this shared condition of needing diverse others in order to encounter that shared humanity. What is crucial about this approach is that any presumption of arrival at some full understanding of "the human" as some fixed, closed, and monolithic conception is, by its very nature, a misunderstanding of that shared humanity (it is, in effect, anti-human). The moment it closes off this essential openness, or posits some *terminus* to the ongoing process of epistemic resistance and friction with regard to our understanding of humanity, it has in effect disavowed what is in truth universal about us, and replaced it with a particular understanding masquerading as the universal.

This means that any assimilationist account of "the Human Project" fails to understand what that project is at heart. There is, clearly, a real danger in this approach if it is understood on a consumerist or exoticist model. The aim here is not simply to recognize that *we* need "others" to show us ourselves, such that the rest of the world exists simply to serve our epistemic ends by being assimilated into this ongoing and narcissistic project of self-understanding. For what is crucial in the account I am attempting to sketch here, and in keeping with the emphasis on sociogeny, dynamism, and openness, is that these productive encounters with resistance and friction fundamentally alter the self that is being understood. There is, in this sense, an ontological shift (dynamism) such that one's encounter with this kind of friction, *if* that encounter is in keeping with the spirit of "the Human Project" as I am suggesting it should be understood here, changes in a fundamental way the participants in that encounter. Thus, the idea that I encounter some diverse other, experience a resistance to some entrenched and hidden aspect of my sense of self, learn a valuable lesson, and then move on utterly fails to grasp what is happening here, for it maintains the model of a closed system. The kind of encounter that will indeed generate the type of resistance and friction necessary here is one in which the participants are *open* to the unsettling of their sedimented sense of self—they are willing to learn *from* (as opposed to just *about*) and be changed by each other.

In this way, the epistemic aspects of "the Human Project" are always also ethical aspects. Coloniality, as a commitment to the view that one's own sense of self if the single, universal, and complete account of the human, is thus also a commitment to the view that *we* have nothing to learn from *them*. We may learn about them, in the same way we might learn about the local flora and fauna in a strange place (and the history of anthropology is rife with examples of this approach to the study of human beings), but *they* have nothing to teach *us*, with the possible exception of a glimpse into our barbarous origins. Following Fanon's claim that in the colonial context, the colonized has no "ontological resistance" from the perspective of the colonizer, it may be added that there is also no *epistemic* resistance.[48] Taking up Wynter's challenge to pursue the Human Project therefore entails not only an epistemic commitment to seeking out and being open to resistance and friction, but also the ethical commitment to the idea that others, especially those who have survived on modernity's underside, *have* resistance to offer.

In other words, one must, if one is committed to the Human Project, affirm (in the broadest sense of the term) the capacity of all, but especially of *les damnés de la terre*, to contest and resist one's sense of self. It is only in this way that we can close the "dangerous gap" and take seriously the significance of the sociogenetic principle. Furthermore, this means that human diversity is not a lamentable obstacle to the dream of a universal humanism, but rather a condition for the possibility of epistemic resistance, learning from each other, and the understanding of truth as *dynamic*. The universality to be found in the Human Project is thus incompatible with homogeneity, or with totalizing and assimilationist politics. Understood in this way, the Americas are not a unique location in and through which to take up this project, but it is one particularly conducive to it. Philosophy and philosophers can either set aside Eurocentrism and parochialism in order to embrace and advance that project, or remain irrelevant at best, and agents of coloniality at worst.

Notes

1. I emphasize the "colonial" here to leave open the possibility that it was not the encounter between Europeans and the peoples of the Western Hemisphere as such that was the problem, but rather the colonial character of that encounter. Further, this leaves open the possibility that encounters prior to 1492 might not have had the same colonial character.

2. Walter D. Mignolo, "Decolonizing Western Epistemology/Building Decolonial Epistemologies," in *Decolonizing Epistemologies: Latina/o Theology and Philosophy*, eds. Ada María Isasi-Díaz and Eduardo Mendieta (New York, NY: Fordham University Press, 2012), 25.

3. Walter D. Mignolo, "Decolonizing Western Epistemology/Building Decolonial Epistemologies."

4. Sylvia Wynter, "On How We Mistook the Map for the Territory, and Re-Imprisoned Ourselves in Our Unbearable Wrongness of Being, of Désêtre: Black Studies Toward the Human Project," in *Not Only the Master's Tools: African-American Studies in Theory and Practice*, eds. Lewis R. Gordon and Jane Anna Gordon (Boulder, CO: Paradigm Publishers, 2006), 260.

5. Sylvia Wynter, "On How We Mistook the Map for the Territory," 117.

6. Sylvia Wynter, "On How We Mistook the Map for the Territory," 125.

7. Sylvia Wynter, "On How We Mistook the Map for the Territory," 125.

8. Of course, my focus on colonialism here makes the European/Non-European distinction central, but even among Europeans, women, the poor, homosexuals, and the disabled were all, in different ways, instantiations of this "human Other to Man".

9. In Wynter's analysis, this positing of the human Other to *Man* as first and foremost a *lack* is characteristic of the colonial condition as such. It is thus not exclusive to the Americas, but evident anywhere on the globe that has been shaped by colonialism. In other words, the notion of *lack* is a universal relation to the *full* humanity of the European male bourgeois *Man* (of Reason), but the exact nature of that lack (ironically, we might say the *content* of that lack) will vary from place to place. What is posited as lacking in the Akan or Arawak may differ somewhat from what is posited as lacking in the Maya or the Maori.

10. Frantz Fanon, *Black Skin, White Masks*, trans. Richard Philcox (New York, NY: Grove Press, 2008), xv; Sylvia Wynter "Towards the Sociogenic Principle: Fanon, Identity, the Puzzle of Conscious Experience, and What It Is Like to Be 'Black,'" in *National Identities and Sociopolitical Changes in Latin America*, eds. Mercedes F. Durán-Cogan and Antonio Gómez-Moriana (New York, NY: Routledge, 2001), 31.

11. Sylvia Wynter, "Towards the Sociogenic Principle," 36–37.

12. Wynter, 53.

13. Lewis R. Gordon, *Existentia Africana: Understanding Africana Existential Thought* (New York, NY: Routledge, 2000), 84.

14. Frantz Fanon, *Black Skin, White Masks*, xiv.

15. W.E.B. DuBois, *The Souls of Black Folk* (New York, NY: Gramercy Books, 1994), 4–6.

16. Lewis R. Gordon, *Existentia Africana*, 87–88.

17. Not to imply that this was a simple or straightforward process, or to deny that there are real and significant internal differences within Europe. Simply as one example, the status of the Spanish as European, from the point of view of Northern Europeans, was always, and in many ways remains, significantly suspect. See Margaret Greer, et. al., *Rereading the Black Legend: The Discourses of Religious and Racial*

Difference in the Renaissance Empires (Chicago, IL: University of Chicago Press, 2007). Thus, I do not wish to suggest that Europe emerged all at once as a monolithic identity free from internal tensions (and even contradictions), but it is significant that such internal differences were far less salient *outside* of Europe. That is, in proximity to that human Other to *Man*, one's status as "European" became as salient, or even more salient, than one's status as English, or Portuguese.

18. Sylvia Wynter, "1492: A New World View," in *Race, Discourse, and the Origin of the Americas: A New World View*, eds. Vera Lawrence Hyatt and Rex Nettleford (Washington, D.C.: Smithsonian Institution Press, 1995), 13–14.

19. See Sylvia Winter "Towards the Sociogenic Principle: Fanon, Identity, the Puzzle of Conscious Experience, and What It Is Like to Be 'Black,'" in *National Identities and Sociopolitical Changes in Latin America*, eds. Mercedes F. Durán-Cogan and Antonio Gómez-Moriana (New York, NY: Routledge, 2001), 43. Enrique Dussel offers an exploration of the contrast between the Christian and the *savage* other in the context of Latin America in "Modern Christianity in Face of the 'Other' from the 'Rude' Indian to the 'Noble Savage,'" *Concilium* 130 (1979): 49–59.

20. Sylvia Wynter, "On How We Mistook the Map for the Territory," 145.

21. Sylvia Wynter, "Towards the Sociogenic Principle," 53.

22. In my own work, I have described this "sense of self" as one in which European Man understands itself as the most *pure* form of the human, and colonialism as an effort to purify the globe by bringing it under the domination of the highest and purest manifestation of humanity. Michael J. Monahan, *The Creolizing Subject: Race, Reason, and the Politics of Purity* (New York, NY: Fordham University Press, 2011), 153–182.

23. Sylvia Wynter, "On How We Mistook the Map for the Territory, 125.

24. Sylvia Wynter "Towards the Sociogenic Principle," 40.

25. My use of the masculine pronoun here is a deliberate acknowledgement of the way in which women were understood as constitutively incapable of such rationality and autonomy. See Genevieve Lloyd, "The Man of Reason," in *Feminist Theory: A Philosophical Anthology*, eds Ann E. Cudd and Robin O. Andreasen (Malden, MA: Blackwell Publishing, 2005).

26. My use of "unruly" here is indebted to Falguni Sheth's *Toward a Political Philosophy of Race* (Albany, NY: State University of New York Press, 2009).

27. Sylvia Wynter, "On How We Mistook the Map for the Territory," 163.

28. Lewis R. Gordon, "African-American Philosophy, Race, and the Geography of Reason," in *Not Only the Master's Tools: African-American Studies in Theory and Practice*, eds. Lewis R. Gordon and Jane Anna Gordon, (New York, NY: Routledge, 2006), 125.

29. Sylvia Wynter, "1492: A New World View."

30. Nelson Maldonado-Torres, *Against War: Views From the Underside of Modernity* (Durham, NC: Duke University Press, 2008), 3.

31. Sylvia Wynter, "Towards the Sociogenic Principle," 60.

32. Sylvia Wynter, "On How We Mistook the Map for the Territory," 134.

33. Lewis R. Gordon, "African-American Philosophy, Race, and the Geography of Reason," 125.
34. Lewis R. Gordon, *An Introduction to African Philosophy.* (New York, NY: Cambridge University Press. 2008), 92.
35. Lewis R. Gordon, *Existentia Africana*, 88.
36. Asian sources fared somewhat better, but still face similar problems.
37. Lewis R. Gordon, "African-American Philosophy, Race, and the Geography of Reason," 36.
38. José Medina, *The Epistemology of Resistance*, (Oxford: Oxford University Press: 2013), 24.
39. José Medina, *The Epistemology of Resistance*, 197.
40. Medina, 204.
41. Medina, 186.
42. Medina, 301–303.
43. To further carry this metaphor, I would point out that sound is always a result of friction (and indeed, unless it is generated in a vacuum, all friction produces sound, even if it is not always audible to humans), and thus we might just as easily call for richer and more productive sounds. There is, to play more loosely with the metaphor, a music to epistemology, something medina himself gestures toward in his concept of polyphonic contextualism (see Medina, 224)
44. Sylvia Wynter, "On How We Mistook the Map for the Territory," 156–7.
45. Sylvia Wynter, "On How We Mistook the Map for the Territory," 161.
46. Miguel León-Portilla, *Aztec Thought and Culture: A Study of the Ancient Nahuatl Mind*, trans. Jack Emory Davis (Norman, OK: University of Oklahoma Press, 1963), 8.
47. See Sybylle Fischer, *Modernity Disavowed: Haiti and the Cultures of Slavery in the Age of Revolution* (Durham, NC: Duke University Press, 2004), 260–271.
48. Frantz Fanon, *Black Skin, White Masks*, 90.

Bibliography

DuBois, W.E.B. *The Souls of Black Folk*. New York, NY: Gramercy Books, 1994.
Dussel, Enrique. "Modern Christianity in Face of the 'Other' from the 'Rude' Indian to the 'Noble Savage,'" *Concilium* 130 (1979): 49–59.
Fanon, Frantz. *Black Skin, White Masks*. Translated by Richard Philcox. New York, NY: Grove Press, 2008.
Fischer, Sybylle. *Modernity Disavowed: Haiti and the Cultures of Slavery in the Age of Revolution*. Durham, NC: Duke University Press, 2004.
Gordon, Lewis R. *Existentia Africana: Understanding Africana Existential Thought*. New York, NY: Routledge, 2000.
———."African-American Philosophy, Race, and the Geography of Reason," in *Not Only the Master's Tools: African-American Studies in Theory and Practice*, eds. Lewis R. Gordon and Jane Anna Gordon. New York, NY: Routledge, 2006.

———. *An Introduction to African Philosophy*. New York, NY: Cambridge University Press, 2008.

Greer, Margaret R., Walter D. Mignolo, and Maureen Quilligan. *Rereading the Black Legend: The Discourses of Religious and Racial Difference in the Renaissance Empires*. Chicago, IL: University of Chicago Press, 2007.

León-Portilla, Miguel. *Aztec Thought and Culture: A Study of the Ancient Nahuatl Mind*. Translated by Jack Emory Davis. Norman, OK: University of Oklahoma Press, 1963.

Lloyd, Genevieve. "The Man of Reason." In *Feminist Theory: A Philosophical Anthology*. Edited by Ann E. Cudd and Robin O. Andreasen. Malden, MA: Blackwell Publishing, 2005.

Maldonado-Torres, Nelson. *Against War: Views From the Underside of Modernity*. Durham, NC: Duke University Press, 2008.

Mignolo, Walter D. 2012. "Decolonizing Western Epistemology/Building Decolonial Epistemologies." In *Decolonizing Epistemologies: Latina/o Theology and Philosophy*. Ada María Isasi-Díaz and Eduardo Mendieta, eds. New York, NY: Fordham University Press

Monahan, Michael J. 2011. *The Creolizing Subject: Race, Reason, and the Politics of Purity*. New York, NY: Fordham University Press.

Sheth, Falguni A. 2009. *Toward a Political Philosophy of Race*. Albany, NY: State University of New York Press.

Wynter, Sylvia. 1995. "1492: A New World View." In *Race, discourse, and the Origin of the Americas: A New World View*. Vera Lawrence Hyatt and Rex Nettleford, eds. Washington, D.C.: Smithsonian Institution Press. pp. 5–57

———. 2001. "Towards the Sociogenic Principle: Fanon, Identity, the Puzzle of Conscious Experience, and What It Is Like to Be 'Black'". In *National Identities and Sociopolitical Changes in Latin America*. Edited by Mercedes F. Durán-Cogan and Antonio Gómez-Moriana. New York, NY: Routledge, 2001.

———. "On How We Mistook the Map for the Territory, and Re-Imprisoned Ourselves in Our Unbearable Wrongness of Being, of *Désêtre*: Black Studies Toward the Human Project." In *Not Only the Master's Tools: African-American Studies in Theory and Practice*. Edited by Lewis R. Gordon and Jane Anna Gordon. Boulder, CO: Paradigm Publishers, 2006

12
Race, Multiplicity, and Impure Coalitions of Resistance
Lee A. McBride, III

As I see it, Inter-American philosophy can be taken in two ways. First, it can be seen as a comparative exercise, a study of the numerous cultural variants encountered in North America, the West Indies, Central America, and South America. We can compare and contrast the languages, the religions, the conventional norms, the cultural products, the waves of immigration, and the enduring marks of colonization, dispossession, and bondage that gave rise to the extant populations throughout this vast territory. Alternatively, Inter-American philosophy can denote any project intent on highlighting and piecing together diffuse diasporic peoples in the Pan-American context. Indigenous, Latinx, or Afro-descended peoples may work to re-establish or nurture a lineage, a coalitional affiliation, a shared identity (despite language barriers, cultural divergences, and genealogical lacunae) to galvanize collective agency or group uplift. In either approach to Inter-American philosophy, there is the potential for nationalisms along racial lines. That is, there is the potential for racialized people to develop chauvinistic loyalties to their assigned racial group. Nationalism, so understood, is a sentiment (based on distinctive phenotypic or cultural characteristics) that binds a population in a chauvinistic manner, often producing a policy of racial or ethnic separatism. Some argue that racial separatism is anthropologically inescapable, meaningful for racialized populations, and required for anti-racist struggle. In contrast, I would suggest that racial separatism is not anthropologically necessary and that a focus on racial distinctiveness comes with its own set of problems. Here, I argue that the multiplicity, the multiculturalism, the intersectionality within these communities of resistance is typically overlooked, disregarded, or erased by the emphasis on racial distinctiveness and racial separatism.[1] I outline an alternative way forward, one that allows for multiplicitous identities extending beyond racial nationalisms and facilitates interracial, multicultural coalitions, opening avenues to intercultural communication and coalitional agency.

Conserving Racial Distinctiveness

In 1897, a 29-year-old W.E.B. Du Bois published "The Conservation of Races." Therein, Du Bois acknowledges that human beings are, in fact, divided into races and seems to suggest that populations have always been separated into three to five distinct races.[2] In this essay, Du Bois offers a definition of race: "A race is a vast family of human beings, generally of common blood and language, always of common history, traditions and impulses, who are both voluntarily and involuntarily striving together for the accomplishment of certain more or less vividly conceived ideals of life."[3] Hence, what binds a race are common blood and language, a common history, common law and religion, similar habits of thought, and conscious striving together.[4] Note, at this point, Du Bois suggests that there are "spiritual and mental differences" between the races. The English contributed constitutional liberty and commercial freedom; the Germans science and philosophy; the Romance nations literature and art; the other races are striving. The Negro race, like other races, has its own distinctive "gift" to contribute to the world: a gift of story and song; a gift of sweat and brawn; and a gift of the Spirit/θυμός.[5] Du Bois argues that black people (or, American Negroes)[6] have a duty to conserve their physical powers, their intellectual endowments, their spiritual ideals. And to accomplish this, black people will need race organizations.[7] It is, thus, the duty of black people to maintain their race identity until the mission of the Negro people is accomplished.[8] It is the duty of black folk to conserve their distinctive race.

In 1996, Lucius Outlaw published "Conserve Races? In Defense of W.E.B. Du Bois," which defends a modern-day conservation of racial distinctiveness. Outlaw portrays racial grouping as a natural, time-tested feature of human anthropology. On this view, human populations inevitably group into "racial/ethnic" populations. Outlaw describes race as "a sociohistorical varying collection of sets of biological, cultural, and geographical factors" characteristic of a particular population.[9] Racial categories, thus, capture biologically related peoples who have shared culture and a marked attachment to a geographic location.

Outlaw admits that efforts to locate a set of necessary and sufficient characteristics for a racial group are especially difficult. This seems to suggest that the boundaries of racial categories are problematic and perhaps arbitrarily demarcated. Nevertheless, Outlaw insists that race is one of the defining characteristics of one's group. Distinctive racial identities are key to the meaningfulness, authenticity, and legitimacy of peoples' lives. Black people only truly understand themselves when they understand themselves as black people, with shared lineage and culture. Asian people will only truly understand themselves when they understand themselves as Asian people, with shared lineage and culture. Racial identity, thus, gives people a sense of heritage and belonging. As such, race is a defining characteristic of human populations and must be taken into account when we discuss the human condition.

Outlaw argues that racial categorization is necessary for just social ordering.[10] Acknowledgement of the racial groups in a particular geography is required for the creation of just principles and social order. The adjudication or amelioration of race-based problems in political, social, and economic life cannot be accomplished without tracking and assessing empirical data pertaining to these distinct racial populations.[11] The abstract, race-less human being evoked in colorblind ideologies is conceptually and practically inadequate in changing the material realities of racially oppressed peoples. As racialized populations are still affected by racist norms and institutions, racial communities of resistance provide the collective agency needed to resist and oppose racist structures and practices. To abandon racial groupings, is to negate the possibility of racial communities of resistance. Thus, Outlaw argues that racial identities are needed to ameliorate past and present injustices.

According to Outlaw, we need not conclude that all regard for raciality must be eliminated to reach further social enlightenment for peoples of color. Advancement in social enlightenment does not require stripping ourselves of race identity. In fact, the elimination of all regard for raciality is unlikely and unnecessary.[12] Outlaw emphasizes that, for some, the continued existence of discernible racial/ethnic communities of meaning is highly desirable and politically necessary. Outlaw is convinced that both the struggle against invidious racism and the struggle of racial groups to share their gift (i.e., their cultural goods) require that we recognize racial groups as political communities that value cultural pluralism and democratic justice.[13] Black folks would then be understood as a racial group that produces distinctive cultural goods and a political community that works to forward the political mission of black folks. Indigenous folks would be understood as a racial group that produces distinctive cultural goods and a political community that works to forward the political mission of indigenous folks. The task, then, is to revise the ways in which we conceive each of the distinct races and strip them of their egregious connotations and legacies of hierarchy and immiseration.

Outlaw, while concerned primarily with the interests of black folk, suggests that this line of thought should be afforded to other racial groups. If it is natural and inevitable for black people to self-segregate and find meaning and authenticity in their blackness, then we should expect white people and Asian people to self-segregate and find meaning and authenticity within their respective racial/ethnic groupings. But, since the eighteenth century, whiteness has been closely tied with European colonization, imperialism, white supremacy, and the exploitation of non-whites.[14] As Outlaw sees it, white people must change; they will have to confront their racial imperialism, their greed, their bigotry.[15] White supremacy must be rooted out, but the dissolution of racial whiteness is not required. Rather, Outlaw advocates for the rehabilitation of racial whiteness (with the intention of undermining white supremacy).[16] Whiteness should be reworked and rehabilitated, not abolished. For racial groupings are instrumental in fulfilling basic anthropological needs. Racial groupings condition:

> anthropologically necessary, socially mediated needs for place and person-securing identity-with-similar-others in a historical circumstance conditioned substantially by an intense "politics of identity and recognition" and by subsequent felt needs for transgenerational, transhistorical, transgeographic sociality of the kinds sought and gained, more or less, in collectives and associations characterized as races and ethnie, tribes, clans, poli, peoples, and nation-cum-nation-states.[17]

On this view, it is in our racial groups that our anthropologically necessary, socially mediated needs are met. Thus, white people will need communion with white people, just as black people will need communion with black people. Note well, race is not in itself the source of racial conflict; rather we are compelled to do away with that which causes racial conflict between the races, be it ideological dispute, competition over scarce resources, or intergroup ignorance.

Additionally, Outlaw argues that the retention of distinctive races supports the heterogeneous nature of democracy in the United States. He explains that a central aspect of democracy is the appreciation or tolerance of racially and ethnically diverse groups and their varied ways of life.[18] To do away with racial groupings/identities (including whiteness) is to commit to homogeneity. But it would be absurd to commit to homogeneity across ethnic and racial lines (in the United States). That would be un-democratic. And thus, if we are truly committed to democracy, racial distinctiveness must be preserved. The rehabilitation of whiteness is then the socially necessary compliment of the reversal work on blackness.[19] And thus the vertical hierarchy of race is laid down horizontally; the distinctiveness of each race remains, but the hierarchic relation between the races is annulled. This allows for just and reciprocal relations between these rehabilitated races. This allows for each distinct race to share its gift with the other racial groups in a democratic fashion—racial egalitarianism.[20]

Shannon Sullivan follows this same line of reasoning, arguing for the preservation of racial distinctiveness and separatism.[21] She develops a notion of transaction that captures the push and pull, the interaction of bodies and environments. The interactions between racial groups is better described metaphorically as a stew than as a tossed salad. Sullivan explains: "In their transaction with each other, the vegetables of a stew dynamically constitute each other as the vegetables they are or that they become in the stew."[22] The vegetables do not lose all flavor, texture, or color in the stewing transaction; they do not become "one indistinguishable lump." Rather, the distinctiveness of each vegetable is altered in the stewing transaction, yet each vegetable preserves distinctive flavors, textures, and contributions to the stew. Unpacking the analogy, races are like vegetables in a stew. Through social and environmental interaction, racial groups are dynamically co-constituting, each bringing a distinct flavor to the democratic stew. Importantly, on this account, the races retain their distinctiveness—yellow, red, brown, black, and white. White and black people do not melt into a homogenous "khaki-colored people"; "the distinctiveness of white and black people is preserved, not eliminated, but it is preserved in a relationship of dynamic connection."[23]

Sullivan, like Outlaw, supports the preservation of whiteness. She argues that the move to preserve whiteness does not necessarily imply white supremacy or the domination of people of color. She argues that the habits of whiteness, especially white racist habits, can be exposed, critiqued, and rehabilitated.[24] On this view, an egalitarian pro-whiteness is possible. That is, a form of white pride that does not inherently presuppose the subordination other racial groups. This would allow white people to celebrate their heritage, their culture, the racial gifts they contribute to society. And, within white communities, white people will be able to have their anthropologically-necessary, socially-mediated needs met. To this end, Sullivan proffers joyous "white self-love": white folks loving each other attentively, rooting out the white supremacist aspects of white identity.[25]

Sullivan openly defends racial separatism.[26] On this account, racial self-segregation or separatism plays an integral role in pluralist, cross-fertilizing relationships. Understood transactionally, self-segregation and separatism name a set of practices that attempt to make greater room for the voices of dominated or oppressed groups in their transaction with dominant culture. This separatism does not eliminate transaction between the races; rather, it attempts "to eliminate a situation in which the dominant group's desires are always or primarily that to which an oppressed group has to respond."[27] Thus, racial separatism is evoked to shield non-white races from hegemonic white supremacy and its structural pressures to assimilate or submit under duress. Sullivan suggests that sometimes it is better for white people "to leave non-white people alone."[28] This allows for the non-white spaces people of color need to build communities of resistance to counter white supremacy.

And thus a multi-pronged case is made for racial separatism and the conservation of racial distinctiveness. We are prompted to imagine a world where distinct racial groups persist and thrive apart from racist practices and institutions, apart from pressures to assimilate to the dominant Euro-American culture; a world where the races are allowed to self-separate and take pride in their racial heritage (without racial hierarchy or persecution) while simultaneously contributing their racial gifts to a heterogeneous, democratic society.

Outliers, Overgeneralization, and Bad Inferences

I stand in antipathy to the racially separatist positions described above. There are several aspects of that position that I am compelled to challenge. First, Outlaw seems to use the term "race" as a synonym for "ethnic group," liberally referring to races as "race/ethnie." But this is misleading. Ethnic groups are populations that share lineage and culture (e.g., language, cultural products, and objects of reverence). Racial groups, according to Outlaw, are biologically related populations that share readily observable phenotypic traits, a distinct culture, and a marked attachment to a geographic location. Note that the various people assigned to a particular racial group may not share the same language, culture, or geographic location. For instance, if we investigate those populations often categorized as black in Límon (Costa Rica), Port-au-Prince (Haiti), and Atlanta (United States), we find Afro-descended populations bearing some shared phenotypic features. And yet these populations speak differing languages, orient their lives around differing religious beliefs, dance to differing melodies and syncopations, and relish differing comfort foods.[29] Racial categorization, so conceived, separates the world into four or five races based on distinct, readily observable phenotypes. Immanuel Kant, circa 1777, recognized the white race, the Negro race, the Hun race, and the Hindustani race; Shannon Sullivan recognizes a white race, a black race, a red race, a brown race, and a yellow race.[30] But these divisions are inadequate to capture the diversity of ethnic and cultural groupings.[31] Ethnic groups do not map cleanly onto these four or five basic categories, especially when we extend our analysis beyond the United States. In fact, regional cultural identities, which are central to ethnicity, often permeate a couple of these purportedly distinct racial groupings at one time. Thus, it seems a mistake to equate "race" and "ethnic group" or to run them together into "race/ethnie."

Now, let us return to what Outlaw claims is anthropologically necessary. Outlaw argues racial groups are required to meet our anthropologically necessary, socially mediated needs. He claims that people require "place and person-securing identity-with-similar-others"; they require "transgenerational, transhistorical, transgeographical sociality."[32] Let us, for the sake of argument, assume that human beings require this "place and person-securing identity-with-similar-others." But why is race the only means to this person-securing sociality? These purported anthropologically necessary, socially mediated needs can be met within other salient forms of sociality: ethnic groups, religious groups, national groups, socioeconomic groups, gender groups, and the like. A dark-skinned, Afro-descended Puerto Rican person may find solace and communion among people in the Latinx community—Spanish-speaking, Catholic, and partial to Bomba and tostones y arroz con gandules. This dark-skinned Puerto Rican person might be assigned to the black race, yet find intimacy and closeness with other Hispanophone Latinx people who may vary from pale-skinned to dark-skinned.[33] In this case, assigned race can be more of a hindrance than a socially binding feature.[34] Race, here, seems to lump all dark-skinned Afro-descended people (despite ethnic and cultural discrepancies) into one racial category, where they are expected to bond and revel in their shared lineage and their shared black culture. But this is dubious. To which black culture do we refer? In any case, if human beings require "place and person-securing identity-with-similar-others" or "transgenerational, transhistorical, transgeographical sociality," it does not follow that racially distinct groups are the only means by which to fulfill these needs. Regarding Latin America, José Martí proclaims:

> There can be no racial animosity, because there are no races. The theorists and feeble thinkers string together and warm over the bookshelf races which the well-disposed observer and the fair-minded traveler vainly seek in the justice of Nature where man's universal identity springs forth from triumphant love and the turbulent hunger for life. The soul, equal and eternal, emanates from bodies of various shapes and colors.[35]

Here, racial identity presents itself as a matter of trammels and impediments.[36] Martí seeks place- and person-securing identity-with-similar-others among his revolutionary comrades, regardless of body shape, hair texture, and skin color.

Let us now turn to the question of race and democracy. Both Outlaw and Sullivan argue that the preservation of racial distinctiveness is essential to the heterogeneous nature of democracy in the United States. We are forced into a dilemma: either (i) we retain racial groupings and cultivate a heterogeneous society or (ii) we eliminate racial groupings and commit ourselves to a homogenous society. And genuine democracy inherently rests upon heterogeneity and pluralism. Thus, genuine democracy requires the preservation of distinct racial groupings. But this argument is not compelling. While the second premise seems like a truism, the first premise forces us into a false dichotomy. Race is not the only variable that establishes heterogeneity. Cultural, linguistic, religious, or ideological pluralism can also establish heterogeneity. So it is not clear to me why I should think that the democracy of the United States stands or falls depending on whether or not racial distinctiveness is conserved. Furthermore, if we look outside of the United States, we might recognize (in, for instance, Brazil) populations within democratic nations that identify as predominantly mixed-race or mestizo, pointedly eschewing notions of racial distinctiveness.[37] Gilberto Freyre asserts that "the Brazilian is a living retort to any exclusivist mystique of racial purity such as the Aryan ideal, or Negritude, or the mystique of 'yellow power' embraced by certain imperialist groups in the Far East."[38]

Now let us consider the specific conception of race that undergirds this account. Outlaw describes race as "a sociohistorical varying collection of sets of biological, cultural, and geographical factors" characteristic of a particular population. While giving a nod to the sociohistorical fabrication of race, the account describes racial categorization as a natural, stable feature of human association. Emphasis is placed on the lineage, the biological relatedness of racialized people—the biological or blood ties. Racial categories, on this view, capture biologically related peoples who have shared culture and a marked attachment to some geographic location. Outlaw allows that these "races/ethnies/tribes" may be constantly evolving, which seems to allow that racial groups may manifest differing phenotypic features over time, that the boundaries between racial categories may meander, that interracial commingling may in fact occur. But Outlaws seems to suggest that the core of the race/ethnie/tribe will remain distinct. Moreover, these racial groups should remain distinct, if we are to conserve the gift and earnestly pursue (heterogenous) democracy.

To push back, I would argue that no human population has escaped the genetic or cultural (transactional) influence of other/opposing populations.[39] If a black man and white woman have a child, surely the white mother who gives birth to this brown child shares genetic material/biology and historical lineage with her child. The white mother is then related to this darker race by lineage or line of descent. Or, this brown child is related to her mother's white lineage (as well as her father's black lineage). In such cases, blood ties and biological lineage do not then separate the modern phenotypic races in any definitive, non-arbitrary way. In 1939, a 71-year-old W.E.B. Du Bois writes:

> It is generally recognized today that no scientific definition of race is possible. Differences, and striking differences, there are between men and groups of men, but so far as these differences are physical and measurable they fade into each other so insensibly that we can only indicate the main divisions in broad outline. . . . Race would seem to be a dynamic and not a static conception, and the typical races are continually changing and developing, amalgamating and differentiating.[40]

Leopold Senghor, in 1961, writes: "there is no such thing as a pure race: scientifically speaking, races do not exist."[41] Indeed, the necessary and sufficient conditions distinguishing each race are elusive.[42] My point is that the categorization of populations along racial lines is not clean and neat, nor is it the natural order of things. I also think it is important to acknowledge that the racial categorization that we acknowledge in the United States today is a social fabrication established in the 18th century largely to support Euro-American colonial aggrandizement, the transatlantic slave trade, and indigenous dispossession.[43] As such, racial categories are suspect.

The conception of race we find in Outlaw and Sullivan is too simple, too neat. It produces a troubling depiction of race and racial distinctiveness. Sullivan writes, "White, black, red, brown, yellow, and mixed-race people co-constitute each other's racial existence at the same time that their racial distinctiveness is dynamically preserved."[44] The complex and dappled populations and cultures of the world are here literally reduced to crayon-box colors. African descendant people—all of them—are black. Indigenous people (across the Americas) are red. Asians, from Northern China to Pakistan, are yellow. Select European people are white. (The whiteness of Jewish people, the Irish, Slavic peoples, Italians, Egyptians, and Hispanidad peoples has been disputed at one time or another.) How are we to categorize all the populations of the world into the crayon-box categories provided? Who exactly are the "brown people"? Is the term "brown people" supposed to denote Hispanidad peoples, Middle Eastern peoples, South Asians, the Coloured people of South Africa, and/or the Pardo of Brazil? There seems to be glaring outliers and overgeneralizations. And Sullivan lists a "mixed-race race." (What!?) How is a "mixed-race race" even possible in this proposed schema of racial distinctiveness? In any case, Sullivan is claiming that these racial populations transact, shaping and influencing one another, while retaining their racial distinctiveness. To the contrary, I think that reducing these racialized populations to five distinct color/racial groups truncates our understanding of geographic location and the particular cultures involved. It distorts our genealogies of interracial mixing, the exchange of cultural products/gifts, and the existence of regional cultures that often pervade and exceed racial groupings.[45] This view seems to reify stereotypes and racial scripts, as it stresses that racial populations retain their racial distinctiveness, despite transaction with other races. This account of race produces and maintains distinct racial populations and fragmented beings, who are reduced to the race to which they are assigned. The multiplicity within these populations is disregarded or erased.

Multiplicity, Erased or Fragmented

My father is African American. When he was young, his family moved from Prichard, Alabama, to Sacramento, California, for a chance at a less-segregated life. My mother is Filipino Mexican American. When she was young, her family settled in the California-San Joaquin River Delta. As such, I am black, mixed-race, *and* multiethnic. I am one generation away from Jim Crow apartheid, one generation away from itinerant farm labor. My footing is complicated, liminal, multiplicitous.[46] Multiplicitous people, like me, do not feature prominently in the philosophy of race. Those who fall outside of the neat racial categories, those who are visibly ambiguous or culturally "bilingual," those who move back and forth between ethnic worlds, those who (for various opaque reasons) do not fulfill the customary racial script are not readily acknowledged. These liminal folks are typically belittled as inauthentic, erased as insignificant, or compelled to embrace a fragment of one's racial and ethnic identity. In the United States, the one-drop rule renders anyone with one-drop of Afro-descended blood as racially black.[47] Beyond the black-white divide, mixed-race people are typically categorized (often arbitrarily) based upon readily discernible features (e.g., style of dress, vernacular, etc.), poorly conceived representative heuristics, and/or racial stereotypes. But the main thrust is to categorize the mixed-race person with one predominant race, to isolate one fragment of their multiplicitous identity so that this person fits squarely into the schema of racial distinctiveness.

María Lugones writes:

> When I think of my own people, the only people I can think of as my own are transitionals, liminals, border-dwellers, world-travelers, beings in the middle of either/or. . . . As soon as I entertain the thought, I realize that separation into clean, tidy things and beings is not possible for me because it would be the death of myself as multiplicitous and a death of community with my own.[48]

The separation into clean, tidy racial categories marks the erasure of multiplicity. It disparages the complexity of heritage, the cultural amalgamations, the variety of lived experiences within our racial groups. As such, the emphasis on racial distinctiveness fragments or erases the multiplicity of my life and my family. It would be the end of me as multiplicitous and the erasure of all of those who do not fit neatly into the distinct racial categories.

People within a (phenotype-based) race can be oppressed differently at the many intersections of race, ethnicity, class, gender, sexuality, age, and ability.[49] How we are oppressed and how we respond to oppression may differ given our corporeal situation. While black women may be oppressed or marginalized qua black women, wealthy black women may be marginalized in differing ways than poor black women (for being black and for being from a lower socioeconomic class). A queer black woman from a lower socioeconomic background may face even more compounded forms of degradation (for being black, for being poor, and for spurning heteronormativity). Notice that if we follow the route of racial distinctiveness, it would seem to suggest that black people are just black people who share a lineage, particular phenotypic traits, a shared culture, and geographic location. But to reduce the black position to one generalized black experience is to reduce a variety of multiplicitous people to one-dimensional, fragmented beings.

Within communities of resistance that endorse racial separatism, conspicuously mixed-race people, racially ambiguous cultural "world" travelers, and people who defy the prevailing norms within racial groupings are often treated with suspicion or not welcomed at all. Lugones writes:

> Where do you go to be seen? To be seen as something other than a more-or-less monstrous imitation, an imaginary being. Where do you go to be seen apart from tests of legitimacy that turn you into an imaginary being? Monstrous to different degrees. Imitation white/ imitation color. Ready to be accused of failing to pass the ethnic legitimacy test of passing; of "git'n over" on Blacks, Latinos, Asians, folk of color.[50]

Within communities of resistance that endorse racial separatism, there are often pressures to follow an idealized racial script. The racial script typically dictates stereotypic comportment, aesthetic preferences, and cultural products. Conceptions of racial authenticity are often tied to this. Those who fail to uphold the racial script with fidelity, those who are insufficiently Asian, indigenous, or black can be disparaged as sellouts, turncoats, or deeply misguided wannabees.

But multiplicitous people are a reality; we do exist. Sometimes, through social and environmental transaction, mixture occurs. Sometimes "bloodlines" cross. Sometimes two or three cultures are hung together in a bricolage. Some of us are "khaki-colored".[51] Some of us are iridescent intercultural polyglots. I mean to suggest that moving away from a focus on racial distinctiveness and separatism may actually invite or welcome multiplicitous people to participate in resistance efforts. We may open ourselves to alternative perspectives, alternative matrices of intersectionality within our racialized groups. Perhaps coalitions of resistance can be built (with full recognition of the intersectional diversity within their ranks.[52]

Impure Coalitions and Intercultural Polyglossia

To be clear, I am not advocating a colorblind ideology or the simple elimination of racial terms and concepts from our vocabularies. Outlaw is right on two points. First, the move to identify as race-less human beings is conceptually and practically inadequate in changing the material realities of racially oppressed peoples.[53] If we cannot reference actual racialized populations, then the effort to ameliorate racist injustices in any real way is rendered moot. Secondly, it is necessary to study the policies, institutions, and the material conditions under which racialized populations live in order to pursue just social structures and the means to adjudicate disputes.[54] In other words, there are good reasons to bind together into racial groups. In fact, "there are compelling reasons for persons terrorized by race to band together, define themselves, and work on behalf of themselves."[55] Victims of racism can find solace in racial identity as long as the source of their victimization is racial and the destruction of racism is aided by racial solidarity among victims.[56] In communities mobilized around racial identities, racially subjugated individuals find emotional, economic, and political support. Moreover, the formation of a race-based adversarial group is an integral step in establishing collective agency and combating racism. To productively work against racial oppression, the racialized person will likely need to work together with other similarly racialized persons to articulate the distinctive nature of their oppression. The creation of an anti-racist, counter-hegemonic perspective and discourse requires the collaborative effort of a community.[57] These adversarial communities, as I conceive them, are strategic coalitions, which construct provisional oppositional political identities for themselves.[58] Coalitions of this sort "allow people with common goals to come together, produce, act, and then disband, reform, or continue as needed."[59]

But I am committed to universal human liberation, the view that all human beings should be liberated from oppressive and debilitating boundaries, especially those boundaries that mark particular populations as subhuman or preclude them from basic human dignities.[60] Leonard Harris points out that those social entities that strive for universal human liberation seem to anticipate the disbanding of these socially-constructed coalitions of resistance. The liberation of the proletariat requires the negation of the class identity for both the proletariat and the bourgeoisie. By the same logic, liberation from racial oppression "requires the negation of the racial identity of the oppressor and the oppressed."[61] That is, racial coalitions of resistance should ultimately strive to negate the social and material conditions that provoke their existence as racial collectives. If we were able to eliminate the social and material conditions that maintain and propagate racial oppression, we could disband racial coalitions of resistance and create alternative forms of human association.[62]

It is important to note that racial groupings, on this account, are contingent social constructions; they are malleable, porous identities.[63] Racial identities may have practical, liberatory import, but I tend to agree with Leonard Harris, who says that "racial identities are inextricably tied to, and inevitably, indebted to, degrading, demeaning, and misguided stereotypes."[64] Racial separatism and its attending sense of "person-securing identity-with-similar-others" have, at best, temporary pragmatic merit.[65] Beyond this, racial identities and separatisms have a tendency to reify racial stereotypes and racial scrips, shaping and confining racialized people in their thinking and comportment, closing off creative possibilities.[66] I, following Toni Morrison, worry that our racial identities establish barriers and assign scripts—a house of race. Sure, we can redefine and redecorate the house; we can add windows and crouch in the backroom where racism does not hurt so much.[67] But does the racial house always confine? Do the doors lock from the outside? (Do you hear the faint clinking of keys?) There is a need to rethink the subtle yet pervasive attachments we have to the architecture of race.[68] Morrison prods us to imagine "a site clear of racist detritus; a place where race both matters and is rendered impotent."[69] What would it be like to leave this house of race, to leave these confines, to walk into the night without fear—no lamp, no faint clinking of keys?

In any event, there are liberatory projects to attend to, projects that motivate people of various phenotypes and ethnic backgrounds to enter into racial coalitions of resistance. And these coalitions of resistance will rely upon a shared identity to harness collective agency. Lugones reminds us:

> Of course, merely remembering ourselves in other worlds and coming to understand ourselves as multiplicitous is not enough for liberation: collective struggle in the reconstruction and transformation of structures is fundamental. But this collective practice is born of dialogue among multiplicitous persons.[70]

If they are serious about opposing oppressive structures and changing material realities, multiplicitous people will need to engage in collective struggle. In other words, if multiplicitous people wish to confront white supremacy or any other form of racism, they will likely need to separate (or self-segregate) into racial coalitions of resistance. In this case, one part of our multiplicity becomes most salient—that part that identifies with the racially oppressed coalition of resistance. This, too, is a form of fragmentation of the self. But rather than falling back upon pure, racially distinctive groups (á la Outlaw and Sullivan), multiplicitous people can enter into coalitions of resistance fully cognizant of multiplicity within the group. Racial coalitions of resistance (and the implied racial separatism) then take an impure or "curdled" form.[71] As Lugones explains, the separation of egg yolk from egg white is an exercise in purity. Analogously, the splitting of human populations into five distinctive racial groups is an exercise in purity. In contrast, the separation that occurs when mayonnaise breaks and curdles, coalescing toward either oily water or watery oil, is representative of impure, curdled separation. The mixed-race, multicultural, LGBTQ person, can separate into impure, curdled coalitions of resistance to fight on behalf of a particular racially oppressed group.[72] Although there is separation, it is neither clean nor comprehensive. To keep the curdled nature of these coalitions salient and pliable, Lugones recommends cultivating:

> Bi- and multilingual experimentation; code-switching; categorical blurring and confusion; caricaturing the selves we are in the worlds of our oppressors, infusing them with ambiguity; practicing trickstery and foolery; elaborate and explicitly marked gender transgression; withdrawing our services from the pure or their agents whenever possible and with panache; drag; announcing the impurity of the pure by ridiculing his inability at self-maintenance; playful reinvention of our names for things and people, multiple naming; caricaturing of the fragmented selves we are in our groups; revealing the chaotic in production; revealing the process of producing order if we cannot help producing it; undermining the orderliness of the social ordering; marking our cultural mixtures as we move; emphasizing mestizaje; crossing cultures; etc.[73]

To conceive racial coalitions of resistance in this manner allows for multiplicitous perspectives within the coalition; it makes it possible to see the ways in which oppressions are intersectional. Within these impure coalitions, the provisional nature of the coalition and the multiplicity of its constituents are foregrounded. It is recognized that the multiplicitous experience of some members of the race-based coalition may be opaque to others. "Part of our intellectual task, then, is to work out how different kinds and types of voices *relate to each other* and open up unexpected and surprising ways to think about liberation, knowledge, history, race, gender, narrative, and blackness."[74] Open and often difficult dialogue is vital to the process of communicating our worries and desires, to deciphering the resistant codes of multiplicitous others within our coalitions. Hence, there is a call for "intercultural polyglots who are disposed to understand the peculiarities of each other's resistant ways of living."[75] Intercultural polyglossia, so understood, opens avenues to intercultural communication and impure coalitions of resistance, coalitions that do not rely upon untenable notions of racial distinctiveness or anthropologically necessary racial separatism.

Notes

1. I repurposed and published an earlier variant of this paper as "Evoking Race (to Counter Race-Based Oppression); Or, Adversarial Groups as Anabsolute" in my *Ethics and Insurrection* (London: Bloomsbury, 2021). In any case, I am indebted to Jacoby A. Carter for his insightful comments and suggestions on the earliest draft of this paper.

2. W.E.B. Du Bois, "The Conservation of Races," in *The Idea of Race*, eds. Robert Bernasconi and Tommy Lott (Indianapolis: Hackett Publishing, 2000), 108–110.

3. Du Bois, "The Conservation of Races," 110.

4. Du Bois, "The Conservation of Races," 111.

5. Du Bois, "The Conservation of Races," 112, 116; W.E.B. Du Bois, *The Souls of Black Folk* (New York: Vintage Books/The Library of America, 1990), 189.

6. It is worth noting the slippage between "the Negro race" and the project of "Negro Americans." On a global scale, black or Negro Americans would only comprise a subset of the purported Negro race.

7. Du Bois, "The Conservation of Races," 114.

8. Du Bois, "The Conservation of Races," 116.

9. Lucius Outlaw, *Critical Social Theory in the Interests of Black Folks* (Lanham: Rowman & Littlefield Publishers, 2005), 145.

10. Outlaw, *Critical Social Theory*, 140.

11. Outlaw, *Critical Social Theory*, 140.

12. Outlaw, *Critical Social Theory*, 146.

13. Outlaw, *Critical Social Theory*, 159.

14. Immanuel Kant, "Of the Different Human Races," *The Idea of Race*, eds. Robert Bernasconi and Tommy Lott (Indianapolis: Hackett Publishing 2000), 9; 19–20; Charles Mills, *Blackness Visible* (Ithaca: Cornell University Press, 1998), 73; Lee McBride, "Racial Imperialism and Food Traditions," *The Oxford Handbook of Food Ethics*, eds. Anne Barnhill, Mark Budolfson, and Tyler Doggett (New York: Oxford University Press, 2018), 334; Lee McBride, "Culture, Acquisitiveness, and Decolonial Philosophy," in *Decolonizing American Philosophy*, edited by Corey McCall and Phillip McReynolds (Albany: SUNY Press, 2021), 21–23.

15. Lucius Outlaw, "Rehabilitate Racial Whiteness?," in *What White Looks Like*, ed. George Yancy. (New York: Routledge, 2004), 165.

16. Outlaw, "Rehabilitate Racial Whiteness?," 161.

17. Outlaw, "Rehabilitate Racial Whiteness?," 167.

18. Outlaw, "Rehabilitate Racial Whiteness?," 161, 164.

19. Outlaw, "Rehabilitate Racial Whiteness?," 162; Shannon Sullivan, *Living Across and Through Skins* (Bloomington: Indiana University Press, 2001), 158.

20. Du Bois, "The Conservation of Races," 116; Shannon Sullivan, "Remembering the Gift: W.E.B. Du Bois on the Unconscious and Economic Operations of Racism," *Transactions of the Charles S. Peirce Society*, 39, no. 2 (2003); Terrance MacMullan, "Is There a White Gift? A Pragmatist Response to the Problem of Whiteness," *Transactions of the Charles S. Peirce Society* 41, no. 4 (2005).

21. Sullivan, *Living Across and Through Skins*, 157ff.

22. Sullivan, *Living Across and Through Skins*, 158.

23. Sullivan, *Living Across and Through Skins*, 158; Lucius Outlaw, *On Race and Philosophy* (New York: Routledge, 1996), 13.

24. Shannon Sullivan, *Revealing Whiteness* (Bloomington: Indiana University Press, 2006).

25. Shannon Sullivan, *Good White People* (Albany: SUNY Press, 2014), 123–125, 145

26. Sullivan, *Revealing Whiteness*, 177.

27. Sullivan, *Revealing Whiteness*, 177.

28. Sullivan, *Revealing Whiteness*, 180; cf. Alison Jaggar, "Global Feminist Ethics," in *Decentering the Center*, eds. Uma Narayan and Sandra Harding (Bloomington: Indiana University Press, 2000), 4–10.

29. The picture only gets more complicated if we add African and Afro-descended populations that do not ascribe to the same racial categories as the United States (for example, Durban [South Africa] and Salvador [Brazil]).

30. Sullivan, *Living Across and Through Skins*, 159; Immanuel Kant, "Of the Different Human Races," 11.

31. Gilberto Freyre, *The Gilberto Freyre Reader*, trans. Barbara Shelby (New York: Alfred A. Knopf., 1974) 110.

32. Outlaw, "Rehabilitate Racial Whiteness?," 167.

33. Freyre, *The Gilberto Freyre Reader*, 84.

34. José Martí, *Our America: Writings on Latin America and the Struggle for Cuban Independence*, trans. Elinor Randall, ed. Philip Foner (New York: Monthly Review Press, 1977), 93–94.

35. Martí, *Our America*, 93–94.

36. In 1940, the 72-year-old Du Bois notes that, as he grew older, "Racial identity presented itself as a matter or trammels and impediments as 'tightening bonds about my feet.'" W.E. B. Du Bois, *Dusk of Dawn* (New Brunswick, NJ: Transaction Publishers, 1984), 130.

37. Gilberto Freyre, *The Gilberto Freyre Reader*, 110–113; Antonio Guimarães, "Racism and Anti-Racism in Brazil," in *Racism*, ed. Leonard Harris. (Amherst, NY: Humanity Books, 1999), 314, 319–320.

38. Gilberto Freyre, *The Gilberto Freyre Reader*, 84.

39. Lee McBride, "Racial Imperialism and Food Traditions," 334–335; Alain Locke, *The Philosophy of Alain Locke*, ed. Leonard Harris (Philadelphia: Temple University Press, 1989), 202.

40. W.E.B. Du Bois, *Black Folk: Then and Now* (New York: Oxford University Press, 2007).

41. Leopold Senghor, "What is 'Negritude?'" in *The Idea of Race*, eds. Robert Bernasconi and Tommy Lott (Indianapolis: Hackett Publishing, 2000), 137

42. Outlaw, *Critical Social Theory*, 141.

43. McBride, "Racial Imperialism and Food Traditions," 334–335.

44. Sullivan, *Living Across and Through Skins*, 159.

45. McBride, "Racial Imperialism and Food Traditions"; Jacoby Adeshei Carter, "Like Rum in the Punch: The Quest for Cultural Democracy," in *African American Contributions to the Americas' Cultures*, ed. Jacoby Adeshei Carter (New York: Palgrave Macmillan, 2016); Alain Locke, *The Philosophy of Alain Locke*, 202.; Alain Locke, *Race Contacts and Interracial Relations*, ed. Jeffrey Stewart (Washington, D.C.: Howard University Press, 1992); Alain Locke, *African American Contributions to the Americas' Cultures*, ed. Jacoby Adeshei Carter (New York: Palgrave Macmillan, 2016).

46. María Lugones, *Pilgrimages/Peregrinajes: Theorizing Coalition against Multiple Oppressions* (New York: Rowman & Littlefield Publishers, 2003).

47. Running in the opposite direction, indigenous tribal affiliations are only recognized by the United States Bureau of Indian Affairs if these people bear a Certificate of Degree of Indian Blood (CDIB) that substantiates a sufficient degree of Native American blood. One has to prove they are indigenous (red?) enough to be recognized as indigenous/Indian. See Kyle Powys Whyte, "Indigeneity and US Settler Colonialism," in *The Oxford Handbook of Philosophy and Race*, ed. Naomi Zack (New York: Oxford University Press, 2017), 97.

48. Lugones, *Pilgrimages/Peregrinajes*, 134.

49. María Lugones, "On Complex Communication," *Hypatia* 21, no. 3 (Summer 2006): 75; Patricia Hill Collins, *Black Feminist Thought* (New York: Routledge, 2006), 14, 245.

50. Lugones, *Pilgrimages/Peregrinajes*, 154.

51. Outlaw, *On Race and Philosophy*, 13; Sullivan, *Living Across and Through Skins*, 158; Freyre, *The Gilberto Freyre Reader*, 110.

52. Lee McBride, "Reweaving the Social Fabric Transversally," *Pragmatist Feminism and the Work of Charlene Haddock Seigfried*, eds. Lee A. McBride III and Erin McKenna (London: Bloomsbury, 2022), 143–163.

53. Outlaw, *Critical Social Theory*, 142.

54. Outlaw, *Critical Social Theory*, 140.

55. Leonard Harris, *A Philosophy of Struggle: The Leonard Harris Reader* (London: Bloomsbury, 2020), 57.
56. Harris, *Philosophy of Struggle*, 58.
57. Leonard Harris, "Universal Human Liberation and Community: Pixley Kalsaka Seme and Alain Leroy Locke," in *Perspectives in African Philosophy*, eds. Claude Sumner and Samuel W. Yohannes (Addis Ababa: Addis Ababa University, 2002), 157–158; Alison Jaggar, "Global Feminist Ethics," 6–7.
58. Chandra Talpade Mohanty, *Feminism without Borders*. (Durham, NC: Duke University Press, 2003), 37; Harris, *Philosophy of Struggle*, 232; Jaggar, "Global Feminist Ethics," 8–11; Kristie Dotson, "On the way to decolonization in a settler colony: Re-introducing Black feminist identity politics," *AlterNative* 14, no. 3 (2018), 192–193.
59. Leanne Betasamosake Simpson, *As We Have Always Done* (Minneapolis: University of Minnesota Press, 2017), 217.
60. Harris, *Philosophy of Struggle*, 108, 216, 244.
61. Harris, *Philosophy of Struggle*, 217.
62. Harris, *Philosophy of Struggle*, 58–59; Angela Davis, *The Angela Y. Davis Reader*, ed. Joy James (Malden, MA: Blackwell Publishing, 1998), 300.
63. Harris, *Philosophy of Struggle*, 57.
64. Harris, *A Philosophy of Struggle*, 57.
65. Harris, *Philosophy of Struggle*, 63; Naomi Zack, "Race and Philosophic Meaning," *Race/Sex*, ed. Naomi Zack (New York: Routledge, 1997), 39–40.
66. Davis, *The Angela Y. Davis Reader*, 300; Harris, *Philosophy of Struggle*, 245, 267.
67. Toni Morrison, *The Source of Self-Regard* (New York: Alfred A. Knopf, 2019), 132.
68. Morrison, *The Source of Self-Regard*, 136.
69. Morrison, 137.
70. María Lugones, *Pilgrimages/Peregrinajes*, 62.
71. Lugones, 144.
72. Lugones, 123.
73. Lugones, 145.
74. Katherine McKittrick, *Dear Science and Other Stories* (Durham: Duke University Press, 2021), 50.
75. Lugones, *Pilgrimages/Peregrinajes*, 84.

Bibliography

Carter, Jacoby Adeshei. "Like Rum in the Punch: The Quest for Cultural Democracy." *African American Contributions to the Americas' Cultures*, Edited by Jacoby Adeshei Carter. New York: Palgrave Macmillan 2016.

Collins, Patricia Hill. *Black Feminist Thought*. New York: Routledge, 2009.

Davis, Angela *The Angela Y. Davis Reader*. Edited by Joy James. Malden, MA: Blackwell Publishing, 1998.

Dotson, Kristie "On the way to decolonization in a settler colony: Re-introducing Black feminist identity politics." *AlterNative* 2018, 14, no. 3 (2018): 190–199.
Du Bois, W.E.B. *Black Folk: Then and Now*. New York: Oxford University Press, 2007.
Du Bois, W.E.B. *Dusk of Dawn*. New Brunswick, NJ: Transaction Publishers, 1984.
Du Bois, W.E.B. "The Conservation of Races." *The Idea of Race*. Edited by Robert Bernasconi and Tommy Lott. Indianapolis: Hackett Publishing, 2000, 108–117.
Du Bois, W.E.B. *The Souls of Black Folk*. New York: Vintage Books/The Library of America, 1990.
Freyre, Gilberto. *The Gilberto Freyre Reader*, trans. Barbara Shelby. New York: Alfred A. Knopf, 1974.
Guimarães, Antonio. "Racism and Anti-Racism in Brazil." *Racism*. Edited by Leonard Harris. Amherst, NY: Humanity Books, 1999, 314–330.
Harris, Leonard. *A Philosophy of Struggle: The Leonard Harris Reader*. London: Bloomsbury, 2020.
Harris, Leonard. "Universal Human Liberation and Community: Pixley Kalsaka Seme and Alain Leroy Locke." *Perspectives in African Philosophy*. Edited by Claude Sumner and Samuel W. Yohannes. Addis Ababa: Addis Ababa University, 2002, 150–159.
Jaggar, Alison. "Global Feminist Ethics." *Decentering the Center*. Edited by Uma Narayan and Sandra Harding. Bloomington: Indiana University Press, 2000, 1–25.
Kant, Immanuel. "Of the Different Human Races." *The Idea of Race*. Edited by Robert Bernasconi and Tommy Lott. Indianapolis: Hackett Publishing, 2000, 8–22.
Locke, Alain. *The Philosophy of Alain Locke*. Edited by Leonard Harris. Philadelphia: Temple University Press, 1989.
Locke, Alain. *Race Contacts and Interracial Relations*. Edited by Jeffrey Stewart. Washington, D.C.: Howard University Press, 1992.
Locke, Alain. *African American Contributions to the Americas' Cultures*. Edited by Jacoby Adeshei Carter. New York: Palgrave Macmillan, 2016.
Lugones, María. *Pilgrimages/Peregrinajes: Theorizing Coalition against Multiple Oppressions*. New York: Rowman & Littlefield Publishers, 2003.
Lugones, María. "On Complex Communication." *Hypatia* 21, no. 3 (Summer 2006), 2006: 75–85.
MacMullan, Terrance. "Is There a White Gift? A Pragmatist Response to the Problem of Whiteness." *Transactions of the Charles S. Peirce Society* 41, no. 4 (2005): 796–817.
Martí, José. *Our America: Writings on Latin America and the Struggle for Cuban Independence*, trans. Elinor Randall. Edited by Philip Foner. New York: Monthly Review Press, 1977.
McBride, Lee. "Culture, Acquisitiveness, and Decolonial Philosophy." In *Decolonizing American Philosophy*. Edited by Corey McCall and Phillip McReynolds. Albany: SUNY Press, 2021, 17–35.

McBride, Lee. *Ethics and Insurrection: A Pragmatism for the Oppressed*. London: Bloomsbury, 2021.
McBride, Lee. "Racial Imperialism and Food Traditions." *The Oxford Handbook of Food Ethics*. Edited by Anne Barnhill, Mark Budolfson, and Tyler Doggett. New York: Oxford University Press, 2018, 333–344.
McBride, Lee. "Reweaving the Social Fabric Transversally." *Pragmatist Feminism and the Work of Charlene Haddock Seigfried*. Edited by Lee A. McBride III and Erin McKenna. London: Bloomsbury, 2022, 143–163.
McKittrick, Katherine. *Dear Science and Other Stories*. Durham: Duke University Press, 2021.
Mills, Charles. *Blackness Visible*. Ithaca: Cornell University Press, 1998.
Mohanty, Chandra Talpade. *Feminism without Borders*. Durham, NC: Duke University Press, 2003.
Morrison, Toni. *The Source of Self-Regard*. New York: Alfred A. Knopf, 2019.
Outlaw, Lucius. *On Race and Philosophy*. New York: Routledge, 1996.
Outlaw, Lucius. *Critical Social Theory in the Interests of Black Folks*. Lanham: Rowman & Littlefield Publishers, 2005.
Outlaw, Lucius. "Rehabilitate Racial Whiteness?." *What White Looks Like*. Edited by George Yancy. New York: Routledge, pp. 159–171, 2004.
Senghor, Leopold. "What is 'Negritude'?" *The Idea of Race*. Edited by Robert Bernasconi and Tommy Lott. Indianapolis: Hackett Publishing, 2000, 136–138.
Simpson, Leanne Betasamosake. *As We Have Always Done*. Minneapolis: University of Minnesota Press, 2017.
Sullivan, Shannon. *Good White People*. Albany: SUNY Press, 2014.
Sullivan, Shannon. *Living Across and Through Skins*. Bloomington: Indiana University Press, 2001.
Sullivan, Shannon. "Remembering the Gift: W.E.B. Du Bois on the Unconscious and Economic Operations of Racism." *Transactions of the Charles S. Peirce Society*, 39, no. 2 (2003): 205–225.
Sullivan, Shannon. *Revealing Whiteness*. Bloomington: Indiana University Press, 2006.
Whyte, Kyle Powys. "Indigeneity and US Settler Colonialism." *The Oxford Handbook of Philosophy and Race*. Edited by Naomi Zack. New York: Oxford University Press, 2017, 91–101.
Zack, Naomi. "Race and Philosophic Meaning." *Race/Sex*. Edited by Naomi Zack. New York: Routledge, 1997, 29–43.

PART VI
Inter-American Feminism

13
La Negra's Provocation: Corporeal Consciousness in *Nuestra Señora de La Noche* by Mayra Santos-Febres

Nadia V. Celis Salgado

> "Los marginados hemos aprendido a hablar con el cuerpo . . . Siempre ha habido dictados en los espacios de poder que te han dicho: ¡te vas a callar la boca! Así que tú tienes que aprender a hablar con otros lenguajes. Un lenguaje bien difícil de codificar es el lenguaje del cuerpo, porque siempre hay en él espacio para la ambigüedad, y hay muchos cuerpos que saben hablar por allí . . . en el Caribe se camina y se es de cierta manera, y esa cierta manera de la que él [Benítez Rojo] habla está referida directamente a esos lenguajes de los cuerpos."
>
> "Marginalized people have learned to speak with our bodies . . . There have been always directives in spaces of power mandating: 'you ought to remain silent.' Hence, you had to speak with other languages. A language very hard to codify is body language, because there is always room for ambiguity in it, and there are many bodies that know how to speak this way . . . in the Caribbean one walks and acts in 'a certain way', and that 'certain way' that he [Benítez Rojo] talks about refers directly to those languages of bodies"
>
> (SANTOS-FEBRES IN INTERVIEW WITH CELIS, *"EL LENGUAJE DE LOS CUERPOS"*)

From the Embodied Archive to "Corporeal Consciousness"

Thinking the Caribbean from and with the body—considering the body politics and embodied stories that shaped the region—is an essential project for a society founded on the violent *incarnation* of colonial and patriarchal power.

Bodies have been recurring yet mostly underestimated actors in both the aesthetic deployment and the academic discussion of Caribbean cultural identity, as well as in the production of its globalized image by and for the tourism industry. The body is a common synecdoche among canonical voices of Caribbean thought such as those of the Martinicans Frantz Fanon and Edouard Glissant, the Guyanan Paul Gilroy, and the Cuban Antonio Benítez Rojo.[1] Rendered as an archive of historical memory, in recent decades Caribbean bodies have also become the pillar of numerous scholarly efforts to understand and rewrite the colonial past, assess its impact on the colonial and postcolonial subjects, and make visible both the resistances from the past and present efforts of decolonization. Nevertheless, obscured by both the Cartesian division that continues to render rationality as the *sine qua non* of the "subject," and by the tendency to reduce resistance to the domain of the mind, the role of bodies in the negotiation of colonial relations remains, among Caribbean thinkers, trapped in the tension between their instillment with exceptional autonomy and their reduction to either a rhetorical resource or the docile recipient of hegemonic power. Meanwhile, philosophical approaches that attribute agency and intelligence to the body continue to be exceptional.[2]

In her brilliant account of the prolific use of bodies in contemporary Caribbean literature and theory, Guillermina de Ferrari documents an "exhibitionist" attitude toward the body gradually displacing the previous preference for the symbolism of nature in fiction, in the discussions of the colonial legacy and in the conceptualization of Caribbean identities.[3] De Ferrari argues that in order to counteract the colonizers' tendency to legitimate domination on the discursive subjection of bodies, contemporary writers have resorted to the "myth of the vulnerable body," as "a productive site of memory and contestation."[4] She also underscores the potential fostered by this shift, "[since] the invention of the modern Caribbean was based on symbolic Acts of Delusion that treated the body of the native *as if it were landscape*, it is precisely in the process of foregrounding the role played by the body *in history* that a symbolic reversal of forces—symbolic decolonization—can occur."[5] The recognition of the body as a site of resistance among Caribbean philosophers and fiction writers is linked by De Ferrari to contemporary theories of the body. Her own analysis is grounded in works by Pierre Bourdieu. The wider research leading to this essay engages Bourdieu and Michel Foucault, among other foundational figures of body theories, in a critical dialogue with feminist theories of subjectivity and postcolonial feminism. Feminist theories of *embodiment* stress the material and situated condition of subjects, allowing me to better illuminate Caribbean writers' depiction of bodies as communicative, creative, and resistant agents. Social scientists and scholars of cultural studies have also approached the body in Caribbean history and society, highlighting the vitality and versatility of inter-bodily relations in Caribbean popular culture. Grounded in an interdisciplinary approach, my research underscores how writers and artists mimic and foreground the eloquence and wisdom that bodies deploy in Caribbean culture, as a means to claim both epistemological status and ontological recognition for bodily praxis.

The sociologist Mimi Sheller emphasizes the materiality of the appropriation of bodies during colonization. Sheller locates in the practices of bodily "consumption" that printed the forces of global economy in the flesh of indigenous and Black people—from forced labor to the confiscation of their progeny—the origin of the sexual and racial politics that continue to define the Caribbean as a space suitable for the exploitation and enjoyment of its nature and population.[6] Cultural studies and studies of sexuality in the region address the paradoxical result of the forms of "intimate violence" documented by Sheller. The deployment of ludic and erotic energy manifested in popular practices such as dancing and performance,[7] or even in sexual transactions, speak of the variety of negotiations with power and the alternative deployments of resistance and freedom that Caribbean people have engaged to contest the subjugation of their bodies and selves.[8] By underscoring the incompleteness of the process of colonizing bodies, historians have also displaced their attention from the hegemonic narratives of imperial projects, to the incongruences and uncontrollable outcomes evident in the "affective grid" of the colonial enterprise, "the instabilities and vulnerabilities of colonial regimes, the internal conflicts among those who ruled, and the divergent and diverse practices among them."[9]

The aforementioned ubiquity of the body as a trope, scenario, and speaker in a variety of cultural, social, and artistic phenomena, in addition to regional literature and scholarship, supports my theory of the prevalence among Caribbean people of an exceptional understanding of the relation between the control and location of bodies and the distribution and sustainment of social power—arguably the most widely accepted premise of theories of the body. In my previous work, I have coined the term "corporeal consciousness" to explain such awareness of the embodied condition of power, the uses of the body enabled by this awareness, and the communicational and cognitive capacities highlighted by corporeal practices of resistance.[10] "Corporeal consciousness" refers, in the first instance, to the expressive and creative condition of bodies, evident in their "intuitive" ability to decode the messages conveyed by movement, gestures, appearance, and sensory stimuli in a variety of inter-bodily experiences. The conscious body is, in this first sense, the "lived body" whose perception Maurice Merleau Ponty credited with the mediation of all emotions and thoughts and claimed as axis of the subject's formation.[11] A second connotation of "corporeal consciousness" refers to the different degrees of understanding of that communicative condition of the body, and to the various forms of agency in the exercise of bodies' creative capacity prior or simultaneous to the rational articulation of the social meanings implicit in bodily practices. A third expression of "corporeal consciousness" is the deliberate use of the languages and knowledge of bodies in exposing, negotiating, and contesting hierarchical power relationships. While "corporeal consciousness" is, in its first dimension, universal, even if we are not rationally aware of its common use, other uses respond to culturally specific practices and meanings of the body. My work examines the prevalence and diversity of expressions of "corporeal consciousness" among Hispanic Caribbean women writers and their characters in particular.

Women writers of the Greater Caribbean and its diaspora, along with the feminist critics that have accompanied their rise since the 1980s, have been particularly fruitful in the representation of embodied history, culture, and social realities. They have used the transgressive condition of body language to highlight the complicity between the representation of Caribbean resources and bodies as "consumable" and the racial and gender hierarchies supported by both colonial and post-colonial body politics. Feminist writers have also contested the symbolic and empirical violence that continues to subordinate the "erotic autonomy" of women and feminized subjects to heteropatriarchal, imperial, and capitalist interests.[12] In this context, *"making public the pubic"* has become a fundamental decolonization strategy among women writers in the region. Caribbean women writers' fiction echoes sociological and historical approaches to sexuality in the Caribbean, urging investigation of the links between sexual privilege in intimate relations and more public forms of domination. Mayra Santos-Febres' work takes this strategy to its peak. Her staging of the body as "a dialectical site of traumatic experience and knowledge, or *connaissance*," where both the silenced memory and the knowledges produced under colonialism can be re-membered and re-incorporated to history,[13] affiliates Santos-Febres with Afro-Caribbean women writers such as Jamaica Kincaid (Antigua) and Marise Condé (Guadeloupe), among the pioneers, or Edwidge Danticat (Haiti), among her contemporaries.[14]

Considered "the first black celebrity of Latin American letters," Mayra Santos-Febres is a prolific poet, narrator, essayist, and professor of literature, a blogger, as well as the director and founder of literary workshops, contests and festivals.[15] From her first novel, *Sirena Selena vestida de pena* (1999), Santos-Febres elicited interest among critics, who have emphasized her unique ability to inquire into and tell stories from the point of view of "the Other," to "direct her gaze within, liberating the body and unconscious desire . . . searching for whatever is prohibited in the body politic and not tolerated by the paternal law."[16] Bodies are the core trope of her poetics: the living record of untold history, the site where all power relations materialize, the narrators and actors of stories of oppression and resistance. Santos-Febres' main characters include trans women, prostitutes, migrants, motels' workers and customers, enslaved and free Black women, all of them highly eroticized subjects. In addition to their social marginalization, those characters share an exceptional awareness of the relation between power and sexuality, which they use constantly in their negotiation with the various forces that aim to subjugate them. Santos-Febres' ability to center these characters and their world visions has been attributed to the filtration to the text of her own embodied experience as a Black woman, which "perspires unto the page a colonial identity that, in a fragmented manner, suggests that subjectivity, in a colonial setting, does not conform to the tired Western model of mind/body split (a Lacanian split) but to a disjointed wholeness."[17] The agency that the writer allots her protagonists is also tied to a unique notion of space, displayed by her characters' mobility, that emulates the "wandering" condition of the Caribbean and its citizens. Santos-Febres not only situates her stories in streets, parks, public bathrooms, planes, boats and hotels, rendering urban life as disintegrated and unfathomable, but she also resorts to spaces of desire. Cabarets, motels, and brothels are the main scenarios of her first three novels *Sirena Selena* (1999), *Cualquier miércoles soy tuya (Any Wednesday I Am Yours)* (2002), and *Nuestra señora de la noche (Our Lady of the Night)* (2006). In these spaces, bodies are rendered as the site and product of the tension between forces of hegemonic power and the active memory of peripheral subjects whose "excessive" energy is constantly in tension with the unstable boundaries of Reason and social norms. Bodies enter the text to "talk" about the systemic violence inscribing them under the colonial rule and its legacy, and, at the same time, to claim desire and eroticism as powerful counterforces.

By writing the body and *from* the body, Santos-Febres not only emulates the versatility of bodies in popular culture but she also calls on the body of readers to the exercise of decoding the experiences embodied by fictional characters, as well as to the deconstruction of the meanings culturally assigned to these experiences. Challenging the imposition of modern rationality and its denial of subjectivity to the "savage" bodies of "Others," Santos-Febres' characters suggest that the intuitive understanding of the dependance of power on the control of bodies has allowed Caribbean people to negotiate agency through bodily energies, contact, and performance, making of bodies quintessential speakers of both the successes and failures of the Colonial project.[18]

A Poetics of "Provocation"

A ver, dime Isabel
cómo fue que el tres de enero,
setenta y cuatro
atraíste ciertas balas hasta Ponce
que se alojaron en tu cuerpo
te arrancaron de tu prostíbulo
encendido y febril . . .
isabel, negra, desdúdame . . .
desde qué parcela aclaras
que los cuerpos de la provocación
atraen plomo.[19]

This essay focuses on the protagonist of Santos-Febres' third novel, *Nuestra señora de la noche* (2006), Isabel Luberza or "La Negra," based on a real woman immortalized in Puerto Rican national memory by short stories, songs, and movies. I argue that La Negra's "corporeal consciousness" allows Santos-Febres to reevaluate the "provocative" condition associated with Black women's sexuality, and to expose the political, economic, and social ramifications of sexuality in the Caribbean, underlining the decolonizing potential of desire. The complexity of factors that intersect in the story of Isabel Luberza is anticipated in the poem that serves as epigraph to this section. Santos-Febres outlines the entanglement of race, sexuality, power, and violence entrapping the subjectivity of Black women, implicit in the ironic "provocation" of Isabel's body that, once emancipated, does not attract desire but bullets. *Nuestra señora* is, in the first instance, an attempt to dissect or "desdudar"—a word play suggesting stripping of both clothes and doubts—the history, and power, of the real Isabel Luberza Openheimer, the owner of the most famous brothel in the history of Puerto Rico.[4]

The novel's first narrative sequence, starting during Isabel's childhood in the early 1900s, depicts how this goddaughter of washerwomen in San Antón, an enclave of slaves' descendants at the margins of Ponce city, challenges her multifaceted marginalization to become a rich and powerful businesswoman. By focusing on her early years, the writer displays the factors and actors oppressing the Black girl's body, emphasizing both the vulnerability and the creative capacity of Isabel's body. According to the African-American feminist Patricia Collins, a paradoxical result of the ubiquity of the degrading images associated with Black women—the seductive "available" body and the working "mule," among others—is that their identity formation occurs necessarily within "the struggle to replace controlling images with self-defined knowledge deemed personally important, usually knowledge essential to Black women's survival."[20] Isabel both embodies and refutes many of the stereotypes associated with Black women's sexuality, illustrating not only their effects on her subjectivity but also the knowledge resulting from her interaction with those stereotypes.

Santos-Febres' novel centers the notions of family and community shared by the working-class men and women from San Antón, tracing back Isabel's ability to survive and to forge her own identity not only to the process of self-definition explained by Collins, but also to an alternative world vision rooted in Afro-descendant values. Santos-Febres claims the character of Luberza to locate her in the context of a Black history, turning her into an emblem of the negotiations with sexuality forced by patriarchal and colonial power. At the same time, Isabel embodies the knowledge-power of Afro-Caribbean women, whose agency the author, as her characters, enacts in opposition to a long tradition of silence, misrepresentation, and misappropriation.[21] As suggested by Elvira Sánchez Blake, Santos-Febres expands a project initiated in her poetry and reaching its peak in her next novel, *Faith in Disguise* (2009), aimed to "validate the 'provocative' subjectivity of Afro-Caribbean woman," whose sexuality is seized from its archetypal construction to enact and celebrate its transgressive power.[22] The liberating condition of this transgression is emphasized by the contrast between Isabel's story and those of her female antagonists, Cristina Rangel, the white woman who ends up marrying Isabel's white lover, Fernando Fornarís, and the Black woman who raises Isabel's child with Fernando, Candelaria or Doña "Montse." While Isabel's sexual power and social transgression make her stronger, Cristina and Candelaria's constant efforts to gain social existence by means of acting as "decent" women are not only unrewarded but they also contribute to the gradual deterioration of their bodies and mental health.

A second narrative line, presented from the perspective of Luis Arsenio Fornarís, the son of Cristina and Fernando, links San Antón to Ponce's ruling class, that continues to depend on the Black *gueto*'s provision of workers, domestic employees, and sexual companions. A core conflict in the novel is the tension between the working class and the elites' realities, grounded in the *contrapunto* between Isabel and Luis Arsenio's perspective, and, as Guillermo Irizarry points out, the violence emerging from the epistemological and ethical clash between the hegemonic and the subaltern world visions.[23] La Negra's story also provides the opportunity to observe the imperial takeover of Puerto Rico. Condensed in the rapid modernization of the old colonial city during the first half of the twentieth century, this process includes the transformation from an agricultural to an industrial economy, the problematic incorporation of sectors of society subjugated under the preceding colonial structure, the establishment of US military bases on the island, and events of global resonance such as the world wars. In addition, Luis Arsenio's trajectory as a college student in the United States and a member of the U.S. Navy documents the connections between the local powers and the racial and economic structures of the new Empire in a transnational context.

Isabel's story locates Afro-Puerto Ricans as witnesses of the shortcomings of modernization in the island, that viewed from *"los bateyes de las casuchas de San Antón"* betrays the "racial democracy" that continued to dominate Puerto Rico's social landscape.[24] *Nuestra señora* focuses on Isabel's struggle to expand the contours of the social body in order to make of herself "a woman of means." The weapons raised by La Negra against her marginalization are her awareness and astute use of the coded language of bodies and the social power of desire. Her sophisticated understanding of sexuality reveals, on the one hand, the political role of controlling bodies under the colonial, postcolonial, and neo-colonial hegemonic structure, as well as the symbolic, physical, and sexual violence that enacted such control over Black women. While working as a maid for a white family—where she is almost raped by her *patrón*—through her relationship with a white man, and at each stage of the building of her empire, La Negra experiences in her very flesh those domestic arrangements, emotional connections and sexual exchanges between lords and servers identified by Ann Laura Stoler as both the ground and the cracks of sexual and racial stratification under colonial rule.[25] On the other hand, Isabel's management of desire suggests a complex understanding of the versatility of "Caribbean sex," according to Santos-Febres an expression of "an afro-diasporic philosophy" that conceives of sexuality as "a social force that works [with] the body from a space of negotiation; you negotiate with other forces through the material and the erotic."[26]

Santos-Febres emphasizes the "intimate" condition of power, recreating regional variations of body politics that, according to contemporary studies of sexuality in the Caribbean, have defined the parameters of citizenship both in the colonial and the postcolonial context. Isabel enacts the personal and social potential of "Caribbean sex" through two primary strategies: the disruption of the bodily and spatial hierarchization of difference, and the inversion of the power implicit in the gaze and touch, displayed as forms of both erotic and social contact. Both strategies are recreated in the actions of the protagonist and reproduced at a formal level in the novel. In the final section of this chapter, I illustrate the first strategy grounding what I call Santos-Febres' "poetics of provocation": breaking with the hierarchization of bodies in the private realm as a means to claim space in the public body.[27]

An Economy of "Contagion": Looking, Touching, Taking Space

La Negra's life trajectory illustrates the racial and sexual substrate of the categories sustaining relations of domination, underscoring, on the one hand, the centrality of the categorization of the bodies of "Others" in the formation of the social order and, on the other hand, the permeability of this order to interbodily contact. In her study of the formation of Latin American nations, Beatriz González designates as its backbone the "management of difference," both the production of an "Other" qualified as "vulgar, rude, sick, wild, dirty" and therefore inadmissible according to new notions of citizenship, and the assimilation of acceptable others willing to remove their "excesses."[28] Trimming the unmanageable excrescences of other subjects, other languages, and the heterogeneities of one's own body was essential to the construction of the nation.[29] Sarah Ahmed records the continuity of politics of "estrangement" in the delimitation of public space in contemporary Western societies, grounded in the creation and continuous recognition of acceptable or foreign bodies. The identity of the "Ones," Ahmed argues, "does not simply happen in the privatized realm of the subject's relation to itself. Rather, in daily meetings with others, subjects are perpetually reconstituted . . . it is only through meeting with another that the identity of a given person *comes to be inhabited as living*."[30] The asymmetry of power implicit in these meetings—that enable the "One" to define the "Other" as "strange"—depends on the ratification, meeting after meeting, of a prior and collective history of encounters.[31] Santos-Febres represents the historical memory embodied in the encounters between bodies defined as "strange" by the colonial sexual and racial boundaries, exposing and subverting the ideological substrate of their differentiation. At the same time, the author reveals and celebrates the vulnerability of hegemonic power to the proximity of those bodies and the varying intensities of their encounters. By insistently displaying the flaws in the modern project's attempts to regulate bodies, Santos-Febres reveals the porosity of hegemonic categories, which she tests through the constant interpenetration between "legitimate" and "strange" spaces and bodies. The author highlights, in particular, the role of the visual and sexual contact in the constitution of urban space, the inequalities that mark these contacts, and their effects on individual and collective identities.

The disruptive nature of encounters is triggered in *Nuestra señora de la noche* by the multiplicity and confusion of narrative voices. Isabel's internal voices overlap with Cristina and Candelaria's similarly fragmented consciousness, creating a sort of multifaceted mirror, blurring both the models of femininity that each of these characters embody and their surrounding realities. This effect is further complicated by Luis Arsenio's vision, whose identity enters in crisis after his erotic encounter with a *mulata* at Elizabeth's Dancing Place. Luis Arsenio's difficulty in trimming his "excesses," as required from the men of his class, deepens while attending college in the United States, after his encounter with American elites who situate him as the colonial "stranger," an unwanted and subordinate second-class citizen.

Isabel's physical and social mobility amplify the disintegrative effects of the confusion not only of the voices and consciences but also of the bodies and places that "strangers" are expected to remain at. The process by which the "stranger" is defined and recognized is firmly anchored, according to Ahmed, in the legitimacy of their presence in certain spaces: "we recognize somebody as a stranger, rather than simply failing to recognize them . . . [and] the recognizability of strangers is determinate in the social demarcation of spaces of belonging: the stranger is 'known again' as that which has already contaminated such spaces as a threat to both property and person."[32] From the very first appearance of "La Negra," in the chapter entitled "Revelation," Santos-Febres records the "contagium" of the white elite's space operated by that iconic "stranger"—Black, female, prostitute—trespassing the boundaries associated with her difference. Sheathed in a white glove, the Black hand of the Madama emerges from her lawyer's Cadillac making way for her unlikely body to enter a dance of the Red Cross. Politicians, businessmen, the Bishop, and good wives watch her, astounded yet unable to dispute her presence, because by then, by holding their secrets and doing them favors, Isabel has bought her right to inhabit and to define herself in relation to that space.[33] In the second chapter of the novel, when introducing Elizabeth's Dancing Place, Santos-Febres remarks the inversion operated by the initial displacement and its multiple connotations. The pillar of La Negra's power is described from Luis Arsenio's perspective during his visit of "initiation" in masculinity, in words that insinuate the endemic relationship of the brothel with Ponce's "legitimate" spaces and citizens:

> That [place] was another dimension . . . People laughed high, drank freely in that place with air to overstuffed divan, to site without eyes but full of hands and loud skins that disguised words said without restrain . . . There were the girls, Isabel's pupils/goddaughters/protégées, spread around the hall as meat gifts . . . wielding little screams and smiles and wobbling on high heels, scented with a thousand fragrances and smoke and the smell of free desire of those who arrived at the Elizabeth's looking for a place to release the moorings of their decency.

> [*Aquello era otra dimensión . . . La gente reía alto, bebía libre en ese lugar con aire a diván mullido, a sitial sin ojos pero repleto de manos y pieles de bullicio que camuflaba las palabras dichas sin reparo . . . allí*

estaban las chicas, las pupilas/ahijadas/protegidas de Isabel, esparciéndose por el salón como carnes de regalo . . . empuñando grititos y sonrisas y bamboleándose sobre tacones altos, perfumadas con mil fragancias y con humo y con el olor al deseo regalado de aquellos que llegaban al Elizabeth's en busca de un lugar donde soltar las amarras de su decencia.][34]

The displacement of La Negra's body, which not only creates a space of her own but, returning to the scene of the Red Cross dance, appropriates the space of the "Ones," enables the penetration of the energy of the brothel into the "decent" city spaces. Her movement in the novel emulates the "claiming of space" that Carole Boyce Davis attributes to the Black female body in the context of Carnival and other forms of performance in the Caribbean. In Isabel's case, such disruptive effect works through different stages, including the acquisition of land that she receives from her white lover at the end of their romance, the building and consolidation of Elizabeth's, and her "invasion" of the white and higher-class sectors of the city, as well as her expansion to other islands in the Caribbean, where the Madama invests and secures her money. At the same time, her displacement is key to redefining the externally sexualized and vulnerable Black female body, transformed by Isabel into an autonomous and powerful body-subject.

The description of Elizabeth's from her own point of view reveals the mechanisms enabling Isabel's power. From her "throne of straw," "converted in a spectacle herself and making a spectacle of everything her eyes may reach," the "benevolent Madama" looks at and runs her kingdom, "guarding the place, alert . . . She walked her gaze along as if she was judging a variety show and as if she weighed defense strategies in a mined territory. Her eyes covered it all. ["Sus ojos] vigilaban el lugar, alertas . . . Paseaba su vista como si estuviera evaluando un espectáculo de variedades y como si sopesara estrategias de defensa en un territorio minado. Todo lo abarcaban sus ojos."][35] The two descriptions of the place, conceived as a space for freedom and wildness by Luis Arsenio, and as a battleground by Isabel, introduce the tension between the visions of the elite and the working class. Meanwhile, by placing the Black woman simultaneously as an object of desire and as the subject of power, the passage highlights Isabel's recognition of herself as an embodiment of the porous limits of the individual and the social body: "that woman knew she was quite a female. She knew also that her skin was a provocation and that it was enough to look at her to impress anyone" ["aquella mujer se sabía mucha hembra. Sabía, además, que su piel era una provocación y que bastaba mirarla para impresionar a cualquiera"].[36] The subjectivity of the Black woman is enhanced by her "corporeal consciousness," which power is further asserted by the reversal of the gaze, by those ubiquitous eyes turning on the "Ones" the estrangement otherwise subjecting Black women's bodies and sexuality.

Santos-Febres emphasizes the power of the gaze as a "technology" of both sexual economy and social power. The narrative goes on to describe Isabel's employees as her "pupils" walking across her customers, in a characterization that amplifies her transgressive power. Santos-Febres uses not only the reciprocal gaze but the amalgam of visual and erotic contact taking place in the brothel, where watching and being watched enable and assume the qualities of friction. The gaze, becoming what Merleau-Ponty describes as a "palpation of the eye," is contaminated with the essential reversibility of touching and being touched, prompting the loss of authority implicit in looking, and making the subject who looks and the object to be looked at observable.[37] In her revision of the "imperial gaze" and how it works in the relationship between tourists and locals in the contemporary Caribbean, Mimi Sheller explains in similar terms the situation of the "First World" visitor, whose implicit right to look carries at the same time the risk of being "touched:" "gazing on another requires a certain degree of proximity, which puts the gazer at risk: Embodied encounters leave a space for the gaze, deflecting the gaze, returning the gaze, appropriating the gaze, and destabilizing the power of the gaze."[38]

The economy of "contagion" marking the social landscape of *Nuestra señora* is the first link of the aesthetics of "provocation" that allows the author to retrieve the objectified body of Black women and their sexuality as a source of an autonomous subjectivity, grounded in the continuum between looking and erotic touching. Those sexual encounters in which working class men, US soldiers, and other foreigners seek to ratify their masculine power, and in which the white men of the Ponce's elites ratify, in addition, their economic and social power, become in Elizabeth's a power supply for Isabel. La Negra will come to capitalize both the reading of the bodily needs of her customers, and the secrets they share in bed. Returning to Ahmed, the creation and recognition of the "other" depends not only on his/her visual recognition, but on a hierarchy of touch, where various forms of touching produce different social space arrangements: "Bodies with skins, while they are already touched in the sense of being exposed to others, are touched differently by near and far others, and *it is this differentiation between others that constitutes the permeability of bodily boundaries.*"[39] La Negra's extraordinary ability to understand and negotiate with desire further allows her to subvert those economies of touching, disrupting the legitimate ways of approaching, by whom and to whom, where and how, that constitute the "social body."

The "corporeal consciousness" that Santos-Febres attributes to her character extends to an understanding of the material and sexual nature of citizenship, which is grounded and asserted, according to Mimi Sheller, both in relations of domination and in sexual relations that allow those with real access to the rights and legal protections of a citizen to take advantage of those not considered full citizens.[40] In her characterization of Caribbean neo-colonial states as "masculine," Jacquie Alexander denounces the role of the co-opting of the erotic autonomy of women and other marginalized subjects in support of an idea of Nation threatened by the non-reproductive sexuality of queer subjects and prostitutes.[41] The "anomalous" sexuality of these non-citizens has allowed to define, by contrast, the borders of respectability and "appropriate" sexuality which entitle subjects to citizenship.[42] Alexander emphasizes the paradoxical condition of the prostitute in the context of Caribbean states economically dependent on tourism. Even though the selling of sex is a well-known component of packages for visitors, these nations continue to depend on the clandestinity and social rejection of prostitution to hold the mask of "respectability" that constitutes their moral axis. The bodies and sexuality of Black women are particularly visible in this drama, given their susceptibility to embody both the local fantasies of sexual ungovernability and global fantasies of conquest of the exotic, primitive, and "dangerous" local bodies.[43]

Nuestra señora underscores both the vulnerability of the body in the context of a patriarchal and colonial economy of desire, and the potential of the relationship with a body "of One's own" to negotiate and subvert the terms of its subordination. Isabel's is not just a body that resists, but a body that "thinks" and acts, anticipating the response and encouraging the rational articulation of the protagonist's resistance to hierarchical power structures. A body that exercises power and that, in the case of La Negra, responds also to Isabel's desire of power, rendering at her service both her own "erotic autonomy" and the libido of her wide range of customers. Throughout Isabel's formation, the novel relies on diverse expressions of "corporeal consciousness," from bodily reactions to look and touching, to dressing and dance, among other sophisticated forms of kinetic communication, to recreate the discourses and practices that named and located Black women, as well as the strategies that Isabel uses in negotiating the conditions of oppression associated with her gender, race, and class. At the core of her exceptional ability to read and rewrite inter-bodily relations is an ancestral knowledge archived in Black bodies, source of the "Afrodiasporic philosophy" that Santos-Febres associates to working with sexuality. By entering in the network of relations shaping Isabel's identity from her early age, Santos-Febres illustrates the formation of an alternative logic and ethics, marked by the material, ideological and spiritual context of San Antón, which social interactions reveal the persistence of African epistemologies in tense coexistence with the Euro-Caribbean ones. Moreover, through the deployment of the experiences and meanings of sexuality that frame the negotiation with the "force" of the sexual by Black, mulata, and white women, as well as Ponce's and Puerto Rican men, Santos-Febres exposes the urgency to think Caribbean sexuality from alternative parameters, reiterating the dilemmas posed by social scientists in their discussions about sex work in the region.

Delving into the intimate spring of the public body, Santos-Febres locates at the core of the negotiations for autonomy between subjects and hegemonic forces, discourses and institutions, the symbolic construction of desire, not only sexual desire but also the desire to achieve social existence—of being yourself while being recognized by others. At the same time, her characters' "corporeal consciousness" enables relations that transcend and challenge the reduction of personhood to the parameters of racialization and sexualization dictated by colonial and patriarchal norms as conditions to achieve such existence. The battle for their bodies that the "provokers" vindicated by Santos-Febres engage in, attests to the persistence of a desire for freedom preceding the subjection and subjugation of the private to the public body. This desire, which coexists with power and as a counterforce to the same, finds preeminent expression—precisely because of the unique history of its violent repression in the Caribbean—through the experience of the body and its permeable conscience.

In assessing the scope of Isabel's "corporeal consciousness," my analysis points to its functions in the reproduction and contestation of historical memory, in the formation of autonomous subjects, and in the formulation of alternative forms of citizenship, "citizenships from below" suggesting a conception of freedom beyond the liberal framework. Caribbean eloquent bodies offer to the reconsideration of regional cultural identity, and to the global project of decolonization, at least three fundamental strategies: an ethic based on the negotiation of forces alternative to dichotomous thinking and the logic of confrontation; the recognition and use of the role of corporeality in these negotiations; and the focus on embodied experience and knowledge as tools for emancipatory practices aimed to claim not the right to have or to control but the right to be.[44]

Notes

1. Frantz Fanon, *Black Skin, White Masks* (London: MacGibbon & Kee, 1968); Edouard Glissant, *Poétique de la Relation* (Paris: Gallimard, 1990); Paul Gilroy, *The Black Atlantic: Modernity and Double Consciousness* (Cambridge, Mass.: Harvard University Press, 1993); and Antonio Benítez Rojo, *La isla que se repite: el Caribe y la perspectiva posmoderna* (Hanover, NH: Ediciones del Norte, 1989).

2. Note as an example the case of Paul Gilroy's celebrated work *The Black Atlantic*. His discussion of the richness and versatility of the communicative culture originated in the African diaspora, and its effects on the "structure of feelings" that transverses the Caribbean and the "Black Atlantic" has been widely welcomed by Cultural studies within and beyond the region. In contrast, the ontological and epistemological implications of his suggestive reflection on "the distinctive relationship with the body" of Afrodiasporique cultures have received little consideration. Gilroy highlights how the tendency to use, expose, and read the body as a privileged means of communication grew "in inverse proportion to the limited expressive power of the language" under the "racial terror" of colonial times (Gilroy, *The Black Atlantic*, 74). The "distinctive quinesia of the post-slavery people" is, he argues, the paradoxical result both of the prohibition of speech and of the inability to express discursively the horror of slave violence. However, Gilroy locates in the richness of the non-verbal expressions of Afro-Atlantique cultures (with particular attention to music) the potential to challenge "the conceptions that privilege language and writing as expressions par excellence of human consciousness" (Gilroy, *The Black Atlantic*, 75).

3. Guillermina De Ferrari, *Vulnerable States: Bodies of Memory in Contemporary Caribbean Fiction* (Charlottesville: University of Virginia Press, 2007).

4. De Ferrari, *Vulnerable States*, 3–4.

5. De Ferrari, *Vulnerable States*, 25.

6. Mimi Sheller, *Consuming the Caribbean: From Arwaks to Zombies* (London: Routledge, 2002).

7. Ángel Quintero Rivera, *Cuerpo y cultura. Las músicas mulatas y la subversión del baile* (Madrid; Frankfurt: Iberoamericana Vervuert, 2009).

8. Kamala Kempadoo, ed. *Sun, Sex and Gold. Tourism and Sex Work in the Caribbean*. Lanham: Rowman and Littlefield, 1999); Kamala Kempadoo, ed. *Sexing the Caribbean. Gender, Race and Sexual Labor* (New York: Routledge, 2004); Kamala Kempadoo, "Caribbean Sexuality: Mapping the Field," *Caribbean Review of Gender Studies* 3 (2009); Mimi Sheller, "Work That Body: Sexual Citizenship and Embodied Freedom," in *Constructing Vernacular Culture in the Trans-Caribbean*, eds. Holger Henke and Karl-Heinz Magister (Lanham, MD: Lexington Books, 2008); Mimi Sheller, *Citizenship from Below: Erotic Agency and Caribbean Freedom* (Durham: Duke University Press, 2012.)

9. Ann Laura Stoler, *Carnal Knowledge and Imperial Power: Race and the Intimate in Colonial Rule* (Berkeley: University of California Press, 2002), 10.

10. See Nadia Celis, "The Rhetoric of Hips: Shakira's Embodiment and the Quest for Caribbean Identity", in *Archipelagos of Sound. Transnational Caribbeanities, Women and Music*, ed. Ifeona Fulani (Kingston: University of West Indies Press, 2012); Celis, "Bailando el Caribe: corporalidad, identidad y ciudadanía en las Plazas de Cartagena." in *Caribbean Studies* 41, no. 1 (January–June 2013): 27–61; and Celis, *La rebellion de las niñas. El Caribe y la "conciencia corporal"* (Madrid, Frankfurt: Iberoamericana Vervuert, 2015).

11. Maurice Merleau Ponty, *Phenomenology of Perception*, trad. Paul Kegan (New York: Humanities Press, 2005).

12. Jacqui Alexander, "Erotic Autonomy as a Politics of Decolonization: An Anatomy of Feminist and State Practice in the Bahamas Tourist Economy," in *Feminist Genealogies, Colonial Legacies, Democratic Futures*, eds. Chandra Talpade Mohanty, and M. Jacqui Alexander. (New York: Routledge, 1997), 64.

13. Brinda J. Mehta, *Notions of Identity, Diaspora, and Gender in Caribbean Women's Writing* (New York: Palgrave Macmillan, 2009), 2.

14. Mimi Sheller, "Work That Body," 357.

15. For a detailed analysis of the multiple facets of Santos-Febres, see Nadia Celis and Juan Pablo Rivera, eds. *Lección errante: Mayra Santos-Febres y el Caribe contemporáneo* (San Juan, P.R.: Editorial Isla Negra, 2011), 7, 17.

16. Alberto Sandoval Sánchez, "*Sirena Selena vestida de pena*: A Novel for the New Millenium and for New Critical Practices in Puerto Rican Literary and Cultural Studies," *Centro Journal* 15, no. 2 (2003): 9.

17. Arleen Chiclana y González, "The Body of Evidence: Body-Writing, the Text and Mayra Santos Febres' Illicit Bodies," in *Unveiling the Body in Hispanic Women's Literature: From Nineteenth-Century Spain to Twenty-First-Century United States*, eds. Renée Sum Scott and Arleen Chiclana y González. (Lewiston, NY: Edwin Mellen Press, 2006).

18. In addition to the songs commemorating her and the film made in her honor, *A Life of sin* (1979), directed by Efraín López Neri, Isabel Luberza appears as a character in Rosario Ferré's short story, "Cuando las mujeres quieren a los hombres" in *Papeles de Pandora* (México: Joaquín Mortíz, 1976) and in "La última plena que bailó Luberza" by Manuel Ramos Otero in *El cuento de la mujer del mar* (Río Piedras: Ediciones Huracán, 1979). Sanchez-Blake traces the genealogy of the character within the work of Santos-Febres, according to the critic present as an embryo in her poetry and in the story "Marina y su olor." *Pez de vidrio*. See Elvira Sánchez-Blake, "De *Anamú y manigua* a *Nuestra Señora de la Noche*: Poética errante en la obra de Mayra Santos-Febres," in *Lección errante: Mayra Santos-Febres y el Caribe contemporáneo*, eds. Nadia Celis and Juan Pablo Rivera. (San Juan: Isla Negra, 2011). 187–205,).

19. Mayra Santos-Febres, *Anamú y manigua*, 46.

20. Patricia Collins, *Black Feminist Thought: Knowledge, Consciousness, and the Politics of Empowerment* (New York: Routledge, 2009), 100.

21. Ríos Ávila, Rubén. "La virgen puta," in *Lección errante: Mayra Santos-Febres y el Caribe contemporáneo*, eds., Nadia Celis and Juan Pablo Rivera. (San Juan: Isla Negra, 2011), 73

22. Elvira Sánchez-Blake, "*De Anamú y manigua*," 190.

The fourth of her novels, *Fe en disfraz* (*Faith in Disguise*) (2009), follows this trend and adds a turn. The protagonist is a Black female professor in the world of American academia, negotiating her difference from a "legitimate" space, yet in conflict with a personal and collective history that Faith continues to embody in spite of her efforts to "disguise" the abject condition associated with Black women's sexuality.

23. Guilermo Irizarry, "Pasión y muerte de la madama de San Antón: Modernidad, tortura y ética en Nuestra Señora de la Noche," in *Lección errante: Mayra Santos Febres y el Caribe contemporáneo*, eds. Nadia Celis and Juan Pablo Rivera (San Juan: Isla Negra, 2011), 208.

24. Hilda Lloréns, "Brothels, Hell and Puerto Rican Bodies: Sex, Race, and Other Cultural Politics in 21st Century Artistic Representations." *Centro Journal* 20, no. 1 (2008): 198.

25. Ann Laura Stoler, *Carnal Knowledge and Imperial Power*.

26. Nadia Celis, "Mayra Santos-Febres, El lenguaje de los cuerpos caribeños (Entrevista)" in *Lección errante: Mayra Santos-Febres y el Caribe contemporáneo*, eds. Nadia Celis and Juan Pablo Rivera (San Juan: Isla Negra 2011), 252–3

27. See Nadia Celis, *La rebelión de las niñas* for an analysis of the remaining strategies.

28. Beatriz Stephan González, "Cuerpos de la nación: Cartografías disciplinarias." *Anales Nueva Época* 2 (1999): 71–106.

29. Beatriz Stephan González, "Cuerpos de la nación," 25.

30. Sara Ahmed, *Strange Encounters: Embodied Others in Post-Coloniality* (London; New York: Routledge, 2000), 7–8.

31. Ahmed, *Strange Encounters*, 8–13.

32. Ahmed, *Strange Encounters*, 22.

33. Ahmed, *Strange Encounters*, 9–10.

34. Santos-Febres, *Nuestra señora*, 33–34.

35. Santos-Febres, *Nuestra señora*, 35–36.

36. Santos-Febres, *Nuestra señora*, 35.

37. In his analysis of the textual use of the senses, William Cohen identifies a similar mechanism among some writers of the Victorian era, who question the distance implicit in the act of looking blurring the boundaries between the subject and the object of the gaze. Returning to the theorization of "the flesh" by Maurice Merleau-Ponty, Cohen points out how the philosopher, as the analyzed writers, conceive of looking as a "palpation of the eye," granting vision the qualities of touch, an analogy that pollutes the act of looking with the essential reversibility of touching and being touched: "Merleau-Ponty lends vision the tactile qualities of proximity and direct contact, turning it from the objective, distant sense into a corporeally grounded and reciprocal one." See William A. Cohen, *Embodied: Victorian Literature and the Senses* (Minneapolis: University of Minnesota Press, 2009), 17.

38. Mary Louise Pratt, *Imperial Eyes: Travel Writing and Transculturation* (London and New York: Routledge, 1992); Mimi Sheller, *Citizenship from Below*, 211–212.

39. Ahmed, Strange Encounters, 49.

40. Sheller, *Citizenship from Below*, 242.

41. Alexander, "Erotic Autonomy," 64.

42. Jacqui Alexander, "Not Just (Any) Body Can Be a Citizen: The Politics of Law, Sexuality and Postcoloniality in Trinidad and Tobago and the Bahamas." *Feminist Review* 48 (1994): 7.
43. Alexander, "Erotic Autonomy," 85–88.
44. Sheller, *Citizenship from Below*.

Bibliography

Ahmed, Sara. *Strange Encounters: Embodied Others in Post-Coloniality*. London; New York: Routledge, 2000.

Alexander, M. Jacqui. "Erotic Autonomy as a Politics of Decolonization: An Anatomy of Feminist and State Practice in the Bahamas Tourist Economy." *Feminist Genealogies, Colonial Legacies, Democratic Futures*. Edited by Mohanty, Chandra Talpade and M. Jacqui Alexander. New York: Routledge, 1997, 63–100.

———. "Not Just (Any) Body Can Be a Citizen: The Politics of Law, Sexuality and Postcoloniality in Trinidad and Tobago and the Bahamas." *Feminist Review* 48 (1994): 5–23.

Celis, Nadia. *La rebelión de las niñas. El Caribe y la "conciencia corporal."* Madrid, Frankfurt: Iberoamericana Vervuert, 2015.

———. "Bailando el Caribe: corporalidad, identidad y ciudadanía en las Plazas de Cartagena", en *Caribbean Studies*. 41.1 (January–June 2013): 27–61.

———."The Rhetoric of Hips: Shakira's Embodiment and the Quest for Caribbean Identity", en *Archipelagos of Sound. Transnational Caribbeanities, Women and Music*. Edited by Ifeona Fulani. Kingston: University of West Indies Press, 2012, 191–216.

———. "Mayra Santos-Febres: El lenguaje de los cuerpos caribeños (Entrevista)." *Lección errante: Mayra Santos-Febres y el Caribe contemporáneo*. Edited by Nadia Celis and Juan Pablo Rivera. San Juan: Isla Negra 2011, 247–65.

Celis, Nadia and Juan Pablo Rivera, eds. *Lección errante: Mayra Santos-Febres y el Caribe contemporáneo*. San Juan, P.R.: Editorial Isla Negra, 2011.

Chiclana y González, Arleen. "The Body of Evidence: Body-Writing, the Text and Mayra Santos Febres' Illicit Bodies." *Unveiling the Body in Hispanic Women's Literature: From Nineteenth-Century Spain to Twenty-First-Century United States*. Edited by Scott, Renée Sum and Arleen Chiclana y González. Lewiston, NY: Edwin Mellen Press, 2006, 161–86.

Cohen, William A. *Embodied: Victorian Literature and the Senses*. Minneapolis: University of Minnesota Press, 2009.

Collins, Patricia. *Black Feminist Thought: Knowledge, Consciousness, and the Politics of Empowerment*. New York: Routledge, 2009.

De Ferrari, Guillermina. *Vulnerable States: Bodies of Memory in Contemporary Caribbean Fiction*. Charlottesville: University of Virginia Press, 2007.

Ferré, Rosario. *Papeles de Pandora*. México: Joaquín Mortíz, 1976.

Gilroy, Paul. *The Black Atlantic: Modernity and Double Consciousness*. Cambridge, Mass.: Harvard University Press, 1993.

González Stephan, Beatriz. "Cuerpos de la nación: Cartografías disciplinarias." *Anales Nueva Época* 2 (1999): 71–106.
Irizarry, Guilermo. "Pasión y muerte de la madama de San Antón: Modernidad, tortura y ética en Nuestra Señora de la Noche." *Lección errante: Mayra Santos-Febres y el Caribe contemporáneo*. Edited by Celis, Nadia and Juan Pablo Rivera. San Juan: Isla Negra, 2011, 206–25.
Kempadoo, Kamala. "Caribbean Sexuality: Mapping the Field." *Caribbean Review of Gender Studies* 3 (2009): 1–24.
———, ed. *Sexing the Caribbean. Gender, Race and Sexual Labor*. New York: Routledge, 2004.
———, ed. *Sun, Sex and Gold. Tourism and Sex Work in the Caribbean*. Lanham: Rowman and Littlefield, 1999.
Lloréns, Hilda. "Brothels, Hell and Puerto Rican Bodies: Sex, Race, and Other Cultural Politics in 21st Century Artistic Representations." *Centro Journal* 20.1 (2008): 192–217.
Mehta, Brinda J. *Notions of Identity, Diaspora, and Gender in Caribbean Women's Writing*. New York: Palgrave Macmillan, 2009.
Merleau Ponty, Maurice. *Phenomenology of Perception*. 1945. Trad. Paul, Kegan. New York: Humanities Press, 2005.
Pratt, Mary Louise. *Imperial Eyes: Travel Writing and Transculturation*. London and New York: Routledge, 1992.
Ramos Otero, Manuel. *El cuento de la mujer del mar*. Río Piedras: Ediciones Huracán, 1979.
Ríos Ávila, Rubén. "La virgen puta." *Lección errante: Mayra Santos-Febres y el Caribe contemporáneo*. Edited by Nadia Celis and Juan Pablo Rivera. San Juan: Isla Negra, 2011, 71–77.
Sánchez-Blake, Elvira. "De *Anamú y manigua* a *Nuestra Señora de la Noche*: Poética errante en la obra de Mayra Santos Febres." *Lección errante: Mayra Santos-Febres y el Caribe contemporáneo*. Edited by Nadia Celis and Juan Pablo Rivera. San Juan: Isla Negra, 2011, 187–205.
Sandoval Sánchez, Alberto. "*Sirena Selena vestida de pena*: A Novel for the New Millenium and for New Critical Practices in Puerto Rican Literary and Cultural Studies." *Centro Journal* 15.2 (2003): 4–23.
Santos-Febres, Mayra. *Nuestra señora de la noche*. Madrid: Espasa Calpe, 2006.
———. *Anamú y manigua*. Río Piedras: Ediciones La iguana dorada, 1991.
Sheller, Mimi. *Citizenship from Below: Erotic Agency and Caribbean Freedom*. Durham: Duke University Press, 2012.
———. "Work That Body: Sexual Citizenship and Embodied Freedom." *Constructing Vernacular Culture in the Trans-Caribbean*. Edited by Holger Henke and Karl-Heinz Magister. Lanham, MD: Lexington Books, 2008, 345–76.
———. *Consuming the Caribbean: From Arwaks to Zombies*. London: Routledge, 2002.
Stoler, Ann Laura. *Carnal Knowledge and Imperial Power: Race and the Intimate in Colonial Rule*. Berkeley: University of California Press, 2002.

14
Decolonial Feminisms and Indigenous Women's Resistance to Neoliberalism: Lessons from Abya Yala

Andrea J. Pitts

Es muy difícil cuestionar, la centralidad de la epistemología de lo occidental en el feminismo desde la academia y las ciudades, pero es evidente que muchas mujeres se encuentran des-centradas—¿libres del cerco?—de ella. Conocer las ideas que las mueven a la acción para mí también ha implicado una acción, un ponerme en movimiento hacia ellas y buscar las vías de entablar un diálogo.[1]

The task of theorizing indigenous paths of resistance against neoliberalism begins with the question of knowledge production. How various communities and institutions are situated with respect to the recognition and circulation of knowledge depends largely on the very dynamics of coloniality that are at stake in a theoretical discourse. In this sense, the positions of enunciation that make possible the legibility of the terms of a given discourse are themselves implicated and enabled by the dynamics of coloniality. We can thus situate the following analysis of indigenous women's resistance to neoliberalism from within the loci of academic, largely Anglophone discourses that must themselves resist homogenizing and commodifying the very textual and hermeneutical resources made possible by indigenous writers working throughout Abya Yala.[2]

The epistemic and political positionings implicated by authors producing from the context of North American Anglophone universities requires a vigilant confrontation with what Walter Mignolo and other theorists describe as "academic colonialism." Cheng-Feng Shih describes academic colonialism in the following manner:

> Academic colonialism stands for how states occupying the centre where knowledge is produced, transmitted, and ordered, in an unfair

academic division of labor at the global level have successfully coerced scholars located in the peripheral states to accept their dominated relations in thoughts and ideas by standardising, institutionalising, and socialising academic disciplines.[3]

Shih's articulation of academic colonialism thus places a significantly high responsibility on the terms of analysis of many of the essays in this volume. Namely, the production of academic information *about* indigenous paths of resistance to neoliberalism must find ways to work *alongside* the decolonial struggles of indigenous communities in the Global South by seeking, as Francesca Gargallo Celentani suggests in the epigraph above, *ways to engage in dialogue* with indigenous communities. To do so requires confrontation with forms of colonial difference and differing decolonial struggles, and it is these forms of difference that this essay seeks to address.

In what follows, I hope to trace several threads of indigenous resistance by women in two distinct geopolitical sites of Abya Yala. The aim of doing so is to help situate and critique modes of gender analysis and feminist theory within the Anglophone North American philosophical academy in an effort to develop coalitional strategies with indigenous scholars and activists working across Abya Yala. With conceptual resources from decolonial theory, this essay examines the writings of several authors based in Bolivia and Mexico who are carrying out distinct forms of political organizing in the service of indigenous rights. In each context, I hope to specify variations within contemporary neoliberal policies and practices, and the counterclaims made by indigenous women in these contexts. I thereby aim to highlight strategies of resistance as well as theoretical methods of critique used by several indigenous women in Abya Yala. Although I draw from a very small sampling of texts from Abya Yala, for the purpose of the paper more generally, the overarching aim will be to link these strategies and methods to discourses on the coloniality of gender and feminist theory in the hope of contributing to a broader network of indigenous philosophical studies across the Americas. Also, although Mexico and Bolivia provide sufficiently distinct loci of enunciation with respect to the analysis provided here, I aim to connect, at various junctures in the paper, to broader discourses of decolonial and anti-imperial struggle as a way to bridge philosophical work across the Americas.

To carry out this work, first, I clarify a set of conceptual issues regarding the functioning of terms such as "neoliberalism" and "indigeneity" in this paper. Then, in the second section, I examine how indigenous women in differing sites of Abya Yala are developing pathways of resistance against neoliberal economic, political, and social policies. This analysis then provides critical tools, offered in the last section, for challenging and reshaping academic philosophical discourses in the U.S. and Canada in efforts of coalition praxis alongside indigenous communities in Abya Yala.[4]

Clarifying Our Terms of Engagement

The first conceptual issue that I would like to raise is the problem of naming the socioeconomic and political contemporary world-system that has given rise to what many theorists now refer to as "neoliberalism." While some theorists have taken as their focus the ways in which liberal political and economic theory and practice in the Global North has expanded into the "neo" iterations of political policies, geopolitical sites of knowledge, and international institutions that we see today, our emphasis will be the distinct functions of "neoliberalism" as a target of critique by indigenous communities and its modes of operation within differing decolonial discourses. As Thomas Perreault states of neoliberalism in Bolivia:

> Caution is warranted, however, in making generalizations about neoliberalism and neoliberalization . . . there is no single, unitary, monolithic neoliberalism; there are, rather, multiple, often contradictory neoliberalisms.[5]

With respect to the following analysis of *terms of resistance* against neoliberalism, it thus helps to locate specific theoretical features that can provide a point of contact with the ways in which specific governmental and economic policies and practices are being challenged by indigenous communities. Nancy Postero has named the problem of neoliberalism as such:

> Neoliberalism is in the first instance a theory of political economic practices that proposes that human well-being can best be advanced by liberating individual entrepreneurial freedoms and skills within an institutional framework characterized by strong private property rights, free markets, and free trade.[6]

She continues that in Latin America this view "was put into practice in the mid-1980s by the so-called Washington Consensus and was diffused throughout Latin America in the form of structural adjustment programs, conditions on loans from the World Bank and the International Monetary Fund."[7] In the context of Bolivia, for example, she claims that the privatization of the hydrocarbon industry opened the country to foreign capital and effectively cut social services and tariffs, and made the products of Bolivian farmers less viable.[8] In this vein, we can thereby locate the terms of neoliberalism around the state-sponsored response from Evo Morales and the Movimiento al Socialismo (MAS) against this hegemonic ordering of monetary flows and trade agreements. Isabel Altamirano-Jiménez (Zapotec) has also proposed through a North-South comparative analysis of indigeneity, nature, and neoliberalism that:

> Although neoliberalism has usually been treated exclusively as an economic project involving deregulation, privatization, individualization, and transformation of state-citizen relationship, neoliberalism also shapes the constitution of identity and the commodification of nation . . . neoliberalism involves not only deregulation but also the re-regulation of nature. Thus neoliberalism involves practices, knowledge, and ways of inhabiting the world that emphasize the market, individual rationality, and the responsibility of entrepreneurial subjects.[9]

This means that our analysis of indigenous responses to neoliberalism must also take up the question of how identity claims and the politics of representation have shifted in the twenty-first century alongside neoliberal economic and political reforms.

Toward this end, several veins of indigenous studies have begun exploring how international discourses have mobilized the conception of indigeneity as a political and social tool. Francesca Merlan has argued for a distinction between criterial conceptions of indigeneity and relational models of indigeneity. She describes the distinction as such:

> By "criterial," I mean definitions that propose some set of criteria, or conditions, that enable identification of the "indigenous" as a global "kind." By "relational," I mean definitions that emphasize grounding in relations between the "indigenous" and their "others" rather than in properties inherent only to those we call "indigenous" themselves.[10]

Often these two approaches cannot be neatly distinguished, and conceptions of indigeneity may offer both relational and criterial components. However, for our purposes here, doing comparative work between such distinct geopolitical sites may require some flexibility with respect to how we identify those groups organizing and acting under the label of "indigeneity." For this reason, because criterial definitions focus on conditions that enable identification of a group as "indigenous," the terms of qualification for inclusion within that group will depend on the specificities of each context that we analyze. For example, examining qualifications for indigeneity in the United States reveals that in places like Virginia, the Racial Integrity Act of 1924 led to strict forms of segregation between Black and Native American communities throughout the Commonwealth.[11] Also, in the 1990s, state approval of tribal recognition suggested that marriages and kinship networks between Native American and African American persons prohibited the conferring of tribal status to groups such as the Buffalo Ridge Cherokee and the Occaneechi Band of the Saponi Nation.[12] However, intermarriages between white and Native American members were not disclosed as prohibitions on tribal status. The state conferral of status for indigeneity rested not solely on whether the group met a criterial set of conditions, but also on considerations regarding *with whom* (i.e., which racial groups) tribal members were intermarrying and developing kinship relations. Such cases offer a significant contrast to the Nicaraguan Autonomy Statute of 1987, wherein little distinction was made between the "the recognized rights of Afro-descendent and indigenous peoples."[13]

Given such diverse practices for considerations regarding native status and state recognition, we can thereby shift the terms of our analysis here away from a criterial definition and move toward a conception of indigeneity that focuses on the representative impact and interpellative effects of claiming indigenous identities. This is significant in the following analysis because it takes up the diverse claims made by indigenous authors, politicians, and those of political movements such as the Ejército Zapatista de Liberación Nacional (EZLN). In the broader relational sense of the term, the meaning of indigeneity arises from the manner in which communities and states negotiate the relationship between peoples, places, and nature. Relational definitions also accommodate how the dispossession of lands, disenfranchisement of political actors, and patterns of extractivism have affected diverse groups of people spanning across various global geopolitical sites, including Afro-mestizos and mulattos, as well as the Afro- and indigenous-descended groups that established distinct cultural traditions, as in the many quilombo and maroon communities across Latin America, the Caribbean, and the U.S.

Merlan marks the beginning of an international discourse on indigeneity in the 1970s, with the founding of the International Indian Treaty Council and the World Council of Indigenous Peoples.[14] This period is significant, according to Merlan, in that the indigenous international organizations forming at the time were emerging in liberal democratic states "after policies aimed at assimilation or absorption had become politically discredited (or marginalized)" in those states.[15] In Mexico, the Caribbean, Central America, and South America, conceptions of "indigeneity" had existed in various forms through the discourses of *el problema del indio, indigenismo*, and other references to original peoples of Latin America and the Caribbean. As Merlan notes, *indigenismo* and other earlier state-sponsored forms of public recognition aimed at the native peoples and cultures of various Latin American nation-states were not engaged by an international audience focusing on human rights, dignity, and the sovereignty of native peoples like the contemporary international indigenous discourses. Rather, the aims of these prior discourses often carried nationalist rhetoric that sought to reinscribe the significance of native communities and cultures into a mestizo conception of identity.[16]

However, these discourses throughout the nineteenth and twentieth centuries in Latin America did provide a political platform for indigenous claims in the later decades of the twentieth century. Anna Tsing writes of this history:

> Contemporary indigenous politics in Mexico is a thorough rejection of indigenismo. Instead of assimilation, indigenous Mexicans demand self-determination and cultural respect. But indigenismo remains salient: It brought Indians ideologically into national development, even as it attempted to erase them. The power of contemporary indigenous claims to enter national debates on democracy depends on this spectral presence. (North American Indians' claims, in contrast, have trouble being heard in nation-state politics.) In Mexico, indigenismo also ushered in a still relevant cast of players, including mobilized peasant communities and applied anthropologists.[17]

Thus, the claims made by indigenous communities in liberal democratic states of the Global North, while receiving salience as a set of claims made to international organizations such as the United Nations, are distinct from those made by Latin American geopolitical sites wherein prior nationalist discourses had already created a discursive space for political and socio-cultural discussions of native communities (albeit these prior discourses often traded in degrading and assimilationist terms for indigenous communities).

Given these variations with respect to framings of indigeneity, I seek to take a relational approach to indigeneity and a contextualist approach to neoliberalism. As Perrault, Postero, and Altamirano-Jimenez each propose, neoliberalism takes shape in variegated and sometimes conflicting manners depending on the context in question. While understanding the contexts of neoliberalism in Bolivia and Mexico requires much more space than we have available here, we can locate some important theoretical points of contact with recent literature on this topic. Namely, neoliberalism, with respect to indigenous women's resistance in Bolivia, can potentially be interpreted via the positionings of such claims in relation to the Bolivian presidency and governmental party, the Movimiento al Socialismo (MAS). These governmental agents situate their political actions against neoliberal political and capitalist orderings of the nation-states of the Global North and in opposition to the rhetoric of neoliberal democratic states. For example, Postero writes of the current president:

[Evo Morales] came to power as the head of the cocaleros' (coca growers') union, asserting the right of Andean peoples to grow the sacred leaf of the Inca in the face of the U.S. war on drugs. Over the past decade, he has worked with social movements of poor and indigenous Bolivians to build a political movement that could enact the agendas of his revolutionary ancestors, Túpac Katari, Túpac Amaru, and Zárate Willka, enabling Bolivia's native and poor peoples' claims to land and dignity. Thus, one of the fundamental themes of his administration is to decolonize Bolivia, thereby ridding the country of its legacy of racism.[18]

Morales and MAS nationalized the hydrocarbon and mining industries following the water and gas crises of the nation throughout the 2000–2005 period, and as Silvia Rivera Cusicanqui (Aymara) remarks, this crisis period was one of indigenous insurgencies as well.[19]

With respect to state-sponsored resistance to neoliberalism, consider too the historic speech made by Morales on December 21, 2012, the *Manifiesto de la Isla del Sol*.[20] The event took place on the turning point of the Mayan Calendar between Macha, or "No Time," beginning in 1492 and the arrival of Pachakuti: "a term taken from the Quechua 'pacha', meaning time and space or the world, and 'kuti', meaning upheaval or revolution. Put together, Pachakuti can be interpreted to symbolize a re-balancing of the world through a tumultuous turn of events that could be a catastrophe or a renovation."[21] With this historic presence to mark the occasion, Morales, to an audience comprised of over 40 indigenous groups from five continents, restated the 10 mandates to confront capitalism and to construct a culture of *Vivir Bien* that he had previously delivered to the Permanent Forum for Indigenous Affairs at the United Nations in New York in 2008. He cited in the manifesto (as does the Bolivian constitution) the discourse of *Buen Vivir /Vivir bien* in Spanish or *Suma qamaña* in Aymaran, which are a related set of discourses circulating around the idea of "living well, not better," that functions against narratives of "development" and progress. Among the 10 mandates, Morales states that Bolivians must:

1. Decolonize themselves of racism, fascism and all types of discrimination.
2. Decolonize themselves of commoditization and consumerism, luxury, egoism and greed, and promote *Vivir Bien*.

Moreover, Morales states that Bolivia "will not accept or permit interventionism or neoliberalism by the United Nations or the institutionality of the empire of capital" and that the nation must promote a South-South alliance to work against interventionism, neoliberalism, and colonialism.[22] However,

Morales also notes in this same speech that uprisings in Canada and the United States by indigenous groups were taking place and challenging neoliberal interventions along coalitional lines. In his opening remarks, he makes references to "the peoples of North America" that were forming the Idle No More movement taking shape in December of 2012 across Canadian cities such as Ottawa, Saskatoon, Winnipeg, Edmonton, and Regina, and in the U.S. in Bloomington, Minnesota.[23]

If we focus on patterns of neoliberalism in Mexico, we see trends that emerged throughout the last decades of the twentieth century serving as a catalyst for indigenous uprisings in the state. For instance, the economic crisis of the 1980s led to the cutting of funds for the Instituto Nacional Indigenista. This institute as well as the Programa de Desarrollo Económico y Social de Chiapas had overseen various educational and development projects throughout Mexico since the 1940s. Often, however, as George Collier writes, the lawyers of these organizations worked "behind the scenes" with municipal governments to ensure the continued political viability of the ruling party, the Partido Revolucionario Institucional.[24] Most of the goals of these state-sponsored organizations were also assimilationist and corporatist, and they often left many communities dissatisfied and without further political avenues for redress.

A tipping point during the early 1990s came when the Mexican government stated that it would no longer process or provide any forms of land redistribution. This dealt a massive blow to indigenous communities who held significant claims against the state for unresolved land disputes. As Lynn Stephen, Shannon Speed (Chickasaw), and R. Aída Hernández Castillo state: "For many, it meant the end of any hope of resolving social inequalities or injustices by petitioning the state for land reform."[25] This proposal, along with policy changes that cut social services and opened domestic markets to imported goods, left many indigenous farming communities with few viable state alternatives. An additionally destructive neoliberal policy was the Mexican government's agreement to the North American Free Trade Act (NAFTA) in 1994. NAFTA came at a time when poor farmers and peasants had begun to organize around the economic and political crises in the state. The formation of a group called "ANCIEZ," which later declared itself the EZLN formed during these years in the Lacandon region of northern Chiapas and held major demonstrations in 1992 against the halting of land redistribution, NAFTA, and the 500th year of colonization in the Americas.[26]

In the context of Mexico, the turn to neoliberal policies and practices came with additional rhetoric for indigenous communities that made the reforms appear to bear some acknowledgement of the self-determination rights of indigenous groups. Legal discourses of "multicultural rights" often coincide with neoliberal reforms, granting group rights that simultaneously reinforce the state's ability to govern indigenous communities.[27] For example, as Speed writes:

> Like the analysis that human rights are the "good side" of globalization processes, this perspective renders multiculturalism something to embrace, disentangling it from the "bad" neoliberal economic reforms. In fact, many in Mexico, including indigenous groups and others struggling for social change, strongly advocate for multicultural reform—understood in this instance as a reorganization of society in ways that allow recognition of and respect for cultural difference. But considering the close relationship of these new recognitions of cultural difference with the neoliberal project, multiculturalism as a goal of social struggle becomes considerably more problematic.[28]

Given this two-sided feature of neoliberal multiculturalism, Speed argues that Mexico's policy changes in the early 1990s led to a new kind of relationship between the state and indigenous communities in Chiapas. The EZLN was well aware of this two-sided element of neoliberal reform and thus only took up cautious and limited engagement with the state.

This point has been especially salient following the Mexican government's refusal to implement the peace agreement with the EZLN that it signed during the 1996 San Andrés Accords. The Accords included language regarding the right to "social, cultural, political, cultural, and economic organization" of indigenous communities, rights to legal self-governance (albeit limited by human rights law of the Mexican state), the right to "freely designate representatives within the community," and the right "to promote and develop their languages and cultures" (Stephen, Speed, Hernández Castillo 2006, xv).[29] However, when Vicente Fox took office in 2000, the legislation that was passed under his presidency held none of the positive rights agreed to in the 1996 Accords. Rather, the new version placed "a series of restrictions on the demands of indigenous peoples for autonomy, betraying the spirit of the San Andrés Accords."[30] This failure of the government to implement new policies protecting the self-determination rights of indigenous communities thus strengthened the indigenous rights movement in the region of Chiapas. This eventually led to the declaration of communities in the region as Autonomous Regions, who would then develop their own health care, educational, and agricultural systems in opposition to Mexican state policy.

Through these trajectories, we can see that it is through the invocation of a "new era" ushered in through Morales and the Movimiento al Socialismo in the Andean region of Bolivia and the EZLN in Chiapas that we can begin to situate the loci of enunciation regarding indigenous communities against neoliberalism. However, one caveat that is important to note here with respect to indigenous women is that their organizing efforts are operating from positions of colonial difference. Thus, in following Mignolo's articulation of the problem of knowledge production above, the political and rhetorical strategies invoked by indigenous communities in Bolivia and Mexico "are struggling to resist modern colonization, including the academic one from" the Global North. As such, our elaboration of the work by indigenous women in Abya Yala should be read in a vein of decolonial critique, and not in a critical vein that rejects the overarching goals of Morales, MAS, the EZLN, or the anti-capitalist praxis demonstrated through the various alliances enacted through the leftist movements of Latin America's "Pink Tide." To carry this out, we must retain a vested interest in understanding the politics of indigenous women's resistance from the matrix of colonial relations.

Indigenous Women's Resistance and South-North Decolonial Dialogue

In this section, I examine the work of several scholars writing on indigenous women's resistance to neoliberalism in the contexts of Bolivia and Mexico. Such critical analyses, I propose, will hopefully aid in connecting Anglophone decolonial theorists in the Global North with the dialogical practices of indigenous women in geopolitical contexts of the Global South. First, I turn to the writings of several members of Mujeres Creando, a self-described "anarchofeminist" group based in La Paz. Then I focus on the work of several members of the EZLN and theoretical writings focusing on indigenous resistance in Chiapas. Finally, I conclude by discussing several theoretical points of contact that may offer Anglophone North American academics pathways to establish dialogue and solidarity with indigenous forms of resistance in the Global South.

Mujeres Creando is an important group comprised of indigenous and non-indigenous members who work as feminist activists and scholars. Julieta Ojeda, a member of Mujeres Creando, states the following in response to a 2014 interview question: "*¿Quiénes son 'Mujeres Creando?'*"

> Mujeres Creando is an anarchist feminist movement that has existed, as a movement, for 22 years. We believe that we are in constant construction, and that we have lived through different stages and times that have been instrumental in this construction. Mujeres Creando is made up of different women from different walks of life, different ages, different

cultures, different sexual preferences, and we find ourselves in different existential moments. . . . Although our movement is still numerically small, for us the differences are a potential rather than a disadvantage, and at the same time these differences allow us to give a more complex analysis of our reality as women.[31]

The group uses a range of social organizing strategies including graffiti, public street performance, and direct action. Their public presence operates through various venues such as the publication *Mujer Pública* a radio station, *Radio Deseo*, street and performance art, and through a community space called *La Virgen de los Deseos* that includes hot showers, internet, a bookstore, public meeting spaces, and offers public lectures, literacy classes, medical consultations every Monday, and an agro-ecological market selling body products and food items.

While the cultural and political work of Mujeres Creando is too expansive to elaborate in detail here, I would like to focus on several recent pieces of writing that employ criticisms of the current Bolivian president and the Bolivian government. It is important to mark here that, unlike in Mexico, where state politics have left many indigenous communities seeking autonomous forms of governance, in Bolivia, the state has directly taken up the rhetoric of indigenous rights, decolonization, and resistance to neoliberal expansion. In this sense, the work of Mujeres Creando and other forms of resistance in geopolitical contexts like Ecuador, Guatemala, and Colombia is distinct in that these states have taken constitutional measures to respect the self-governing rights of indigenous groups.[32] Thus, as I note below in states like Mexico, the U.S., and Canada, the strategies for coalitional resistance to neoliberalism and the collective rights of indigenous peoples have taken much different routes. To highlight these differences, let us consider these geopolitical contexts in further detail.

Consider, first, the rhetorical strategy employed by member of Mujeres Creando María Galindo in her essay "If Evo had been born a woman." Here Galindo notes the seemingly heroic narrative written through Morales' work in the coca industry, his union organizing, and his rise to political power in Bolivia. She remarks that had Evo Morales been *Eva* Morales, an indigenous peasant woman, her opportunities in Bolivia would still remain quite limited even under the state's current policies. She writes that first, Eva would not have been encouraged to marry outside of her community, and if she did decide to migrate, as did Evo, this would have been considered turning her back on her community. Moreover, were she to flee domestic life to work in the city, she most likely would have made it to the city with "at least one traumatic experience of rape or sexual harassment."[33] The story continues that she most likely would not have been asked to join the union, and probably would have had three to four children under her charge. She most likely would not have been allowed to leave the care of her children elsewhere in an effort to move more concretely into union politics. However, if Eva did leave the children to her husband (a husband who probably had to take out a microloan to support their children), and did become president, Galindo states,

> Don't doubt for a minute that she would decriminalize abortion, condemn rape within the party and other social organizations, and require that each and every member of the Movimiento al Socialismo provide financial compensation to families caring for the children they abandoned along the way. Eva would understand each and every one of the dreams of Bolivian women.[34]

This method for calling to mind the discrepancies of the Bolivian government and the lived realities of indigenous women in the state is reinforced through Galindo's other writings. Among the concerns that Galindo raises are the ways in which, in her words, "the technocratic neoliberal criteria" of gender quotas for the state's representative democracy "inhibits all forms of alliance between women by needing to alternate each woman with a man."[35] Moreover, the state's convocation laws have foreclosed direct representation from social movements, requiring such movements to form alliances with the MAS party to propose candidates or to remain shut out of socio-political decision-making. On this point, she continues later in the piece:

> As feminists we want to be neither underneath nor on top of anyone. That is why we will not find our own place in this process. As quasi undesirable tenants of the candidacy that we postulate, we use this space to affirm that the decolonization of the State is not possible without its depatriarcalization.[36]

This depatriarcalization centers on, for example, a kind of androcentrism that views cultures as static and inherently conservative sites of civic production. She writes in this vein:

> Our society is not a society of pure, original, indigenous people versus undesirable mestizo white-oids. It is much more complex than that; ours is a society of disobediences and cultural mutations in which the technological revolution is sugar to the soul of all kids who, thanks to piracy, conquer it in their everyday chatting and navigating through the world. It is a society like all societies of the world where we as social actors also construct culture and thus we can talk about youth

culture, about an urban culture, about this, that and the other culture, about a culture of queers and a culture of the street and the street venders and who culturally transform the meaning of the street and public space, for example.[37]

With this dynamic view of social space and culture she proposes concrete policy recommendations as well, such as the claim that men refuse military service on grounds of conscientious objection to the militarization of masculinity, and that children bear the last names of their mothers first in their surnames in an effort to help restore women as "subjects of maternity and not objects of reproduction."[38]

Galindo's claims that indigenous cultures are transforming under neoliberal shifts across the globe. Thus, to resist exoticizing or romanticizing indigenous forms of resistance, we, in the Global North must seek to listen and learn from the practices of communities that are affected through matrices of colonial difference. In this way, the demands for sociocultural and political changes by Mujeres Creando propose that the states' efforts to decolonize the country and the rest of the Global South cannot occur without "depatriarcalizing" these systems as well. The state's own professed commitments to decolonization are thereby in tension with the view that attention to economic and racial inequalities will suffice to address gender inequalities.

However, unlike in many Anglo-centered contexts of the Global North wherein the struggles to recognize gender oppression through feminist loci of enunciation have often meant running the risk of erasing of race and class dynamics, in many decolonial feminist articulations of both the Global North and South, indigeneity and gender as relational and racialized points of contact have remained salient.[39] Consider in this case, the work of the EZLN in Mexico. The gender politics of the EZLN are complex and have included various forms of organized activity and leadership by indigenous women. One particularly important event in which women's direct participation in the leadership and representation of the Zapatistas was the speech by Comandanta Esther in front of the Mexican Congress of the Union on March 28, 2001. Comandanta Esther states the following several lines in her speech:

> We are thus demonstrating that we are not interested in provoking resentments or suspicions in anyone. And so it is I, an indigenous woman. No one will have any reason to feel attacked, humiliated or degraded by my occupying the podium and speaking today. Those who are not here now already knew that they would refuse to listen to what an indigenous woman was coming to say to them, and they would refuse to speak because it would be I who was listening to them. My

name is Esther, but that is not important now. I am a Zapatista, but that is not important at this moment either. This platform is a symbol. That is why it caused so much controversy. That is why we wanted to speak in it, and that is why some did not want us to be here. And it is also a symbol that it is I, a poor, indigenous and Zapatista woman, who would be having the first word, and that the main message of our word as Zapatistas would be mine.[40]

Comandanta Esther's declaration points to the politics of representation and relationality that are at stake in her speech in front of the Mexican congress. Her disavowal of her personal story as well as her commitment to the EZLN also point toward her direct engagement with the representative politics of the nation-state. Toward this end, Comandanta Esther used this platform to reinforce and defend a legislative proposal that would recognize and respect the self-governing rights of indigenous communities, including the preservation of natural resources within the territories of indigenous communities, cultural and language rights that legally protect the multiethnic and pluricultural identities of indigenous communities in the state, and political negotiations between indigenous communities and the state with respect to infrastructural and developmental changes.[41] The speech by Comandanta Esther also carried with it an important message about how neoliberal state policies directly affected indigenous and poor women in the state. She states:

> We, the indigenous women, do not have the same opportunities as the men, who have all the right to decide everything. Only they have the right to the land, and women do not have rights since we do not work the land and since we are not human beings, we suffer inequality. The bad governments taught us this entire situation. We indigenous women do not have good food. We do not have dignified housing. We do not have health services, or education. We have no work programs, and so we scrape by in poverty. This poverty is because of abandonment by the government, which has never taken notice of us as indigenous, and they have not taken us into account. They have treated us just like any other thing. They say they send us help like Progresa, but they do so for the purpose of destroying us and dividing us. And that is simply the way life, and death, is for us, the indigenous women.[42]

She cites, in addition to these concerns, the problem of domestic violence, forced marriages, and how migration affects women in indigenous communities.

However, another significant moment in the speech emerges when, rather than pitting cultural rights against women's rights, as debates in liberal multiculturalism have done,[43] the women of the EZLN made a call to their audience to reject the simple individual versus collective dichotomies that treat indigenous cultures as static and primitive. In this vein, Comandanta Esther states: "We know which are good and which are bad uses and customs."[44] Comandanta Esther is thus pointing to a dynamic and complex relationship between cultural identities and gender identities. Speed writes of this relationship that:

> Not only Zapatistas but women of many indigenous communities are facing the challenges of renegotiating gender relations in the context of the movement that they support and in the communities they call home. These women struggle to change gendered relations of power in the cultural context of their communities while simultaneously defending the rights of the community to define for themselves what that cultural context is and will be.[45]

This public avowal of a dynamic stance on cultural and gender politics among the EZLN thereby dismisses the state's imposition of individualizing neoliberal laws that would seek to reduce the protection of group rights by reinforcing individual and entrepreneurial forms of subjecthood.[46]

Lessons from Abya Yala

Thus, from the Anglophone academic Global North, what are we to glean from this work by indigenous women in the Abya Yala? There are many important lessons to learn from understanding the struggles of indigenous communities in the Global South. However, to conclude this essay, I will highlight three main points.

First, at a general level, it is important to note that the struggles of indigenous communities cannot be reduced to their efficacy for the ends of academics in the Global North. Often, the discursive effects of our academic platforms are minimal. Although many of us seek to extend our influence and representational capacities beyond academic publications and teaching, our extended institutional networks may remain insufficient for challenging, and may even be complicit with the policies and economic trajectories of neoliberal expansion. In this sense, the goals of decolonial praxis through scholarship must also seek non-academic forms of engagement and dialogue. This may include making one's scholarly findings accessible to audiences who do not have institutional access through university databases or by producing texts and resources that are not addressed to academic audiences. This may also mean finding what specific communities may seek from global audiences, including finding out which forms of representation and involvement a given community may desire.

Second, and more directly relevant to the work highlighted above by indigenous women in Mexico and Bolivia, the workings of Bolivian state politics, the EZLN, and the feminist leaders who are seeking social justice and respect for indigenous communities point to the need to move beyond liberal conceptions of *autonomy* and the *nation-state*. Thinking through transnational forms of struggle may help locate geopolitical sites of contact among communities that are mutually affected due to structural adjustment policies, trade sanctions, and austerity measures. Consider, for example, the manner in which indigenous communities have been challenging individualistic conceptions of autonomy and proposing collective forms of self-governance structures and relations to the land. Consider in this sense, the contrast between liberal conceptions of autonomy, and the use of "autonomy" by the EZLN as a reference to the practice of *mandar-obedecer*, to rule by obeying. As Alvaro Reyes and Mara Kaufman argue in their reading of the distinctions between a position taken under state sovereignty and those taken by the EZLN that "reject sovereignty as a viable strategy,"[47] the Treaty of Westphalia proposed a suprastate system that effectively spanned the entire globe. The EZLN, they propose, recognize this historical trajectory of power, and thus have foregone forms of negotiations with the Mexican state for the affording of land rights and political reparations.[48] Their strategy has been instead to *exercise power* rather than asking for or demanding it from the Mexican state. This exercise of power of ruling by obeying, rather than serving as a parallel measure to top-down models of state power or through representative democratic participation, relies on non-state sanctioned forms of regional organization called *Caracoles*, which are supported by rotating councils that share and distribute community governance.[49]

In a similar vein regarding African and Asian forms of sovereignty developed through the United Nations, Kwame Nimako has argued that the modern conception of the nation-state beginning with the 1648 Treaty of Westphalia continues to normatively construct the architecture of political discourse worldwide. He states:

> At the bureaucratic level, the Peace of Westphalia set the contours and parameters for competition and cooperation within European statecraft. These in turn formed the basis of European sovereign states and the related inter-state systems. This process went hand in hand with the institutionalisation of the Atlantic slave trade and chattel slavery in the Americas.[50]

The functioning matrix of this form of statecraft thereby consolidated, at national and cultural levels, the dynamics at play among varying geopolitical locations. Again, quoting Nimako:

> At one level, this process gave rise to the mutual recognition of the signatories of the Treaty of Westphalia. Following this, reciprocal recognition became fundamental to the legitimacy of sovereignty. In practice it implied that, once one major European country recognised another's existence, other nations were likely to fall in line or form alliances. For the "outside world," the importance of the Peace of Westphalia did not lie in the reciprocal recognition of the signatories but rather the non-recognition of the sovereignty of "others."[51]

Thus, Nimako proposes that a reorientation away from Western markets and international financial institutions will provide the possibility for challenges to Westphalian models of statecraft.

Moreover, there are other proposals and forms of nationalism and spatial formation that have attempted to challenge the Westphalian model as well. Although beyond the scope of this paper, these readings of sovereignty invite scholarship that seeks to connect indigenous resistance projects in Latin America and the Caribbean to the various forms of Native American, Black, and Chicanx nationalisms in the U.S. that have attempted to function against or beyond the Westphalian model.[52] Importantly, many Black revolutionary leaders, such as Huey P. Newton and Bobby Seale, for example, were well-versed in the writings of revolutionary anticolonial thinkers in Latin America, such as Che Guevara and Fidel Castro. The task remains today to find out how revolutionary movements in Latin America such as those of the EZLN and the efforts of Mujeres Creando have shared mutual relations with resistance movements in the U.S. and Canada. While news articles on Mujeres Creando have been published in Canadian and U.S. news sources, it is difficult to gauge the extent of their impact on various contemporary anti-racist challenges to neoliberalism, such as Black Lives Matter and Idle No More. However, the influence of the EZLN has mobilized many organizers across the globe, including in Canada and the U.S. For example, research conducted by Alex Khasnabish focuses on the specific challenges facing indigenous groups in Canada and the U.S. and the impact of Zapatismo in these differing sites.[53] Finding these points of convergence thereby brings communities struggling for social justice and change into relational networks of meaning-making, and, as such, build points of contact that aid in the distribution of shareable resources.[54]

Lastly, a third point is that the work from scholars and activists in the Global North must seek to retain the cultural specificity of the contexts in which they seek to engage in coalitional resistance. This, as Latina theorists such as Ofelia Schutte and María Lugones have poignantly argued, requires leaving one's hermeneutical possibilities open for unexpected forms of difference.[55] While colonial difference, as Mignolo and other decolonial theorists have highlighted is not geographically relegated solely to contexts in the Global South, and in this sense can be taken up by thinkers affected by coloniality at any site, the linking of decolonial struggles from one's local situation in the Global North is vitally important, including, for example, the land struggles of indigenous nations in the settler U.S. Respecting the differences of decolonial struggles requires learning from and adjusting to the meanings of decolonial and depatriarchal struggles in contexts different than one's own.

In this manner, fighting for decolonization alongside depatriarcalization in solidarity with Mujeres Creando can be an important link to preserve with the struggles against racism, sexism, and classism in the U.S. and Canada. Understanding how the political struggles of the U.S. and Canada have been situated against the alliances of various Latin American leftist movements emerging throughout the 2000s is also part of this process. Moreover, supporting the decolonial politics of Morales and MAS also requires critical attention to the policies affecting women and gender variant peoples in the nation. From the positioning of our Anglophone and geopolitical problem-spaces, however, the task cannot be in response to these gender politics to condemn Bolivian representative democracy or social policy. Such a dynamic would reiterate a Eurocentered feminist response that attempts to place the category of "women" under an umbrella of sameness wherein the so-called "freedoms" of one social group are compared negatively against those of another. Rather, perhaps our task is to ally ourselves with and amplify the strategies of decolonization and depatriarcalization through differing transnational strategies. By denying the Bolivian state our political support on the basis of gender rights, this parallels Sylvia Wynter's excellent analysis of the "aculturalism of Western Feminist Thought." She writes:

> So it is only within the terms of our contemporary culture that the eradication of these specific cultural practices, rather than, for example, the eradication of hunger, can be seeable as the indispensable condition of being human, of being, for feminist thinkers and writers, an autonomous and fully realized woman.[56]

Such a hierarchical ordering of human needs thus reiterates what she describes as the "modality of being both biological beings and homo economicus, for whom human fulfillment would come to equal, on the one hand, the experience of sexual pleasure, and on the other, the realizing of the American Dream of higher and higher material standards of living, and therefore of being."[57] This is the decolonial feminism that we, in our Global Northern problem-spaces must move beyond through our engagements with writers, artists, and organizers from the Global South. Furthermore, from what we can see through the coalitional praxis of indigenous women in Bolivia and Mexico, they seem to have, perhaps, never needed *this* lesson.

Notes

1. Francesca Gargallo Celentani, *Feminismos desde Abya Yala: Ideas y proposiciones de las mujeres de 606 pueblos en Nuestra América* (Ciudad de México: Editorial Corte y Confección, 2014).

2. Abya Yala is a Kuna term for the geographical landmasses of the Americas prior to the naming of the continent by Spanish colonizers as América. It signifies "land in its full maturity" or "land of vital blood" in English. The term has been adopted by indigenous activists and scholars throughout various Central and South American contexts as a way of shifting the epistemic terms of reference away from colonial meanings of place, peoples, and time.

3. Cheng-Feng Shih, "Academic Colonialism and the Struggle for Indigenous Knowledge Systems in Taiwan," Social Alternatives 29, no. 1 (2010): 44.

4. While engaging with indigenous studies focusing on communities in the U.S. and Canada is an important vein of scholarship and certainly worthy of further analysis, our work here does not focus directly on resistance movements by indigenous communities in the U.S. and Canada. One important contemporary study that does this type of comparative work is Isabel Altamirano-Jiménez, *Indigenous Encounters with Neoliberalism: Place, Women, and the Environment in Canada and Mexico* (Vancouver: UBC Press, 2013).

5. Thomas Perreault, "From the Guerra Del Agua to the Guerra Del Gas: Resource Governance, Neoliberalism and Popular Protest in Bolivia," *Antipode: A Radical Journal of Geography* 38, no. 1 (2006): 153.

6. Nancy Postero, "The Struggle to Create Radical Democracy in Bolivia," *Latin American Research Review* 45 (2010): 60.

7. Postero, "The Struggle," 60.

8. Postero, "The Struggle," 60.

9. Isabel Altamirano-Jiménez, *Indigenous Encounters*, 70.

10. Francesca Merlan, "Indigeneity: Global and Local," *Current Anthropology* 50, no 3 (2009): 305.

11. Arica Coleman, *That the Blood Stay Pure: African Americans, Native Americans, and the Predicament of Race and Identity in Virginia* (Bloomington: Indiana University Press, 2013).

12. Coleman, *That the Blood Stay Pure*, 209–212.

13. However, this document also contained vague language regarding the conferring of land rights and control over natural resources. Subsequent legislation

has led to multiethnic regional councils, wherein Afro-descendent groups like the Creole and Garifuna are minorities (see Miguel González, "Indigenous, Afro-descendant, and Mestizo Costeños: Limited Inclusion in the Autonomy Regime of Nicaragua," in *Blackness and Mestizaje in Mexico and Central America*, eds. Elisabeth Cunin an Odile Hoffman [Trenton, NJ: African World Press, 2014], 7, 9–12). Such forms of difference, are not, however, meant to suggest that geopolitical contexts in Latin America do not enact anti-Black racism. While beyond the scope of this chapter, forms of marginalization and disenfranchisement of Afro-descended Latin Americans and the relationship to anti-indigenous racism remains an important topic for further analysis.

14. Merlan, "Indigeneity," 307.

15. Merlan, "Indigeneity," 306.

16. The manner in which Bolivia and Mexico have both adopted differing responses to the demands made by indigenous groups in the 1980s and 1990s points to the much more complex histories of these differing geopolitical regions.

17. Anna Tsing, "Indigenous Voice," in *Indigenous Experience Today*, eds. Marisol de la Cadena and Orin Starn (New York: Routledge, 2007), 45.

18. Nancy Postero, "The Struggle," 60.

19. Silvia Rivera Cusicanqui, *Ch'ixinakax utxiwa: Una reflexión sobre prácticas y discursos descolonizadores* (Buenos Aires: Tinta Limón, 2010), 58.

20. Evo Morales, *Manifiesto de la Isla del Sol: Alocución del presidente del Estado Plurinacional de Bolivia, Evo Morales, el 21 de diciembre de 2012 tiempo del Pachakuti* (Caracas: Gobierno Bolivariano de Venezuela, 2012).

21. Bob Thompson, "Pachakuti: Indigenous Perspectives, buen vivir, sumaq kawsay, and Degrowth," *Development* 54, no. 4 (2011): 450.

22. Morales, *Manifiesto*, 7.

23. Morales, *Manifiesto*, 2.

24. George Collier, "The New Politics of Exclusion: Antecedents to the Rebellion in Mexico." *Dialectical Anthropology* 19 no. 2, 1994:.

25. Shannon Speed, R. Aída Hernández Castillo, and Lynn M. Stephen, eds. *Dissident Women: Gender and Politics in Chiapas* (Austin: University of Texas Press, 2006), xiv.

26. Speed et al., *Dissident Women*, xiv.

27. Shannon Speed, *Rights in Rebellion: Indigenous Struggle and Human Rights in Chiapas* (Stanford: Stanford University Press, 2008), 31.

28. Speed, *Rights in Rebellion*, 31–32

29. Speed et al, *Dissident Women*, xiv.

30. Speed et al, *Dissident Women*, xvi.

31. Julieta Ojeda, "¿Qué es y cuáles son las bases ideológicas de Mujeres Creando?" MujeresCreando.org (2014). http://www.mujerescreando.org/.

32. R. Aída Hernández Castillo, Lynn M. Stephen, and Shannon Speed, "Introduction" in *Dissident Women: Gender and Politics in Chiapas*, Shannon Speed, R. Aída Hernández Castillo, and Lynn M. Stephen, eds. (Austin: University of Texas Press, 2006), 46.

33. María Galindo, "Si Evo hubiera nacido mujer." MujeresCreando.org (2014). http://www.mujerescreando.org/.

34. Galindo, "Si Evo hubiera nacido mujer."

35. María Galindo, "Un análisis feminista sobre el proceso a la Asamblea Constituyente en Bolivia." Mujeres Creando.Org (2006). http://www.mujerescreando.org/.

36. Galindo, "Un análisis feminista."

37. Galindo, "Un análisis feminista."

38. Galindo, "Un análisis feminista."

39. It is important to note that there have also been forms of feminist and gender-identified organizing and theorizing within the United States and Canada that have offered innovative ways to address the intersections of race, class, and gender. Black feminism, womanism, Latina feminism, mujerista theology, aboriginal feminism, and Native American feminism all remain important exceptions from the claims made above. However, examining the specific critical responses to neoliberalism from each of these distinct forms of organizing and theorizing is beyond the scope of this paper. Developing such conceptual and historical links, however, points toward the need for further Inter-American forms of philosophical and political analysis.

40. Comandanta Esther, "Speech before the Mexican Congress," in *Dissident Women: Gender and Politics in Chiapas*, eds. Shannon Speed, R. Aída Hernández Castillo, and Lynn M. Stephen (Austin: University of Texas Press, 2001), 17

41. Unfortunately, Vincente Fox never ratified the proposal and instead passed a law that, in Shannon Speed's words, "set indigenous rights back by limiting indigenous jurisdiction, by denying rights to territory and to natural resources, and by passing the definition of indigenous peoples and what rights pertain to them on to the individual state-level governments." See Shannon Speed, "Rights at the Intersection: Gender and Ethnicity in Neoliberal Mexico," in *Dissident Women: Gender and Politics in Chiapas*, Shannon Speed, R. Aída Hernández Castillo, and Lynn M. Stephen, eds. (Austin: University of Texas Press, 2006), 218.

42. Comandanta Esther, "Speech before the Mexican Congress," 22.

43. See, e.g., Susan Moller Okin, "Is Multiculturalism Bad for Women?" in *Is Multiculturalism Bad for Women?* Joshua Cohen, Matthew Howard, and Martha C. Nussbaum, eds. (Princeton: Princeton University Press, 1999).

44. Comandanta Esther, "Speech before the Mexican Congress," 23.

45. Speed, "Rights at the Intersection," 215.

46. Speed, "Rights at the Intersection."

47. Alvaro Reyes and Mara Kaufman, "Sovereignty, Indigeneity, Territory: Zapatista Autonomy and the New Practices of Decolonization," *The South Atlantic Quarterly* 110, no. 2 (2011): 511.

48. Reyes and Kaufman, "Sovereignty," 514.

49. Subcomandante Insurgente Marcos, *¡Ya Basta! Ten Years of the Zapatista Uprising* (Oakland: AK Press, 2003), 47.

50. Kwame Nimako, "Reorienting the World: With or Without Africa." MnM Working Paper No. 5, International Centre for Muslim and Non-Muslim Understanding (Adelaide: University of South Australia, 2011), 6.

51. Nimako, "Reorienting the World," 6.

52. See, for example, Paul Gilroy, *The Black Atlantic: Modernity and Double Consciousness* (New York: Verso, 1993); Rafael Pérez-Torres, "Refiguring Aztlán," in *Postcolonial Theory and the United States: Race, Ethnicity, and Literature*, Amritjit Singh and Peter Schmidt, eds. (Jackson: University Press of Mississippi, 2000); María Josefina Saldaña-Portillo, *The Revolutionary Imagination in the Americas and the Age of Development* (Durham: Duke University Press 2003); William Van Deburg, *Modern Black Nationalism: From Marcus Garvey to Louis Farrakhan* (New York: NYU Press, 1997).

53. Alex Khasnabish, *Zapatismo Beyond Borders: New Imaginations of Political Possibility* (Toronto: University of Toronto Press 2008); Alex Khasnabish, *Zapatistas: Rebellion from the Grassroots to the Global* (Black Point, NS: Fernwood Publishing, 2010).

54. As a practical example of such shareable resources, while operating under very different sets of colonial and racial dynamics, consider how Palestinians in Gaza have been using social media to teach demonstrators fighting against racist police violence in Ferguson, Missouri how to protect themselves when being attacked with teargas. See Zak Cheney-Rice, "The People of Palestine Have a Message for #BlackLivesMatter Protestors in the U.S," Identities.mic. 2015. http://mic.com/articles/121826/palestines-have-message-for-black-lives-matter-protesters-in-us.

55. Ofelia Schutte, "Cultural Alterity: Cross-Cultural Communication and Feminist Theory in North-South Contexts," *Hypatia* 13, no. 2 (1998): 53–72; María Lugones, *Pilgrimages/Peregrinajes: Theorizing Coalition against Multiple Oppressions* (Lanham: Rowman & Littlefield, 2003); María Lugones, "Heterosexualism and the Colonial/Modern Gender System," *Hypatia* 22, no. 1 (2007); María Lugones, "Toward a Decolonial Feminism," *Hypatia* 25, no. 4 (2010).

56. Sylvia Wynter, "'Genital Mutilation' or 'Symbolic Birth?' Female Circumcision, Lost Origins, and the Aculturalism of Feminist/Western Thought." *Case Western Reserve Law Review* 47 (1996): 505.

57. Sylvia Wynter, "'Genital Mutilation' or 'Symbolic Birth?'" 534.

Bibliography

Altamirano-Jiménez, Isabel. *Indigenous Encounters with Neoliberalism: Place, Women, and the Environment in Canada and Mexico*. Vancouver: UBC Press, 2013.

Cheney-Rice, Zak. "The People of Palestine Have a Message for #BlackLivesMatter Protestors in the U.S." *Identities.mic*, 2015. https://www.mic.com/articles/121826/palestines-have-message-for-black-lives-matter-protesters-in-us.

Coleman, Arica L. *That the Blood Stay Pure: African Americans, Native Americans, and the Predicament of Race and Identity in Virginia.* Bloomington: Indiana University Press, 2013.

Collier, George. "The New Politics of Exclusion: Antecedents to the Rebellion in Mexico." *Dialectical Anthropology* 19, no 2 (1994): 1–44.

Comandanta Esther. "Speech before the Mexican Congress." Shannon Speed, R. Aída Hernández Castillo, and Lynn M. Stephen, eds. *Dissident Women: Gender and Politics in Chiapas.* Austin: University of Texas Press, 2001.

Galindo, María. "Si Evo hubiera nacido mujer." *MujeresCreando.org*, 2014. http://www.mujerescreando.org/.

———. "Un análisis feminista sobre el proceso a la Asamblea Constituyente en Bolivia." *MujeresCreando.org*, 2006. http://www.mujerescreando.org/.

Gargallo Celentani, Francesca. *Feminismos desde Abya Yala: Ideas y proposiciones de las mujeres de 606 pueblos en Nuestra América.* Ciudad de México: Editorial Corte y Confección, 2014.

Gilroy, Paul. *The Black Atlantic: Modernity and Double Consciousness.* New York: Verso, 1993.

González, Miguel. "Indigenous, Afro-descendant, and Mestizo *Costeños*: Limited Inclusion in the Autonomy Regime of Nicaragua." *Blackness and* Mestizaje *in Mexico and Central America,* eds. Elisabeth Cunin an Odile Hoffman. Trenton, NJ: African World Press, 2014.

Hernández Castillo, R. Aída. Lynn M. Stephen, and Shannon Speed. "Introduction." In *Dissident Women: Gender and Politics in Chiapas.* Edited by Shannon Speed, R. Aída Hernández Castillo, and Lynn M. Stephen. Austin: University of Texas Press, 2006.

Khasnabish, Alex. *Zapatismo Beyond Borders: New Imaginations of Political Possibility.* Toronto: University of Toronto Press, 2008.

———. *Zapatistas: Rebellion from the Grassroots to the Global.* Black Point, NS: Fernwood Publishing, 2010.

Lugones, María. "Heterosexualism and the Colonial/Modern Gender System." *Hypatia* 22, no. 1 (2007): 186–209.

———. "Toward a Decolonial Feminism." *Hypatia* 25, no. 4 (2010): 742–759.

———. *Pilgrimages/Peregrinajes: Theorizing Coalition against Multiple Oppressions.* Lanham: Rowman & Littlefield, 2003.

Merlan, Francesca. "Indigeneity: Global and Local." *Current Anthropology* 50, no. 3 (2009): 303–333.

Morales, Evo. *Manifiesto de la Isla del Sol: Alocución del presidente del Estado Plurinacional de Bolivia, Evo Morales, el 21 de diciembre de 2012 tiempo del Pachakuti.* Caracas: Gobierno Bolivariano de Venezuela, 2012.

Nimako, Kwame. "Reorienting the World: With or Without Africa." MnM Working Paper No. 5, International Centre for Muslim and Non-Muslim Understanding, Adelaide: University of South Australia, 2011.

Ojeda, Julieta. "¿Qué es y cuáles son las bases ideológicas de Mujeres Creando?" *MujeresCreando.org*, 2014 http://www.mujerescreando.org/.

Okin, Susan Moller. "Is Multiculturalism Bad for Women?" In *Is Multiculturalism Bad for Women?* Edited by Joshua Cohen, Matthew Howard, and Martha C. Nussbaum. Princeton: Princeton University Press, 1999.

Pérez-Torres, Rafael. "Refiguring Aztlán." Amritjit Singh and Peter Schmidt, eds. *Postcolonial Theory and the United States: Race, Ethnicity, and Literature.* Jackson: University Press of Mississippi, 2000.

Perreault, Thomas. "From the Guerra Del Agua to the Guerra Del Gas: Resource Governance, Neoliberalism and Popular Protest in Bolivia." *Antipode: A Radical Journal of Geography* 38, no. 1 (2006): 150–172.

Postero, Nancy. "The Struggle to Create Radical Democracy in Bolivia." *Latin American Research Review* 45 (2010): 59–78.

Reyes, Alvaro, and Mara Kaufman. "Sovereignty, Indigeneity, Territory: Zapatista Autonomy and the New Practices of Decolonization." *The South Atlantic Quarterly* 110, no. 2 (2011): 505–525.

Rivera Cusicanqui, Silvia. *Ch'ixinakax utxiwa: Una reflexión sobre practices y discursos descolonizadores.* Buenos Aires: Tinta Limón, 2010.

Saldaña-Portillo, María Josefina. *The Revolutionary Imagination in the Americas and the Age of Development.* Durham: Duke University Press, 2003.

Schutte, Ofelia. "Cultural Alterity: Cross-Cultural Communication and Feminist Theory in North-South Contexts." *Hypatia* 13, no. 2 (1998): 53–72.

Shih, Cheng-Feng. "Academic Colonialism and the Struggle for Indigenous Knowledge Systems in Taiwan." *Social Alternatives* 29, no. 1 (2010): 44–47.

Speed, Shannon. *Rights in Rebellion: Indigenous Struggle and Human Rights in Chiapas.* Stanford: Stanford University Press, 2008.

———. "Rights at the Intersection: Gender and Ethnicity in Neoliberal Mexico." In *Dissident Women: Gender and Politics in Chiapas.* Edited by Shannon Speed, R. Aída Hernández Castillo, and Lynn M. Stephen. Austin: University of Texas Press, 2006.

Speed, Shannon, R. Aída Hernández Castillo, and Lynn M. Stephen, eds. *Dissident Women: Gender and Politics in Chiapas.* Austin: University of Texas Press, 2006.

Subcomandante Insurgente Marcos. *¡Ya Basta! Ten Years of the Zapatista Uprising.* Oakland: AK Press, 2003.

Thompson, Bob. "Pachakuti: Indigenous Perspectives, buen vivir, sumaq kawsay, and Degrowth." *Development* 54, no. 4 (2011): 448–454.

Tsing, Anna. "Indigenous Voice." In *Indigenous Experience Today*, eds, Marisol de la Cadena and Orin Starn. New York: Routledge, 2007.

Van Deburg, William L. *Modern Black Nationalism: From Marcus Garvey to Louis Farrakhan.* New York: NYU Press, 1997.

Wynter, Sylvia. "'Genital Mutilation' or 'Symbolic Birth?' Female Circumcision, Lost Origins, and the Aculturalism of Feminist/Western Thought." *Case Western Reserve Law Review* 47 (1996): 501–552.

15
The Menstruating Body Politic: José Martí, Gender, and Sexuality

Stephanie Rivera Berruz

Introduction

Contemporary Latin American philosophy in the United States has notably given attention to the essays of José Martí. Specifically, the scholarly attention that Martí has received within the world of U.S.-based Latin American philosophy identifies his work as providing a unique conceptualization of race as a social construction that interrupts problematic essentialized notions of race from a non-European perspective. Nevertheless, Martí's philosophy has received less philosophical attention with respect to his use of concepts of gender and sexuality. In this chapter I argue that gender and sexuality are truncated in Martí's notions of politics and social reproduction in ways that reify coloniality. This predicament in Martí's political writings is problematic when considered against the backdrop of his political construction of nationhood, which envisions America as a unified collectivity. However, as this essay demonstrates, the America that Martí envisions may in fact not belong to everyone.

In order to advance this argument the chapter takes the following form: I begin with a brief description of the role that gender and sexuality play in Martí's key works: "Madre America" and "Nuestra America." I then take up the task of highlighting the manner in which the political project of articulating "our" America necessitates the use of an essentializing notion of gender that is buttressed by presumptions of heteronormativity that frame the possibilities of social reproduction. I argue that given Martí's positionality as a subject of modernity, we ought to read his structuring of gender and sexuality through the lens of Lugones' coloniality critique. The result of this reading reveals that "nuestra" America is itself predicated on the production of a particular gender discourse that essentializes the female body to its reproductive capacities by collapsing it into its maternal capabilities.

José Martí: A Trans-American Writer

Jose Martí's influence as a trans-American political writer is monumental. Martí was a prolific writer whose life only spanned 42 years (1853–1895), but his impact on Latin American studies and Latin American thought has been and continues to be deeply influential. His complete works reach to nearly thirty scholarly volumes.[1] His life witnessed political imprisonment and exile, which eventually brought him to the United States, where to make a living he dedicated his time to journalism and translation. Between 1881 and 1895 Martí mainly lived in New York City. The body of articles that he wrote while residing in New York City for newspapers in Venezuela, Guatemala, and Argentina kept his readership abreast of the development of the United States as an imperial power.[2] His unique position as an exile, a migrant, and linguistic border dweller provided a lens through which to articulate the rise of the United States as an imperial power from within its boundaries. Laura Lomas, one of the foremost contemporary Martí scholars, describes him in the following fashion: "As a stateless, nonassimilating migrant, a colonized and linguistically marginalized translator, José Martí elucidates an alternative to the modernity that serves imperial expansion."[3] His contemporary scholarly impact is most notably felt in the decades of the 1990s when critics note his 1891 essay "Nuestra América" as a touchstone that remapped the field of American studies because it actively reflected on the North-South axis of power.[4]

Martí is definitionally a modern trans-American writer. In 1870, at the age of 17, Martí was arrested and convicted of anti-Spanish activities, which resulted in six months of political prison.[5] After serving six months he became ill and was called to serve out his sentence in exile. He was deported to Spain in January of 1871.[6] After three years of exile in Spain, Martí commenced his trans-American travels. He visited New York City en route to Mexico, traveled extensively throughout Central America and South America, residing along the way in Mexico, Guatemala, and Venezuela, always leaving in disagreement with their oppressive political systems.[7] He returned to Cuba in 1879 as a result of an amnesty following the Ten Years' War (1868–1878).[8] However, he was quickly deported for participating in anti-Spanish sentiments. It is during this period of exile that Martí came to live in New York City for 14 years.

The wake of the Ten Years' War left dissatisfaction with Spanish colonial rule in Cuba that materialized in various ways. The political camps of Cuba were divided among those who wished to have Cuba annexed to the United

States, those who wanted a fully independent Cuba, and those who wished Cuba to become an autonomous region of Spain.[9] It is important to note that Cuba at this point in time was an economic colony of the United States as a result of the boom in the sugar industry. The Haitian Revolution (1791–1804) had left a void of sugar production, as Haiti had been the world's principal provider of sugar.[10] The cultivation of sugar brought with it drastic changes to Cuba's economy, demography, politics, and ecology.[11] Modern industrial practices were imported from both England and the United States (e.g., ideas and technology). Therefore, by the second half of the nineteenth century, Cuba had significant commercial and cultural ties with the United States.[12] Although Cuba gained independence in 1898, U.S. involvement was attached to its constitution through the Platt Amendment (est. 1902), which gave the United States the right to intervene in the country in the event of political unrest and gave it land access to install two naval bases.[13] Cuban- U.S. relationships cannot be understated as one explores the work and political life of Martí. His status as a modern trans-American figure is shaped by the development of the United States as an imperial power during the span of Martí's life, as can be seen in the bulk of writing that he produces during his residence in New York City.

Martí's published work from New York City can be differentiated into three stages.[14] The beginning stage dates from 1881–1884 in which Martí grapples with his arrival to New York City during the Gilded Age in all of its enigmas and splendors.[15] The second stage, taking place between 1884–1892, marks Martí's critical radicalization, which was brought on by the United States' disadvantageous commercial treaty with Mexico and the possibilities of purchasing Cuba from Spain.[16] It was during this time that "Madre América" (1889) and "Nuestra América" (1891) were written. His final stage of U.S.-based writing marks his break with Latin American newspapers and the founding of the Cuban Revolutionary Party (1892).[17] His notable essay "Mi Raza" was written in 1893. By 1895 Martí set off on his final journey to Cuba. On May 19, 1895, against the advice of the military leader of the Cuban insurgent army General Máximo Gómez, Martí rushed into battle. He died as the result of bullet injuries to the head, chest, and thigh.[18]

América: Madre y Nuestra

Given that the focus of this essay is the role that gender plays in constructing the body politic of nationhood in Martí's thought, I make use of the most notable essays on these topics from Martí's second and final stages of writing in New York City. In these essays Martí reflects on the conditions of imperial modernity from within the empire itself.[19] In 1889 Martí was invited to address delegates participating in the first International Conference of American States gathering in New York City for a party hosted by the Spanish-American Literary Society.[20] The essay he delivered in a speech on December 19, 1889, is called "Madre América." In this essay Martí elaborates identity in the development of América for Latin Americans. Through the use of gendered maternal tropes, Martí elaborates the history of Latin America's identity forged through colonial-independence struggles. In doing so, he makes a case for the importance of Latin American unity in spite of its conflict-ridden foundations. Unity is a trans-American experience. Martí notes that although located within the boundaries of Lincoln's America (the United States), the América of Juárez (president of Mexico from 1861 to 1871) or "Our" América, could still be honored.[21]

"Mother America" opens with the following words: "What can the imprisoned son say when he sees his mother again from behind the bars of his cell? . . ."[22] Implicit in the title of the essay as well as its opening lines is a framework that is determined within the confines of the language of motherhood. However, it is not an open definition of motherhood. Rather, Martí deploys a specific conceptualization of motherhood, one that positions the situation of the male political exile as the son who cannot be reunited with his mother—the "other" America, Latin America. Hence, motherhood is constructed around normative masculine and gender roles whereby the status of the male/son as citizen is read against the status of the female/mother as nation.

The essay genders the nation as female. Martí notes: "Where is America going, and who will unite her and be her guide? Alone and as one people she is rising. Alone she is fighting. Alone she will win."[23] A further example is found in the closing of the essay where Martí characterizes America as "mistress, hope, and guide: Mother America, we found brothers . . . Mother America you have sons. . . ."[24] Hence, there is a dichotomy between the political citizen and the nation. The political citizen is gendered male through the identification of progeny in the use of terms like sons and brothers. Meanwhile, the nation is constructed as female through both its ability to reproduce male citizen subjects as well as to care for them. Motherhood entails both the reproductive capacity for birth as well as the care labor typically associated with the labor of mothering. However, it is a labor that is directed toward male subjects so as to produce the sons and brothers that will ascend to citizenship and participate in collective unity. By relying on the use of gender and the maternal to configure his sense of the nation, Martí constructs a framework through only a portion of the population; her sons (not children) are guided "home."

Furthermore, Martí closes the essay by juxtaposing the terms: mistress, hope, and guide. The use of the term mistress can be definitionally interpreted in a variety of ways. The term can refer to a woman in a position of authority or mastery over a particular subject or situation. It can capture the female head of household. Or it can refer to a woman in an extramarital relationship. Archaically, it may have also been used to refer to a woman courted by a man. Given that Martí uses this term once in the essay and in closing it is not a term that is heavily elaborated on. However, even among its various definitions, the term is gendered female through roles that are for the most part relegated to private spaces: households or bedrooms. If the mistress is to be a woman in a position of authority, we could still ask what the object of mastery would be in Martí's larger framework given its use of gendered maternal tropes. Finally, the understanding of mistress as a woman engaged in extramarital relationships is gendered. However, this understanding of the use of the term has to be read against the backdrop of female figures, like La Malinche,[25] who are identified as illegitimate "mothers" of nations. To identify America as a mistress is to evoke one if not all of these gendered tropes for the configuration of the nation. For Martí, however, it is not just that the nations is female, but rather that the reproduction of the body politic of the nation aims at the production of male bodies. The status of women is determined through its capacities to participate in this national project.

Nevertheless, independent of how we understand the definitional use of the term "mistress," Martí constructs a sense of nationhood that is read on and through the reproductive female body. There is an important note of translation that is worth making here. The term for nation (*la nación, la América*) is gendered female in Spanish. Some might argue that this is merely an issue of linguistic style wherein nation is gendered female and that hence Martí deploys the appropriate use of Spanish in his writing—nothing more. However, this critical response does not account for Martí's use of the language of sons and brotherhood, which is indicative of a very specific relationship of citizenship to nation state. Notably, Martí is anchoring his sense of the body politic to an essentialized notion of gender that is produced through the status of the son and brother as political actors. Femininity, on the other hand, is only ever disclosed through a language of the maternal. The maternal is the only locus through which feminine embodiment is possible. This problematically suggests that the only place where we could begin to articulate the role of any feminized political subject is from a sense of the maternal; an activity that is normatively bound up with essentialized notions of sex and gender, as well as heteronormative reproduction. Normative understandings of the possibilities of motherhood are bound up with biological reproduction. Hence, the possibilities of biological reproduction inform how we understand female sex categorization. In this instance, the status of femaleness is overdetermined by the possibilities of biological reproduction to the extent that women are only as good as their reproductive capacities to engender the body politic. From this framework the possibilities of biological reproduction are constructed through heteronormativity. The orientations of female sexuality are determined by the possibilities of biological reproduction. As a result, the default mode of understanding feminine desire is through its participation in heterosexuality. The feminine gender is essentialized to the sex category of female, and the status of female is determined through its biological capacities to participate in heterosexual reproduction.

In 1891 Martí's most influential and widely read essay, "Nuestra América," was published in newspapers in New York and Mexico City.[26] The publication of this essay came at a time when Puerto Rico, Cuba, Panama, the Phillipines, Guam, and Hawaii were not part of the United States' field of imperial control.[27] However, Martí pays close attention to the way in which the impetus that drove the machine of U.S. westward expansion that yielded the annexation and colonization of half of Mexico's territory is not satiated.[28] Hence, the goal of "Nuestra América" was to call attention to the fact that the United States was flexing its imperial muscles southward. Martí had very good reasons to be concerned given the subsequent annexation of Hawaii and the expansion into the Spanish-controlled Caribbean, Pacific, and Panamá.[29] Hence, the essay expounds a specific "Latin" perspective that is reflective of Latin America's weaker hemispheric geopolitical position.[30]

In order to capture the geopolitical situation of "Our" or "Nuestra" América, Martí continues to deploy maternal gendered tropes in a manner consistent with "Madre América." In this essay Martí deploys gendered language to refer to the Latin American state. For instance, he makes use of the pronoun "her" and employs terms like: "sweetheart" and "mother." However, in this essay, Martí notably intertwines what he takes to be the achievement of appropriate masculinity with pride in the status of "sons of America." The failures of men to admit their heritage for Martí are indicative of a failure of manhood. He writes:

> These men born in America who are ashamed of their mother that raised them because she wears an Indian apron, these delinquents who disown their sick mother and leave her alone in her sickbed! Which one is truly a man, he who stays with his mother to nurse her through her illness, or he who forces her to work somewhere out of sight, and lives off her sustenance in corrupted lands, with a worm for his insignia, cursing the bosom that bore him . . . ?[31]

There are three important points to note from this quote. First, Martí ties the achievement of masculinity to the maternal relationship, whereby to be a true "man" is to be in a biologically linked mother-son relationship. The loss of masculinity or manhood, that is, the production of "delinquents," is generated through the disavowal of the mother-son relationship. The mother is determined through a biological relationship constructed on and through the "bosom" of the female body, which generates the production of a male-centered body politic. The mother is the one that bears the possibility of the male political citizen. To the extent that the male political subject cannot identify with his mother, he fails in the participation of normative masculinity. Second, the role that women play in this framework is only configured through the possibilities of begetting the conditions for sustaining the men of América. Although the achievement of normative masculinity is configured through the maternal relationship, Martí also sets up the conditions whereby the status of womanhood is rendered through the gendered roles of the maternal and the racialized laborer of the house. As he notes that she wears an "Indian apron," the nation is read against her racialized gendered labor that is encapsulated in the domestic space. Moreover, her status of "illness" is also one that is spatially part of the private domestic sphere as she is "alone in her sickbed," and in need of care from her sons who exist outside in the public political space. The gendered dichotomy between the private and the public permeates Martí's political schema. The female body and her racialized gendered roles in the private sphere give rise to the public male citizen. However, this is a false dichotomy. The public/private dichotomy is foreclosed through the relationships between both spaces, and hence everything is always already political. That is to say that all spaces are permeated by politics, particularly those that are described as giving rise to political participants. Finally, it is important to note the role that race plays in the construction of the nation. After all, the nation wears an "Indian apron." Hence, the nation is racialized through her participation in indigeneity although this is described through the use of an apron, a gendered household tool predominantly used in the activity of cooking, in this instance at the behest of sons.

"Nuestra América" further emphasizes power differentials through the use of gendered and sexualized terms.[32] Reflecting on possible U.S.—Latin American relations, Martí writes: "The hour is near when she will be approached by enterprising and forceful nation that will demand intimate relations with her, though it does not know her and disdains her."[33] Latin America is femininized and the United States is masculinized through essentialized notions of gender that work on and through the body. Forcefulness and demandingness are read as part of a level of intimacy that structures unequal power distributions. However, contact or intimacy is necessarily violent as the possibilities of rape or assault are at stake in the analysis. Femininity is read through its reproductive maternal capacities that are fragile and require defense and help. Hence, Martí deploys a highly romanticized notion of gendered norms that configure his sense of masculinity and femininity.[34] The female gendered body is one that must be protected, but only to the extent that it can reproduce the nation/state through the production of male citizens. Should the United States interrupt her capacity to do this then the true danger lies in the thwarted possibilities of male existence.

A Defense of Martí

How can we make sense of Martí's deployment of gender and sexuality? To be clear, I am not advocating for reading Martí as a feminist or for a feminist reading of his thought, but rather I am interested in how to approach or understand Martí's political thought so as to best comprehend the deployment of gender and sexuality in his work. Reflecting on the deployment of gender and sexuality in Martí, Laura Lomas has argued: "Martí's discourse on gender and sexuality proves so contradictory that he simultaneously reproduces and unravels this bond between nationalism and masculinism."[35] On the one hand, Martí reproduces problematic masculine hegemonic norms that link the nation and heteronormative manhood, and on the other hand he does take note of gender practices that are altering the course of American modernities that can be found in other locations of his work.[36]

Notably, Lomas has argued that the masculinist discourse that surrounds Martí's work merits further attention. Specifically, she makes use of Gabriela Mistral's work on Martí in order to illustrate the contestation of masculinist logics. She invites a reading of Martí through Mistral that undermines the masculinist character of Martí's arguments by considering his use of poetic language as an intervention on the hegemonic masculinity that constructs nationhood. Mistral is an important figure to juxtapose with Martí, as she dissented from normative heterosexual roles as a prominent lesbian in Chile who has been known as the queer mother of the nation.[37] Under consideration are Mistral's essays "La Lengua de Martí" and "Los Versos Sencillos de José Martí" ("Martí's Tongue" and "The Simple Verses of José Martí"). In "La Lengua de Martí" Lomas argues we can read Martí as capable of ingesting colonizing cultures, all the while maintaining his own accent. Mistral's lexicon affords us the ability to read Martí as an adept writer that is not bound by the virility of his sex, but rather as adept at the use of trope.[38] Moreover, in "Los Versos Sencillos de José Martí" the presence of poetic language places blood and pleasure at the centerfold of the body politic and allows readers to reimagine Martí's works in a different light. Mistral reads the tropes of blood through menstruation as a non-reproductive capacity of the female body. Lomas argues that the construction of menstruation as non-reproductive cuts through Martí's concept of the nation, which is dominantly interpreted as excluding women.[39] As Lomas states: "Mistral's essay offers an unexpected reading of these images of blood. It glosses this figure as an affirmation of non-normative virilities and non-reproductive female bodies. No longer causes for exclusion from revolutionary belonging, these bodies and minds represent an unfulfilled potential for creativity, energy and strength within the body politic."[40] Hence, according to Lomas, Mistral offers a different vision of Martí that departs from participation in heroic masculinism.[41]

A further defense of Martí's work can be found in the essay "Resistance to Colonialism: The Latin American Legacy of José Martí" by Ofelia Schutte, which argues that the exclusion of gender from the construction of the nation, albeit problematic, should not deter from reading his works as resistant to colonial structures. She notes that Martí foresaw a hemispheric pattern of domination that would severely affect the "America" that is the Global South.[42] Hence, he warns against this imminent threatening imperial relationship that allows us to read his work as de-colonial in nature. For instance, he opens "Our America" by stating: ". . . weapons of the mind, which vanquish all others. Trenches of ideas are worth more than trenches of stone."[43] In so doing, Martí leads by underscoring the importance of ideas for intervening on imperial pressures and can hence be understood as resisting impending colonial pressures. If we can change the landscape of ideas, then we can resist the impending imperial imposition of the United States. Furthermore, his ideas about race found in "Nuestra América" as well as in "My Race" elaborate on racial identity as a social construction imbued with social meaning that ought not to be understood as a dividing factor. As Martí writes in "My Race": "Affinity of character is more powerful than affinity of color."[44] It is clear both from Martí's own words, as well as Schutte's analysis, that Martí's system of thought attempted to counteract colonial forces. Writing from within the boundaries of the United States, and attending to the way in which the United States was setting itself up as an imperial power, Martí was very much in line with de-colonial resistant strategies. Central to his task was the advancement of de-colonial arguments that exposed the constructivist nature of racial categories in order to resist further imperial impositions.

Both defenses of Martí (Lomas or Schutte) overlook one key relationship between modernity and coloniality. The conditions of modernity are made possible by a global order that is heir to a colonial system, but whose impact is notably felt through the articulation of specific concepts of race *as well as* gender and sexuality. Lomas has argued that we ought to understand Martí as an unequivocally modern trans-American writer reflecting on the conditions of modernity from within "the belly of the beast" that attempts to offer alternative narratives to modernity by rejecting discourses that take Europe as their origins.[45] Moreover, Schutte's attention to his arguments about de-colonization position Martí at the forefront of modern resistance to colonial structures. Nevertheless, neither defense draws attention to the way in which his modern condition and scholarly reflection therein is also shaped by a coloniality that inform his attention to race, but also necessarily inform his use of gender and sexuality. We cannot read the deployment of colonial resistance and concepts of racial identity as de-linked from his visions of gender and sexuality.

Coloniality of Gender and The Construction of "Nuestra" América

In "Coloniality of Power, Eurocentrism, and Latin America," Aníbal Quijano argues for the importance of calling attention to the invention of racial categories as part of the colonial processes that made modernity possible. In this essay Quijano notes that the modern idea of race does not make sense prior to the historical moment of colonization.[46] To this point he writes: "Insofar as the social relations that were being configured were relations of domination, such identities were considered constitutive of the hierarchies, places, and corresponding social roles, and consequently of the model of colonial domination that was being imposed."[47] The social relations that drop out of the invention of the categories of race prove to be shaped by systems of domination that plague contemporary global power structures and continue to be justified by Eurocentric perspectives. Race then comes to track the hierarchical dispersal of global power as it served as the justification for colonial conquest.

In the scholarship of María Lugones, particularly in the positions she articulates in "Heterosexualism and the Colonial/Modern Gender System," she argues that race is not the only category invented as a tool of domination; gender similarly functions as an imposed modern category supported through the perspectives of Eurocentrism. Hence, she argues that we should seek to understand the "modern/colonial gender system," which Quijano fails to take into serious consideration. According to Lugones, Quijano presumes the givens of a dichotomous sex/gender system that is underpinned by heteronormativity. In other words, Quijan's analysis of race presumes hegemonic understandings of gender that are articulated in terms of presumed biological dimorphism, heterosexuality, and patriarchal relations that are themselves products of Eurocentric colonial impositions.[48] Coloniality permeates all aspects of life. In Lugones' view, Quijano's analysis implies that gender difference is constituted through disputes over sex and its resources whereby sex is rendered a biological attribute elaborated through social categories.[49] She advocates for an expansion of Quijano's model of coloniality so as to include the invention of hegemonic gender norms of sexual dimorphism and heterosexuality as part of the colonial project that we are heir to today.

In light of Lugones' critique, we can return to the work of Martí. It is clear that Martí is operating from a framework that essentializes gender through sexual dimorphism and hence understands the nation as participant in patriarchal gender roles reproduced through heterosexism. Women are relegated to the domestic sphere and are constructed around their possibilities for biological social reproduction. The only true subject of the nation is the male political citizen, which is begotten through the reproductive capacities of women's bodies. The role of women can only be conceptualized vis-à-vis "our" América through her potential participation in maternal reproductive roles. The framework also presumes heterosexuality as a norm of social reproduction. Therefore, Martí participates in the modern colonial/gender system as described by Lugones. Although his analysis on race may have been apt to capture the social construction of race, it nevertheless participates in the colonial gender system that problematically positions women solely as potential resources for the reproduction of a male body politic.

We should then recall Lomas' charitable reading of Martí's use of gendered tropes. Lomas' take on Martí makes use of non-reproductive gendered capacities as the foci of her analysis. Her account fails to take into consideration the way in which gender still operates within a logic of exclusion. Her position does not appreciate the way in which menstruation, although a non-fetus-producing process, still figures as part of a gendered reproductive capacity that is often construed as essential to the category of woman. Gender continues to be encapsulated in bodily reproductive processes that only matter to the extent that they birth male political participants and citizens. Thus, gender is only meaningful to the extent that it participates in a discourse of social reproductive processes that if otherwise not present, would relegate non-menstruating "female" bodies to a place of total exclusion.

Non-menstruating female bodies pose a problem for the nation as they lack the capacity to produce male citizens. Although menstruation is an instantiation of the lack of reproduction, its value still operates from within a matrix of sexual dimorphism that solidifies gender. So, although menstruation does not symbolize reproductive processes (e.g., the presence of a fetus), it does capture the female body's capacity to reproduce. Femaleness continues to be constructed through sexual dimorphism whereby gender is essentialized through the role of bodily capabilities. If menstruation is not present then neither is the nation.

Given Lugones' insights that gender was just as much a colonial invention as racial categories we ought to land on a different reading of Martí on gender and sexuality. The focus of Lomas' analysis on the capacities of the female body necessarily link to social reproduction. Menstruation, albeit in a non-reproductive capacity, is a gendered bodily capacity that drops out of a modern/colonial gender system and classifies bodies in terms of "biological" dichotomous categories of male and female.

Martí's failures to include gender as a focus of his analysis of "our" America moves beyond a mere exclusion of women as true subjects of the body politic. The use of gender as a method for constructing the nation and its citizen rests on the dimorphism that defines male and female bodies. Sexual dimorphism is reinforced through the resources it produces. In Martí's analysis the status of the female body is only valuable to the extent that it reproduces male political citizens. Hence, "our" América is a resource upon which to build a nation of sons on and through the reproductive labor of female bodies. This labor of production is underpinned by heterosexual norms that dictate not only the structure of desire, but also the formation of the family through the construction of nation. The progeny of the nation, the masculine male body, is the materialization of heterosexual values that vision men as the bodies upon which progress is founded. As a result, Martí's framework for understanding gender reinforces the modern/colonial gender system that makes use of a heteronormative dichotomous classificatory system. These are the conditions for the exclusion. It is an exclusion that is built upon the reading of the female body as deriving its identity through its reproductive capabilities and nothing more. Understanding femininity through its maternal capabilities (menstruation included) derives its power from a system that identifies woman as fragile and in need of saving. This is José Martí's América. She is the product of a modern colonial gender system that not only invents race, but also gender through heteronormative sexuality. So, although Martí can attend to some of the impacts of this system through his reflections on race and the United States as a global imperial power, his attention on gender and sexuality remains constrained by the very system he is attempting to resist. In light of Lugones' analysis we have to remember that we must understand race, gender, and sexuality as co-constitutive dimensions of the coloniality of power. Hence, even Martí's ideas about race have to be read against the conditions of the modern colonial gender system, which introduces the values used to advocate for social reproduction. You cannot arrive at national or racial identity without social reproduction, and this requires attending to the norms of sex categorization, gender, and sexuality. The focus on gendered bodily processes that Lomas suggests fails to consider how the very categories at stake are already a part of a system of coloniality.

Therefore, even the most charitable of readings of Martí on this point will not suffice unless we consider the coloniality of gender that generates the conditions of exclusion.

Conclusion

José Martí is an iconic modern political figure situated at the fringes of a trans-American experience. The entirety of his work reveals commitment to the project of nation building as well as to struggles of resistance. In spite of these commitments, Martí falls prey to the binds of colonialism that attune him to some important dimensions (e.g., race and nation), but occlude his appreciation of others (e.g., gender, sex, and sexuality). Hence, if we are to herald Martí for giving voice to the troubles of nation building, we also have to attend to the way in which that project is constructed in and through his condition of modernity that is shaped by the particular constructions of gender and sexuality that impact his overall project. Writing across the Americas, Martí reveals the ways in which coloniality is a power that we are beholden to, regardless of the location or locution. Hence, I maintain we should continue to read Martí, but we should read him cautiously as he too is a product of the very forces he is attempting interrupt. A nation constructed around gender exclusivity and compulsory ascension into heterosexuality is not a shared América and therefore does not warrant the claim of "ours" or "*nuestra*."

Notes

1. Julio Rodríguez-Luis. "Introduction: On the Re-Evaluation of Martí," in *Re-Reading José Martí: One Hundred Years Later*, ed. Julio Rodríguez-Luis (Albany: SUNY Press, 1999), x.

2. Jeffery Belnap and Raúl Fernández. "Introduction: The Architectonics of José Martí's 'Our Americanism,'" in *José Martí's "Our America": From National to Hemispheric Cultural Studies*, ed. Jeffery Belnap and Raúl Fernández (Durham: Duke University Press, 1998), 1.

3. Laura Lomas, *Translating Empire: José Martí, Migrant Latino Subjects, and American Modernities* (Durham: Duke University Press, 2008), ix.

4. Laura Lomas, *Translating Empire*, 2.

5. John M. Kirk, "José Martí and the United States: A Further Interpretation," *Latin American Studies* 9.2 (1977): 276.

6. John M. Kirk, "José Martí and the United States."

7. Kirk.

8. Kirk.

9. Roberto González Echevarría, introduction to *Jose Marti: Selected Writings*, by José Martí (New York: Penguin Books, 2002), xiii.

10. Roberto González Echevarría, introduction to *Jose Marti*, xii.
11. González Echevarría, xii.
12. González Echevarría, xiii.
13. González Echevarría, xvi.
14. Susana Rotker, "Jose Marti and the United States: On the Margins of the Gaze," in *Re-Reading José Martí: One Hundred Years Later*, ed. Julio Rodríguez-Luis (Albany: SUNY Press, 1999), 23.
15. Susana Rotker, "Jose Marti and the United States," 23.
16. Rotker, "Jose Marti and the United States," 23.
17. Rotker, "Jose Marti and the United States," 24.
18. Roberto González Echevarría, introduction to *Jose Marti*, ix.
19. The United States is characterized as an imperial power through the length of this chapter. Historically, the acquisition of Mexican lands via the Mexican-American war (1846–1848) as well as the acquisition of Puerto Rico, Guam, and land access to Cuba via the Spanish-American war (1898) function as the touchstones for the development of the United States as an imperial power.
20. José Martí, "Mother America," in *José Martí Reader: Writings on the Americas*, ed. Ivan A. Schulman (Victoria, Australia: Ocean Press, 2007), 101.
21. Martí, "Mother America," in *José Martí Reader*, 102, 109.
22. José Martí, "Mother America," in *Writings on Latin America and the Struggle for Cuban Independence*, ed. Phillip S. Foner, trans. Elinor Randall (New York: Monthly Review Press, 1977), 69.
23. Martí, "Mother America," in *Writings on Latin America*, 79.
24. Martí, "Mother America," in *Writings on Latin America*, 83.
25. For instance, Octavio Paz actively refers to *los hijos de la chingada* (sons of the fucked one) to discuss the formation for Mexican identity. In this process he links "the fucked one" to La Malinche or Malitzin, who is historically identified as an indigenous woman that served as translator and object of desire to Hernán Cortés during the conquest. See *The Labyrinth of Solitude* (1950).
26. Jeffery Belnap and Raúl Fernández. "Introduction: The Architectonics of José Martí's 'Our Americanism,'" 5.
27. Belnap and Fernández, 5.
28. Belnap and Fernández, 5.
29. Belnap and Fernández, 5.
30. Lomas, *Translating Empire*, 220.
31. José Martí, "Nuestra America" in *José Martí: Selected Writings* (New York: Penguin Books, 2002), 289.
32. Beatrice Pita, "Engendering Critique: Race, Class, and Gender in Ruiz de Burton and Martí," in *José Martí's "Our America": From National to Hemispheric Cultural Studies*, ed. Jeffery Belnap and Raúl Fernández (Durham: Duke University Press, 1998), 139.
33. Martí, "Nuestra America," 295.
34. Pita, "Engendering Critique," 139.
35. Lomas, *Translating Empire*, 245.

36. Lomas, *Translating Empire*, 245.

37. Laura Lomas, "Redefining the American Revolutionary: Gabriela Mistral on José Martí," *Comparative American Studies* 6.3 (2008): p 243.

38. Laura Lomas, "Redefining the American Revolutionary," 250.

39. Lomas, "Redefining the American Revolutionary," 242.

40. Lomas, "Redefining the American Revolutionary," 254.

41. Lomas, "Redefining the American Revolutionary," 241.

42. Ofelia Schutte, "Resistance to Colonialism: The Latin American Legacy of José Martí," in *Colonialism and its Legacies*, ed. Jacob T. Levy (Maryland: Lexington Books, 2011), 184.

43. Martí, "Our America," in *Selected Writings*, 288.

44. José Martí, "Mi Race," in *Latin American Philosophy for the 21st Century*, ed. Jorge J.E. Gracia and Elizabeth Millán-Zaibert (Amherst: Prometheus Books, 2004), 254.

45. Lomas, *Translating Empire*, 9.

46. Aníbal Quijano, "Coloniality of Power, Eurocentrism, and Latin America," *Nepantla: Views from the South* 1.3 (2000): 534.

47. Aníbal Quijano, "Coloniality of Power, Eurocentrism, and Latin America," 534.

48. María Lugones, "Heterosexualism and the Colonial/Modern Gender System," *Hypatia* 22.1 (2007): 190.

49. María Lugones, "Heterosexualism and the Colonial/Modern Gender System," 193.

Bibliography

Belnap, Jeffrey and Raúl Fernández. "Introduction: The Architectonics of José Martí's 'Our Americanism.'" In *José Martí's "Our America": From National to Hemispheric Cultural Studies*, edited by Jeffery Belnap and Raúl Fernández, 1–23. Durham: Duke University Press, 1998.

González Echevarría, Roberto. Introduction to *Jose Marti: Selected Writings*, by José Martí, ix–xxv. New York: Penguin Books, 2002.

Kirk, John M. "José Martí and the United States: A Further Interpretation." *Latin American Studies* 9, no. 2 (1977): 275–290.

Lomas, Laura. "Redefining the American Revolutionary: Gabriela Mistral on José Martí." *Comparative American Studies* 6, no. 3 (2008): 241–264.

———. *Translating Empire: José Martí, Migrant Latino Subjects, and American Modernities*. Durham: Duke University Press, 2008.

Lugones, María. "Heterosexualism and the Colonial/Modern Gender System." *Hypatia* 22, no. 1 (2007): 186–209.

Martí, José. "Mother America." In *José Martí Reader: Writings on the Americas*, edited by Ivan A. Schulman, 101–110. Victoria, Australia: Ocean Press, 2007.

———."Mother America." In *Writings on Latin America and the Struggle for Cuban Independence*, edited by Phillip S. Foner, trans. Elinor Randall, 69–83. New York: Monthly Review Press, 1977.

———. "Nuestra America." In *José Martí: Selected Writings*, 288–295. New York: Penguin Books, 2002.

———. "Mi Race." In *Latin American Philosophy for the 21st Century*, edited by Jorge J.E. Gracia and Elizabeth Millán-Zaibert, 253–256. Amherst: Prometheus Books, 2004.

Pita, Beatrice. "Engendering Critique: Race, Class, and Gender in Ruiz de Burton and Martí." In *José Martí's "Our America": From National to Hemispheric Cultural Studies*, edited by Jeffrey Belnap and Raúl Fernández, 129–144. Durham: Duke University Press, 1998.

Quijano, Aníbal. "Coloniality of Power, Eurocentrism, and Latin America." *Nepantla: Views from the South* 1, no. 3 (2000): 533–580.

Rodríguez-Luis, Julio. "Introduction: On the Re-Evaluation of Martí." In *Re-Reading José Martí: One Hundred Years Later*, edited by Julio Rodríguez-Luis, vii–xxiii. Albany: SUNY Press, 1999.

Rotker, Susana. "Jose Marti and the United States: On the Margins of the Gaze." In *Re-Reading José Martí: One Hundred Years Later*, edited by Julio Rodríguez-Luis, 17–34. Albany: SUNY Press, 1999.

Schutte, Ofelia "Resistance to Colonialism: The Latin American Legacy of José Martí." In *Colonialism and its Legacies*, edited by Jacob T. Levy, 181–204. Maryland: Lexington Books, 2011.

Contributors

Stephanie Rivera Berruz is an associate professor of philosophy at Marquette University. She was the recipient of the Woodrow Wilson Career Enhancement Fellowship for her work on Latin/a American philosophy for the academic year of 2017–2018. Her main research interests lie in Latin American philosophy and Latinx feminisms as well philosophy of race, gender, and sexuality. She recently co-edited an anthology: *Comparative Studies in Latin American and Asian Philosophies* (2018), and her publications appear in *Hypatia, Inter-American Journal of Philosophy*, and *Essays in Philosophy*. Originally from Bayamon, Puerto Rico, Dr. Rivera Berruz has lived both inside and outside of the continental United States. She credits her migrations as inspirations for her interests in philosophies that explore myriad dimensions of identity.

Jacoby Adeshei Carter is an associate professor of philosophy, and chair of the Department of Philosophy at Howard University. He is the director of the Alain Leroy Locke Society, author of *African American Contributions to the Americas' Cultures: Lectures by Alain Locke* and co-editor of *Philosophic Values and World Citizenship: Locke to Obama and Beyond* and *Insurrectionist Ethics: Radical Perspectives on Social Justice*. He is also series editor of *African American Philosophy and the African Diaspora*, published by Palgrave/Macmillan.

Nadia V. Celis Salgado is a professor of Latin American, Caribbean and Latinx studies at Bowdoin College. She received her PhD in literature from Rutgers University, where she also specialized in gender and women's studies. Her research explores embodiment, subjectivity and intimacy in Hispanic Caribbean literature and popular culture. Her publications include articles on Colombian Caribbean authors Marvel Moreno, Fanny Buitrago, and Gabriel García Márquez, as well as essays on dance and performance. Celis is the author of *Cronica de un amor terrible: La historia secreta de la novia devuelta en la muerte anunciada de García Márquez* (Lumen, 2023) and *La rebelión de las niñas: El Caribe y la "conciencia corporal"* (Iberoamericana Vervuert, 2015), which received the

Nicolás Guillén Award from the Caribbean Philosophical Association, and an Honorable Mention of the Premio Iberoamericano by LASA. She is also co-editor of the collection *Lección errante: Mayra Santos–Febres y el Caribe contemporáneo* (Isla Negra, 2011).

Tommy J. Curry is professor of philosophy at the University of Edinburgh. His research interests are in Africana philosophy, the Black radical tradition and Black male studies. He is author of *The Man-Not: Race, Class, Genre, and the Dilemmas of Black Manhood* (Temple University Press 2017), which won the 2018 American Book Award. He is the author of *Another white Man's Burden: Josiah Royce's Quest for a Philosophy of Racial Empire* (SUNY Press 2018), and has re-published the forgotten philosophical works of William Ferris as *The Philosophical Treatise of William H. Ferris: Selected Readings from The African Abroad or, His Evolution in Western Civilization* (Rowman & Littlefield 2016). He is also the editor of the first book series dedicated to the study of Black males entitled *Black Male Studies: A Series Exploring the Paradoxes of Racially Subjugated Males* published by Temple University Press. Dr. Curry is currently co-editing (with Daw-nay Evans) the forthcoming anthology *Contemporary African American Philosophy: Where Do We Go from Here* for Bloomsbury Publishing (2019).

Hernando A. Estévez was educated at DePaul University and Indiana University. He works on Latin American philosophy, political philosophy and continental philosophy. He is currently chair and professor of the Department of Philosophy, Arts and Literature, and former Dean of the School of Philosophy at Universidad de La Salle in Bogotá. Hernando is the editor and contributor of *Teaching to Discern: forming connections, decolonizing perspectives* (Bogotá: Ediciones UniSalle, 2019).

Daniel Fryer is assistant professor of law at the University of Michigan. His work draws on scholarship in social and political philosophy, law, the social sciences, and public policy. He is also influenced by social movements and intellectual discourse outside the academy. His writing has appeared or is forthcoming in *Criminal Law and Philosophy*, *Ethics*, *Journal of Criminal Law and Criminology*, and *The Washington Post*.

James B. Haile, III is an associate professor of philosophy at University of Rhode Island. Haile specializes in philosophy and literature, philosophical aesthetics, and Africana philosophy. His most recent book, *The Buck, the Black, and the Existential Hero* was published by Northwestern University Press in 2020.

Chike Jeffers is an associate professor of philosophy at Dalhousie University and Canada Research Chair in Africana Philosophy. His research interests include Africana philosophy, philosophy of race, social and political philosophy, and ethics. He is the co-author of *What Is Race? Four Philosophical Views* (2019) and editor of *Listening to Ourselves: A Multilingual Anthology of African Philosophy* (2013).

Lee A. McBride, III is professor of philosophy at the College of Wooster (Ohio). McBride specializes in American philosophy, ethics, political philosophy, and philosophy of race. He is the author of *Ethics and Insurrection: A Pragmatism for the Oppressed* (Bloomsbury, 2021). He is the editor of *A Philosophy of Struggle: The Leonard Harris Reader*

(Bloomsbury, 2020) and co-editor with Erin McKenna of *Pragmatist Feminism and the Work of Charlene Haddock Seigfried* (Bloomsbury, 2022). Additionally, McBride has published articles on pragmatist feminism, racism, food ethics, anger, leftist politics, and decolonial philosophy.

Michael Monahan is a professor of philosophy at the University of Memphis. His teaching and research focus primarily on the philosophy of race and racism, political philosophy, Hegel, and phenomenology. He is the author of *Creolizing Practices of Freedom: Recognition and Dissonance* (Rowman and Littlefield).

Adriana Novoa is a cultural historian whose specialty is science in Latin America, and with Alex Levine she has written two books about Darwinism in Argentina: *From Man to Ape: Darwinism in Argentina, 1870–1920* (University of Chicago Press) and *Darwinistas: The Construction of Evolutionary Thought in Nineteenth-Century Argentina* (Brill). She is currently completing another manuscript on this topic, which treats the politics of evolutionism and its relationship to gender and race: *From Virile to Sterile: Masculinity and National Identity in Argentina, 1850–1910*. Dr. Novoa's articles have been published in the *Journal of Latin American Studies, Science in Context, The Latinoamericanist, Cuban Studies,* and *Revista Hispánica Moderna,* among others.

Susana Nuccetelli is professor of philosophy at St. Cloud State University, Minnesota. She is the author of *Latin American Thought* (2002) and co-author of *Latin American Philosophy: An Introduction with Readings* (2004). She co-edited the *Blackwell Companion to Latin American Philosophy* (with Ofelia Schutte and Otávio Bueno, 2009) and is a contributor to the *Stanford Encyclopedia of Philosophy.*

Andrea J. Pitts is professor of comparative literature at the University of Buffalo, and author of *Nos/Otras: Gloria E. Anzaldúa, Multiplicitous Agency, and Resistance* (SUNY Press 2021). They are also co-editor of *Beyond Bergson: Examining Race and Colonialism through the Writings of Henri Bergson* with Mark Westmoreland (SUNY Press 2019) and *Theories of the Flesh: Latinx and Latin American Feminisms, Transformation, and Resistance* with Mariana Ortega and José M. Medina (Oxford University Press, 2020).

Dwayne A. Tunstall is professor of philosophy and associate dean of inclusive excellence and curriculum at Grand Valley State University. His areas of specialty are African American philosophy, classical American philosophy (especially Josiah Royce), and existentialism. His research interests include moral philosophy, phenomenology, philosophy of religion, and social and political philosophy. He is the author of two books: *Yes, But Not Quite: Encountering Josiah Royce's Ethico-Religious Insight* (Fordham University Press, 2009) and *Doing Philosophy Personally: Thinking about Metaphysics, Theism, and Antiblack Racism* (Fordham University Press, 2013). He is also author of numerous articles and book chapters, including "Royce's Ethical Insight and Inevitable Moral Failure," in Joshua R. Farris and Benedikt Paul Göcke, eds., *The Routledge Handbook on Idealism and Immaterialism* (Routledge, 2021) and "The Spiritual Significance of Curry's The Man-Not by Critic Tunstall," in *The Acorn* (2018).

Alejandro A. Vallega is a professor of philosophy at the University of Oregon. He is also Research Fellow at the Center for Gender and African Studies, University of the Free State, South Africa. Among his publications are *Tiempo y Liberación* (Editorial Akal, 2021), *Latin American Philosophy from Identity to Radical Exteriority* (Indiana University Press, 2014), *Sense and Finitude: Encounters at the Limits of Art, Language, and the Political* (SUNY Press, 2009), and *Heidegger and the Issue of Space: Thinking on Exilic Grounds* (Penn State Press, 2003). His work focuses on aesthetics, Latin American thought, decolonial thought, decolonial epistemologies, and Continental philosophy.

Index

Abya Yala, 326–328, 335, 340
aesthetics, 25–26, 75, 139, 160, 188, 240–241, 258, 260, 294, 318, 368, 370
African American experience, 15, 17–19, 197, 220
African American philosophy, 1–26
Africana experience, 94, 194–196, 202
Africana existentialism, 30, 194. *See also* existentialism
Africana phenomenology, 195, 204. *See also* phenomenology
Africana philosophy, 1–3, 27, 38–46, 193–194, 195, 202–204, 206, 220–229, 267–268
Afro-American existentialism, 198. *See also* existentialism
Afro-Caribbean: culture, 33–34, 40; experience, 94, 205, 211; people, 32, 38, 94; philosophy, 1, 21–22, 28–31, 35–38; thought, 7, 38; women, 310, 313
Afro-Cubans, 76, 78–79, 82–84
Afro-experience, 197, 207, 209
Afro-Latin philosophy, 28, 41, 46, 95
Alcoff, Linda Martín, 77, 183–184
American philosophy, 2–8, 12–13, 20–24, 85–94, 121, 124, 127, 141, 148, 152, 157, 163, 226, 298, 368–369
American Revolution, 58, 121
anarchofeminism, 335
ante-theory, 106, 108, 112
anti-racist, 284, 295, 342

Black experience, 14–15, 19, 294
Black women, 294, 311–312, 314, 318–319
Bolívar, Simón, 240, 246
Bolivia, 327–328, 331–332, 334, 336–337, 341, 343–344
border: dwellers, 293, 351; experiences, 164; philosophy, 183; thinking, 162–163, 177–178
born of struggle, 14–15, 20–21: African American philosophy *as*, 14–15, 18–19; American philosophy, 22; "born of struggle," 12, 17, 22; expression, 12, 14–15; Harris's use, 12, 14–15; interpretation, 17–19; label, 11–16, 23; philosophy (*see* philosophy: born of struggle); philosophy *as*, 12–13; phrase, 11, 13; texts, 11, 16–17; *the* philosophy, 14

Caribbean: Caliban of, 208; culture, 33, 37, 308–309; colonies, 123; history, 309; hybridity, 34; islands, 73–74, 218, 220; literature, 308; people, 309, 311; philosophy, 30, 35–36; sexuality, 314, 320; states, 319; women, 310
citizenship, 50, 54, 58–59, 61, 63, 71, 73, 319; democratic, 71; denial of, 72; forms of, 320; ideas of, 62; nature of, 318; notion of, 51, 53, 55, 58, 60, 64, 315; origins of, 60; parameters of, 314; rights of, 72; sense of, 57; status of, 64; rights of, 72; understanding of, 59; values of, 60; world, 237, 239

371

coalitions, 80, 284, 333; multicultural, 285; of resistance, 295–298, 336, 343–344; strategic, 295, 327–328
coloniality, 6–7, 94, 263, 265–266, 323–327, 343, 350, 358–362, 364–365; agents of, 279; of being, 178–179; concept of, 171; dynamics of, 326; of gender, 180–181, 327; of knowledge 177; perspective of, 94; of power, 171, 173, 177, 179–180, 184
Cooper, Anna Julia, 7
corporeal consciousness, 294, 309–310, 312, 317–320
cosmic race, 235–36, 239–242
cosmopolitanism, 75, 235, 237–239, 242–243, 247, 254
creolization, 33–35, 41–44, 46, 221, 271
Cuba, 41, 57, 68, 73, 75, 82–84, 93, 97, 123, 125, 134, 246; Africans in, 70, 72; annexation of, 68–71, 351; independent, 79, 95, 352; libre, 68, 80; race-neutral, 68–78, 80–81
Cuban, 69, 83, 96–99, 248, 235, 308, 352
Creoles, 75; expatriates, 79; identity, 78, 80–81, 84; independence, 66, 68, 74, 77, 82, 246; nationalists, 78; resistance, 79
Cuban Independence, 77–79, 246; from Spain 68, 78; movement, 79, 97; war of, 82; writings on, 74
Cuban Revolution, 74, 239, 246
Cuban Revolutionary Board, 96, 98
Cuban Revolutionary Party, 79, 352

Darwin, Charles, 129–130, 132–134
Darwinists, 138
decolonial, 7, 176, 183, 328, 340; alternative, 178, 181; feminism, 7–8, 180, 338, 344; struggle, 182, 327, 343; theory, 327, 335, 343; thought, 163, 169, 171, 176
decoloniality, 183, 263
decolonization, 263, 308, 310, 320, 336–338; decolonize, 2, 107, 312, 332
deconstruction, 23, 163, 175–176, 178, 311
Delany, Martin R., vii, 2, 7, 68–89, 99
democracy, 6, 290, 337, 343; heterogenous nature of, 287, 289, 291; in the United States, 287, 291; racial, 314; rhetoric of, 182
democratic, 15, 119, 288–289; citizenship, 71; liberal states, 250, 330–331; justice, 286; process, 182, 341
Du Bois, W. E. B., 138, 285, 292

Dussel, Enrique, 164, 170, 221, 263

eliminativism, 84, 88, 241, 254, 286, 291, 295–296; racial, 236, 238, 248–249
eliminativist, 80–81, 235, 247
embodied, 18, 94, 217, 307, 309, 318; experience, 179, 206, 311, 313, 320
embodiment, 204, 268, 308, 317, 354
embody, 76, 238, 249, 319
enlightenment, 117–119, 130, 268–269; Iberian, 120, 121, 125; ideal, 172, 263; modernity, 262, 277
evolution, 106, 130; technological 105; German science, 129; stages of, 213
evolutionary, 132–133; biologists, 137; ideas, 131; science, 138
evolutionism, 130
evolutionist, 135
existential, 7, 32, 111, 171, 199, 201, 237, 336; challenges, 4; condition, 179; concepts, 203; reality, 201–202; sense of being, 166; struggles, 15, 18
existentialism, 31, 148; Africana, 30, 194; Afro-American, 198; European, 30, Latin American, 166
existentialist, 29, 208, 220
exteriority, 170, 228. *See also* radical exteriority

Fanon, Frantz, 7, 29–30, 32, 34, 263–268, 272–273, 279, 308
feminism, 7–8, 180, 308
feminist, 180, 337, 341, 343, 357; activists, 335; African American, 7, 312; critical, 310; Inter-American, 8; philosophy, 3, 5, 21–22; theorists, 8, 308; theory, 327
First Inter-American Conference of Philosophy, 21
French Revolution, 58, 121
Freyre, Gilberto, 291

gender, 2, 8, 183, 294, 298, 319, 352, 357; coloniality of, 180–181, 327, 359; *See also* coloniality: of gender; concept of, 350; difference, 180, 359; gendered existence, 180, 357; gendered force, 21; gendered maternal tropes, 353–355; groups, 290; hierarchies, 310; identities, 340; issues, 184; oppression, 7, 338; politics, 338, 343; quotas, 337; racialized, 180–181; roles, 353, 356, 360–362; transgressions, 297
Glissant, Edouard, 33, 308

Gómez, Máximo, 79, 352
Gordon, Lewis, 42, 184, 193–198, 211, 216, 220, 262; concept of experience, 211, 216, 266; geography of reason, 202–206, 265, 273–274
Gracia, Jorge E., 156, 183

Haiti, 43, 78–79, 93, 246
Haitian Independence, 121
Haitian Revolution, 121–122, 272, 352
heterogeneity, 22, 135, 176, 291, 315
heteronormative, 361
heteronormative manhood, 357
heteronormative reproduction, 354
heteronormativity 4, 294, 350, 355, 359
heteropatriarchal, 310
heterosexism, 360–361
heterosexual, 22, 180, 355, 360–361
heterosexuality, 355, 359, 360, 362
Harris, Leonard, 11–19, 21–22, 257, 259, 296
Henry Blake, 74–75
Henry, Paget, 28–32, 36, 40, 205–206, 211; Africana philosophy, 29, 37; author of *Caliban's Reason*, 35; creolization 33, 38, 41–43. See also creolization; critics of, 39; experiences, 195–196, 216; racial essentialism, 31, 34
Hilst, Hilda, 2

Iberian, 118–120, 128, 148
Iberian Peninsula, 249, 271
identity, 4, 17, 22, 101, 182–183, 197–198, 205, 210, 219, 222, 248, 315; African, 34, 37, 42, 94; Black, 70, 97–99; claims, 23; collective, 60; colonial, 311–313; common, 56; conception of, 331; constitution of, 329; Cuban, 78, 80–84; cultural, 56–58, 62, 211, 308, 319; ethnic, 81, 96, 293; European, 166; human, 218, 272; individual, 57; Latin American, 163–167, 173–177, 235, 353; mestizo, 240; multiplicitous, 293; national, 2, 68, 80–81, 239, 243; notion of, 61; place and person-securing, 287, 290, 296; political, 50–51, 53, 56, 61–63, 81; politics of, 287; racial, 80, 83, 96, 98, 239–240, 242, 247, 252, 254, 285–286, 295–296, 358–359, 361; shared, 71, 284, 296 slave, 74; spiritual, 245; white, 288
Inter-American: context, 4, 256; dialogue, 28; discourse, 14, 24; exchanges, 236; experience, 162; philosophy, 1–9, 236, 255, 257, 284

Indigenous, 171, 175, 196, 284, 294, 309; American, 274; communities, 60, 328, 336, 339; culture, 2, 215, 338; dispossession, 292; enslaved, 246; identities, 330; origins 224; peoples, 77, 168, 172, 223, 286; resistance, 329, 332–334; thought, 165, 174, 184; traditions, 180; women, 335, 337–344; writers, 326

Lamming, George, 2, 194, 204–205, 229–230
Latin American experience, 166,173–177, 183
Latin American philosophy, viii, 1–3, 6–7, 21–46, 77, 93, 99, 142, 147–170, 174–187, 189–191, 220, 280–283, 350–351, 364–370
Locke, Alain, 2, 235–238, 240–241, 248, 250–257, 300–302, 367
Lugones, Maria, 180, 184, 263, 293, 343, 359

Maceo, Antonio, 79, 99
Maldonado-Torres, Nelson, 178–179, 184, 271
Martí, José, vii–viii, 2, 7, 68–89, 95, 98, 134, 142, 144, 184, 235–302, 350–365
Medina, José, 262, 275–277
Medina, Vicente, 125
Mendieta, Eduardo, 183
mestizaje, 57, 241, 297; biological, 251–252; Caribbean, 96; concept of, 240, 248; idea of, 239, 249–250
mestizo, 57, 82–83, 238, 246, 330–31, 337; identity, 239–242; modernity, 172; race, 249–250, 252, 291
Mexico, 120, 138, 327, 330–338, 344, 351–355
Mignolo, Walter, 176, 178, 184, 263, 326
Mujeres Creando, 335–336, 338, 342–343

Negro Society for Historical Research, 99–100, 102

Outlaw, Lucius, 39, 41, 285–292, 295, 297

philosophy: born of struggle 11–13, 15, 17 (*see also* born of struggle); of the Americas, 38; of the Black experience, 14; of Black history, 102; of evolution, 137; of experience, 220; of history, 99,102; of identity, 176; of language, 157; of liberation, 22, 167, 169–171, 183–184; of literature, 2, 107, 148, 194, 226–231, 368; of mind, 254, of place, 194, 203; of race, 237, 240–241, 249–250, 253, 293; science, 130, 149

Quijano, Aníbal 7, 171, 263, 359

racial: anti-realism, 235; apparatus, 99; ascription, 81; creed, 238; development, 105; eliminativism, 81, 235–236, 247–248; equality, 80, 82, 288; essences, 32, 81; essentialism, 28, 32–34, 37; hierarchy, 42, 253, 310; humanity, 103; identity, 98, 239, 242, 285, 358, 361; inferiority, 111, 245, 249; integrity, 94, 100, 104–105, 329; internationalism, 97; oppression, 4, 83–84, 295–296; politics, 96, 117, 309; practices, 254; purity, 239, 248, 291; realism 2, 212, 235, 237; separatism, 284, 289, 294, 298; temperament, 101; thinking, 239
racialism, 82, 235, 245–246; advocacy of, 251; biology, 248, 250, 253; classical, 75; consequences of, 237, 244, 354; Delany's, 76, 83; divisiveness of, 236, 244, 250; forms of, 238, 252; good, 254, 353. *See also* racism; good harm, 247; rejection of, 249
racialized, 296, 338; as black, 11, 17, 70, 241, 244; as white, 243,245, 248; caste system, 240; gender 180–181, 356; people's humanity, 247, 284, 291; populations, 249, 256, 286, 292, 295; self, 178; thought, 221
racism, 23, 81, 110–112, 236–237; anti-Black, 221, 271; colonial, 266; context of, 265; eliminate, 84; forms of, 76, 251, 296–197; good, 83, 244–246, 251–253; history of, 184; justification of, 247; legacy of, 332; mechanisms of, 267; struggles against, 286, 295, 343; victims of, 295; violence of, 213
racist, 22, 179, 243, 295–296; anti-Black, 75; beliefs, 246; colonialism, 111, 266; discourses, 30; good, 247; habits, 288; ideas, 32; order, 110; practices, 75, 289; structure, 93, 286
radical exteriority, 162–163, 171, 174, 184
revolution, 58, 68, 71, 240, 255; aim of, 6; Black, 72, 74; Delany's call for, 70; Darwinian, 130; scientific, 118; violent, 77
revolutionary, 16, 83, 98, 104, 134, 139, 358; Black, 342; comrades, 290; Darwinian evolution, 129; spirit, 95; struggle, 84; thought, 4
Revolutionary War, 43

Salazar Bondy, Augusto, 150, 156, 167–170, 174
Santos-Febres, Mayra, 307, 310–316, 318–320
Schomburg, Arturo Alfonso, vii, 2, 93, 97, 114
Schutte, Ofelia, 184, 343, 358
Sullivan, Shannon, 288–289, 290, 292, 297

Traditions, 1–4, 7, 12–13, 16, 22, 31, 37, 118, 152, 154–155, 157, 168, 174, 184, 285; African, 31–32, 34, 36–37, 39, 41, 43; American, 5–6, 162, 273; cultural, 330; European, 8, 120, 162, 273; Indigenous, 180; intellectual, 1, 30, 204, 220; literary, 31; oral, 31; philosophical, 1–2, 4–5, 12, 15, 22–23, 34, 39, 152–153, 157, 236; political, 52; precolonial, 28; western, 162, 171

Vasconcelos, José, 2, 44, 235–260

Wynter, Sylvia, 2, 7, 196, 216–228, 261–283, 343, 347, 349

www.ingramcontent.com/pod-product-compliance
Lightning Source LLC
Chambersburg PA
CBHW020350080526
44584CB00014B/960